Adding Ajax

Other resources from O'Reilly

Related titles
Ajax and Web Services
Ajax Design Patterns
Ajax Hacks™
Ajax on Java
Ajax on Rails
Head Rush Ajax

Head First Servlets and JSP
JavaServer Pages
Learning JavaScript
RESTful Web Services
Securing Ajax Applications

oreilly.com
oreilly.com is more than a complete catalog of O'Reilly books. You'll also find links to news, events, articles, weblogs, sample chapters, and code examples.

oreillynet.com is the essential portal for developers interested in open and emerging technologies, including new platforms, programming languages, and operating systems.

Conferences
O'Reilly brings diverse innovators together to nurture the ideas that spark revolutionary industries. We specialize in documenting the latest tools and systems, translating the innovator's knowledge into useful skills for those in the trenches. Please visit *conferences.oreilly.com* for our upcoming events.

Safari Bookshelf (*safari.oreilly.com*) is the premier online reference library for programmers and IT professionals. Conduct searches across more than 1,000 books. Subscribers can zero in on answers to time-critical questions in a matter of seconds. Read the books on your Bookshelf from cover to cover or simply flip to the page you need. Try it today for free.

Adding Ajax

Shelley Powers

O'REILLY®

Beijing · Cambridge · Farnham · Köln · Paris · Sebastopol · Taipei · Tokyo

Adding Ajax
by Shelley Powers

Copyright © 2007 Shelley Powers. All rights reserved.
Printed in the United States of America.

Published by O'Reilly Media, Inc., 1005 Gravenstein Highway North, Sebastopol, CA 95472.

O'Reilly books may be purchased for educational, business, or sales promotional use. Online editions are also available for most titles (*safari.oreilly.com*). For more information, contact our corporate/institutional sales department: (800) 998-9938 or *corporate@oreilly.com*.

Editor: Simon St.Laurent	**Indexer:** Lucie Haskins
Production Editor: Laurel R.T. Ruma	**Cover Designer:** Karen Montgomery
Copyeditor: Amy Thomson	**Interior Designer:** David Futato
Proofreader: Reba Libby	**Illustrators:** Robert Romano and Jessamyn Read

Printing History:

June 2007:   First Edition.

 This book uses RepKover™, a durable and flexible lay-flat binding.

ISBN-10: 0-596-52936-8
ISBN-13: 978-0-596-52936-9
[M]

Table of Contents

Preface

Ajax: It is part revolution, part evolution, and some would say all hype. Ajax is an umbrella term used to encompass a set of technologies including:

- Markup, such as HTML, XHTML, XML, and SVG
- JavaScript
- CSS and XSLT
- Last but not least, browser objects, including the canvas object and the object that really makes Ajax, `XMLHttpRequest`

Despite all of the recent interest, most of these technologies have been around for about a decade. Why the interest now?

Ajax is more than just a set of technologies—it's also a determination to take web pages and applications in new directions. We've had this determination in the past, but we never had the tools with which to build these applications. Now, the specifications that were all new ten years ago have reached maturity, and, even more importantly, have broad support in web browsers. New specifications continue to appear, and tool makers cooperate much more than they did a few years ago.

Years ago when web developers made first tentative motions to add interactivity to web pages, we were constrained by browsers that supported completely different models, and at times, even different scripting languages. The use of Cascading Style Sheets (CSS) as a uniform way of adding presentation to a page was hampered by differing interpretations, not to mention proprietary extensions.

Now, CSS has almost universal support, and though there are still "quirks" in the system, most browsers support most of the specifications, and we're at a stage where what we can do exceeds what we can't do. As for scripting, through the efforts via the ECMA standards organization, we have a released version of JavaScript known as ECMAScript that is accepted and supported in all the major tools, in the Web and out.

The markup has become more sophisticated, and we're moving from the HTML with its vagaries to XHTML with its discipline. We're also adding new XML vocabularies, such as Scalable Vector Graphics (SVG)—a way of adding interactive graphics that don't depend on plug-ins and external objects. This is matched by the introduction of the Canvas object, both separate from any markup and included as part of the upcoming work on HTML5—the intermediate step between the older HTML and the more rigorous XHTML.

Yet we haven't completely abandoned the old proprietary objects. Now, rather than being implemented in one browser, their use is becoming universal. One such object is XMLHttpRequest, which allows us to make calls to web services directly from pages and then process the results dynamically without ever having to reload the page.

What does that mean to developers and consumers? It means being able to read an article, click it, and then edit it in place—all in the same page. We can also delete rows from a table and have the deletion happen instantaneously. Updates, too.

We can also add categories to a photo without reloading either the page or the photo. Or expand that photo to a larger size just by clicking on a thumbnail.

Our use of web forms has changed considerably. We can make a selection in one list and have another selection list automatically populated. We can sort a table using drag-and-drop, collapse fields to make room, or click on tabbed pages to fill in other parts of a large form or to see other information, again without having to reload the page.

Of course, what we think of as a "page" has changed, and there's good and bad with this new viewpoint. It's difficult to figure out how much to charge for ads by "page view" when a hundred pages can be loaded without once using a refresh. Search engine companies don't particularly understand dynamically generated links, and neither do screen readers. As for cases where scripting is disabled or nonexistent, well, that's a nonstarter when it comes to Ajax, with its dependence on JavaScript.

That's where the concept of *progressive enhancement* enters into the picture. Coined by Steven Champeon, progressive enhancement is based on the philosophy that Ajax effects are added as enhancements to existing web technologies, rather than as replacements. In other words, you still build the more traditional web application that's based on submitting a form to update a table, but then you enhance it by adding the capability to update the table with changes to the form fields without actually having to submit the form.

That tabbed page can become a series of vertical sections within a page if scripting is disabled; the data will still be there, just arranged differently. A slideshow can serve its content whether requested by an application created in PHP and residing on a Unix box, or via a JavaScript call from within Firefox, Safari, or Internet Explorer.

With the use of progressive enhancement, it doesn't matter if scripting is disabled or not, because no functionality is lost; it's just different. At the same time, the efficiencies that Ajax can add to a web application—and they are numerous—can still be provided to the 80 percent or so of people who do use an applicable browser and who do have scripting enabled.

The best thing of all for you? You're already halfway there.

Audience

One major assumption about the audience of a book about adding Ajax is that you're already a web developer looking to take your more traditional web applications to the next level by adding Ajax effects. Chances are, you already have the web forms, the server-side-driven pages, and the static content—or at a minimum, you are familiar with how traditional web applications work. You're actually lucky—you have the "business side" of the application down. Now it's time to take your page to the next level.

First though, a more in-depth look at the assumptions about the audience that drove this book. This book is intended for those who:

- Have some degree of experience with web markup, including HTML and XHTML.
- Understand the basics of XML, including the necessity of it being both valid and well-formed.
- Are familiar with relational databases and have worked with them at least once in either a production environment or just for your own interest.
- Have worked with CSS and can read most CSS stylesheets.
- Have worked with JavaScript and feel comfortable with it, and have a good idea of how object-oriented JavaScript works.
- Are more interested in extending existing applications than in creating what are known as Rich Internet Applications (RIA).

This book does not assume you're an expert in any one of the technologies just listed, only that you've had some experience and with a little help (from either an online resource or an other technology-specific book) can follow along with any of the applications.

The last item in the list of requirements is really the most important. This book does not cover the concepts needed for building a PowerPoint replacement within a web page or for creating online games and other purely scripted solutions.

This book focuses purely on enhancing existing web applications by adding Ajax effects—not replacing existing applications, and not building pure Ajax solutions from scratch. O'Reilly has other fine books focused more for those who are interested in writing the next web-based spreadsheet program; we just want to make livelier, fun, interesting, and much more interactive web pages.

Contents of This Book

This book does not require you to start from the beginning and read it all the way to the end. I've tried to make each chapter as standalone as possible. Having said that, there is some small degree of building on a previous chapter's work, primarily in the use of an Adding Ajax library that is created as the book proceeds. However, all of the material is included in the downloadable examples. I would, however, recommend that you read Chapters 1 and 2 before you read any other chapters.

The following is a brief synopsis of each chapter:

Chapter 1, *Getting Ready to Make a Move to Ajax*
> Provides an overview of the Ajax technologies, but also covers the importance of developing a strategy for change to your site before sitting down to code. It covers the importance of discovering your audience and provides tips on how you can accomplish this task. It also covers the importance of standards and making sure you have a good, solid web page before you begin to add any Ajax effects. Once you've read this chapter, you're ready to add any of the Ajax effects covered in the later chapters.

Chapter 2, *The Ajax Bits*
> Provides a nuts-and-bolts coverage of the heart and soul of Ajax: how to work with the XMLHttpRequest object. In this chapter, I cover how to request a web service using both a GET and a POST request, as well as how to use dynamic scripting for cross-domain data requests. As for types of data, I cover HTML, XML, as well as the newer JavaScript Object Notation (JSON). I also discuss the asynchronous nature of Ajax requests and cover some of the potential gotchas and performance issues.

Chapter 3, *Ajax Tools and Terminology*
> Introduces and demonstrates several of the more important Ajax libraries, including Prototype, script.aculo.us, Rico, MochiKit, and so on. Though most of the examples don't use an external library, each chapter does have a sprinkling of examples using some of the libraries so that you can become familiar with the effect, learn how to extend libraries, package your own libraries, and discover some of interesting challenges associated with multilibrary Ajax development.

Chapter 4, *Interactive Effects*
> Gets into the interactive element that is Ajax, including how to work with events and event handlers that works across browsers, and what works if more than one library is used. In addition, we'll look at building tool tips, pulling in help data from external sources, creating an Ajax "fade" to signal changes, live previews, and merging live previews with live updates.

Chapter 5, *Space: The Final Frontier*
> Explores the concept of web page as space, and covers three popular approaches to managing web space. These include the accordion, where space is collapsed vertically; the tabbed page, where pages are served when tabs are clicked; and

the overlay, where the page is overlayed with a message, photo, or other material. This chapter also explores how to package complete "effects" so that one library can provide effects for any number of applications and pages. This chapter also looks at how these effects can be integrated with web service requests.

Chapter 6, *Dynamic Data*

This is a real nuts-and-bolts chapter. It gets into how to make data updates, including adding new data, deleting, and making updates, all from within a single page. It focuses on extending existing web applications so that form updates and Ajax updates coexist harmoniously. It also incorporates the use of "fades" to add polish and feedback to your application users. Some of the performance and security issues associated with database access through Ajax are also covered, as is the use of "live" updates and effects like drag-and-drop sorting.

Chapter 7, *History, Navigation, and Place with Single-Page Applications*

This is where we explore the Ajax effects on the Web, including breaking the Back button, losing the browser history, dynamic effects that disappear when the page is refreshed, and being able to link or bookmark an Ajax "page." In this chapter, we explore the approaches that can be taken to restore much of the lost web effects, and we will develop a better sense of how far we can take Ajax and still keep the best part of the Web.

Chapter 8, *Adding Advanced Visual Effects*

This chapter is pure fun. We've worked hard and now we can take out the paintbrush and fingerpaint set and go wild. This chapter covers some advanced CSS effects, including drag-and-drop "scrollbars," pagination, and the use of SVG, and the Canvas object. Though the support for the latter two items is not universal, support is growing and if used to supplement data presented in more traditional ways, can be both fun and effective.

Chapter 9, *Mashup Your Site*

Explores mashups. One of the most powerful aspects of Ajax is the ability to bring in web services, our own and others, and combine the data in any number of ways directly in our web pages. This chapter takes maps from Google, photo information from Flickr, and weblog information from Technorati, mashes it all up in a nice tabbed page interface, and then shows how all of that can be implemented in such a way that it works whether scripting is enabled or not.

Chapter 10, *Scaling, Infrastructure, and Starting from Scratch*

This chapter is both the long breath after the many code examples and a second look at issues of performance, architecture, and security. Privacy of web services is touched on, as well as distributing resource needs and how tightly coupled you want your server and client components to be. The chapter also looks at starting Ajax from scratch by briefly introducing some of the many frameworks available in so many languages: Java, .NET, PHP, Perl, Ruby, Python, and so on.

The PHP language is probably one of the most ubiquitous and pervasive programming languages in use for web applications today, and it's what I used for all of the server-side components of the Ajax applications. The reasoning is that while some of you might know Python, and others Ruby, and still others .NET or Java, most people know PHP. Or if not, you can get up to speed with PHP more quickly than with the other languages. Plus, every web host I know of provides support for PHP.

Conventions Used in This Book

The following typographical conventions are used in this book:

Italic
> Indicates new terms, URLs, filenames, and file extensions.

`Constant width`
> Indicates computer code in a broad sense. This includes commands, options, switches, variables, attributes, keys, requests, functions, types, classes, namespaces, methods, modules, properties, parameters, values, objects, events, event handlers, XML tags, HTML tags, macros, the contents of files, and the output from commands.

`Constant width bold`
> Shows commands or other text that should be typed literally by the user.

`Constant width italic`
> Shows text that should be replaced with user-supplied values or by values determined by context.

 This icon signifies a tip, suggestion, or general note.

 This icon indicates a warning or caution.

Web sites and pages are mentioned in this book to help the reader locate online information that might be useful. Normally both the address (URL) and the name (title, heading) of a page are mentioned. Some addresses are relatively complicated, but you can probably locate the pages easier by using your favorite search engine to find a page by its name, typically by typing it in quotation marks. This may also help if the page cannot be found by its address; it may have moved elsewhere, so the name may be the only way to find the page.

Using Code Examples

This book is here to help you get your job done. In general, you may use the code in this book in your programs and documentation. You do not need to contact us for permission unless you're reproducing a significant portion of the code. For example, writing a program that uses several chunks of code from this book does not require permission. Selling or distributing a CD-ROM of examples from O'Reilly books does require permission. Answering a question by citing this book and quoting example code does not require permission. Incorporating a significant amount of example code from this book into your product's documentation does require permission.

We appreciate, but do not require, attribution. An attribution usually includes the title, author, publisher, and ISBN. For example: "*Adding Ajax* by Shelley Powers. Copyright 2007 Shelley Powers, 978-0-596-52936-9."

If you feel your use of code examples falls outside fair use or the permission given above, feel free to contact us at *permissions@oreilly.com*.

We'd Like to Hear from You

Please address comments and questions concerning this book to the publisher:

O'Reilly Media, Inc.
1005 Gravenstein Highway North
Sebastopol, CA 95472
800-998-9938 (in the United States or Canada)
707-829-0515 (international or local)
707-829-0104 (fax)

We have a web page for this book, where we list errata, examples, and any additional information. You can access this page at

http://www.oreilly.com/catalog/9780596529369

To comment or ask technical questions about this book, send email to:

bookquestions@oreilly.com

For more information about our books, conferences, Resource Centers, and the O'Reilly Network, see our web site at:

http://www.oreilly.com

Safari® Enabled

 When you see a Safari® Enabled icon on the cover of your favorite technology book, that means the book is available online through the O'Reilly Network Safari Bookshelf.

Safari offers a solution that's better than e-books. It's a virtual library that lets you easily search thousands of top tech books, cut and paste code samples, download chapters, and find quick answers when you need the most accurate, current information. Try it for free at *http://safari.oreilly.com*.

Acknowledgments

A book of this nature does not come about through one person's imagination and work—it comes about through the effort of many people, including those who define the concepts, work through the problems, and create the libraries.

I want to thank the creators of all the libraries mentioned in this book for providing them so willingly and freely. Most of these library developers do not earn anything for such labor, and yet they provide polished sites, documentation, bug fixes, and new releases—all of which can be downloaded and used in any of our applications.

I also want to thank Jon Sullivan at Public Domain Photos (*http://pdphoto.org/About. php*) for all the photos he's given away freely to use, including the one of the "appletini" used in the application in Chapter 2.

I want to thank those who worked with me on the book, including my reviewers: Elaine Nelson, Dare Obasanjo, Roger Johansson, Jesse Skinner, Roy Owens, Anthony Holder III, Anne Zalenka, and Kathy Sierra. I also want to thank my editor, Simon St.Laurent. This now makes my third solo book for O'Reilly, and those who know me admire him greatly for his patience.

I'd also like to thank the folks that helped put this book together, including Lucie Haskins, Reba Libby, Laurel Ruma, and Amy Thomson.

This book is a better book because of all the support I've received.

CHAPTER 1

Getting Ready to Make a Move to Ajax

Ajax brings a whole new level of feedback and flexibility to web applications. Gone, or at least pushed gently aside, are the days when web page forms produced a result only after being submitted to a server. Gone also are static web pages of frozen HTML (Hypertext Markup Language) that could be read, but were unresponsive to the page reader's actions. Nowadays, web page developers can provide, directly within the page, much of the same functionality that used to require a round trip to the server.

Using Ajax, page components can be collapsed or expanded as required, populated on demand, and feedback to the user can range from a color fade to a system of strategically placed messages. Every element of the page can be used to make web service requests, thus creating more responsive pages and less frustration for the users. The end result is a sharper, tighter application.

Ajax applications can also make use of a host of Ajax-enabled libraries and web services from companies such as Google, Amazon, Adobe, Microsoft, and Yahoo!, as well as independent libraries such as Prototype, Dojo, MochiKit, and jQuery. Existing web services can often be used as they are or easily modified to work with Ajax.

Ajax is unique in that it's a cutting edge concept that's based on rather mature technology. Even some of the more esoteric effects can be created comfortably and with confidence; developers can be secure in the knowledge that any particular effect should work in most, if not all, modern browsers.

Ajax development has some challenging aspects, but it really is an 80–20 technology: 80 percent of the people interested in the technology need only about 20 percent of the capability. Much of the discussion related to Ajax is based on explorations in how far the concept can be pushed. Because of this, it may feel as if you're working with an extremely complex framework. This can be intimidating when you're just starting to consider how you can use Ajax in your sites, but in general, using the Ajax group of technologies is relatively simple with few moving parts.

You don't have to spend months reading all that's been written or trying all of the libraries in order to create efficient and interesting Ajax functionality *if*, and this is a big if, you start out small and work your way up to bigger effects.

This book assumes you're one of the luckier Ajax developers: you already have a web application or pages in place, and you're now looking to add some new effects. This puts you solidly on the *progressive enhancement* road, which automatically makes you a good Ajax developer.

The term progressive enhancement originated with Steven Champeon in a series of articles for Webmonkey and as part of an SXSW presentation (see the Wikipedia page at *http://en.wikipedia.org/wiki/Progressive_enhancement* for more history). It implies that you start with a site or application that is already clean, standardized, and accessible, and only *then* do you add special effects using application techniques such as Ajax. Other developers and designers such as Dave Shea and Jeremy Keith have expanded on this. The Wikipedia article on progressive enhancement lists the following guidelines:

- All basic content should be accessible to all browsers.
- All basic functionality should be accessible to all browsers.
- Sparse, semantic markup organizes the content.
- Enhanced layout is provided by externally linked CSS.
- Enhanced behavior is provided by unobtrusive, externally linked JavaScript.
- End user browser preferences are respected.

We can also use terms such as *graceful degradation* to refer to progressive enhancement. It all means the same thing—the pages and applications will work with any type of browser, mouse, or keyboard, regardless of the presence of a screen reader, and even if scripting is turned off.

I subscribe to the concept of progressive enhancement (or graceful degradation, or unobtrusive scripting, or whatever you want to call it), and the examples in this book are based on this premise. While it's true that you cannot reproduce all types of effects in a nonscript environment (such as those used in Google Maps, which demand Ajax), I believe that we shouldn't limit access to our core site content and functionality merely for the sake of adding eye candy.

As you begin to work with Ajax and consider which effects you want to use, it's important to remember that the simplest effects most often provide the greatest return for your time and effort. Most of us are not trying to recreate the desktop in the browser, or the browser in the desktop for that matter. We simply want to add to or enhance the basic functionality of our existing web pages and applications. We're the lucky ones, as half our job—providing the basic, non-Ajax functionality—is already finished. Now comes the fun part.

The term Ajax originated in an article by Jesse James Garrett titled "Ajax: A New Approach to Web Applications" (see the article at *http:// www.adaptivepath.com/publications/essays/archives/000385.php*).

Is it Ajax or AJAX? Is it a single word or an acronym for Asynchronous JavaScript and XML? Garrett used AJAX as a handy nickname for the set of technologies discussed in this chapter. However, the concept has since expanded beyond the technology itself; it's a whole new way of looking at the web and pushing beyond the boundaries of a traditional browser page. It is now very common to use the term Ajax to refer to this overall capability.

For the sake of simplicity, following what has become more or less a de facto standard, this book uses Ajax.

The Technologies That Are Ajax

Ajax is not built on new technologies, but focuses instead on the refinement and maturing of existing tools and environments. When Jesse James Garrett originally defined Ajax, he listed the associated technologies as:

- XHTML (Extensible HTML) and CSS (cascading stylesheets) for page layout and presentation
- XML (Extensible Markup Language) and XSLT (Extensible Stylesheet Language Transformations) for data interchange
- Document Object Model (DOM) for interactivity
- A specialized object (`XMLHttpRequest`) for client-server interaction
- JavaScript (or JScript) to act as glue

All of these technologies have been around in one form or another for years.

Though most of the emphasis of Ajax is on the web service request, the concept extends beyond simple data access within the page. It's a way of looking at a web page and using existing and new technologies to make it more interactive and responsive. This includes a new way of looking at JavaScript and more sophisticated JavaScript libraries, as well as a fresh new look at dynamic HTML techniques from the 1990s. It's thinking outside the web page box, whether you are using these technologies to create desktop applications, or, as in our case, to add usefulness, sparkle, and spontaneity to existing web pages.

A Natural Progression

Ajax is the result of a natural progression of client-side functionality. If Garrett hadn't boxed the concept into one name, chances are good that someone else would have; the web development environment was already heading toward a new explosive interest in the combined technologies.

In the earliest days of the Web, all of an application's functionality resided on the server. Netscape introduced client-side scripting with JavaScript, which allowed some client-side interactivity, but web pages remained static. Other browsers that followed, such as Microsoft's Internet Explorer (IE), had their own implementations of scripting, and eventually an effort arose to provide a minimum definition of scripting standards; the result was ECMAScript.

However, it wasn't until the W3C specification work with the DOM and CSS that pages became more dynamic and script could be used to modify, move, hide, create, or remove individual web page elements. At that time, dynamic web page effects were given the term *dynamic HTML* or DHTML—a concept that's now been subsumed into Ajax.

While advancements were being made in scripting and presentation, efforts were also underway to create a markup language that wasn't dependent on any specific vocabulary and could be extended without being overly complicated to implement. The result, XML, was released in 1998.

From this point, progress took multiple paths, and we entered an era of great expansion in functionality. This divergence naturally led to the advent of cross-browser incompatibilities, some of which still exist to this day. Among the browser-proprietary objects was one that would become the heart and soul of Ajax—Microsoft's IE 5 ActiveX object, `Microsoft.XMLHTTP`. Though it might have remained an IE-specific object, the concept caught the interest of other browser developers, and Mozilla created a variation called `XMLHttpRequest`.

`XMLHttpRequest` is special because it allows users to directly access asynchronous web services from within a web page. Rather than submitting data to the server through a form and then displaying the result in a separate page, `XMLHttpRequest` lets scripts invoke a server function and process the result without having to reload the page. The asynchronous aspect of the web service request means that the page isn't locked on hold while it waits for the service to respond.

Garrett also mentioned the use of XSLT, which can be partnered with XML to present the results of web service requests. However, a more popular approach is to use the DOM and new object notation such as JSON (JavaScript Object Notation) in addition to XML to manipulate existing page elements and manage the results of the web requests.

In summary, the development of web page functionality has led us from simple static web pages to all the functionality currently supported in Ajax today, with a few stops along the way:

- Static web pages with HTML-managed presentation and formatting
- Interactive functionality using JavaScript and variations such as JScript
- Separation of presentation and markup through the use of CSS

- Exposure of page elements to dynamic manipulation through the use of scripting
- Extensible markup provided by XML
- Web service requests and in-page XML processing

The Technologies: Book View

The JavaScript incorporated into the majority of Ajax applications in use when this book was written is based on the ECMAScript specification ECMA 262. It is more or less equivalent to the version of Microsoft's JScript found in IE 6.x and IE 7. It is also roughly equivalent to JavaScript 1.5 in Gecko-based browsers such as Firefox and Camino, and it is supported in Opera (9x), Safari 1.2, the Safari WebKit (development version for future versions of Safari), Konqueror, and other modern graphical browsers. This version of JavaScript is also supported in other user agents, for example personal assistants such as BlackBerry and iPhone.

Our next technology, the DOM, allows access to unique page elements and their attributes. The techniques and examples in this book are based on the Browser Object Model, or BOM (typically thought of as DOM Level 0), as well as DOM Levels 1 and 2. These are supported, with varying degrees of success and completeness, by the browsers mentioned above. As we examine Ajax, I'll note where the differences are.

Because this book focuses mainly on adding Ajax to existing sites and applications (from the client side), I will keep the discussion of server-side applications to a minimum. However, when required, PHP is the scripting language used to provide server-side functionality throughout this book. It is one of the simplest and most common server languages.

All of the examples in the book are XHTML-compliant, except where XHTML is not supported by the Ajax effect. For instance, Google Maps doesn't work in XHTML and the page is formatted as HTML 4.01 strict.

Additionally, all the examples are run in standard mode (rather than quirks mode) by providing a DOCTYPE for the page—either HTML 4.01 strict or XHTML 1.0 strict.

 Quirks mode allows a browser to maintain backward compatibility with older browsers and stylesheets. For instance, IE uses an older CSS box model when no DOCTYPE is provided or when the DOCTYPE is not a standard variation.

Changing a file's extension to *.xhtml* and adding the DOCTYPE may not be enough to run some of the examples on particular browsers. For example, Internet Explorer doesn't support the application/xhtml+xml MIME type, and Firefox defaults to

HTML. In an Apache environment, one trick to get XHTML documents to serve correctly in various agents is to make the following modifications to an *.htaccess* file:

```
AddType text/html .xhtml
RewriteEngine on
RewriteBase /
RewriteCond %{HTTP_ACCEPT} application/xhtml\+xml
RewriteCond %{HTTP_ACCEPT} !application/xhtml\+xml\s*;\s*q=0
RewriteCond %{REQUEST_URI} \.xhtml$
RewriteCond %{THE_REQUEST} HTTP/1\.1
RewriteRule .* - [T=application/xhtml+xml]
```

If the use of *.htaccess* is restricted or not supported by the web server, you can specify the MIME type in the applications that return the pages. For example, you can make the following PHP modification:

```
<?php
if ( stristr($_SERVER["HTTP_ACCEPT"],"application/xhtml+xml") ) {
  header("Content-type: application/xhtml+xml");
}
else {
  header("Content-type: text/html");
}
?>
```

Another alternative in getting an example to work properly is to simply give it a *.html* extension. This works with all the book examples except for those using PHP and those using embedded Scalar Vector Graphics (SVG), which is covered in Chapter 8.

All of the examples make use of CSS Levels 1 and 2. In order to avoid the workarounds caused by browser oddities, the examples in this book deal with the CSS features supported by all the browsers.

To ensure the examples and HTML/XHTML markup are valid, they have been run through one of the following validators:

- The Total Validator at *http://www.totalvalidator.com*
- The W3C's XHTML/HTML validator at *http://validator.w3.org*
- The W3C's CSS validation service at *http://jigsaw.w3.org/css-validator*
- The Cynthia Says accessibility validator at *http://contentquality.com* using the Section 508 guidelines

If you are using Firefox for development, all of these services can be accessed through the Web Developer Toolbar for Firefox or through the Total Validator Firefox extension. Though the examples work in all the target browsers (discussed later), for development purposes I recommend and assume you are using Firefox with Firebug installed as your primary development browser. This browser works in all target environments, and I've found no other tool as effective for development and debugging than Firebug. I'm so impressed with it that I consider it absolutely essential for Ajax development.

Download Firefox from *http://www.mozilla.com/en-US/firefox/*. Download Firebug from *http://getfirebug.com/*.

Start Clean

Adding Ajax to your site is an opportunity to do that page cleanup you've probably been wanting to do for a long time, but couldn't find the time. Dynamic effects and the use of old and outdated HTML don't go together well, particularly if you're moving objects around, collapsing and expanding columns, or doing in-place editing or help.

In a weblog post at O'Reilly Radar, Nat Torkington wrote the following account of Mark Lucovsky's attempt to implement the same bit of Ajax functionality into two very different web sites; one clean and the other with a large amount of "baggage" (*http://radar.oreilly.com/archives/2006/08/the_value_of_web_standards.html*):

> While at OSCON, Mark Lucovsky of Google sent us a bit of HTML that'd embed a slender map search widget into our conferences web site. It's an easy way for attendees to find restaurants, hotels, parks, bars, etc. near the conference venue. Great idea, and an elegant demo of the Ajax Search API that Mark's been working on.
>
> Mark's next speaking gig was at the Search Engine Strategies (SES) conference, so naturally he reached for the find-me-stuff-around-the-conference example. However, he rapidly ran into the messy HTML that is the SES web site. Whereas it had been a matter of seconds to add the JavaScript into the O'Reilly web page, adding it to the SES page was an ordeal.
>
> That's a vindication of the large amount of hard work that [the] O'Reilly design team put into redesigning pages so they were XHTML and CSS. It's also a vindication of the standards themselves: we sometimes lose track of the bigger picture when we're fighting our way through a twisty maze of namespaces, all alike. The point of the standards is not just to ensure that browsers can display the pages. The standards also ensure the pages form a platform that can be built upon; a hacked-together platform leads to brittle and fragile extensions.

Ajax is heavily dependent on CSS and even more dependent on the DOM. In Ajax applications, we can access individual elements and move them about, create them, or remove them on the fly. Due to the dependency on DOM, we can't just embed script in a page, throw a couple of ID attributes on elements, and expect our effects to work. Ajax is really dependent on the page being clean before we begin.

Before jumping in and tearing web pages apart in order to add Ajax effects, it's a good idea to first run your pages against various validators provided by the W3C (and others) to find and fix the current problem areas. Validation can help you determine how much work your pages need and can help you plan accordingly. Even if you're going to redesign the pages, you'll find that it's easier to convert from one design to another if you start with a clean design.

XHTML and HTML Validators

The granddaddy of all validators is the W3C's Markup Validation Service. To use the validator, enter a URL or upload a web page and the service will list, in minute detail, all those components that aren't valid (or are valid but not encouraged).

The Markup Validation Service supports a variety of doctypes, such as XHTML 1.0 Transitional, HTML 4.01 Strict, XHTML 1.1, and even custom doctypes. Normally a doctype is given in the document, using syntax such as the following:

```
<!DOCTYPE html PUBLIC "-//W3C//DTD XHTML 1.0 Transitional//EN" "http://www.w3.org/TR/
xhtml1/DTD/xhtml1-transitional.dtd">
```

You can override the doctype in the validation service in order to see how the page does with stricter specifications. You can choose to display the source with line numbers (helpful in debugging), or you can specify verbose mode for more detailed output. Figure 1-1 shows the output of the validator, listing several errors.

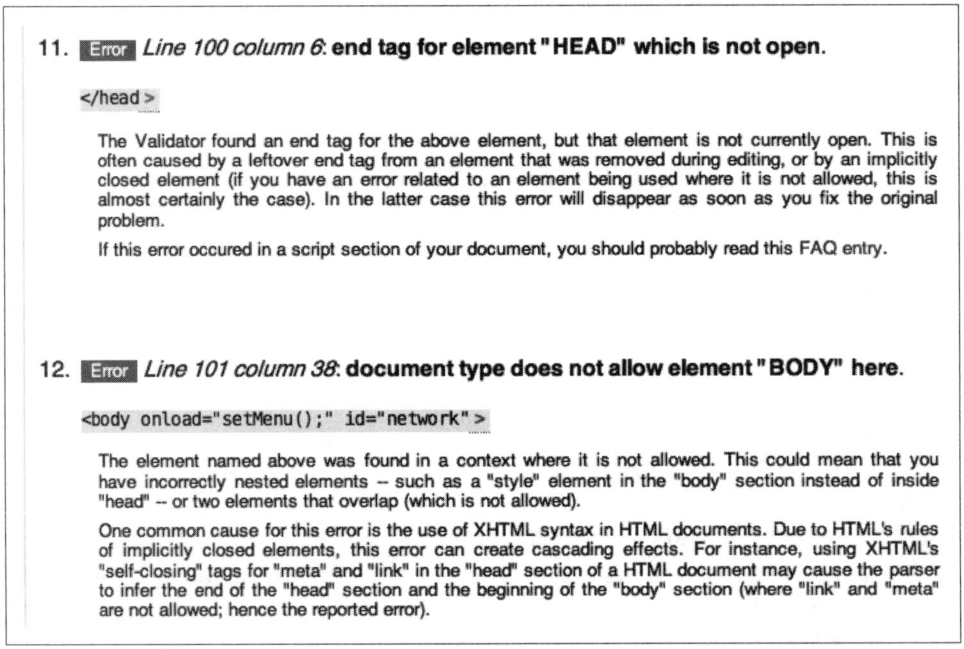

11. **Error** *Line 100 column 6*: **end tag for element "HEAD" which is not open.**

`</head >`

The Validator found an end tag for the above element, but that element is not currently open. This is often caused by a leftover end tag from an element that was removed during editing, or by an implicitly closed element (if you have an error related to an element being used where it is not allowed, this is almost certainly the case). In the latter case this error will disappear as soon as you fix the original problem.

If this error occured in a script section of your document, you should probably read this FAQ entry.

12. **Error** *Line 101 column 38*: **document type does not allow element "BODY" here.**

`<body onload="setMenu();" id="network" >`

The element named above was found in a context where it is not allowed. This could mean that you have incorrectly nested elements -- such as a "style" element in the "body" section instead of inside "head" -- or two elements that overlap (which is not allowed).

One common cause for this error is the use of XHTML syntax in HTML documents. Due to HTML's rules of implicitly closed elements, this error can create cascading effects. For instance, using XHTML's "self-closing" tags for "meta" and "link" in the "head" section of a HTML document may cause the parser to infer the end of the "head" section and the beginning of the "body" section (where "link" and "meta" are not allowed; hence the reported error).

Figure 1-1. The W3C's Markup Validation Service tells you how clean your page's markup is

Another validator is the Total Validator, created by Andy Halford. This validator can take longer than the W3C's, but you have an option (in the Advanced form) of providing an email address to have the results sent to you. The reason Total Validator takes so long is because of its impressive array of options. In addition to validation errors, the site also finds bad or missing links and misspelled words (which can be both localized and customized)—a nice double-check on the site.

One of the options is to check the accessibility of the site, and you can choose from a list of levels, including U.S. Section 508, and the three W3C Web Accessibility Initiative (WAI) levels. Another option allows you to set the number of pages validated (up to 20) and the depth (as defined in the site map). You can also skip specified paths within the site's navigation.

The tool also provides a screenshot based on your browser, operating system, and screen resolution. This is a very handy option if you don't have access to a specific browser in a particular operating system.

Figure 1-2 displays the results of running the validator against the O'Reilly main web page, including a screenshot taken in Konqueror v3.4 in Linux.

Figure 1-2. Using the Total Validator's many options to closely examine a web page

CSS Validators

I use Firefox for most of my browsing, and it's also my primary target browser for testing. The reason I use it more than other browsers is because of all the extensions, including those for web developers. Among these is the aforementioned Firebug, which is used extensively throughout this book. Web Developer Toolbar (*https:// addons.mozilla.org/firefox/60*) is another.

Among the features of Web Developer is a drop-down list with various validations that can be run on whatever page you're currently viewing. The HTML option uses the W3C Markup Validation Service, discussed in the previous section. There's also an option to validate the page's stylesheet using the W3C CSS Validator.

The CSS validator accepts the URL of a site or an uploaded file. If you want to try out the CSS before you put it into a stylesheet and you're not sure whether the syntax is valid, you can simply type in the CSS and have it checked. This option is handy—I tried it with the following code, which is from a stylesheet on one of my sites:

```
.comment-number {
       text-align: right;
       display: inline;
       font-size: 48pt;
       opacity: .3;
       filter: alpha(opacity=30);
       z-index: 3;
       padding-bottom: 0px; margin-bottom: 0px;
}
```

The result is shown in Figure 1-3. As you can see, the validator rejects the use of the nonstandard opacity settings.

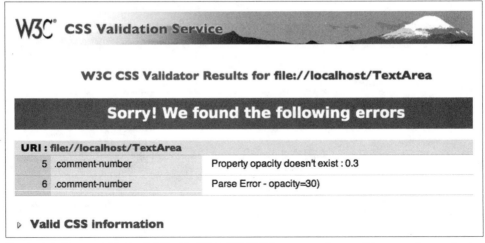

Figure 1-3. Testing a block of CSS with W3C CSS Validator to see how well it meets the standard

Checking Accessibility

Why is accessibility so important? I've heard the argument that only five percent of page readers are impacted by page functionality that may fail these accessibility guidelines. However, ethical considerations aside, accessibility is becoming mandated more and more by law—many countries now mandate that all government pages meet accessibility guidelines. Accessibility is also becoming an important consideration for commercial sites. In fact, there's currently a case pending against Target (a large chain of stores in the U.S. and elsewhere), where the company was successfully sued for not providing an accessible online web store (the case is under appeal). I expect this to be a continuing trend.

An excellent one-page listing of the best articles on accessibility and Ajax can be found at the Stanford Online Accessibility program at *http://soap.stanford.edu/show.php?contentid=65.*

Unlike validating CSS or XHTML, determining whether a page meets an accessibility guideline is as much inspection and personal interpretation as it is automated test results. The results from running an accessibility test at the Cynthia Says site can be quite extensive, and you'll probably need to read the guidelines associated with the test. One of the most critical factors in using this site is choosing which standard you're running the test against: one of the three W3C WAI 1.0 guidelines—Priority 1, 2, or 3—or the U.S. Section 508 guidelines.

Read more on the W3C WAI 1.0 guidelines at *http://www.w3.org/TR/ WCAG10/*, and Section 508 at *http://www.access-board.gov/sec508/ standards.htm* (Subpart_b).

The Total Validator also performs accessibility checks, again providing options for you to choose WAI or Section 508. Even with these tests, though, you'll need to manually check your effort against the guidelines when finished. Something like a meaningful alt attribute description for an image element (which will help readers who can't interpret images to know what's missing) can't be deduced from automatic testing.

Converting Tables to CSS Layouts

Page layout problems that trigger an error message are easy to identify. However, some page changes that are required to make a site optimal for Ajax development (and all other uses) don't result in validation errors or accessibility warnings. One of the most common old layout tricks before the advent of CSS was using HTML tables to manage the page contents, regardless of content type. However, HTML tables were meant for tabular data, such as a listing of records from a database. For our purposes, HTML tables are not very adaptable to many Ajax effects. As I'll demonstrate later in this chapter, and also in Chapter 6, updating a dynamic table is trickier than updating a discrete div element. In addition, you can't necessarily move a table row or handle a table cell as a distinct object. HTML tables also drive the semantic web people batty—if you use HTML tables to present all of the information on a web page, the tabular data will not stand out.

Here are some of the issues with using HTML tables for all of your page content:

- HTML table elements were created specifically for tabular data.
- HTML tables add an extra layer of complexity when using JavaScript.
- HTML table elements, such as rows and cells, exist within a framework that makes it awkward to work with an element individually.
- HTML table elements can't be easily collapsed, moved, or removed from the display without adversely effecting other elements.
- Some JavaScript-based effects, such as layering, opacity, and other subtle effects can have a negative impact when used with an HTML table.

Based on all this, one of the most common Ajax preparation tasks is converting HTML tables to valid XHTML elements and CSS. Converting the page to CSS is going to make creating Ajax effects easier, and it is going to make site maintenance easier, too. Contrary to expectation, the conversion is actually not as hard as you may think. The next couple of sections explore how to do this, along with a few other conversion efforts. If your web site is already valid and making use of CSS and XHTML, you may want to skip these sections.

 HTML tables were designed to display related data, such as a list of stores and locations or the results of a survey. Using them for general page layout is not semantically correct. You'll hear mention of the *semantics* of an approach throughout the book. What this means (no pun intended) is that the elements used in the page are used in ways that are appropriate for their defined usage, not just for formatting. This can help screen readers and other devices to process the page more accurately. It can also help *web bots*, automated web robots used by search engines and other sites, process the data more efficiently.

Here's a typical web page design: the header and footer extend the width of the page or the content, and the body of the page is broken into two vertical components, one as a sidebar and the other as main content. The sidebar can be on the left or right, and the page can be sized and centered or extended to the width of the browser window.

Using an HTML table in this case is simple: create one table with two columns and three rows, and use colspan to expand the column in the first and third rows to the width of the table. There are several different methods you can use to recreate this effect using XHTML and CSS. One is to create three blocks using div elements, each expanded to 100 percent of the container space, stacked one after the other, as shown in Figure 1-4.

To create the two columns in the middle space, add two div elements side by side instead of stacked, and sized so that the content column is wider. List the content column first in the actual page markup so that it will be the first one read by text-to-screen readers.

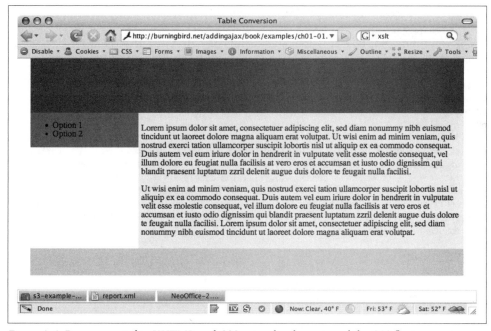

Figure 1-4. Page converted to XHTML and CSS using div elements and the CSS float property

Normally div elements are block-level elements, which means they stack vertically. To align the columns side-by-side, use the CSS float property to float the block to the left or right, effectively removing the item from the vertical page flow. If the sidebar is going on the left, set its float value to left and set the content column's float value to right. Example 1-1 shows the complete page.

Example 1-1. XHTML page with converted two-column page

```
<!DOCTYPE html PUBLIC "-//W3C//DTD XHTML 1.0 Strict//EN"
    "http://www.w3.org/TR/xhtml1/DTD/xhtml1-strict.dtd">
<html xmlns="http://www.w3.org/1999/xhtml">
<head>
<meta http-equiv="Content-Type" content="text/html; charset=utf-8" />
<title>Table Conversion</title>
<style type="text/css">
body { margin: 0; padding: 0 }
#wrapper { width: 800px; margin: 0 auto; }
#header { height: 100px; background-color: #00f; }
#sidebar {  width: 200px; background-color: #f00; float: left; }
#content {  width: 590px; background-color: #ff0;  padding: 5px; float: right; }
#footer { clear: both; background-color: #0f0; height: 50px; }
</style>
</head>
<body>
<div id="wrapper">
<div id="header">
</div>
```

Example 1-1. XHTML page with converted two-column page (continued)

```
<div id="content">
<p>Lorem ipsum dolor sit amet, consectetuer adipiscing elit, sed diam nonummy nibh euismod
tincidunt ut laoreet dolore magna aliquam erat volutpat. Ut wisi enim ad minim veniam,
quis nostrud exerci tation ullamcorper suscipit lobortis nisl ut aliquip ex ea commodo
consequat. Duis autem vel eum iriure dolor in hendrerit in vulputate velit esse molestie
consequat, vel illum dolore eu feugiat nulla facilisis at vero eros et accumsan et iusto
odio dignissim qui blandit praesent luptatum zzril delenit augue duis dolore te feugait
nulla facilisi.
</p><p>
Ut wisi enim ad minim veniam, quis nostrud exerci tation ullamcorper suscipit lobortis
nisl ut aliquip ex ea commodo consequat. Duis autem vel eum iriure dolor in hendrerit in
vulputate velit esse molestie consequat, vel illum dolore eu feugiat nulla facilisis at
vero eros et accumsan et iusto odio dignissim qui blandit praesent luptatum zzril delenit
augue duis dolore te feugait nulla facilisi. Lorem ipsum dolor sit amet, consectetuer
adipiscing elit, sed diam nonummy nibh euismod tincidunt ut laoreet dolore magna aliquam
erat volutpat. </p>
</div>
<div id="sidebar">
    <ul>
       <li>Option 1</li>
       <li>Option 2</li>
    </ul>
</div>
<div id="footer">
</div>
</div>
</body>
</html>
```

To remove the float property from the footer (so that it will appear below, rather than beside, the sidebar and content pages) the CSS clear property is set to both.

Viewing the page in Figure 1-4, notice that the left column, which is the sidebar, doesn't extend all the way down if the content isn't long enough. This is the drawback of using CSS-positioned XHTML: the column background extends only the length of the content.

One way of working around this problem is to set the same background color for all of the containers—this will hide the column length differences.

Another approach (and the one I prefer) is to create an image that is the same width and color of the sidebar, and then use it as a background image for the sidebar container. To use this method, set the background repeat attributes so that the image does not repeat horizontally or vertically, and position it where the sidebar would start. You can also set the background color of the container to be the same as the content column—this will fill in any area not covered by the background image. With this modification, both columns appear to be the same length. The modified style setting is:

```
#wrapper {
            background-image: url(ajaxbackground.jpg);
            background-position: top left;
            background-repeat: repeat-y;
            background-color: #ff0;
            width: 800px;
            margin: 0 auto;
            }
```

The page with the modified container style setting is shown in Figure 1-5.

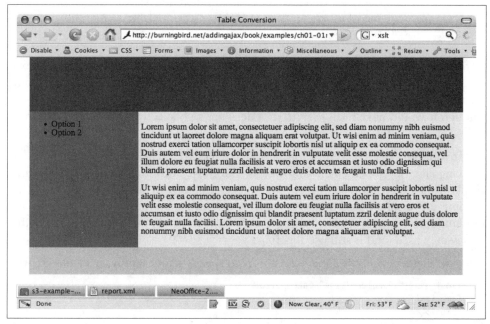

Figure 1-5. Modified container style settings make both columns appear to be the same length

This is just one approach. There are many CSS-based layout possibilities. The one just described is a *fixed* layout. In a *fluid* layout, the column sizes change to fit the page size, and in an *elastic* layout, the column sizes are based on page size, but are not to exceed a maximum width. For additional reading on CSS layouts, search the Web for "fluid fixed elastic CSS layout."

It can be difficult to get sites switched over from HTML tables to CSS because the tables are so handy and simple to use, and CSS can be a little daunting. Furthermore, a page will validate as XHTML regardless of whether it uses HTML tables. However, some web page elements simply will not validate and must be converted. In the next section, we'll look at the most common of these elements.

Continuing the Conversion: Element by Element

Converting a page to XHTML and CSS is one major change, but there are a host of smaller, easier changes to make before the page validates as XHTML. These changes will make the page elements accessible for script access, which I'll be demonstrating throughout this book.

 There are a number of tools that can assist you in cleaning up your web pages and converting them from HTML to XHTML. A popular tool used for this purpose is HTML Tidy, available at *http://tidy. sourceforge.net/*.

In the early days of the browser, one of the first items people wanted to control was the font. If the entire page were black and white, with font family and size based only on the type of element, our sites would have been too uniform and far too dull (though it would have been easy from a designer's perspective, not to mention fully accessible).

To provide for page customization, a few new HTML elements were introduced as the language developed, including one of the most notorious of all bad elements: blink. This element caused objects (text, images, etc.) to blink on and off. It has become universally hated and is a poster child for separation of page markup and presentation. Luckily, people only toyed briefly with blink, but another element that was widely used (and is still used) is font.

The font element gives designers the ability to specify a font family, size, and color:

```
<font size="4" color="blue" face="arial">
Some text
</font>
```

The font element lets us make our text more distinctive, but it does have a drawback: if we want to make a change to the font in our web content, we have to hunt down the use of font in all of our web pages and make the change manually. This can make page maintenance excruciating.

With the advent of CSS, the push is on to remove the use of font (and it has disappeared, more or less, from most pages). If the font element is present in your web sites or applications, you'd be wise to remove it and use a stylesheet setting instead. The following is the CSS setting for the font of a specific element:

```
#test { font-family: arial; font-size: 4em; color: #0000ff }
```

Other position- and style-specific elements have been deprecated or conflict with the use of Ajax and should be removed. Among these are:

center

This element is used to center objects. Use CSS to achieve this effect instead.

menu
> This element is used to create menu lists. This effect should be replaced using unordered lists (UL).

Strike
> This element creates strikethrough text (use CSS or DEL).

dir
> This element is used to create a directory list and should be replaced using UL.

Applet
> This element was used to include Java applets, but you should use object now.

The best way to determine whether a page contains deprecated elements is to set the DOCTYPE to the specification you want to support and then run the page through the validator. You will be notified by the validator if there are any unsupported elements.

Another aspect of HTML that is not compatible with XHTML is the use of tag closure with elements that may or may not have a terminating end tag. For instance, the img element has no end tag, as all the information about an image is included in the element tag. In XHTML, this tag should be closed with a forward slash just before the closing bracket:

```
<img src="some.jpg" alt="alternative text" />
```

When adding Ajax, it's especially important that elements in a web page are properly closed; otherwise, you may get unexpected side effects when you begin to add dynamic effects. Among the more commonly unclosed elements are paragraphs (p) and list items (li). Closing them may seem like a minor headache, but it's one that may prevent much larger headaches later on.

So, what happens once you've eliminated the obvious problems? Will all web browsers look and act the same? Oh, we can only wish.

Dealing with Browser-Specific Quirks

It may seem like every HTML element has predefined style settings. Headers are block-level elements, larger than paragraph text, increasing in size from h6 to h1. Each HTML list item has a default padding value. Paragraphs are block elements with specific margins and padding, fonts, and line spacing.

At first glance, these defaults appear to be relatively the same across browsers, but even minor variations can have significant impact on page design and Ajax effects. Browsers provide their own internal stylesheets that define these values, and though there are some constraints on the styling (such as paragraphs being block-level elements), other settings are based on the browser developers' interpretation of W3C-specified guidelines.

Due to these variations, the amount of spacing between letters, sizes, and so on can differ. Link colors, list icons, and relative header sizes can also differ—significantly at times. This can cause a lot of problems in the page design and can produce unexpected side effects when adding Ajax.

Controlling the Page and Adding Ajax

Many effects in Ajax, such as just-in-time (JIT) help (in-page messages that are hidden until needed), placement, color fades, collapsible elements, and so on can only work effectively across browsers when the browsers' various quirks are eliminated.

For example, Safari supports a different line height than Firefox—a quirk that doesn't impact pages containing a great deal of text, but one that can create major problems for an Ajax application that positions text in a small box for a help system. If the text ends up being too large for some browsers and too small for others, the overall system is going to look amateurish or may be hard to read.

One of the worst offenders for invalid CSS has been IE, and some of the workaround hacks have actually been given names, such as Peekaboo Bug, Border Chaos, and the Guillotine Bug; entertaining names, but they're a pain to work with.

 Microsoft has made an effort in IE 7 to fix most of the browser's CSS problems; for more information see *http://blogs.msdn.com/ie/archive/2006/08/22/712830.aspx*. Unfortunately, the browser isn't perfect and still has quirks.

IE isn't the only browser that has quirks, though—there is no gold standard. Each browser has its own personality. Unfortunately, personality isn't necessarily a positive attribute in the browser marketplace. Perhaps if it were easy, it wouldn't be as much fun.

If the font sizes, margins, and padding differ between browsers, even by minor amounts, elements serving as containers for dynamic text, such as list items or box elements, may be too small for the text, and the result will be wrapping or truncation. You'll have far fewer of these problems if you use XHTML and comprehensive CSS stylesheets.

Taking Control

One approach to resolving cross-browser stylesheet differences is to create a custom stylesheet that optimizes each of the elements for a single browser, then add the necessary tweaks to make it look the same for the second browser (trying not to break the first), and then move on to the third, and so on. This can be a major job, especially for a site that's using sophisticated styling and relatively complex Ajax.

Another approach is to remove all style settings from the stylesheet and add in only the ones that are needed. This can be a drastic change, but it will provide you with absolute control over the page layout, thereby ensuring that Ajax effects work as expected.

If you want to change style settings for all of your web elements, you can apply global settings—it's as simple as typing the asterisk (*) character. The following code sets the margin and padding to 0, and sets the font (font-family) to Arial for all elements:

```
* { padding: 0; margin: 0; font-family: Arial }
```

It's a simple style setting, but when applied to a page, the effects are dramatic.

Of course, removing or adjusting the settings for all elements means that you have to go through and define a style setting for every element, which can get tedious. A better approach might be to adjust the settings for just those elements that tend to give you the most problems across browsers, and leave the others at the default values. You can then package these defaults into a stylesheet that will be included in all pages just before a second stylesheet that contains each page's unique settings.

One such global change you might consider is removing the underline from all hypertext links. The underline can mess up the page's look and prove distracting, especially when you have a group of items that are all underlined. Underlines can also cut off the lower part of the letters with some fonts, making the words hard to read. The following setting will remove the underline from all links:

```
a { text-decoration: none}
```

The underline can then be added back in (again using CSS) for links within specified elements, such as an element containing a great deal of text and few links. Of course, one of the problems with using this approach is that the hypertext links aren't as apparent on the page. What I do with my sites is use a font that's compatible with link underlines and keep the underlines in my main content text. In sidebars and menus, the context should be enough to highlight that the text is wrapped in a link. Since the font can be smaller, or many linked items listed one after another, I remove the underline for a cleaner, easier-to-read page.

Another major cleanup task is setting headers to use the same size, padding, and margin using syntax similar to the following:

```
h1, h2, h3, h4, h5, h6{ font-size:  1em; padding: 0; margin: 0 }
```

These are really semantic elements, providing information for search engine bots and screen readers about the outline in the page:

```
h1 header one
    h2 header two
        h3 header three
        h3 header three
    h2 header two
```

We've gotten into the habit of using these header elements for boldness and size, which is completely contrary to their purpose. By removing these elements, we're forced to use headers appropriately and use font styling where appropriate to create a visual effect. If you provide a graphical header, provide an h1 header for the content. If you don't want it showing, turn off its visibility, but don't remove it; it's necessary for search engine optimization. A good compromise is wrapping the image in an h1 element, with the exact text in the alt attribute.

Once you've removed the most obvious errors, continue creating your own default stylesheet, removing or normalizing any element that proves itself problematic across browsers.

 Threr is an interesting article by Tantek Çelik about creating a default scaffolding stylesheet at *http://tantek.com/log/2004/09.html#d06t2354*. A follow-up by Eric Meyer is located at *http://meyerweb.com/eric/thoughts/2004/09/15/emreallyem-undoing-htmlcss*.

After validating and cleaning up existing sites and applications, the next step in the process of adding Ajax is defining a plan for the type of changes you want to make to your site, including which frameworks to use and which target browsers and other user agents you need to support. To do all of this, you need to have a good understanding of your client base: your web page readers and your web application users.

Understanding Your Client Base

The amount of Ajax functionality that you introduce to your site depends on more than just how much you're willing to add and maintain. Even the niftiest technology is going to fall flat if it doesn't provide an added value, or worse, locks your users out of the site. What you will discover, though, is that if you listen to the feedback from your client base, you'll be able to use a little scripting and a few in-page web services to really increase the usability of your site.

Discovering Your Clients

The first step in your Ajax makeover is discovering all you can about the people who visit your site so that you plan accordingly. Your best friends in this regard are your site's logs. The following log entry is from one of my sites, and it is a fairly typical example:

```
5x.x2.x8.xx0 - - [31/Aug/2006:03:09:27 +0000] "GET /wp-content/themes/bbgun/bbgung.
png HTTP/1.1" 200 90338 "http://burningbird.net/wp-content/themes/bbgun/style.css"
"Mozilla/5.0 (Windows; U; Windows NT 5.1; en-US; rv:1.8.0.6) Gecko/20060728 Firefox/
1.5.0.6"
```

This log displays the date, the resource accessed, and a string containing information about the client's operating system and browser. In this case, the browser is Firefox version 1.5.0.6, and the operating system is Windows. Another line from the log is:

```
x0.xx3.1xx.xx4 - - [31/Aug/2006:03:14:48 +0000] "GET /wp-content/themes/words/
eyesafe.png HTTP/1.1" 404 9058 "http://burningbird.net/" "Mozilla/5.0 (Macintosh; U;
PPC Mac OS X Mach-O; en-US; rv:1.8.1b1) Gecko/20060707 Firefox/2.0b1"
```

This client is using Firefox 2.0, the first beta release, and the operating system is Mac OS X.

This information will help you determine which user agents (browsers and mobile devices) to support, and will allow you to compensate for the image, image resolution, font support, and tool support differences that exist between operating systems.

You can look at a logfile directly or you can use one of a variety of web tools such as AWStats or Webalizer to analyze the log. You can find these and others just by searching for "logfile analyzer" with your favorite search engine.

Other resources you can use to explore web access are the sites that track browser statistics, such as the W3 Schools at *http://www.w3schools.com/browsers/browsers_stats.asp* or The Counter at *http://www.thecounter.com/stats*.

To determine how many users have JavaScript enabled, add a NOSCRIPT section that loads a unique image, one that doesn't impact on the page, and then check the logs to see how often the image has been accessed. With recent high-profile script-based security violations at Google and elsewhere, you'll find that more people are disabling script as a security measure. Others may be using tools such as NoScript (*http://noscript.net*), a Firefox extension that allows you to enable JavaScript on a site-by-site basis. When designing your web content, expect that people will have script turned off, and unless the application is completely based on scripting, don't put up notices about how people should turn scripting on for a better experience; this has become the equivalent of an Ajax blink.

An Open-Door Policy

I once asked readers at one of my sites which specific uses of Ajax they'd like to see on the site. One of the options I listed was a drop-down menu that popped open either when the mouse was over a top-level menu item or when the item was clicked—a quite common use of DHTML frequently extended to Ajax.

Surprisingly, the behavior of the drop-down menu wasn't especially interesting to my readers. They tended to be more interested in having control over their interaction with the site than they were controlling the navigation between pages.

Now, if I had a more complex site structure, the menu might have been more essential. However, the difference between what I thought would be important to the page readers and what they actually reported demonstrates that you can't assume what your page readers will want. Before you begin the process of adding Ajax to your site, it's a good idea to get your readers involved—ask what they want to see, or test new technology in specific places and solicit feedback. Don't be surprised, though, if you have to change both your assumptions and your implementation plan.

What if my page readers had wanted the DHTML drop-down menu? If my site structure had been more than two levels deep, I would agree, but I wouldn't just implement the menu and then walk away. Dynamically generated navigation makes your site inaccessible for those who have turned off JavaScript, have difficulties using a mouse, or are using a text-to-speech browser.

Even if you find that 95 percent of your readers turn on script, use a mouse, or use a browser like Firefox, making your site inaccessible punishes those people who may already have enough challenges in their lives. Consider also that the most popular extension for Firefox is one that turns scripting off for sites by default (NoScript). You shouldn't make any assumptions about how many people are using JavaScript, either. Finally, search engine web bots, such as Google's and Yahoo!'s, can't follow script-generated links, and therefore won't pick up the material accessible only through the menu.

Some features may require JavaScript or the mouse. These might include online word processors, spreadsheets, or games, but should never include critical features such as the ability to navigate to main content pages and application documentation. Use the following recommendations when you are determining how to best incorporate your page readers' needs:

- Forget the surprise rollout; ask your page readers what they'd like to see before you begin.
- Consider beta testing a change in one portion of your site and soliciting feedback before rolling it out across the site.
- Balance requests against the amount of work required; the more moving parts the more things can break, and no reader likes a broken page.
- Listen to people. If you roll out a change and it doesn't work, be prepared and ready to pull it back and try something else.

The Plan

Now that you have a better idea of your page readers' environments and preferences, it's time to develop a plan for adding Ajax to your site. The difference between adding Ajax to a small site versus a big one is in the number of hours it will take, not in the steps you take.

The object that you change first is dependent on your reasons for adding Ajax. For instance, if you have an extensive customer application with lots of form pages, this would be an ideal place for adding Ajax; it's an isolated application that could have big returns in terms of satisfaction, quality of response, and resource use once it's Ajax-enabled. Ajax can also improve the overall performance of the application, making it even more of a win–win situation.

Other target areas are any pages where your readers have the ability to update or modify information. Adding Ajax to make the changes in-place can add enormously to the client's satisfaction, while still being completely accessible.

Providing JIT help or feedback is an excellent use of Ajax. Just make sure that the same information is available if scripting is disabled or if clients are using a text-to-speech browser.

The addition of visual elements should not be your highest priority, but it's a legitimate use of Ajax. These changes can add a nice "Wow" factor with minimum disruption of the site's primary functionality.

Ajax should be added gradually, and you should back the site up before you add even one line of code. If you do need to add something globally, like a new Ajax-enabled menu that will appear on all of your site's pages, encapsulate the code into a file that can then be incorporated into all your pages—such as a header file that's incorporated into each page using server-side functionality.

Minimize the amount of code you'll add to each page by organizing code into libraries and including only the desired library on each page. Or consider using one of the freely available Ajax libraries. Several Ajax libraries are covered in Chapter 3 and are used throughout this book.

When creating your plan, consider the following:

- This is a nag, but can never be said too much: back up your site before you start and when each addition is published.
- Determine your starting point; an isolated application makes a good candidate.
- Examine areas where your site or application is already interactive and explore how Ajax can be used for improvement.
- Make liberal use of JIT help and feedback, providing alternatives for clients who have scripting disabled.
- Visual effects to enhance or accompany existing functionality add sparkle and effect, usually at minimum cost.
- Look for opportunities to encapsulate reusable chunks of code, such as menu functions or online help.
- Use existing libraries.

Designing a Framework for Your Site

The most important decision facing you now is whether to add Ajax to existing pages or to start from scratch. This book is based on an assumption that web developers begin by introducing Ajax into existing pages and applications rather than scrapping a site and starting anew. In other words, the client-side functionality is adapted, and the server-side component of the site is left as-is, more or less.

The next step in the decision process is to determine the extent of the Ajax modifications. If you're changing a static web page form to one that uses script and `XMLHttpRequest` to support in-page edits, your use of the new technologies is relatively isolated and will have little impact on the overall site application.

However, if you're adding a site-wide help system, a new dynamic menu, or an in-place search feature, all of your pages will be impacted, and you might want to consider some additional architecture changes, such as splitting out your header and all the script into separate files that can be included in all of your pages. This approach allows you to make sure all of the appropriate JavaScript libraries are included, and allows you to isolate objects like event handlers.

Many of the new content management systems are based on a modular approach that allows you to reuse the sidebar, headers, and footers as much as possible. If your site doesn't use a modular system and the pages are managed manually, you might want to add this to your to-do list for future designs.

 Whether you modularize your web pages or not, all of your custom JavaScript should be created in separate files that are included into the appropriate pages. When you change in the code in a script, it will automatically be propagated out to all the pages using that script.

Meet Your Reader

Earlier, I covered the importance of discovering your web page readers' environments, including their browsers and operating systems, and determining whether they have JavaScript enabled. You'll also need to work through an accessibility plan, including criteria used to judge each web page as it's converted to Ajax. This will help to ensure the plan's requirements are met.

I remember reading somewhere once that you only have to meet the needs of 90 or 95 percent of your web page readers. That may be true of people using older browsers, such as IE 5.5 for the Mac, but it isn't true for people who face enough challenges in life without having more thrust on them just to access your site. This may include:

- The visually impaired, who may use a text-to-speech browser
- Those physically incapable of using a mouse

- People who suffer from color blindness
- The hearing impaired, who may not be able to listen to a podcast or hear auditory instructions
- People with attention-deficit disorder or other learning-comprehension challenges, who may not be able to quickly comprehend fast-moving text or flashed messages
- The tired, time-challenged, distracted, and stressed

In other words, all of us. Your readers may have a hard time reading font that's tiny enough to require a magnifying lens to view. Adding in-page editing or dynamic search functionality doesn't amount to much if you have to cram the additions into a space too small to be readable. Additionally, there are few things more irritating than having to wave the mouse around the page like a magic wand in order to discover where the site's navigation objects are or which elements can be clicked to get access to critical information.

Safe and Secure

A site's readers are also dependent on the developers providing a usable and safe environment. Part of a web site's architecture is the inclusion of test procedures that check to make sure the page is still accessible in all of the target browsers and environments each time a change is added. Included in your upgrade plan should be procedures to stress test the changes.

You should also run tests to make sure the code isn't taking more than its share of space on a reader's computer. Most JavaScript applications use client-side storage for one reason or another and for the most part JavaScript cookies are sufficient for an application's needs. However, several Ajax libraries have provided facilities to store additional data on the client's computer using Flash or some other external storage. When developing your plan, investigate how much data must be stored on the client compared to the server. Client-side storage is an inherent security risk in any web application, Ajax-based or not.

You will also have to include security issues in your plan. As we progress through the book, I'll point out areas of vulnerability with the different Ajax effects we explore. Still, the more moving parts your pages have, the more important it is to monitor sites that issue security releases and test your pages when browsers release updates.

 Since this is a general-purpose book on adding Ajax, I can't provide complete details on security issues. Instead, I recommend Christopher Wells' book, *Securing Ajax Applications* (O'Reilly), which provides detailed coverage of Ajax and security.

Tight Coupling and Loose Coupling

As part of the framework for adding Ajax, web developers also need to decide on how tightly coupled client and server applications are.

A *tightly coupled* application is one in which most of the client side of the application is generated by or dependent on the server. In other words, there's no way to really separate the two or the whole thing breaks.

A *loosely coupled* application, on the other hand, is one in which the web services could be called by an Ajax application, but could likewise be called by another web service. In addition, the client side of the application interfaces only with the API (application programming interface), so it is not affected by how the web service was developed or which language is used.

If you're choosing a loosely coupled solution, it means that you're developing your server application to provide web services that may be called by other server-side applications in addition to an Ajax application. This approach is the most disciplined because it makes no assumption about the capability of the client. A change in the client doesn't impact the server, and a change in the implementation of the server doesn't impact the client.

If, however, you're using a more tightly coupled approach (for example, a Java library such as Google's Google Web Toolkit (GWT), then the tool itself is going to determine the extent of what you can do with the page or even what's generated.

For the most part, if you're adding Ajax to an existing site, you're going the loosely coupled approach. When you're starting from scratch, you have the option to use tight coupling as an approach, though you should be cautious in tying the server and client sides so closely together.

Progressive Enhancement Versus Massive Overhaul

As stated earlier, you're one of the luckier Ajax developers because you have a site or an application that already has all the basic functionality, and now you're looking to enhance and improve it through the use of Ajax. This might require some preparation ahead of time, but anything done to make the pages better for Ajax also makes the site better.

Supported Browsers

It's always difficult to determine which browsers and other user agents to support when writing a book. I checked my own logs at a number of my sites to see what people are using, and it runs the gamut from Firefox 2.x to IE 3.x. People access the pages from PDAs, cellphones, and other mobile devices, and even WebTV.

Most of the examples I provide in this book would not look good on the small screen of an iPhone or equivalent device, regardless of whether Ajax is used or not. The way I provide content for mobile devices is to use a separate mobile stylesheet, which renders the content legible in a small device. We can also use this as a way of determining whether to turn off our Ajax effects. I vote for off, myself.

As for browsers, I decided on testing the examples with all of the following:

- IE 6.x on Windows 2000
- IE 7 on Windows XP
- Firefox 2.x, on both Windows and Mac
- Camino 1.0 for Mac
- Safari 2.0.4
- WebKit 420+
- Opera 9.x and later on Windows and Mac
- OmniWeb 5.x
- Konqueror

I made a decision, after much internal deliberation, not to support IE 5.5 or earlier versions of IE. These earlier versions are no longer supported by Microsoft and are insecure, not to mention grossly incomplete in their implementations of standard web technology. For all environments where IE 5.5 or earlier is used, there are replacements. This includes the Mac, as well as earlier versions of Windows. Needless to say, the examples don't provide Ajax support to browsers such as Netscape 4.x, either.

The approach I used was to emulate an effect where scripting was disabled and clients were receiving non-Ajax web pages. This provides access without having to go through the considerable pain of dealing with a world of infinite varieties.

I don't equate accessibility with masochism. One has to draw the line somewhere.

A summary of what's been covered in this chapter gives us the following set of steps for simplifying and preparing for your Ajax development:

1. Validate the existing pages for target XHTML and CSS specifications and make required corrections.

2. Convert old HTML table layouts to CSS/XHTML, clean up deprecated or out-of-date HTML elements, and convert HTML to XHTML.

3. Define a plan for adding Ajax effects, including which sections of the site are going to be completely rewritten, which will be modified, and which effects will be incorporated.

4. Study your readers; determine which pages they access and which tools they use.

5. Get your web page readers' involvement, including results of prototype tests.

6. Create a framework for change; minimize the amount of code by making as much of it reusable as possible. Now would be a good time to consider bringing in a content management system if you aren't already using one.

Once you've formed a plan, defined a framework for rolling out Ajax additions to your site, converted the pages into valid XHTML and CSS, and reduced the CSS variations among browsers, you're ready to begin adding Ajax.

CHAPTER 2

The Ajax Bits

What sets Ajax apart from JavaScript is its use of in-page requests for external data and its ability to return the results without reloading the page. The request can be as simple as loading a new image or stylesheet, or as complex as loading an entire XML document that updates many parts of the page. The data from the web service can be integrated into the page through *dynamic scripting*—creating a scripting block that consists of a callback function and the returned data. Typically, though, the request is made to a web service through a key object, `XMLHttpRequest`.

The concept of an object that manages web service requests from script within a web page originated several years ago with Internet Explorer 5.0. The original object was an ActiveX object, and Microsoft continued to support that approach with IE 6.x. Now, though, like the other browsers, Microsoft supports the `XMLHttpRequest` object.

The `XMLHttpRequest` object is one of the simpler browser objects to work with: a web service request is created, the request is sent, and a callback function is invoked to process the response. Rather than all of this activity spread across many pages, as is the case with traditional web applications, it's all accomplished within the same web page, without any page reloads.

 There are so many acronyms in this business. I use `XMLHttpRequest` throughout much of the book, but I, and other developers, also sometimes just say *XHR* to save both time and typing.

The Web Application

For this chapter, I created a simple application, Drinks, where the web page reader selects the name of a drink and the drink recipe is printed out. Though it's fairly trivial, it does serve to demonstrate the server-client communication implicit in web applications without getting too bogged down with extraneous functionality.

The server-side functionality is created using PHP, and for this simplified example, the recipes are stored within the PHP page. The client side contains a form with a list of drink names and a submit button. When the page reader clicks the submit button, the form is sent to the web server, and the associated recipe is retrieved and printed to the page.

Before getting into the Ajax functionality, let's look at an application as it might be constructed without any use of JavaScript.

For a simple application, it's not unusual to combine the client and server within the same file, with the server-side functionality printing out pertinent client-side elements. The only tedious part of creating this application is ensuring the selected drink reappears in the list as the selection; otherwise, the first drink in the list will be displayed, making it out of sync with the printed recipe. Example 2-1 shows the complete application, with one page containing both client and server components.

Example 2-1. Complete one-page Drinks application

```php
<?php

//If no search string is passed, then we can't search
$drink = $_REQUEST['drink'];
if (empty($drink)) {
    $drink = 'TEA';
} else {
    //Remove whitespace from beginning & end of passed search.
    $search = trim($drink);

    switch($search) {
      case "TEA" :
        $result = "<h3>Hot Tea</h3><p>Boil water. " .
                   "Pour over tea leaves. Steep five minutes. " .
                   "Strain and serve</p>";
        break;
      case "APPLETINI" :
        $result = "<h3>Appletini</h3><p>Mix 1 oz vodka and 1/2 oz Sour Apple Pucker or " .
                   "apple schnapps in a glass filled with ice. Strain into martini glass. " .
                   "Garnish with an apple slice or raisin.</p>";
        break;
      case "NONCHAMP" :
        $result = "<h3>Non-Alcoholic Champagne</h3><p>Mix 32 ounces club soda" .
                   " with 12 ounces frozen white grape juice concentrate.</p>";
        break;
      case "SWMPMARGARITA" :
        $result = "<h3>Swamp Margarita</h3>" .
                   "<p>Mix 1 1/2 ounce good quality tequila, 3/4 ounce Cointreau, " .
                   "3/4 ounce Grand Marnier, 1/2 ounce lime juice, and 2 ounces sour mix.
        Chill an hour. " .
                   "Fill bottom of tall glass with several green olives and a few drops
        olive juice. " .
                   "Pour margarita over the olives and let sit for ten minutes. " .
                   "Strain and serve with a few olives stuffed with pimento on a
        toothpick.</p>";
        break;
```

Example 2-1. Complete one-page Drinks application (continued)

```
        case "LEMON" :
          $result = "<h3>Lemon Drop</h3><p>Mix 1 ounce lemon vodka " .
                    "with 1 ounce lemon juice and 1 teaspoon sugar. Shake with ice, " .
                    "strain and serve.</p>";
          break;
        default :
          $result = "No recipes found";
          break;
      }
}
?>
<!DOCTYPE html PUBLIC "-//W3C//DTD XHTML 1.0 Strict//EN"
  "http://www.w3.org/TR/xhtml1/DTD/xhtml1-strict.dtd">
<html xmlns="http://www.w3.org/1999/xhtml" xml:lang="en" lang="en">
<head>
<meta http-equiv="Content-Type" content="text/html; charset=utf-8" />
<title>Drinks</title>
<link rel="stylesheet" href="drink.css" type="text/css" media="screen" />
</head>
<body>
 <body>
    <h1>Drinks</h1>

    <div id="drinkblock">
      <form action="" id="myform" method="get">
        <fieldset legend="drinks">
          <label for="drink">Select drink:</label> <select
          name="drink" id="drink">
            <option value="TEA" <?php if ($drink == 'TEA')
                                       printf('selected="selected"'); ?>>
              Hot Tea
            </option>

            <option
            value="APPLETINI" <?php if ($drink == 'APPLETINI')
                                         printf('selected="selected"'); ?>>
              Appletini
            </option>

            <option value="NONCHAMP" <?php if ($drink == 'NONCHAMP')
                                          printf('selected="selected"'); ?>>
              Non-alcoholic Champagne
            </option>

            <option
            value="SWMPMARGARITA" <?php if ($drink == 'SWMPMARGARITA')
                                             printf('selected="selected"'); ?>>
              Swamp Margarita
            </option>

            <option
            value="LEMON" <?php if ($drink == 'LEMON') printf('selected="selected"'); ?>>
              Lemon Drop
```

Example 2-1. Complete one-page Drinks application (continued)

```
            </option>
          </select> <input type="submit" value="Get Recipe" />
        </fieldset>
      </form>
    </div>

    <div id="drinkblock">
      <?php echo $result; ?>
    </div>
  </body>
</html>
```

Since no target is specified in the form's action attribute, the same page is invoked on the server to process the form results, with drink passed as part of a GET request. The drink name is used to find the appropriate recipe, which is assigned to a variable. Later in the page, in a second PHP block, the recipe is printed out to the page just below the form.

The drink value is compared to the name for each select option, and if a match is found, the item is selected. It's important to refresh the form as well as the results, or the two may differ.

The only external file to the application is the one that contains the CSS, shown in Example 2-2. It's the same CSS file used for all of the drink examples with an addition described later in this chapter.

Example 2-2. CSS for all of the Drinks applications in this chapter

```
html
{
        background: #fff url(drink.jpg) no-repeat fixed top left;
        color: #000;
}
body
{
        font-family: Verdana, Arial, sans-serif;
}
form
{
        color: #000;
        padding: 20px;
        text-align: left;
}
h1
{
        margin-left: 380px;
}
label
{
        display: block;
        margin-bottom: 10px;
}
```

Example 2-2. CSS for all of the Drinks applications in this chapter (continued)

```
#drinkblock
{
        margin-left: 380px;
        width: 500px;
}
```

The code, markup, and style settings represented in Examples 2-1 and 2-2 form a perfectly good application, but if the functionality is to be used by another application, it must be duplicated. A better approach is to place the server-side functionality into a separate web application and use a PHP include statement in other server-side code to incorporate that functionality wherever it's needed:

```
require_once("./recipe.php");
```

This also simplifies the client since the server-side functionality is kept to a minimum. Example 2-3 demonstrates the use of PHP to process the form request.

Example 2-3. PHP to process Drink request

```php
<?php

//If no search string is passed, then we can't search
$drink = $_REQUEST['drink'];
if(empty($drink)) {
    $drink = 'TEA';
} else {
    //Remove whitespace from beginning & end of passed search.
    $search = trim($drink);

    switch($search) {
      case "TEA" :
        $result = "<h3>Hot Tea</h3><p>Boil water. " .
                  "Pour over tea leaves. Steep five minutes. " .
                  "Strain and serve</p>";
        break;
      case "APPLETINI" :
        $result = "<h3>Appletini</h3><p>Mix 1 oz vodka and 1/2 oz Sour Apple Pucker or " .
                  "apple schnapps in a glass filled with ice. Strain into martini glass.
                  " .
                  "Garnish with an apple slice or raisin.</p>";
        break;
      case "NONCHAMP" :
        $result = "<h3>Non-Alcoholic Champagne</h3><p>Mix 32 ounces club soda" .
                  " with 12 ounces frozen white grape juice concentrate.</p>";
        break;
      case "SWMPMARGARITA" :
        $result = "<h3>Swamp Margarita</h3>" .
                  "<p>Mix 1 1/2 ounce good quality tequila, 3/4 ounce Cointreau, " .
                  "3/4 ounce Grand Marnier, 1/2 ounce lime juice, and 2 ounces sour mix.
        Chill an hour. " .
                  "Fill bottom of tall glass with several green olives and a few drops
        olive juice. " .
                  "Pour margarita over the olives and let sit for ten minutes. " .
```

Example 2-3. PHP to process Drink request (continued)

```
                    "Strain and serve with a few olives stuffed with pimento on a
            toothpick.</p>";
        break;
    case "LEMON" :
        $result = "<h3>Lemon Drop</h3><p>Mix 1 ounce lemon vodka<br />" .
                    "with 1 ounce lemon juice and 1 teaspoon sugar. Shake with ice, " .
                    "strain and serve.</p>";
        break;
    default :
        $result = "No recipes found";
        break;
    }
}
?>
```

Again, simple and functional. Figure 2-1 shows the application after processing a Drink request. It's guaranteed to work in pretty much any browser or environment—a property of the application we don't want to lose when we add Ajax functionality.

Figure 2-1. A basic application response, showing that our PHP script behaves as expected

One restriction with the use of the application is that the form elements have to use the same names. It is important to note that the form elements have to be updated to match the recipe so that the form contents are kept in sync with the printout. Depending on the form, this can be a lot of work. A workaround is to print the drink results on a separate results page. The file name for this page is given in the action attribute for the form. The resulting form is much simpler since we don't have to worry about syncing the select contents:

```
<form action="drink.php" id="myform" method="get">
  <fieldset legend="drinks">
    <label for="drink">Select drink:</label> <select name="drink" id="drink">
      <option value="TEA" selected="selected">
        Hot Tea
      </option>

      <option value="APPLETINI">
        Appletini
      </option>

      <option value="NONCHAMP">
        Non-alcoholic Champagne
      </option>

      <option value="SWMPMARGARITA">
        Swamp Margarita
      </option>

      <option value="LEMON">
        Lemon Drop
      </option>
    </select> <input type="submit" value="Get Recipe" />
  </fieldset>
</form>
```

The page that processes the form results is formatted to appear the same as the original client page, thus maintaining continuity between the two. The result page's only functionality is to include the server-side application (*recipe.php*) and print out the selected recipe:

```
<!DOCTYPE html PUBLIC "-//W3C//DTD XHTML 1.0 Strict//EN"
  "http://www.w3.org/TR/xhtml1/DTD/xhtml1-strict.dtd">
<html xmlns="http://www.w3.org/1999/xhtml" lang="en" xml:lang="en">
  <head>
    <title>Drinks</title>
    <link rel="stylesheet" href="drink.css" type="text/css" media="screen" />
    <meta http-equiv="Content-Type" content="text/html; charset=utf-8" />
  </head>
  <body>
    <h1>Drinks</h1>
    <div id="drinkblock">
      <?php
      require_once("./recipe.php");
```

```
        print($result);
        ?>
    </div>
  </body>
</html>
```

This method of using a separate results page means that the application user has to browse back to the original form page and start the whole process over again if he wants to find another recipe.

Rather than having to submit the form, either to the same page through a reload or to a separate page, the Ajax approach gives us the option to make a call to a web application to get the data and then process the result directly in the page. It does this without a reload and without having to worry about refreshing the page form to keep it in sync. It's this approach that we'll look at for the remainder of this chapter.

The XMLHttpRequest Object Structure

The W3C, the organization responsible for most of the specifications we use in our web applications, is currently working on a standard definition of the XMLHttpRequest object. The latest working draft (at the time of this writing) is dated September 2006 and can be examined at *http://www.w3.org/TR/XMLHttpRequest*. Most instances of XMLHttpRequest, though, derive from common usage: first in IE and then in Gecko-based browsers such as Firefox. There might be some differences in implementation between the applications, but in this book, we'll focus on the most important and common functionalities.

The XMLHttpRequest object is quite simple. The following methods are available in all of the target browsers discussed in this book:

open
> The syntax is open(*method*,*url*[,*async*,*username*,*password*]). This method opens a connection to the given URL using the specified method (such as GET or POST). Optional parameters are *async*, a boolean value that sets the requests to be asynchronous ('true') or synchronous ('false'), and a *username* and *password* if required by the server process. If the *async* parameter is not provided, the request is asynchronous by default.

setRequestHeader
> The syntax is setRequestHeader(*label*,*value*). This method adds a label/value pair to the header in the request.

send
> The syntax is send(*content*). This method is used to send the request with any associated data. If the request is made using an HTTP method such as POST, where parameters aren't attached to the URL, all required parameters are passed using this method; otherwise, the *content* is set to null.

getAllResponseHeaders

> The syntax is getAllResponseHeaders( ). This method returns all HTTP response headers as a string. Among the information included is the keepalive timeout value, content type, information about the server, and date.

getResponseHeader

> The syntax is getResponseHeader(*label*). This method returns the specific HTTP response header identified by *label*.

abort

> The syntax is abort( ). This method aborts the current request.

XMLHttpRequest also has the following properties:

onreadystatechange

> This property holds a handle to the function that will be called when the ready state of the request changes.

readyState

> This property has one of five values: 0 for uninitialized, 1 for an open request, 2 for a request that has been sent, 3 when a response is being received, and 4 when the response is finished loading. For the most part, we're interested in a readyState of 4.

responseText

> This property specifies that the response will be formatted as a text string.

responseXML

> Use this property to format the response as XML.

status

> This property refers to the server status, such as 404, 500, and 200, when the request is successful.

statusText

> This property specifies the text message associated with the status.

The rest of this chapter examines and demonstrates these properties and methods in detail, beginning with creating the XMLHttpRequest object.

Preparing the Object for Use

One of the first decisions to make when creating the XMLHttpRequest object is whether your application will support IE 6.x. In IE 7, and in newer versions of the other browsers (Opera, Firefox, Safari, Netscape, and so on), the server request object is simply XMLHttpRequest, and the browsers all support similar behavior. However, IE 6.x still supports the older Microsoft ActiveX object. Since older Windows operating systems, such as the very popular Windows 2000, cannot support the newer IE 7, you have to decide whether you will provide support for people using Windows 2000 (or those using Windows XP who have not upgraded their browsers).

This is where you return to your logs and see how many people access your site using IE 6.x. If you have even five percent using IE 6.x, you're most likely going to want to support this older browser. Fortunately, the additional code doesn't take a lot of extra space.

The next issue when working with the ActiveX object is determining which object ID to set in the function call to create the object. Unfortunately, Microsoft was not consistent with the name of this object by operating system, and we have variations such as MSXML2.XMLHttp, MSXML2.XMLHttp.3.0, and MSXML2.XMLHttp.4.0. Most Ajax libraries focus on two of these, the older ID, Microsoft.XMLHttp, and the more common of the newer ones, MSXML2.XMLHttp.

Since most browsers that access the site will have access to the now-standard XMLHttpRequest object, it's most efficient to test for its presence first. If this test fails, test for the two Microsoft-specific objects. Since we'll be making a great deal of use of XHR, packaging it into a reusable function simplifies its inclusion in a library. Example 2-4 shows the code for a typical XMLHttpRequest object function.

Example 2-4. Typical XMLHttpRequest object creation function

```
function getXmlHttpRequest() {

    var xmlHttpObj;
    if (window.XMLHttpRequest) {
        xmlHttpObj = new XMLHttpRequest();
    } else {
        try
            {
                xmlHttpObj = new ActiveXObject("Msxml2.XMLHTTP");
            }
        catch (e)
            {
                try
                    {
                        xmlHttpObj = new ActiveXObject("Microsoft.XMLHTTP");
                    }
                catch (e)
                    {
                        xmlHttpObj = false;
                    }
            }
    }
    return xmlHttpObj;
}
```

From the top, if the window object has an XMLHttpRequest method, it's used to create the XMLHttpRequest object; otherwise the ActiveX object is created within a try/catch block to provide graceful error handling (in this case, setting the object to false). The resulting object is returned from the function.

We'll be using this object throughout the book, so it makes sense to begin a global JavaScript library that we'll use with all the examples and add this function as the first entry. By doing this, we can code the function once and forget about it.

For simplicity, the library is called *addingajax.js*, after this book. Because the examples in the book use other libraries, from time to time all functions and objects in the library are prefaced with "aa_" to distinguish them from other library functions that might otherwise have the same name—for example, aaGetXmlHttpRequest instead of the plain getXmlHttpRequest. It's a small library now, but it will be growing.

> Just a quick reminder: all the example code, including the *addingajax.js* library in its final state, can be downloaded from the book support site at *http://www.oreilly.com/catalog/9780596529369*.

Recall the JavaScript in Example 2-4. The handling of the returned object depends on how the object is to be used. Typically, the XMLHttpRequest object is assigned to a global variable so that it may be accessible via different functions at different times. As we'll see later, at a minimum, the instantiated XMLHttpRequest object has to be accessible in the callback function. This is one of the few cases where the use of global variables in JavaScript is accepted practice (albeit reluctantly). Other libraries incorporate its use into more complex objects.

> One other aspect of cross-browser incompatibility is that some older Mozilla-based browsers may not properly handle the request if the result does not return with a proper XML MIME header of text/xml. There is an additional method in Mozilla-compatible browsers, overrideMimeType (with a parameter of text/xml) to correct for this occurrence. However, this method is not available on XMLHttpRequest for all browsers, such as IE 7.

Now that the XMLHttpRequest object has been created, what do we do with it?

Preparing and Sending a Request

Preparing and sending a web service request is probably one of the easiest aspects of Ajax. A few decisions about parameters, a couple of function calls, and you're done.

When preparing a request, the first decision to make is which HTTP verb to use with the request. When adding Ajax to a site, chances are you'll be working with existing web services, and you'll have to build your JavaScript client interface accordingly. However, if you're also modifying the web service interface, it'll be worth your time to review the HTTP methods that can be used between the client and the web service in order to maximize the efficiency and security of the application.

HTTP GET, POST, and RESTful Friends

I'm assuming you've probably worked with web applications before and are familiar with the GET and POST HTTP requests. XMLHttpRequest supports both of these, and a variety of other verbs. Many of those verbs don't make a lot of sense for Ajax applications, but there are four in particular that are well suited:

GET

Used to retrieve information from the web server, parameters attached to the URL, and the URL exposed in the request.

POST

Used to send information to the web server. Data is passed to the server via the function parameter.

DELETE

Used to send a request to delete a specific object. Data is passed to the server via the function parameter.

PUT

Used to send an update to the web server. Data is passed to the server via the function parameter.

The first two, GET and POST, are commonly used in web applications, but the latter two may not be familiar to you. All four of these HTTP methods are supported by web services that are considered *RESTful*—applications based on Representational State Transfer (REST), a recommended approach to providing web services.

The need for four separate methods isn't just one of semantics. A GET request is one that shouldn't have a side effect—it's used to retrieve information only. Google once came up with beta functionality, the Google Web Accelerator, which promised more efficient applications by automatically prefetching all GETs within a page and caching the data. Unfortunately, some of the GETs on pages that users visited were actually used to delete or update data. Accessing a page with a browser equipped with this Google functionality created all sorts of havoc.

Though Google's use of GET was hasty at best, the lesson learned was valuable: GET should be used to retrieve data only; POST, PUT, and DELETE are used to create, update, and delete data:

- GET retrieves data.
- POST creates a new object.
- PUT updates an existing object.
- DELETE deletes an object.

However, these rules aren't always followed. POST can also be used for retrieval to provide added security of parameters, as well as for managing web server requests where the number of parameters or the size of any individual parameter may be quite large.

GET and POST are universally supported by web browsers; PUT and DELETE, unfortunately, are not. This lack of support means that while PUT and DELETE could be very useful, they are simply not appropriate for Ajax applications (at the time of this writing), so they won't be used in the examples in this book.

After settling on GET and POST, our next task, described in the following section, is to examine how to pass parameters with each HTTP request. Depending on which type of method is used, parameters are either passed as part of the URL or through one of the XMLHttpRequest methods.

The Parameters

More than one parameter can be passed to whatever web service is requested. Each parameter uses the format *keyword=value* and each pair is separated from one another with an ampersand (&).

If the HTTP method is POST, the parameters are passed in the object's send method:

```
xmlhttp.send(params);
```

With a POST request, you'll also need to set the content type of the request header before sending the request. Set the value to form encoding:

```
xmlhttp.setRequestHeader('Content-Type','application/x-www-form-urlencoded');
```

If the GET HTTP method is used, the parameters are attached to the end of the URL for the web service request, separated from the URL with a question mark (?):

```
http://somewebserver.com/someapp.php?param=value&param2=value2
```

If the parameters contain HTTP-sensitive characters, such as spaces, ampersands, or HTML characters such as angle brackets, you'll need to escape the parameters. You can use the JavaScript built-in encodeURIComponent function to do this:

```
var paramvalue = encodeURIComponent(value);
```

Because the Drinks application is performing a simple query and we're not concerned about hiding the parameter, the GET method is used with the drink name attached to the web service URL. The JavaScript to create the XHR object and the request URL follows:

```
if (!xmlhttp) xmlhttp = aaGetXmlHttpRequest();
if (!xmlhttp) return;
var drink = encodeURIComponent(document.getElementById('drink').value);
var qry = 'drink=' + drink;
var url = 'drink.php?' + qry;
```

Sending the Request

To send an HTTP request, we must first open the XHR object. The open method's first parameter is the HTTP request method, followed by the URL, and then a boolean true to specify an asynchronous request:

```
if (!xmlhttp) xmlhttp = aaGetXmlHttpRequest();
if (!xmlhttp) return;
var drink = encodeURIComponent(document.getElementById('drink').value);
var qry = 'drink=' + drink;
var url = 'drink.php?' + qry;
xmlhttp.open('GET', url, true);
```

Whatever the nature of the request, there is always a response, even if it is only an error message. Since the request is asynchronous, though, the browser isn't waiting for the response. To handle the response in an asynchronous environment, we need to assign a *callback* function to be invoked when the XHR request is finished.

 A callback function is any method or function to be called at some future time based on some event, such as when the web service request completes in Ajax.

On the next line in the code, this callback function, printRecipe, is attached to the onreadystatechange event handler. This indicates that the printRecipe function will be called whenever the request object's state is changed. We'll look at the response in more detail in the next section, but for now, the request object's send method is called, passing in a null parameter (because this is a GET request) and the parameters are attached to the URL. The entire request is incorporated into a function, getRecipe:

```
function getRecipe() {
    if (!xmlhttp) xmlhttp = aaGetXmlHttpRequest();
    if (!xmlhttp) return;
    var drink = encodeURIComponent(document.getElementById('drink').value);
    var qry = 'drink=' + drink;
    var url = 'drink.php?' + qry;
    xmlhttp.open('GET', url, true);
    xmlhttp.onreadystatechange = printRecipe;
    xmlhttp.send(null);
}
```

If the request were a POST request instead of a GET, the only differences in the client application would be in the getRecipe function. Instead of attaching the parameters to the URL, they'd been passed in the send method call. Additionally, the request encoding would have be made before the request was sent, as shown in bold text in the following code snippet:

```
function getRecipe() {
    if (!xmlhttp) return;
    var drink = encodeURIComponent(document.getElementById('drink').value);
    var qry = 'drink=' + drink;
```

```
        var url = 'drink.php';
        xmlhttp.open('POST', url, true);
        xmlhttp.onreadystatechange = printRecipe;
        xmlhttp.setRequestHeader('Content-Type',
          'application/x-www-form-urlencoded');
        xmlhttp.send(qry);
    }
```

The application needs some event to trigger the function call to getRecipe. In the
newly reengineered Drinks application, there are a couple of ways to approach this.
The first is to assign a function to the select element's onchange event handler, which
is then activated when the list's selected item has changed. The problem with this
approach, though, is that the first item on the list would require that the web page
reader select another item first, just so the reader could select the first item and trigger this change.

Another approach is to capture the button submit event and use the Ajax request
rather than letting the form submission continue. This could confuse the application
user, though, as submit buttons represent form submissions, and one of the rules of
good Ajax design is to minimize how far we "break" fundamental page behavior. In a
web article titled "Ajax Accessibility Overview," Becky Gibson of IBM wrote, "…when
people explicitly request an update by selecting a link or button, they may be surprised
when the entire page does not reload."

Of course, this is the entire basis of Ajax. The point is that if we do break the
"accepted" behavior, we do so in an unsurprising manner (see Chapter 7).

Even with concerns about "breaking" web behavior, of the two options just
described, interceding in the form submission is the better option because it ensures
that users can access any option in the selection list. However, we can't just intercede in the form submission—we have to cancel the submission event and also
ensure it doesn't "bubble" up to the default form handling. The application uses
direct assignment of the getRecipe function to the form's onsubmission event handler, and then cancels the event using preventDefault for Firefox, Opera, Safari, etc.,
and returns false for IE.

 Chapter 4 extends *addingajax.js* with several functions to manage
events. For now, IE must have different event handling incorporated,
as it doesn't support preventDefault.

Example 2-5 shows the application-specific JavaScript.

Example 2-5. JavaScript that uses Ajax to get the drink recipe

```
var xmlhttp;

function getRecipe(evnt) {
    if (!xmlhttp) xmlhttp = aaGetXmlHttpRequest();
    if (!xmlhttp) return;
```

Example 2-5. JavaScript that uses Ajax to get the drink recipe (continued)

```
  var drink = encodeURIComponent(document.getElementById('drink').value);
  var qry = 'drink=' + drink;
  var url = 'drink.php?' + qry;
  xmlhttp.open('GET', url, true);
  xmlhttp.onreadystatechange = printRecipe;
  xmlhttp.send(null);
  if (evnt && evnt.preventDefault)
    evnt.preventDefault( );
  return false;
}

function printRecipe( ) {
  if(xmlhttp.readyState == 4 && xmlhttp.status == 200) {
    alert(xmlhttp.getAllResponseHeaders( ));
    alert(xmlhttp.responseText);
  }
}

window.onload=function( ) {
  document.getElementById('myform').onsubmit=getRecipe;
};
```

In the callback function to manage the Ajax request printRecipe, two properties are tested on the XMLHttpRequest object. The first is a check to see whether the readyState is equal to 4. As mentioned earlier, a request goes through stages until a response is returned, signaled by a readyState of 4. In addition, a successful response returns an HTTP status of 200. Both of these values should be present for a successful Ajax request.

 For a successful Ajax request, the XMLHttpRequest object's readyState property equals 4, and the status property equals 200.

Currently, the callback function prints out the XMLHttpRequest object's response text (responseText), as well as the response headers (getAllResponseHeaders). The next section shows how to do something with that text. The new application client page is similar to the previous ones, with the addition of the two JavaScript script blocks:

```
<script type="text/javascript" src="addingajax.js">
</script>
<script type="text/javascript" src="getdrink1.js">
</script>
```

Even if the JavaScript is turned off, the original application still provides the original forms-based functionality.

One last thing before we look more closely at the response: in Chapter 1, I mentioned dealing with older versions of IE by defaulting to a script-disabled functionality.

Years ago when dealing with cross-browser functionality, we used to parse the Navigator object's appName and appVersion properties to detect browser and version. Eventually this was abandoned in favor of object detection, such as that demonstrated in Example 2-4 with the XMLHttpRequest. However, when specifically filtering one browser, in our case, older versions of Internet Explorer, parsing out the Navigator properties is an effective approach.

In the *addingajax.js* library, create the function aaScreenIE to return false if the browser is either not Internet Explorer or is IE 6.x or later. Otherwise, the value true is returned:

```
// screen out older IE versions
function aaScreenIE( ) {
    if (navigator.appName == 'Microsoft Internet Explorer') {
      msie=navigator.appVersion.split("MSIE")
      version=parseFloat(msie[1]);
      if (version >= 6) return false;
    } else return false;
    return true;
}
```

Next we modify the window onload event handler function so that it will not add the event handlers if a version of IE older than 6 accesses the application:

```
// intercede in form submission
window.onload=function( ) {
    if (aaScreenIE( )) return;
    document.getElementById('myform').onsubmit=getRecipe;
    alert(navigator.appName + " " + navigator.appVersion);
};
```

With this filter, we don't have to worry about older, noncompatible versions of IE accessing the Ajax application and most likely breaking. Instead, people using the older browser will get the traditional form functionality.

Now on to the Ajax response.

Processing the Ajax Response

To process the Ajax response and display the recipe, we must make two changes in our existing application. The first is embedding the request response directly in the page and the second is modifying the page layout to provide a place for the response.

In the last example in the previous section, the getRecipe function makes its request to the same *drink.php* web application used with the earlier, traditional web application, and the existing server-side application is designed to create a web page rather than to return data. This functionality is apparent when reviewing the data returned in the XHR object's responseText property. Both the page formatting and the data are returned, but an Ajax application needs only the data.

We must therefore change the server program from a web application to a *web service* that will support machine-to-machine interaction over a network. Specifically, we want the web service to return the data using a predetermined web service protocol (in this case, REST), rather than the simpler approach of setting application variables. Since the same functionality still has to be available to the nonscripted application, whatever approach we use must work whether the application is used within a traditional web application or invoked as a web service.

For our purposes, the change is simple: add echo $result at the end of the *recipe.php* application to print the result out. With this one small change, the application works whether embedded in a PHP block in a web page or called as a REST service.

The Ajax request in the getDrink function is modified to call the *recipe.php* web service:

```
// get recipe using Ajax
function getRecipe(evnt) {
    if (!xmlhttp) xmlhttp = aaGetXmlHttpRequest();
    if (!xmlhttp) return;
    var drink = encodeURIComponent(document.getElementById('drink').value);
    var qry = "drink=" + drink;
    var url = 'recipe.php?' + qry;
    xmlhttp.open('GET', url, true);
    xmlhttp.onreadystatechange = printRecipe;
    xmlhttp.send(null);
    if (evnt && evnt.preventDefault())
      evnt.preventDefault();
    return false;
}
```

When running the application using the modified getRecipe function, the processed response text now shows an HTML fragment rather than the entire web page. That's the minimum an Ajax application requires of a response—data formatted in such a way that the application can do something with it.

The formatting of the returned data depends on what you plan to do with such formatting using JavaScript and which other applications are going to be making use of the service. For existing applications, the service itself will determine the format; if the service returns the data with a particular format, it's up to the client program to adjust it.

Once this example returns an HTML fragment, we can incorporate it into a document.

A Quick and Easy Response: HTML Fragment and innerHTML

One of the simplest ways to add Ajax response text to a page is to add an HTML fragment by using the nonstandard but ubiquitous innerHTML property. Using this property approach, if the data returned from the web service is formatted as text-based HTML, it can be appended directly to the document with little or no intervention.

As demonstrated in examples from the previous section, the response is already formatted as HTML. To complete the effort, all that's needed is to integrate the response into the page. That leads to the second key part of the Ajax application—how to add the new data to the page.

When embedding a response in a page, one approach is to manually add an empty element into the page to serve as a placeholder for the returned data. However, a better approach is to create the element dynamically so that if scripting is disabled, the output element doesn't impact the page. More importantly, if the element is created dynamically, you don't have to modify every individual page that will use the output element.

Once the new recipe placeholder object is added to the page, we can either access the element and reuse it, or access the element, remove it, and then create it anew each time the application is run. The latter approach has appeal because we don't have to worry about emptying out the element before we add new material.

In the current application, the output is added to a div element and given the identifier recipe. This new element is added into the web page following the block containing the search form.

To provide proper presentation, we could extend the dynamic aspect of the application further by not creating individual style settings for the new element. It's a simple matter to adjust an element's style setting by using the style property:

```
elem.style.backgroundColor="#fff";
```

However, unless the style settings undergo many changes (in which case, trying to create new CSS classes for each could become burdensome), a better approach would be to assign the element's className property to a predefined stylesheet rule:

```
obj.className = 'someclass';
```

If the className doesn't exist, we could create the new stylesheet rule and use it with the new element. Unfortunately, there are significant browser differences associated with this effort, and the support varies drastically between the different browsers. What we can do instead is create the class name manually and add to the overall application stylesheet. See the excellent *How to Create* series by Mark "Tarquin" Wilton-Jones, specifically his tutorial in dynamic stylesheets for details on creating and adding stylesheet rules dynamically: *http://www.howtocreate.co.uk/tutorials/javascript/domstylesheets*. Because the stylesheet is shared across pages, we can add the rule directly to the *drink.css* file:

```
#recipe
{
        margin-left: 400px;
        margin-top: 30px;
        background-color: #E6F990;
        width: 350px;
        padding: 10px;
}
```

The web client page links to a new JavaScript file, *getdrink2.js*. This script file is a copy of the JavaScript shown in Example 2-5, except that the getRecipe function calls the newly created web service, *recipe.php*. The printRecipe function now processes the response text by embedding the returned HTML fragment into the page, as shown in Example 2-6.

Example 2-6. Appending the HTML fragment with recipe to the page

```
var xmlhttp;

// get recipe using Ajax
function getRecipe(evnt) {
   if (!xmlhttp) xmlhttp = aaGetXmlHttpRequest( );
   if (!xmlhttp) return;
   var drink = encodeURIComponent(document.getElementById('drink').value);
   var qry = "drink=" + drink;
   var url = 'recipe.php?' + qry;
   xmlhttp.open('GET', url, true);
   xmlhttp.onreadystatechange = printRecipe;
   xmlhttp.send(null);
   if (evnt && evnt.preventDefault( ))
     evnt.preventDefault( );
   return false;
}

// Add recipe to page
function printRecipe( ) {
   if(xmlhttp.readyState == 4 && xmlhttp.status == 200) {

      var body = document.getElementsByTagName('body');

      // remove, if exists
      if (document.getElementById('recipe')) {
         body[0].removeChild(document.getElementById('recipe'));
      }
      var recipe = document.createElement('div');
      recipe.id = 'recipe';
      recipe.className = 'recipe';
      recipe.innerHTML = xmlhttp.responseText;
      body[0].appendChild(recipe);
   }
}
// intercede in form submission
window.onload=function( ) {
   if (aaScreenIE( )) return;
   document.getElementById('myform').onsubmit=getRecipe;
};
```

The recipe div element is accessed, the found recipe text is appended to it using innerHTML, and it's formatted using the recipe class name. Figure 2-2 shows the page when one of the recipes is accessed.

Figure 2-2. Drinks application displaying recipe retrieved using Ajax request and incorporated with innerHTML

Any HTML element that can be accessed using script can be modified with the HTML that is returned as a text fragment from a web service. This is why Ajax requests formatted as HTML fragments and the use of innerHTML are so popular for applications that both query data and use that data directly in the page.

This is the quick and easy approach to Ajax, but there is some risk to this technique: you have to have a great deal of trust in the web service to embed the HTML directly without knowing what it contains. Even when we provide our own services, we can make mistakes and the result can be an illegible page. If the application is hacked in some way, the application could end up embedding script that can cause problems for our web page readers. You should keep the following in mind when using this approach:

- Embedding XHTML fragments using innerHTML means that you really must trust the web service.

- Embedded fragments may be incorrectly formatted and make the page illegible.

- Hackers could intercede in the request and embed markup dangerous to application users.

There is another approach to working with XHTML, but first we'll look at processing an XML document rather than an HTML fragment.

Working with a More Traditional XML

When Ajax was originally defined, the idea was that all responses would be formatted as well-defined XML, and XSLT would be used to transform the data. If individual components of the response had to be accessed, XML could be parsed using the JavaScript engine's own XML built-in parsing functionality.

Of course, nothing is ever as simple as it first seems, and using XML as a format brings its own challenges, not the least of which is the amount of code necessary to effectively work with XML.

To demonstrate using an XML-formatted response, I changed the PHP program in Example 2-3 to format the drink title, ingredients, and instructions as individual XML elements. I also used an XML header to set the MIME type of the data to text/xml. By formatting the data this way, two things happen: first, the XML is loaded and parsed as an XML document, retrievable via the responseXML property rather than responseText; second, each of the data objects can be accessed using DOM methods. Example 2-7 shows the new web service code, saved in a file called *recipe2.php*.

Example 2-7. Drink recipe web service; response formatted as well-defined XML

```php
<?php

//If no search string is passed, then we can't search
$drink = $_REQUEST['drink'];
if(empty($drink)) {
    echo "<title>No drink name sent</title>";
} else {
    //Remove whitespace from beginning & end of passed search.
    $search = trim($drink);
    switch($search) {
      case "TEA" :
        $result = "<title>Hot Tea</title>" .
                  "<ingredient>tea leaves</ingredient>" .
                  "<instruction>Boil water. Pour over tea leaves. " .
                  "Steep five minutes. Strain and serve.</instruction>";
        break;
      case "APPLETINI" :
        $result = "<title>Appletini</title>" .
                  "<ingredient>1 ounce vodka</ingredient>" .
                  "<ingredient>1/2 ounce Sour Apple Pucker or apple schnapps</ingredient>
        " .
                  "<instruction>Mix vodka and schnapps in a glass filled with ice. Strain
            into martini glass. " .
                  "Garnish with an apple slice or raisin.</instruction>";
        break;
```

Example 2-7. Drink recipe web service; response formatted as well-defined XML (continued)

```
    case "NONCHAMP" :
      $result = "<title>Non-Alcoholic Champagne</title>" .
                "<ingredient>32 ounces club soda</ingredient>" .
                "<ingredient>12 ounces frozen white grape juice concentrate</
            ingredient>" .
                "<instruction>Mix club soda" .
                " with grape juice concentrate.</instruction>";
      break;
    case "SWMPMARGARITA" :
      $result = "<title>Swamp Margarita</title>" .
                "<ingredient>1 1/2 ounce good quality tequila</ingredient>" .
                "<ingredient>3/4 ounce Cointreau</ingredient>" .
                "<ingredient>3/4 ounce Grand Marnier</ingredient>" .
                "<ingredient>1/2 ounce lime juice</ingredient>" .
                "<ingredient>2 ounces sour mix</ingredient>" .
                "<ingredient>several green olives</ingredient>" .
                "<instruction>Mix all ingredients. Chill an hour. " .
                "Fill bottom of tall glass with several green olives. " .
                "Pour margarita over the olives, let sit for ten minutes, and serve." .
                "</instruction>";
      break;
    case "LEMON" :
      $result = "<title>Lemon Drop</title>" .
                "<ingredient>1 ounce lemon vodka</ingredient>" .
                "<ingredient>1 ounce lemon juice</ingredient>" .
                "<ingredient>1 teaspoon sugar</ingredient>" .
                "<instruction>Shake with ice, " .
                "strain and serve.</instruction>";
      break;
    default :
      $result = "<title>No recipes found</title>";
      break;
  }

  $result ='<?xml version="1.0" encoding="UTF-8" ?>' .
          "<recipe>" . $result . "</recipe>";

  header("Content-Type: text/xml; charset=utf-8");

  echo $result;

}
?>
```

Since XML is a picky format, you might first want to test the web service by itself by running the application and manually passing in a drink:

```
http://someapp.com/recipe2.php?drink=LEMON
```

If the XML returned from the server is well-formed and no problems occur in the application, the result should show up in the responseXML object. In Example 2-7, the XML is handcoded in the PHP appliation. In a production application, though,

---

XML libraries should be used to provide the XML formatted data. For the same reason, it's better to use the DOM to create content rather than document.write in the client, using XML functions in the server-side application ensures that the XML is well-formed, all elements are properly terminated, and no unexpected side effects will occur because of "bad" XML.

PHP 5 has DOM XML functionality similar to that available in JavaScript. The following is an example of how the hot tea recipe could be formed using the DOM:

```php
// create the new XML document
$dom = new DOMDocument('1.0', 'iso-8859-1');

// root element
$recipe = $dom->createElement('recipe');
$dom->appendChild($recipe);

// create the title
$title = $dom->createElement('title');
$title->appendChild($dom->createTextNode("Hot Tea"));
$recipe->appendChild($title);
```

Formatting the response as XML in the web service is easy; processing it in the Ajax client is a little more complicated. The printRecipe function must be completely rewritten and, as you'll see, a lot more code is needed. Because we have access to individual elements, the ingredients are listed in a ul element, the title is given a header, and the instructions are inserted into a paragraph (see Example 2-8). All elements are embedded in the same recipe block.

Example 2-8. Ajax client using XML-formatted data

```javascript
// Add recipe to page
function printRecipe( ) {
   if(xmlhttp.readyState == 4 && xmlhttp.status == 200) {

      var body = document.getElementsByTagName('body');

      // remove, if exists
      if (document.getElementById('recipe')) {
         body[0].removeChild(document.getElementById('recipe'));
      }
      var recipe = document.createElement('div');
      recipe.id = 'recipe';
      recipe.className='recipe';

      // add title
      var title = xmlhttp.responseXML.getElementsByTagName('title')[0].firstChild.
      nodeValue;
      var titleNode = document.createElement('h3');
      titleNode.appendChild(document.createTextNode(title));
      recipe.appendChild(titleNode);

      // add ingredients
```

Example 2-8. Ajax client using XML-formatted data (continued)

```
    var ul = document.createElement("ul");
    var ingredients = xmlhttp.responseXML.getElementsByTagName('ingredient');
    for (var i = 0; i < ingredients.length; i++) {
        var x = document.createElement('li');
        x.appendChild(document.createTextNode(ingredients[i].firstChild.nodeValue));
        ul.appendChild(x);
    }
    recipe.appendChild(ul);

    // add instruction
    var instr = xmlhttp.responseXML.getElementsByTagName('instruction')[0].firstChild.
    nodeValue;
    var instrNode = document.createElement('p');
    instrNode.appendChild(document.createTextNode(instr));
    recipe.appendChild(instrNode);

    // add to body
    body[0].appendChild(recipe);
  }
}
```

Looking at the code in printRecipe in more detail, the DOM function getElementsByTagName is used to access the elements associated with each element: title, ingredient, and instruction. There can be more than one ingredient, so these are accessed as an array and processed accordingly.

For each element, the text value of the child node associated with the element is accessed and used to populate a DOM textNode, which is then appended to a newly created element, whether the element is the header, the individual list items, or the instructional paragraph. The element is then appended to the recipe object in the main document. These are the steps:

1. Get the elements by tag name (element name):

   ```
   titleObj = xmlhttp.responseXML.getElementsByTagName('title');
   ```

2. Once the collection is accessed (getElementsByTagName returns a nodeList, which is processed as an array), access each node (or the first for a single element), find the first child node for this node, and get its value:

   ```
   title = titleObj[0].firstChild.nodeValue;
   ```

3. Create a new h3 element to hold the content:

   ```
   titleNode = document.createElement('h3');
   ```

4. Create a textNode to hold the value of the text from the XML:

   ```
   titleText = document.createTextNode(title);
   ```

5. Append the textNode to the newly created node:

   ```
   titleNode.appendChild(titleText);
   ```

6. Append this node to the containing element:

   ```
   recipe.appendChild(titleNode);
   ```

Once the data for the title, ingredients, and instruction is processed, the page should look like the one shown in Figure 2-3.

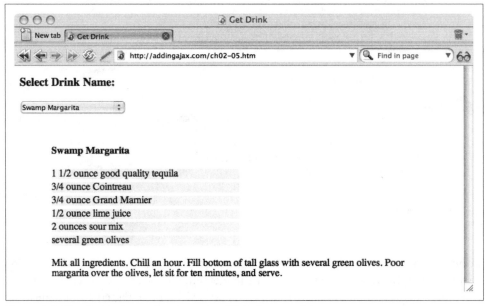

Figure 2-3. The Get Recipe application, using XML-formatted data

Example 2-8 uses considerably more code than `innerHTML`, though the results are nicer because we can format the individual elements in the browser rather than on the server. There's yet another approach that can cut down on the complexity of accessing the data but still allow us to format individual elements. This approach uses the scripting notation known as JSON.

Simplifying Processing with JSON

JavaScript Object Notation, or *JSON,* is a way of specifying response data in text-based JavaScript object notation. The data is accessible in traditional Ajax applications through the use of the eval function to "instantiate" the object defined in the data.

JSON takes the form of keyword/value pairs:

    object { keyword : value}

Or it can take the form of an array:

    array[value, value,...,value]

Or both:

    object { keyword: [{ keyword: value}, {keyword: value}] }

Instantiating the object takes a form similar to the following, using the `responseText` property to build the eval statement:

```
eval("theObj = (" + xmlhttp.responseText + ")");
```

Or if the object name is given in the returned data, it can take the following form:

```
eval(xmlhttp.responseText);
```

The eval function instantiates the object, which can now be accessed as regular Java-Script objects and/or arrays, rather than having to use the DOM methods to work with XML, as demonstrated in the previous section.

 A quick reminder: the eval function interprets text as JavaScript and processes whatever is included within the text, as if it were actual JavaScript.

Of course, if we thought that embedding HTML as-is directly in a web page was scary, using eval on possibly unknown data should probably be more so. If you know or control the data source, you should be relatively safe. If not, or if you want to be extra secure, use a JSON parser, such as `parseJSON`, provided at the JSON web site, *http://www.json.org/js.html*:

```
var obj = xmlhttp.responseText.parseJSON( );
```

To simplify the script in the examples in this chapter, I have used eval directly.

Using JSON requires changes in both the web service and the Ajax client. Focusing on the service first, Example 2-9 contains the PHP web service *recipe3.php*, modified from Examples 2-3 and 2-7, and now returning text-based JSON formatting data.

Example 2-9. Drink web service with JSON-formatted data

```php
<?php

//If no search string is passed, then we can't search
$drink = $_REQUEST['drink'];
if(empty($drink)) {
    echo "{'title': 'No drink name sent'}";
} else {
    //Remove whitespace from beginning & end of passed search.

    $search = trim($drink);
    switch($search) {
      case "TEA" :
        $result = "{ 'title' : 'Hot Tea'," .
                  " 'ingredients' : [ {  'ingredient' : 'tea leaves' }," .
                  "   {'ingredient' : 'water'}]," .
                  " 'instruction' : 'Boil water. Pour over tea leaves." .
                  " Steep five minutes. Strain and serve.'}";
        break;
      case "APPLETINI" :
```

Example 2-9. Drink web service with JSON-formatted data (continued)

```php
        $result = "{ 'title' : 'Appletini', " .
                  " 'ingredients' : [ { 'ingredient' : '1 ounce vodka' }, " .
                  " { 'ingredient' : '1/2 ounce Sour Apple Pucker or apple schnapps'}]," .

                  " 'instruction' : 'Mix vodka and schnapps in a glass filled with ice.
              Strain " .
                  "into martini glass. Garnish with an apple slice or raisin.'}";
        break;
    case "NONCHAMP" :
        $result = "{ 'title' : 'Non-Alcoholic Champagne', " .
                  " 'ingredients' : [ { 'ingredient' : '32 ounces club soda' }, " .
                  " { 'ingredient' : '12 ounces frozen white grape juice concentrate'}]," .

                  " 'instruction' : 'Mix club soda with grape juice concentrate.'}";
        break;
    case "SWMPMARGARITA" :
        $result = "{ 'title' : 'Swamp Margaria', " .
                  " 'ingredients' : [ { 'ingredient' : '1 1/2 ounce good quality
              tequila'}, " .
                  " { 'ingredient' : '3/4 ounce Cointreau'}, " .
                  " { 'ingredient' : '3/4 ounce Grand Marnier'}, " .
                  " { 'ingredient' : '1/2 ounce lime juice'}, " .
                  " { 'ingredient' : '2 ounces sour mix'}, " .
                  " { 'ingredient' : 'several green olives'}]," .
                  " 'instruction' : 'Mix all ingredients. Chill an hour. " .
                  "Fill bottom of tall glass with several green olives. " .
                  "Pour margarita over the olives, let sit for ten minutes, and serve.
              '}";
        break;
    case "LEMON" :
        $result = "{ 'title' : 'Lemon Drop', " .
                  " 'ingredients' : [ { 'ingredient' : '1 ounce lemon vodka'}, " .
                  " { 'ingredient' : '1 ounce lemon juice'}, " .
                  " { 'ingredient' : '1 teaspoon sugar'}]," .
                  " 'instruction' : 'Shake with ice, " .
                  "strain and serve.'}";
        break;
    default :
        $result = "{ 'title','No recipes found'}";
        break;
    }
    echo $result;
}
?>
```

The structure used for each recipe in Example 2-9 is an object (delimited by the curly braces), with the title and instruction as property/value pairs, and the ingredients as an array of objects.

Just as with the XML, most languages used to create web services also have libraries to create JSON. An example for PHP is *php-json*, which is now part of PHP 5.2.0.

The modified `printRecipe` function is shown in Example 2-10. Notice that the only difference in the code between it and Example 2-8 is in how the data is retrieved; creating the new page elements is identical.

Example 2-10. JSON Drinks application client

```
// Add recipe to page
function printRecipe( ) {
   if(xmlhttp.readyState == 4 && xmlhttp.status == 200) {

      var body = document.getElementsByTagName('body');

      // remove, if exists
      if (document.getElementById('recipe')) {
         body[0].removeChild(document.getElementById('recipe'));
      }
      var recipe = document.createElement('div');
      recipe.id = 'recipe';
      recipe.className='recipe';

       var recipeObj = eval("(" + xmlhttp.responseText + ")");

        // add title
        var title = recipeObj['title'];
        var titleNode = document.createElement('div');
        titleNode.className='title';
        titleNode.appendChild(document.createTextNode(title));
        recipe.appendChild(titleNode);

        // add ingredients
        var ingredients = recipeObj.ingredients;
        for (var i = 0; i < ingredients.length; i++) {
           var x = document.createElement('div');
           x.className = 'ingredient';
           x.appendChild(document.createTextNode(ingredients[i].ingredient));
           recipe.appendChild(x);
        }

      // add instruction
      var instr = recipeObj.instruction;
      var instrNode = document.createElement('div');
      instrNode.className='instruction';
      instrNode.appendChild(document.createTextNode(instr));
      recipe.appendChild(instrNode);

      body[0].appendChild(recipe);
}
```

The result of using the JSON-formatted data in the application is the same as that for the XML, except that the data is generally simpler to access and JavaScript-friendly. That's one reason why many of the language-based frameworks manage data interchange between the server and client through JSON. Evaluating the JSON object is also more efficient than many of the XML parsers built into the browsers, though unless the data is really large or complex, the differences won't be that noticeable. JSON is also a popular format to use to get around the JavaScript security sandbox, discussed later in this chapter.

 Though JSON developed in a somewhat ad hoc manner, there is an effort to standardize on the syntax. For instance, all strings in JSON must be in double quotes, not single. All keywords must also be in quotes. For more on this, read "Keep your JSON valid" by Simon Willison at *http://simonwillison.net/2006/Oct/11/json*, and "JSON is not just Object Notation" by Jesse Skinner (who tech-reviewed this book) at *http://www.thefutureoftheweb.com/blog/2006/8/json-is-not-just-object-notation*.

JSON and XML are both much easier to use when you want to differentiate the elements being returned, though using innerHTML and an HTML fragment can be faster. However, one significant difference between the three formats just explored is that the service that's providing the data for the application is also providing the content for the nonscript-enabled application. The page that processes the form submission for the nonscript option could parse the XML or the JSON—there are PHP libraries to manage most of the work for us.

The better approach would either be to provide different formats for the data— HTML, XML, or JSON—and let the client specify the format (using something like a format=JSON parameter), or to use XHTML, making sure it is formatted as an XML format that can either be plunked into a web page as-is or fed into an XML parser.

(X)HTML Fragment

There's no reason why an Ajax application can't process XHTML using XML techniques. All that's needed is a little cleanup and preparation of the data.

One change to the earlier example with an HTML fragment is to convert the example into a more formalized format, including creating the ingredients as an unordered list, the title as a heading, and the instructions as paragraphs. In other words, the format matches the output.

One other change is that the data has to be enclosed within one single element. We'll use the recipe div for this. Example 2-11 shows the modified program, *recipe4.php*.

Example 2-11. XHTML-formatted data

```php
<?php

//If no search string is passed, then we can't search
$drink = $_REQUEST['drink'];
if(empty($drink)) {
    echo "<h3>No drink name sent</h3>";
} else {
    //Remove whitespace from beginning & end of passed search.
    $search = trim($drink);
    switch($search) {
      case "TEA" :
          $result = "<h3>Hot Tea</h3>" .
                    "<ul><li>tea leaves</li><li>water</li></ul>" .
                    "<p>Boil water. Pour over tea leaves. " .
                    "Steep five minutes. Strain and serve.</p>";
          break;
      case "APPLETINI" :
          $result = "<h3>Appletini</h3>" .
                    "<ul><li>1 ounce vodka</li>" .
                    "<li>1/2 ounce Sour Apple Pucker or apple schnapps</li></ul>" .
                    "<p>Mix vodka and schnapps in a glass filled with ice. Strain into
martini glass. " .
                    "Garnish with an apple slice or raisin.</p>";
          break;
      case "NONCHAMP" :
          $result = "<h3>Non-Alcoholic Champagne</h3>" .
                    "<ul><li>32 ounces club soda</li>" .
                    "<li>12 ounces frozen white grape juice concentrate</li></ul>" .
                    "<p>Mix club soda" .
                    " with grape juice concentrate.</p>";
          break;
      case "SWMPMARGARITA" :
          $result = "<h3>Swamp Margarita</h3>" .
                    "<ul><li>1 1/2 ounce good quality tequila</li>" .
                    "<li>3/4 ounce Cointreau</li>" .
                    "<li>3/4 ounce Grand Marnier</li>" .
                    "<li>1/2 ounce lime juice</li>" .
                    "<li>2 ounces sour mix</li>" .
                    "<li>several green olives</li></ul>" .
                    "<p>Mix all lis. Chill an hour. " .
                    "Fill bottom of tall glass with several green olives. " .
                    "Pour margarita over the olives, let sit for ten minutes, and serve." .
                    "</p>";
          break;
      case "LEMON" :
          $result = "<h3>Lemon Drop</h3>" .
                    "<ul><li>1 ounce lemon vodka</li>" .
                    "<li>1 ounce lemon juice</li>" .
                    "<li>1 teaspoon sugar</li></ul>" .
                    "<p>Shake with ice, " .
                    "strain and serve.</p>";
          break;
```

Example 2-11. XHTML-formatted data (continued)

```
    default :
        $result = "<h3>No recipes found</h3>";
        break;
    }

    $result = "<div id='recipe' class='recipe'>" . $result . "</div>";

    echo $result;
}
?>
```

The nonscript form-submission page is modified slightly to embed the results of the PHP application directly into the page body, as shown in Example 2-12.

Example 2-12. Modified form-submission page for nonscript solution

```
<!DOCTYPE html PUBLIC "-//W3C//DTD XHTML 1.0 Strict//EN"
  "http://www.w3.org/TR/xhtml1/DTD/xhtml1-strict.dtd">
<html xmlns="http://www.w3.org/1999/xhtml" lang="en" xml:lang="en">
<head>
<meta http-equiv="Content-Type" content="text/html; charset=utf-8" />
<title>Drinks</title>
<link rel="stylesheet" href="drink.css" type="text/css" media="screen" />
</head>
<body>
<h1>Drinks</h1>
<?php

require_once("./recipe4.php");
?>

</body>
</html>
```

The client web page remains the same except that the form is submitted to *drink2. php* and the embedded script is named *getdrink5.js*. This new JavaScript is very similar to that in Example 2-8, except that we're not accessing a generic XML document—we're accessing standard XHTML. To trigger the XMLHttpRequest into processing the document as XML, the application needs an XML header in the web service. However, the web service is being embedded into another document where the header has already been sent, and a second header can't be returned. What we need is a way to parse the XML without being dependent on XMLHttpRequest.

To work around the header problem, the JavaScript client creates an instance of an XML parser and loads the XHTML formatted string that is returned as plain text into this newly created parser. I used a cross-browser technique to do this (thanks to the W3 Schools entry *http://www.w3schools.com/dom/dom_parser.asp*), using DOMParser for all W3C-compatible browsers (Safari, Gecko-based browsers, Opera, etc.) and ActiveXObject for IE:

```
  // code for IE
  if (window.ActiveXObject)
    {
    var doc=new ActiveXObject("Microsoft.XMLDOM");
    doc.async="false";
    doc.loadXML(recipeObj);
    }
  // code for Mozilla, Firefox, Opera, etc.
  else
    {
    var parser=new DOMParser();
    var doc=parser.parseFromString(recipeObj,"text/xml");
    }
  xDoc = doc.documentElement;
```

We can use the DOM methods to process the data in this newly created XML document the exact same way we can process XML coming in through the responseXML object. Example 2-13 contains the new printRecipe JavaScript, which does just that.

Example 2-13. Using an XML parser with an XHTML fragment

```
// Add recipe to page
function printRecipe( ) {
   if(xmlhttp.readyState == 4 && xmlhttp.status == 200) {

      if (window.ActiveXObject) {
         var doc=new ActiveXObject("Microsoft.XMLDOM");
         doc.async="false";
         doc.loadXML(xmlhttp.responseText);
      } else {
         var parser=new DOMParser( );
         var doc=parser.parseFromString(xmlhttp.responseText,"text/xml");
      }
      var xDoc = doc.documentElement;

      var body = document.getElementsByTagName('body');

      // remove, if exists
      if (document.getElementById('recipe')) {
         body[0].removeChild(document.getElementById('recipe'));
      }
      var recipe = document.createElement('div');
      recipe.id = 'recipe';
      recipe.className='recipe';

      // add title
      var title = xDoc.getElementsByTagName('h3')[0].firstChild.nodeValue;
      var titleNode = document.createElement('h3');
      titleNode.appendChild(document.createTextNode(title));
      recipe.appendChild(titleNode);

      // add ingredients
      var ul = document.createElement("ul");
      var ingredients = xDoc.getElementsByTagName('li');
```

Example 2-13. Using an XML parser with an XHTML fragment (continued)

```
        for (var i = 0; i < ingredients.length; i++) {
            var x = document.createElement('li');
            x.appendChild(document.createTextNode(ingredients[i].firstChild.nodeValue));
            ul.appendChild(x);
        }
        recipe.appendChild(ul);

        // add instruction
        var instr = xDoc.getElementsByTagName('p')[0].firstChild.nodeValue;
        var instrNode = document.createElement('p');
        instrNode.appendChild(document.createTextNode(instr));
        recipe.appendChild(instrNode);

        // add to body
        body[0].appendChild(recipe);
    }
}

// intercede in form submission
window.onload=function() {
    if (aaScreenIE()) return;
    document.getElementById('myform').onsubmit=getRecipe;
};
```

The resulting page will look the same regardless of whether the Ajax-enabled approach is used to fetch the drink recipe, or the nonscript processing is used.

As you can see, you have a lot of options as to how the data is processed by an Ajax request. One thing they all have in common, though, is that they're all limited by the JavaScript sandbox. All of the web services have to be based in the same domain that served up the client pages.

In the next section, we'll look at how we can "route" around the security protection, a necessity when creating or using widgets in an application.

Endpoints, the JavaScript Sandbox, and Widgets

The use of XMLHttpRequest has one significant limitation: the *same-domain restriction*. A request through this object can be made only to the same domain from which the page was first requested, a key part of the JavaScript security sandbox (you can play only in your own "sandbox," thus avoiding the chaos that could result if code could connect anywhere). Among the reasons for this restriction is to ensure that the web page that contains the XHR request can't be used by a malicious site to access resources on a company intranet living behind a firewall. There are ways around this restriction, such as through signed script or setting security parameters in the browsers, but these options are being phased out as new browser versions are released.

Cross-domain access restrictions aren't normally a problem in a web application. After all, most of the web services are accessed from the same domain. In addition, if data is pulled from another domain, we can create proxies—server-side applications that access the data and then pass it on to the client—to assist us.

There is one circumstance, though, where we can't depend on the server to manage the data access of external data for us: the use of widgets.

Widgets have a history on the desktop and other environments, but they are fairly new in web development. Widgets are small objects, usually embedded in a sidebar, that provide a simplified application or access to data, such as getting weather conditions from a weather site or tag data from del.icio.us. Chapter 3 provides a screenshot of a weather.com widget created using the Rico Ajax library.

Sometimes the JavaScript file providing the functionality is hosted completely on the remote server, which means there's no problem with cross-domain access—both JavaScript and data reside on the same server. This is how Google Maps works. However, sometimes the widget requires local JavaScript but remote data and web services. What's a developer to do?

JSON Endpoints and Dynamic Script Creation

This is where JSON really proves its power. JSON is more than just a format and a structure—it's a doorway. You can create a script object within one document and within one domain, set its `src` attribute to the returned data from a JSON call made to an *endpoint* in another domain, and the data is then incorporated as objects within the client page.

 All web services are "endpoints," providing services that can be called by Ajax or other applications. In this book, I use the term endpoint to specifically denote a service that provides callback capability, as will be demonstrated in this section.

For this to work, the remote service must provide the functionality to allow us to pass the name of a callback function within the service call—a callback parameter in the GET request. The following script demonstrates this concept by making a call to a del.icio.us JSON endpoint passing in a callback function:

```
var script = document.createElement('script');
script.type = 'text/javascript';
script.src = 'http://badges.del.icio.us/feeds/json/url/blogbadge?

hash=b543788c882e78ef73bc012fbe4c4eb1&callback=myFunction';
document.getElementsByTagName('head')[0].appendChild(script);

function myFunction(data) {
    var obj = eval(data);
    alert(obj[0].hash);
}
```

The request returns text formatted as JSON, wrapping the data structure within a function call to the callback routine provided in the passed callback parameter:

```
myFunction([...data])
```

Because this is used as the src attribute for the newly created scripting element, it's virtually the same as loading in a JavaScript file with the existing object.

Creating the script element, adding it to the document, and setting the src to the returned function-encapsulated data is the same as running the script within the page. The only difference is that the data for the function call argument comes from a remote server, rather than in code.

The following example takes the code from Example 2-12, but this time uses a dynamic script block and a callback function instead of the eval function to create the JavaScript object. The web page remains the same, other than calling a different JavaScript file. When the request is received, both parameters—drink name and callback function—are derived from the request, and the callback function is used to wrap the JSON object in the server:

```
echo $callback . '(' . $result . ')';
```

In the client, getRecipe and printRecipe are modified accordingly, as shown in Example 2-14. The printRecipe function is relatively the same, except that we don't have to create the object, nor do we have to test to see whether the request is finished and the status equal to 200—the results of the endpoint are added to the web page document, like another script file.

Example 2-14. The script in Example 2-12, modified to use a JSON callback function

```
function getRecipe( ) {
   var drink = escape(document.forms[0].elements[0].value);
   var qry = "drink=" + drink;
   var url = 'http://burningbird.net/addingajax/examples/recipe3json.php?' + qry;
   var script = document.createElement('script');
   script.type = 'text/javascript';
   script.src = url + '&callback=printRecipe';
   document.getElementsByTagName('head')[0].appendChild(script);
}

// Add recipe to page
function printRecipe(recipeObj) {

      var body = document.getElementsByTagName('body');

      // remove, if exists
      if (document.getElementById('recipe')) {
         body[0].removeChild(document.getElementById('recipe'));
      }
      var recipe = document.createElement('div');
      recipe.id = 'recipe';
      recipe.className='recipe';
```

Example 2-14. The script in Example 2-12, modified to use a JSON callback function (continued)

```
    // add title
    var title = recipeObj['title'];
    var titleNode = document.createElement('h3');
    titleNode.appendChild(document.createTextNode(title));
    recipe.appendChild(titleNode);

    // add ingredients
    var ul = document.createElement('ul');
    var ingredients = recipeObj.ingredients;
    for (var i = 0; i < ingredients.length; i++) {
        var x = document.createElement('li');
        x.appendChild(document.createTextNode(ingredients[i].ingredient));
        ul.appendChild(x);
    }
    recipe.appendChild(ul);

    // add instruction
    var instr = recipeObj.instruction;
    var instrNode = document.createElement('p');
    instrNode.appendChild(document.createTextNode(instr));
    recipe.appendChild(instrNode);
    body[0].appendChild(recipe);
    }
}
```

The domain used for the dynamic script and JSON endpoint is burningbird.net, while the page was pulled from Addingajax.com. Most widgets that use local script to make remote web service calls use this approach, as wel as JSON data.

 Later in the chapter, we will examine the security implication of this cross-domain web service access.

So, does it have to be JSON-formatted data? Actually, no. The only critical part of this application is that the web service appends the callback function to the response, and formats that response as one or more function arguments. This means that the data could be in another format, such as XML.

Dynamic Scripting with XML

The common understanding about the approach just outlined is that the data returned is always formatted as JSON. This isn't a requirement, though. You can use any data format that can be wrapped as a function parameter. The only requirement is that the server has to process the callback parameter, and your Ajax application has to manage whatever data gets returned. It doesn't even have to be just one parameter if there's agreement between you and the web service, though going beyond one parameter should be avoided (for simplicity if for no other reason).

To demonstrate that this approach won't lock you in to JSON, I modified the PHP program that created XML-formatted data to also process a callback function request. The only changes are that the program pulls in the callback parameter from $_GET and then processes the callback, if any, before the result:

```
$callback = $_GET['callback'];
...
    $result = "<recipe>" . $result . "</recipe>";

    if ($callback) {
        $result = $callback . '("' . $result . '")';
        echo $result;
    } else {
        header("Content-Type: text/xml; charset=utf-8");
        echo $result;
    }
```

The application provides the header response only when a callback is not provided. We don't want the XML header when we're using the response from the application to create a function call with a parameter. We want this response to be treated as plain text, and we don't want any extraneous material outside of the XML elements. Sending an XML header would cause the application to fail.

Unlike JSON, which is already a JavaScript object when it's loaded as a parameter, the XML document has to be imported into the application for us to access it using the built-in browser XML parser:

```
function printRecipe(recipeObj) {

    // load xml
    // code for IE
    if (window.ActiveXObject)
      {
      var doc=new ActiveXObject("Microsoft.XMLDOM");
      doc.async="false";
      doc.loadXML(recipeObj);
      }
    // code for Mozilla, Firefox, Opera, etc.
    else
      {
      var parser=new DOMParser();
      var doc=parser.parseFromString(recipeObj,"text/xml");
      }
    xDoc = doc.documentElement;
...
```

Once the XML document is loaded into a document via the DOM parser, manipulating the data is no different than that shown in Examples 2-8 and 2-13. You could use any format, as long as it either can be returned in an XMLHttpRequest or packaged as a function argument (if you are using dynamic scripting).

That Security Stuff

I imagine by this point you've torn great furrows into your scalp by the number of ways I've demonstrated of opening your web page to the worst sort of damage.

In particular, working around the security restrictions in the browser by using dynamic scripting with a call to an external service, which you do not control, *means that your application is open to potential security violations.*

Just such a security violation was discovered in Google's popular Gmail application in 2006. One service associated with the application would return a list of contacts for a given individual. This functionality was created as a JSON web service, and as long as the user was logged in, a call to this service returned the user's list of contacts. However, calls of this nature could be placed from any location, and the web service didn't check to ensure that they were from a "safe" domain. As such, a web site could easily make the call to the JSON service and then send the contacts list using an Ajax call to another service, or even an XHR request on its own site, thus opening up the contacts for yet more spam email.

Creating a JSON or even an XML service endpoint for sensitive data makes no sense, and neither does making a call on an endpoint service from a nontrusted site. Keeping these security issues in mind is important, though, because these kinds of services are important for implementing widgets.

If you read through the Ajax security restrictions at the Open Web Security Project (OWASP) wiki at *www.owasp.org/index.php/OWASP_AJAX_Security_Guidelines*, you might think that there is no use of Ajax that's safe, and that's true—there is no safe use of Ajax. There are only safeguards you can put in place.

As mentioned earlier, Douglas Crockford provides a JSON parser at *http://www.json.org/js.html* that you can incorporate into your application rather than using eval. His parser ensures that there's no hidden scripting embedded in the object that can bite you. Using XML within the DOMParser is actually a safer bet for dynamic scripting. None of these options is going to be completely secure unless you either control the endpoint or web service, or you have a high degree of confidence and trust in a service you're using externally.

Now that we've figured out how to violate browser security, what about those other two essentials of web application development: performance and accessibility?

 Chapter 10 examines scaling and building a site from scratch, and will discuss overall Ajax security concerns.

A First Look at Performance

Throughout this book, especially in the later chapters, we'll look at some performance issues and tweaks associated with Ajax applications. I did want to mention one first, though, and that is HTTP's two-connection limitation that most browsers put on pages pulled from a specific domain.

When you open a web page and download material from the Web, only two parallel connections to the same domain are opened at any one time. This means that if you're downloading images, JavaScript files, and other material embedded into the page, the download will queue based on the number of connections. This becomes a more acute problem when you're using Ajax calls in your script, all of which could be held up waiting on connections to open from processing other calls or downloading other material.

One way to improve performance is to consider offloading some of the incidental material, such as images, to another domain so that you free up connections from the current domain specifically for Ajax calls. The other domain can be on the same server, as the connection limitation built into browsers is based on domain name, not IP address. So you can create *CNAME* subdomains such as images.sitename. com, js.sitename.com, or database.sitename.com, effectively allowing your browser to create more than two concurrent connections, thus increasing the speed with which the page and the Ajax requests are made.

 Using multiple subdomains to increase the number of parallel HTTP requests can frustrate dial-up modem users who have only limited bandwidth. Still, as broadband use increases significantly, this becomes less of an issue. You need to be aware of who your customers are and plan accordingly.

Another performance enhancement could be to compress your JavaScript so that the file sizes are smaller. However, this can obscure your JavaScript code, making it more difficult to read and reuse, if this is of interest to you. You can easily find and try out several JavaScript compression tools by searching for "javascript compression."

Rather than using small JavaScript files, each of which has to be loaded individually, you might consider packaging JavaScript files that are used together most frequently into one file. However, balance this with loading code that might not be used in a specific application. It's better to have smaller files than to load unnecessary code.

One Last Word on Asynchronous Versus Synchronous

Though the "A" in Ajax stands for "asynchronous," the XMLHttpRequest object doesn't have to be used asynchronously. A *synchronous* request is one where the browser is locked up waiting for a response. An example of this behavior would be the following:

```
var state = document.forms[0].elements[0].value;
var url = 'ajax.php?state=' + state;
xmlhttp.open('GET', url, false);
xmlhttp.send(null);
alert(xmlhttp.getAllResponseHeaders());
```

In this code, a string representing a state is accessed from a form field and used to build an HTTP GET request on the web service, *ajax.php*. The third parameter in the open method is false, which means the request is made synchronously. The request is sent without any parameters (the null value), and immediately after the send, an alert message box is opened and the response headers are printed out.

Now, if the service is quick, the response is almost immediate. However, if the service is slow, no other page activity can happen until the request finishes. The effect is little different from when you first open a web page and you can't typically do anything with the page until it's finished loading.

Most Ajax applications use the XMLHttpRequest object asynchronously. In this case, an asynchronous request is sent, but the browser continues processing the code following the request rather than waiting for a response from the server. To process the response when it is sent, a function is assigned to the onreadystatechange property of the XMLHttpRequest object. In the function, then, the ready state and request status are tested, and when the ready state is equal to 4, the request is finished.

The asynchronous version of the above code could be like the following:

```
    // get recipe using Ajax
function getRecipe(evnt) {
    if (!xmlhttp) xmlhttp = aaGetXmlHttpRequest();
    if (!xmlhttp) return;
    var drink = encodeURIComponent(document.getElementById('drink').value);
    var qry = "drink=" + drink;
    var url = 'recipe.php?' + qry;
    xmlhttp.open('GET', url, true);
    xmlhttp.onreadystatechange = printRecipe;
    xmlhttp.send(null);
    if (evnt && evnt.preventDefault())
      evnt.preventDefault();
    return false;
}
```

The advantage of an asynchronous request is that the web page reader can continue to interact with the page (and the browser) while the request is being processed. Even if you want to prevent any other actions on the part of the web page reader while the process is being completed, you're still going to want to run the request asynchronously. If the request is synchronous, and the service is delayed or takes too long, the page seems to "freeze up," giving an impression that something may be broken.

To better get an idea of what a delay in a request "feels" like when working either asynchronously or synchronously, add a `sleep` function to any of the recipe PHP applications that are accessed through an Ajax request (XMLHttpRequest):

```
// delay
sleep(10);
//Remove whitespace from beginning & end of passed search.
$search = trim($drink);
```

The current setting is a 10 second delay, but you can adjust it to be as long as you'd like. I suggest strongly, though, that you try it at 10 seconds at first. Believe me, you'll get the effect.

When you access the page and make a drink selection, you'll find that the page seems to "freeze" and the selection box remains open; everything is waiting now for the request to return, including the functionality to repaint the page. In other words, the page acts "broken."

If you return the function back to asynchronous operation, there's a noticeable delay in the answer and you might want to think about adding a message box or some other indicator that the application is working, but at least the page is not frozen—the worst of all possible impressions you want to give with your site.

 Regardless of which approach you use, if the service request takes longer than the request timeout (depending on settings, but typically over 30 seconds), the request will fail. Scattered throughout the examples are simple ways you can add a "working…" indicator to your applications.

CHAPTER 3

Ajax Tools and Terminology

JavaScript has undergone a metamorphosis since its earliest beginnings. With newer versions, in addition to more complex and rich JavaScript libraries, it may seem as if you're using an entirely new language—full of strange and odd operators and functions. The popularity of Ajax has generated interest in more formal approaches to JavaScript development and this has led to the creation of new concepts and associated terminology and coding syntax. The positive effect of such effort is more robust and richer applications. The downside, however, is having to learn the lingo of the Ajax development community, as well as having to spend a considerable amount of time with the libraries before you can incorporate them into your own applications.

This chapter looks at some of the more popular Ajax libraries, both as an introduction to the library and as a way of introducing some of the more commonly occurring Ajax concepts and terminologies. In addition, it also covers some of the more common "gotchas" associated with using the libraries, many of which were designed more for developing a new form of desktop application than adding Ajax to existing web sites and applications.

Most Ajax libraries provide a basic set of functionality, such as methods that can access any web page object without having to use the DOM methods. Most libraries also provide the ability to communicate with a web service. The major difference between library types is whether they contain functions to do specific tasks or contain frameworks to provide infrastructure support on which other libraries are built.

Libraries can also be layered, one building on another, or mashed together, which provides its own challenges. For example, if two libraries assign a different function to a window onload event handler, they must be set up correctly or one library will overwrite the other and the setup routine may not be properly executed. These library conflicts can be the worst to debug, too, because if you're not familiar with either library's code, you're also not familiar with how they can compete with each other.

The server-side development communities are also getting into the Ajax thing, either by designing new client-side technologies to work with their services, language, or infrastructure, or by incorporating existing technologies into their tool bases. We'll examine many of these in the final chapter of this book. This includes a quick look at Ruby on Rails (RoR), which is tightly integrated with the granddaddy of all Ajax libraries, Prototype.

Prototype

Probably the best known of the Ajax libraries, and one of the most used, is Prototype. It's actually a fairly small and self-contained library. It loads quickly and forms a core on which other libraries are built, including script.aculo.us and Rico, both of which are discussed later.

Prototype is less a framework than a scripting language *equalizer*, providing a set of objects that cut through some of the complexity of accessing and working with page elements across different browsers. It was created and is still maintained by Sam Stephenson, and the latest version (Prototype 1.5 at the time of this writing) can be downloaded from *http://prototypejs.org*. This site also has documentation for the library's API, as well as articles and tutorials on its use.

Adding Prototype to your projects is simple; you can include it in an application using the following:

```
<script type="text/javascript" src="/path/to/prototype.js"></script>
```

One of the defining characteristics of Prototype is its incorporation of several Ruby language-like functions and behavior. Ruby is a simple-to-use language, but it's also cryptic, and Prototype's use of these functions in JavaScript can cause confusion, particularly if you're not familiar with Prototype's unique components. Key among these components are functions known as the *dollar* and *dollar F*.

The dollar function, $( ), returns a reference to the element whose name is passed into the function:

```
var elem = $('some_element');
```

The element is identified using the id attribute:

```
<div id="some_element">
...
</div>
```

This is equivalent to using the following DOM method call:

```
var elem = document.getElementById('some_element');
```

In addition to returning the element, the $( ) function also appends several Prototype-specific properties.

The function $F( ) returns the value of a form field, given its identifier:

```
var value = $F('form_field');
...
<input type="text" id="form_field" />
```

This is equivalent to:

```
var value = document.getElementById('form_field').value
```

Prototype doesn't provide new functionality as much as it repackages commonly needed functionality into handily accessible units. Using document.getElementById is simple, but $( ) is even simpler, especially when functionality is added.

Another key component in Prototype is the Enumerable object, which provides iterative capability within JavaScript. Traversing collections of data, such as arrays, has always been somewhat primitive in JavaScript, at least compared to other languages. It's also an area undergoing change in new versions of JavaScript, such as the addition of the forEach and filter functionalities in JavaScript 1.6 and the iterative functionality added in JavaScript 1.7. Until such change is widespread among all browser providers, though, the use of Prototype's Enumerable object can be used to emulate much of the behavior of these built-in capabilities.

Prototype also provides objects to manage XMLHttpRequests. They're not complicated to use, and they simplify the code to make a web service request. The base Ajax object is called, appropriately enough, Ajax, but most of the work is done through the Ajax.Request object. An example of using this object to make a request is the following:

```
var myAjax = new Ajax.Request( url, {
    method: 'get',
    parameters: qry,
    onComplete: printRecipe });
```

The first parameter is the URL for the web service request, and the second parameter takes an object that has an HTTP request method, the service request parameters, and a function to call when the request is complete.

The XMLHttpRequest response is wrapped within Prototype; you can't intercept the different stages of the request. Instead you handle onComplete, onLoading, onLoaded, and onInteractive events to process each stage. For most applications, though, you'll probably be interested only in onComplete, or onSuccess, which applies only if the request is a success.

Prototype also provides ways to emulate the DELETE and PUT HTTP request methods, using the alternative POST approach discussed in Chapter 2. The library also has a way to automatically evaluate the returned data. If the data is formatted as HTML, the Ajax.Updater method can process the response and insert the data in a specified element. If the data is marked as JSON, Prototype can autoevaluate it and pass it as an object in the callback function. The operative phrase here is "marked as JSON," which requires an X-JSON header. This is supported by Ruby on Rails, the de facto server-side environment for Prototype. Unfortunately, using a custom header can fail, especially because of the size of data returned. Rather than using a nonstandard custom header, the examples in this chapter and throughout the book return the JSON data within the response object and either use eval directly or use json.org's JSON evaluator.

The best way to conclude our examination of the Ajax and enumeration objects, as well as the dollar functions, is with an example. Example 3-1 demonstrates how to use Prototype to make a web service request using the Ajax object. The web service is similar to that used in Example 2-9 in Chapter 2, except that rather than sending along a drink search term, the web service returns *all* the drink recipes, formatted as JSON.

Example 3-1. PHP application returning list of drink recipes, formatted as JSON

```php
<?php

    $result = "'drinks' : [{ 'drink' : 'TEA', 'makings' : { 'title' : 'Hot Tea'," .
                " 'ingredients' : [ { 'ingredient' : 'tea leaves' }]," .
                " 'instruction' : 'Boil water. Pour over tea leaves." .
                " Steep five minutes. Strain and serve.'}}";
    $result .= ", { 'drink' : 'NONCHAMP', 'makings' : {'title' : 'Non-Alcoholic Champagne',
                " .
                " 'ingredients' : [ { 'ingredient' : '32 ounces club soda' }, " .
                " { 'ingredient' : '12 ounces frozen white grape juice concentrate'}],"
                .
                " 'instruction' : 'Mix club soda with grape juice concentrate.'}}";
    $result .= ", { 'drink' : 'APPLETINI', 'makings' : { 'title' : 'Appletini', " .
                " 'ingredients' : [ { 'ingredient' : '1 ounce vodka' }, " .
                " { 'ingredient' : '1/2 ounce Sour Apple Pucker or apple schnapps'}],"
                .
                " 'instruction' : 'Mix vodka and schnapps in a glass filled with ice.
            Strain " .
                "into martini glass. Garnish with an apple slice or raisin.'}}";
    $result .= ", { 'drink' : 'SWMPMARGARITA', 'makings' : {'title' : 'Swamp Margaria', " .
                " 'ingredients' : [ { 'ingredient' : '1 1/2 ounce good quality
            tequila'}, " .
                " { 'ingredient' : '3/4 ounce Cointreau'}, " .
                " { 'ingredient' : '3/4 ounce Grand Marnier'}, " .
                " { 'ingredient' : '1/2 ounce lime juice'}, " .
                " { 'ingredient' : '2 ounces sour mix'}, " .
                " { 'ingredient' : 'several green olives'}]," .
                " 'instruction' : 'Mix all ingredients. Chill an hour. " .
                "Fill bottom of tall glass with several green olives. " .
                "Poor margarita over the olives, let sit for ten minutes, strain and
            serve.'}}";
    $result .= ", { 'drink' : 'LEMON', 'makings' : {'title' : 'Lemon Drop', " .
                " 'ingredients' : [ { 'ingredient' : '1 ounce lemon vodka'}, " .
                " { 'ingredient' : '1 ounce lemon juice'}, " .
                " { 'ingredient' : '1 teaspoon sugar'}]," .
                " 'instruction' : 'Shake with ice, " .
                "strain and serve.'}}] ";
    echo $result;

?>
```

When the service request returns, the JSON is processed through the eval function, forming a JavaScript object with a group of drink objects. Each drink object is identified by a drink name, and each contains a further object, makings, which includes title, ingredients, and instructions.

In the client portion of the Ajax application, shown in Example 3-2, when a drink is selected from the drop-down list, the Prototype Ajax.Request object is created, passing in the web service URL. Other information, including which function to call when a successful request is completed, is also passed into the request. If there had been parameters, they would have been assigned to the parameters property of the object. In the callback function, the response text is used within an eval function call to create a recipe object containing the recipes for all of the drinks, and the printRecipe function is called to process the results.

In printRecipe, the $F( ) function is used to get the drink name, and the $( ) function is used to get the element that contains the printed recipe.

What's next is the really interesting part of the application. To retrieve the drink that is selected from the list, we'll use the Prototype Enumerable object's find method, passing in an anonymous function, which performs the comparison—in this case, a comparison on drink name. If a match is found, a specific drink object is then returned with all the information about that drink.

The drink object has a second property, makings, which includes the drink's title, ingredients, and instruction. The title and instruction are retrieved using straight item access, but the ingredients property, which is an array of individual ingredients, is processed using two other Prototype Enumerable objects: collect, and then join. The whole lot is concatenated to a string that is used to update the recipe object's existing contents. The JavaScript for this application is shown in Example 3-2.

Example 3-2. Using Prototype's Enumerable object to search within drink objects

```
var recipeObj;

Event.observe(window,'load',function( ) {
   Event.observe('myform','submit',getRecipe);
});

function getRecipe(evnt) {
   Event.stop(evnt);
   if (recipeObj) {
      printRecipe( );
      return;
   }
   var url = 'query1.php';
   var myAjax = new Ajax.Request( url,
{
   method:'get',
```

```
  onSuccess: function(transport){
    eval("recipeObj = {" + transport.responseText + "}");
    printRecipe();
  },
  onFailure: function(){ alert('Something went wrong...') }
  });

}
function printRecipe() {

    // get drink name and recipe space obj
    var drinkName = $F('drink');

    // search for drink name
    var drinkObj = recipeObj.drinks.find(function(drink) {
        if (drink.drink == drinkName) {
          return drink;
        }
    });

    if (!drinkObj) return;

    var recipe = document.createElement('div');
    Element.extend(recipe);
    recipe.id = 'recipe';
    recipe.addClassName('recipe');

    var str = "<h3>" + drinkObj.makings.title + "</h3>";
    var ingredients = drinkObj.makings.ingredients.collect(function(ingredient) {
        return ingredient.ingredient;
    });
    str += ingredients.join('<br />');
    str += "<br /><br />" + drinkObj.makings.instruction;
    if ($('recipe'))
        $('recipe').remove('recipe');
    var recipe = document.createElement('div');
    Element.extend(recipe);
    recipe.id = 'recipe';
    recipe.addClassName('recipe');
    recipe = recipe.update(str);
    document.body.appendChild(recipe);
}
```

In the getRecipe function, if the recipeObj is already instantiated, the printRecipe function is called; otherwise, the Ajax request is made and the object is built in the processRecipe function. This prevents multiple calls to the web server.

Unless there's a delay at the server for the first request, the recipe is printed out almost immediately when a drink name is selected.

The web page itself is identical to that in Example 2-10 in Chapter 2, except that it uses the Prototype library. The application-specific JavaScript is located in a file called *getalldrinks.js*. The example files for the book reference it from *ch03-02.xhtml*.

The "Rubification of JavaScript" enabled by Prototype may or may not be sufficient to justify its use, but the Enumerable object does provide intriguing functionality. How does it work, though? After all, it's not as if any specialized object was created. For all that we know, we're just dealing with straight JavaScript objects.

Enumerable and many other objects in Prototype work via the JavaScript prototype property, hence, we suppose, the name. If you haven't been exposed to the use of prototype, you can get the basics of it in the overview presented in the next section. The use of prototype to extend objects is not uncommon in Ajax—not uncommon, and not without controversy. If you're familiar with the prototype property, feel free to skip the section.

The JavaScript Prototype Property

JavaScript does not provide for a traditional class structure where you extend a class by inheriting from it and then adding new functionality. Instead, the language uses the prototype property to extend existing objects and all their instances.

prototype is a collection of properties and methods that are defined at runtime and are available for every instance of an object, whether the instance was created before or after the prototype modification was made.

How the prototype works in JavaScript is that when an object property is accessed, the browser's scripting engine first looks for that property among the native properties, then searches within the prototype properties. If it is not found among the prototype properties, the instance-level properties are checked.

In the following code, the prototype property is used to extend the Number object, in this case by adding a new property, percentage, and a new method, adjustValue:

```
Number.prototype.percentage=0.15; // 15 percent
Number.prototype.adjustValue = function( ) {
        return this * this.percentage;
}
```

To use the new properties, access them as if they were native properties:

```
var someValue = 3.0;
alert(someValue.adjustValue( ));
```

In the application, a message displays the adjusted value based on the initial number 3.0 multiplied by the percentage 0.15.

The Prototype library makes use of this prototype capability to add extensions for certain built-in objects, such as String, Array, and Function. An example is the extended method stripTags, which strips all element tags from a string:

```
var str = "<p>This is a paragraph</p>";
var newStr = str.stripTags(); // result is "This is a paragraph"
```

The use of JavaScript's prototype property is very powerful and forms the basis for much of the Prototype library. However, it's also risky.

Associative Arrays and the Risks of Prototype

JavaScript objects can all be treated as associative arrays (also called a *hash*, *hash structure*, or *hash table*). This means that you can access an object property using the dot notation:

```
someObject.objProperty
```

You can also access a property using array notation, given the property's name as the index:

```
someObject["objProperty"]
```

Mapping between key and value pairs is an inherent component of an associative array. Because JavaScript objects can be treated as associative arrays, you can use the JavaScript for...in notation to iterate through the object's properties:

```
for (props in obj) {...}
```

You can also use any JavaScript object to create a new associative array, including Array, RegExp, Object, String, and so on. The following code uses the Array object, which would seem to be the most appropriate:

```
var newArray = new Array();
newArray['1'] = 'one';
newArray['3'] = 'three';
```

It seems simple enough, but this can trigger some of the most passionate discussions among those who use JavaScript, particularly those who use Prototype.

There are some who say there are no associative arrays in JavaScript, that the functionality is a way of adding runtime properties. Regardless of semantics, the functionality does match that of an associative array (array elements assigned by key or name rather than number), so for all intents and purposes, it is an associative array.

Then there are those who say that associative arrays in JavaScript are wrong or harmful. Their reasoning is that using an Array object to create an associative array isn't natural—that the array methods that normally give you information about the array, such as length, no longer work, and that only using Array objects for traditional numeric arrays supports expected behavior.

This is particularly acute for Prototype, as it extends the basic `Array` object through the prototype property. If you create an associative array from an `Array` object that has itself been extended through a library such as Prototype, when you use the `for...in` loop on it, you may get unexpected results, most likely a break in the application.

Instead of using `Array` for associative arrays, the Ajax pundits say you should use `Object`. Version 1.4 of Prototype also extended the basic JavaScript `Object` using the prototype property, but due to popular demand, Stephenson pulled this in version 1.5. Still, it does extend `String`, `Array`, and others, and as such you need to be aware if you use associative array functionality to access object properties in your application.

 You also need to be especially aware of this prototype extension capability if you're using more than one library, each of which could be creating its own extensions on the primary JavaScript objects. Conflicts between the libraries can cause subtle problems that are difficult to debug.

External Libraries: Risks and Benefits

Concerns about Prototype really are concerns about any external library. Among the more common are:

- The library size can be large.
- It can make application problems very difficult to debug.
- It can introduce hidden customizations that cause unexpected behaviors.
- It can clash with homegrown libraries, as well as other external libraries.

You can see how much a library can add to an application just by using Firebug to step through a typical Ajax request. When I tried this with Prototype, I think I counted about 50 different statements executed above and beyond what normally happens with an Ajax request.

Prototype is a very small, compact library, less than 15k in size. Other libraries though, like Dojo (discussed in the upcoming "Dojo" section), are much larger and can cause slow page loading.

The most frustrating aspect for me in using an external library is when something goes wrong and it becomes very difficult to determine exactly what, even when stepping through the code with Firebug.

Balance this, though, with the benefits of the library. Prototype provides a great deal of cross-browser management so we don't have to deal with all the quirks and fidgets that all the various browsers add on to the web development process. In particular, its ability to handle differences when accessing page element styles is very attractive, as is its event management and other DOM extensions.

The bottom line is that I wouldn't use Prototype or any library just for small applications or to make an Ajax request. However, if I were creating a very large, very extensive Ajax application that was going to be used site-wide, one that must work with all sorts of browsers and be robust, I would use Prototype or possibly one of the other libraries, such as jQuery, Dojo, or MochiKit.

Most of this book uses JavaScript from scratch to demonstrate the functionality, but many of the sections will also either feature the use of another library or explore how one of the libraries would implement the same feature. This will help you become familiar with at least a handful of popular and robust Ajax libraries. You will also learn how to generate the same functionality using standard JavaScript functionality so that you can judge for yourself when to use a library and when not to.

 If I seem overly critical of Prototype or any library in this chapter, it's only because I want to ensure that you, the reader, are aware of the potential problems with using an external library. However, I feel that all of the libraries covered in this chapter are wonderfully useful tools, and commend the developers not only for providing them, but also for doing so freely.

script.aculo.us

The script.aculo.us library is based on Prototype, extending the functionality with higher-level features and providing a framework in which to create more sophisticated Ajax effects. It got its name using a variation of domain naming of the social bookmarking site, del.icio.us, though there is no association between the two. It can be downloaded from *http://script.aculo.us*. The version used in the examples in this chapter is 1.7.0.

To use script.aculo.us, you'll need to include both the Prototype and script.aculo.us JavaScript files. You don't need to download Prototype, though, as it's bundled with the script.aculo.us download package:

```
<script src="javascripts/prototype.js" type="text/javascript"></script>
<script src="javascripts/scriptaculous.js" type="text/javascript"></script>
```

The script.aculo.us library consists of different effects, each in its own separate file. If you're using only one script.aculo.us effect, you can specify it as part of the URL of the script file within the script src attribute:

```
<script src="scriptaculous.js?load=effects" type="text/javascript"></script>
```

This script tag loads the main script.aculo.us.js library, which is primarily nothing more than a loader program. The URL in the tag triggers the loader to also load the *effects.js* file. How this occurs is that the loader gets the script URL, parses out the library (or libraries) to load, and then calls a function that uses document.writeln to "add" the libraries. If no library is named, the script.aculo.us loader pulls in all of the libraries.

Adding JavaScript using document.write or the DOM to insert new script elements is also called *On-Demand JavaScript*, a known Ajax pattern, as defined in Michael Mahemoff's book, *Ajax Design Patterns* (O'Reilly).

At the time of this writing, the different libraries that could be included are:

- builder
- effects
- dragdrop
- controls
- slider

There are dependencies between libraries, which are detailed in the script.aculo.us documentation.

Using document.writeln or document.write to add script tags to include new JavaScript libraries is a handy way to dynamically "load" libraries as they're needed. Unfortunately, this doesn't work if you serve the document up as XHTML, since dynamically adding what could be crufty markup into a properly formatted XHTML document isn't allowed. In fact, script.aculo.us doesn't work in a properly formatted XHTML document.

The script.aculo.us Effects

Once loaded, script.aculo.us has some nice effects: drag and drop, autocompletion, sliders and controls, and list sort capabilities. It also has a set of visual effects that script.aculo.us refers to as "combination effects," which are available through an object appropriately named Effect. The effects available in this object are listed in Table 3-1.

Table 3-1. script.aculo.us visual effects

Effect name	Effect behavior
Effect.Appear	Display a hidden element.
Effect.Fade	Gradually hide an element by fading it from view.
Effect.BlindDown	Scroll an element down, moving from top to bottom.
Effect.BlindUp	Scroll an element up, moving from bottom to top.
Effect.SwitchOff	Flash the image before dropping it from view.
Effect.SlideDown	Slide an element down from the top to the bottom. The content of the element slides down with the container.
Effect.SlideUp	Slide an element from the bottom to the top. The content of the element slides up with the container.

Table 3-1. script.aculo.us visual effects (continued)

Effect name	Effect behavior
Effect.DropOut	Emulate a dropping of the element before hiding it.
Effect.Shake	Shake the element.
Effect.Pulsate	Fade the element in and out rapidly, creating a pulse effect.
Effect.Squish	Shrink the element up and left until it disappears.
Effect.Fold	Scroll the element up (BlindUp), then end by scrolling horizontally inward.
Effect.Grow	Expand the element from nothing.
Effect.Shrink	Shrink the element down and right until it disappears.
Effect.Highlight	Highlights the element, typically by flashing a yellow color. This is also called a *fade* by many Ajax developers.

Example 3-3 is based on the same code as that shown in Example 3-2. Here, the script.aculo.us Shake effect is used on the updated recipe element to highlight that the element's contents have changed using, I think, a very appropriate effect. Since the page is rather long, the code displayed in this example only lists the changed function. Remember, though, that the page must be served as HTML, not XHTML, since the most recent version of script.aculo.us doesn't work with XHTML.

Example 3-3. Trying out the script.aculo.us library

```
function printRecipe( ) {

    // get drink name and recipe space obj
    var drinkName = $F('drink');

    // search for drink name
    var drinkObj = recipeObj.drinks.find(function(drink) {
        if (drink.drink == drinkName) {
          return drink;
        }
    });

    if (!drinkObj) return;

    var str = "<h3>" + drinkObj.makings.title + "</h3>";
    var ingredients = drinkObj.makings.ingredients.collect(function(ingredient) {
        return ingredient.ingredient;
    });
    str += ingredients.join('<br />');
    str += "<br /><br />" + drinkObj.makings.instruction;

    if ($('recipe'))
        $('recipe').remove('recipe');
    var recipe = document.createElement('div');
    Element.extend(recipe);
    recipe.id = 'recipe';
    recipe.addClassName('recipe');
```

Example 3-3. Trying out the script.aculo.us library (continued)

```
    recipe = recipe.update(str);
    document.body.appendChild(recipe);
    new Effect.Shake(recipe);
}
```

In this example, all of the script.aculo.us libraries are loaded to give you an idea of how much delay the script library can add to page load times. Even with broadband, it is noticeable.

In the example, the recipe block shakes after the fetched drink recipe is displayed. The effect doesn't add significantly to the functionality of the application—it's visual candy, like many effects used in Ajax. As long as the effect doesn't impact adversely on the user experience with longer load times and such, it can provide nice feedback.

In Chapter 4 and later in Chapter 6, I'll demonstrate how fade and effects like this are used to provide feedback to the web page reader—they can be particularly useful for marking successful Ajax updates and deletions.

> Note the use of new in front of the script.aculo.us effect. Object instantiation is a part of the effect, but it may not be as obvious or intuitive. It's not uncommon for people to forget to use new.

Rico

Rico is another Ajax library built on Prototype. Like script.aculo.us, Rico includes several packaged effects, including fade, and like all Ajax frameworks, it includes functions to simplify Ajax service calls. Rico can be downloaded from *http://openrico.org*. Rico also has a nicely implemented round corner effect that can be added to page elements. However, whether you want the overhead for this is debatable. I have a feeling that rounded corners will begin to lose some of their popularity—at least until they're available in most browsers as CSS.

Rico has an interesting LiveGrid, which connects to a data source through an Ajax request and serves up new data as the page reader scrolls down the data table. This effect is also known as *Ajax pagination* or *live scrolling*.

Ajax Pagination

Ajax pagination is a mixed bag. When implemented properly, it's a terrific way to pull in external data without your readers even being aware that it is happening. Google uses this approach when it brings in a seemingly never-ending map with the Google Maps web services.

However, done incorrectly, pagination can be a nightmare. Recently, Yahoo! reworked its Yahoo! TV web site to include several Ajax effects, including Ajax pagination. The performance and "busyness" of the site due to the pagination change in particular raised howls of protest from current users. The pagination added an over-all burden to page load times, and the effect wasn't implemented with any form of caching to create a smooth "endless scrolling" effect.

Rico provides encapsulated behavior called the LiveGrid, which supports pagination by working with a live backend database to query the data as needed. The Rico developers provide a demonstration of a LiveGrid Yahoo! search at *http://openrico.org/rico/demos.page*.

The Rico Weather Widget

Like script.aculo.us, Rico provides demos of functionality but not a lot of formal documentation. The typical approach in learning how to use any of these libraries is to find an example and take a look at the source. One of my favorite examples is the Rico Weather Watch (*http://openrico.org/demos/weather_demo*), which is shown in Figure 3-1.

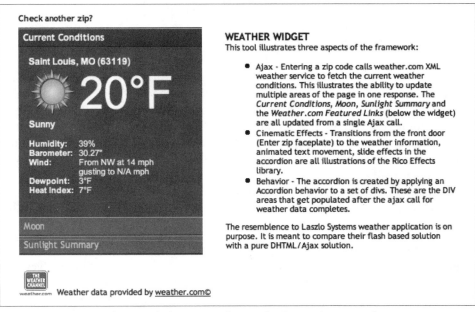

Figure 3-1. Rico's Weather Watch demo, a good example of using Ajax accordions

The demo uses three *accordions*—collapsible panels—to hide and show each piece of weather data. Each, in turn, uses the Rico round corner effects to give it that Ajax feel. An Ajax accordion is really a combination of effects, either displaying an element immediately, resizing it so that it goes from zero height to full height, or increasing the area that shows using CSS clipping regions. In addition, it's layered with other elements, so that as one displays more fully, the others around it alter their positions, making room for the element's new size.

We'll get into how to craft the accordion effect in Chapter 5.

The Rico Weather Watch application calls a web service function that runs local to the Rico effort, which then makes the web service call to Weather.com for the weather information. The returned data is displayed in the different categories. The Weather.com web service request can't be made directly from the client page because of the JavaScript sandbox and security.

The JavaScript Sandbox and Proxies

In Chapter 2, I discussed how the JavaScript sandbox model limits browsers to actions that reference only resources on the same domain from which the script itself was loaded. In other words, Ajax calls can be made only to the same web server domain that served up the original page. Therefore, if your web page comes from the domain somedomain.com, then the web service request must also be made to some-domain.com.

I also discussed how security can be bypassed by altering your security settings, digitally signing your script, or using the dynamically loaded script and callback function—the latter being the only one that will work in all of the browsers. A third approach, demonstrated by Rico with the Weather widget, and one that doesn't bypass the JavaScript security model but does allow cross-domain web service access, is to use a proxy. An Ajax proxy is a web server application (in the local domain) that makes the remote service calls for the client side scrip and then passes the results to the client. In Chapter 9, I'll demonstrate how the use of a proxy works in more detail. Now, back to the Ajax libraries.

An *Ajax proxy* is a web application (in the local domain) that serves up the script that makes calls to the remote web service (there is no inherent limitation on domains for server-server access). The proxy then passes the results back to the client. With a proxy application, your client Ajax program can then make the web service request on the local domain, but still access the numerous web services.

Dojo

Dojo is an open source effort managed by the Dojo Foundation. Unlike the other libraries, which are maintained by individuals or small groups, the Dojo effort actively encourages additions to the Ajax library from various sources.

The basic Dojo Toolkit is actually quite large and provides a rather complex "pluggable" framework, which allows for the development of Dojo-style widgets—external extensions that don't impact the underlying code. You can download the toolkit at *http://dojotoolkit.org*.

The released version of the library provides both human-readable source and Java-Script source that has had all extraneous whitespace removed (which makes the library smaller and more or less impossible to read).

 There are several tools and sites that provide JavaScript compression. A good place to start is to simply search for "JavaScript compression" in your favorite search engine.

Dojo has extensive documentation, accessible at *http://manual.dojotoolkit.org/index.html*. The mechanics of widget-building for Dojo are beyond this book, and I'll refer you to a tutorial on the subject at *http://openrico.org/demos/weather_demo*.

Like other Ajax libraries, Dojo originally had little documentation. Considering how complex it was, this was more than a small handicap in using the toolkit. Luckily, the project did start a wiki (a site where more than one person can edit the contents) for documentation, though like all wikis, the coverage can be sketchy. Another place to find documentation is at *http://dojotoolkit.org/docs*.

Dojo provides its own cross-browser and JavaScript language functionality, but unlike Prototype, it also provides a framework for developing extensions and boot-strapping the Dojo environment. According to the Dojo site's documentation, Dojo consists of several modules, including the following (just a sampling):

dojo
: The Dojo bootstrap, which loads whatever modules are being used

dojo.lang
: JavaScript utilities

dojo.string
: JavaScript string utilities

dojo.dom
: DOM manipulation routines

dojo.style
: CSS manipulation routines

dojo.html
: HTML specifications

Dictionary
: A dictionary/hash object

dojo.animation.Animation
: Animation support

dojo.crypto
: Cryptographic routines

The list goes on and on. As you can see, Dojo is not a small library. Luckily, you don't have to load all of Dojo to access a subset of the functionality.

I tried out Dojo at one of my sites because I wanted to play around with one of the effects, specifically a fisheye menu. If you're familiar with Apple's OS X operating system, you might be familiar with the fisheye menu effect—when you move your mouse over the Dock, the items expand but in a way that emulates a "fish-eye" magnifier. A sample from the Dojo web site is shown in Figure 3-2.

Figure 3-2. Sample of a fisheye menu, expanding with a mouseover

I included the bootstrap Dojo library, but I also included the `fisheye` module, using the Dojo require function:

```
<script type="text/javascript" src="/dojo/dojo.js"></script>
...
dojo.require("dojo.widget.FisheyeList");
```

The *dojo.js* bootstrapping script also references other modules it needs to operate, regardless of module used. It also defines the function that includes the libraries, though following that code becomes a lesson in obfuscation.

Dojo provides functionality for everything you can think of and probably everything you can't think of. This includes Ajax, cryptography, extended client-side storage beyond cookie use, most visual effects, and so on. To support this, the infrastructure is complex, and the source code is extremely difficult to read and follow.

Even with the ability to minimize the code loaded, Dojo is still a slow library. It also has its own side effect when it comes to playing well with other libraries.

However, unlike Prototype, Dojo's side effects are based on standard rather than nonstandard use of JavaScript, and are related to event handlers.

 The Dojo Foundation has been hard at work optimizing Dojo to create a smaller footprint, as well as a slimmed-down widget core. You might find that by the time you read this book, Dojo is a much more attractive choice, with faster, leaner code.

Event Handler Chaining

Before the W3C released the DOM Level 2, events were handled by assigning an event handler to an object, such as in the following:

```
event.onload=functionToRun;
```

This code is still supported, but assigning a new function overwrites any previous function assignment to the onload event handler, including those that Dojo assigns, which means Dojo's setup functions aren't able to run.

Instead of overriding event handler function assignments, in DOM Level 2, a new method of assigning event handlers was created that provides for handler function chaining. The following assigns the function functionToRun to the load event:

```
window.addEventListener("load",functionToRun,false);
```

Unfortunately, though, Microsoft does not support this new method, providing its own proprietary event handler:

```
window.attachEvent("onload",functionToRun);
```

The following works through the cross-browser differences:

```
if (window.addEventListener) {
   window.addEventListener("load",finish,false);
} else if (window.attachEvent) {
   window.attachEvent("onload", finish);
}
```

We'll look at events and event handlers in more detail in Chapter 4, but this serves as a quick note that when using external Ajax libraries, you'll need to plan on using event handler function assignment such as that just shown. For the most part, the examples in this book will use this or a variation of this functionality.

Declarative HTML

Another old HTML problem that is unfortunately resurfacing with newer Ajax uses is the use of nonstandard or deprecated element attributes. There are a number of older attributes no longer supported, such as align with HTML tables and images, bgcolor for all table elements, border for images, tables, and the document body, and so on.

Now, though, there's a whole host of nonstandard attributes being introduced by Ajax libraries. The reason? The library developers are trying to create effects that don't require the users to actually touch JavaScript. I'll demonstrate this with an example.

Earlier I mentioned Dojo's fisheye effect. This isn't a trivial effect to create. You not only have to capture the web page reader's mouse movements, you also have to size objects in relation to each other and the mouse. It's not something I'd be interested in creating. Luckily, through the use of Dojo, I don't have to.

To use the Dojo fisheye widget functionality, create a series of div elements: one outer element, another element that acts as control, and several inner elements, one for each menu item. Each element is given a specific Dojo class name, as well as element attributes providing information for the menu caption, source file for the icon, minimum and maximum image sizes, and so on. The menu page elements are shown in Example 3-4.

Example 3-4. Using the Dojo fisheye widget

```
<div class="outerbar">
<div class="dojo-FisheyeList"
    dojo:itemWidth="50" dojo:itemHeight="50"
    dojo:itemMaxWidth="200" dojo:itemMaxHeight="200"
    dojo:orientation="horizontal"
    dojo:effectUnits="2"
    dojo:itemPadding="10"
    dojo:attachEdge="top"
    dojo:labelEdge="bottom"
    dojo:enableCrappySvgSupport="false"
>
    <div class="dojo-FisheyeListItem" onClick="load_app(1);"
        dojo:iconsrc="images/icon_browser.png" caption="Web Browser">
    </div>
    <div class="dojo-FisheyeListItem" onClick="load_app(2);"
        dojo:iconsrc="images/icon_calendar.png" caption="Calendar">
    </div>
    <div class="dojo-FisheyeListItem" onClick="load_app(3);"
        dojo:iconsrc="images/icon_email.png" caption="Email">
    </div>
    <div class="dojo-FisheyeListItem" onClick="load_app(4);"
        dojo:iconsrc="images/icon_texteditor.png" caption="Text Editor">
    </div>
    <div class="dojo-FisheyeListItem" onClick="load_app(5);"
        dojo:iconsrc="images/icon_update.png" caption="Software Update">
    </div>
    <div class="dojo-FisheyeListItem" onClick="load_app(6);"
        dojo:iconsrc="images/icon_users.png" dojo:caption="Users" >
    </div>
</div>

</div>
```

Known as *declarative HTML*, this is an interesting approach to take: embed the necessary information as element attributes so that the web page reader doesn't have to touch code. However, using custom attributes has two major drawbacks: it doesn't validate, and it's not accessible.

Dojo, like many other new Ajax libraries, makes use of custom attributes on standard HTML and XHTML objects, which don't validate as strict HTML or XHTML. In addition, the menu is JavaScript-driven, so a user who doesn't have JavaScript enabled in the web browser won't have access to the menu. The approach is also mouse-driven, which makes it unusable for most keyboard-only access.

Later in the book, I'll briefly explore how to make menus that are both valid and accessible, but for now I'll focus on valid. Modifying the code so that it validates is a bit tricky, but doable. What is required is removing the tag attributes for the elements and adding them using the DOM.

Using JavaScript to Bypass Nonstandard Attributes

In Example 3-4, there are six menu items. To alter the application so that it validates, the custom attributes for the one controller and six menu item div elements must be removed:

```
<div class="dojo-FisheyeList" id="controller">

        <div id="menu1" class="dojo-FisheyeListItem">
        </div>
...
        <div id="menu6" class="dojo-FisheyeListItem">
        </div>

</div>
```

In JavaScript, the application uses the document object to get access to each element, and then uses the DOM method setAttribute to reset the custom attributes. The following code resets the attributes for the controller element object:

```
var cont = document.getElementById("controller");
cont.setAttribute("itemWidth","60");
cont.setAttribute("itemHeight","100");
cont.setAttribute("itemMaxWidth", "200");
cont.setAttribute("itemMaxHeight", "300");
cont.setAttribute("orientation","horizontal");
cont.setAttribute("effectUnits","2");
cont.setAttribute("itemPadding","10");
cont.setAttribute("attachEdige","top");
cont.setAttribute("labelEdge","bottom");
cont.setAttribute("enableCrappySvgSupport","false");
```

These attribute settings are exactly as they were found in the tag attributes (other than an alteration to the image sizes to fit my own images).

For each of the menu options, the identifier accesses the element and adds attributes with setAttribute. The following sets the attributes for the first menu item; all other menu objects are modified using the exact same code (except for the images and captions):

```
var menu1 = document.getElementById("menu1");
menu1.setAttribute("onClick","load_page('http://learningjavascript.info')");
menu1.setAttribute("iconsrc","/dotty/dotty.gif");
menu1.setAttribute("caption","Learning JavaScript");
```

Since the Dojo library functionality requires that these attribute settings exist on the elements before its own functionality is processed, and since it processes the data right after the page loads, the function that contains the attribute setting has to be called right after the div elements are created in the page. One way is to embed a script block calling the function in the web page right after the div elements are created:

```
<script type="text/javascript">
//<![CDATA[

setMenuProps();

//]]>
</script>
```

Notice the use of the CDATA section surrounding the script; this is required in order for the page to validate as XHTML.

Once the attributes are set, the Dojo fisheye menu loads cleanly without having to use custom attributes. However, something is still missing: the required attributes. Each img tag is missing an alt attribute—an attribute required for the page to validate.

Unlike setting the initial attributes, the alt attribute has to be added after Dojo has done its work and created the menu. Dojo captures the window.onload event, which must also be captured. However, this must be done in such a way as to not "break" or override Dojo's event handler.

For this purpose, we can use the DOM to attach an event handler on the window onload event, chaining it with the Dojo event handler. The following code does the trick:

```
function addWindowOnLoad(func) {
    // test for object model
    if (window.addEventListener) {
        window.addEventListener("load",finish,false);
    } else if (window.attachEvent) {
        window.attachEvent("onload", finish);
    }
}

addWindowOnLoad(finish);
```

The finish method accesses each image in the page, checks for class name, and when the class name matches the Dojo class name, checks the src attribute on the image. Based on the text, the related alt attribute value is set:

```
function finish() {
  for(var i = 0; i < document.images.length; i++) {
    var crntimg = document.images[i];
    if (crntimg.className == "dojoHtmlFisheyeListItemImage") {
      switch(crntimg.src) {
        case "http://scriptteaser.com/dotty/dotty.gif" :
          crntimg.alt="Learning JavaScript";
          break;
        case "http://scriptteaser.com/dotty/doomed.gif" :
          crntimg.alt="Three Ps and your little R, too";
          break;
        case "http://scriptteaser.com/dotty/falling.gif" :
          crntimg.alt="Web Services";
          break;
        case "http://scriptteaser.com/dotty/impatience.gif" :
          crntimg.alt="Odds n Ends";
          break;
        case "http://scriptteaser.com/dotty/mad.gif" :
         crntimg.alt="Mad Tech Woman on the Loose";
         break;
        case "http://scriptteaser.com/dotty/home.png" :
          crntimg.alt="Home";
          break;
      }
    }
  }

}
```

The page now validates as XHTML. Though it takes more code, this technique is preferable to just blowing off XHTML or valid markup as "not useful" or unimportant. Companies, government agencies, and other organizations are now specifying that their web content must be both valid and accessible. Some browsers and other tools could react oddly to invalid, and therefore unknown, attributes.

As more Ajax libraries are using the nonstandard element attributes to manage effects, keep this approach in mind when you encounter them.

Other Libraries

There are a growing number of Ajax libraries available to use, from the simple to the complex. We'll briefly examine a few others to give you an idea of the wealth of useful functionality already created for your use.

A handy list of many of the Ajax libraries can be found at the eDevil weblog at *http://edevil.wordpress.com/2005/11/14/javascript-libraries-roundup*.

jQuery

One library that's quickly gaining popularity is jQuery, available at *http://jquery.com*. It's small, fast, and provides fundamental cross-browser methods to work with the DOM rather than higher-order effects.

The Interface library, found at *http://interface.eyecon.ro*, provides higher-order effects for jQuery, similar to what script.aculo.us provides for Prototype.

Unlike the other libraries, though, jQuery has only one object, the jQuery object. Unfortunately, jQuery uses the dollar sign shortcut, $( ), to reference this object. If you want to use jQuery with other libraries, especially Prototype, you have to use the jQuery.noConflict( ) function call at the very start of any script block to restore the other libraries back to their normal behavior. The literal jQuery object is then used as a way of accessing all of the functionality.

jQuery provides a high degree of *chainability*, which is the ability to chain function calls, one after another. This type of functionality requires that the library object methods return a reference to the object itself, which is used in the next method in the chain. Creating effects using jQuery is greatly simplified because of this chaining. In the code shown here, when the user clicks a button, the application finds the fourth paragraph and then slides it down:

```
$("input.buttonBslidedown").click(function( ){ $("div.contentToChange").find("p.
fourthparagraph:hidden").slideDown("slow"); });
```

Adding a new element is also trivial thanks to the add method, which takes HTML as input; finding all elements by class is simplified with the use of children:

```
$("div").children(".className");
```

You can also use the library to find text strings within content, not just DOM elements.

Interest in JQuery has increased so rapidly that even by the time this book went through the editing process, the importance placed on it has brought it to the same level as Prototype and Dojo. I would strongly recommend placing this library among the first to check out when you start working with Ajax libraries. I'd also recommend checking out Dean Edwards base2 and base2.DOM, found at *http://dean.edwards.name/weblog/2007/03/yet-another/*. This new, extremely lean "standardization" library was released after this book was initially written.

MochiKit

MochiKit is another all-in-one Ajax library with one big difference: excellent documentation. Both the library and the documentation can be accessed at *http://www.mochikit.com*. MochiKit has a regular expression explorer, which is handy when you're validating form content. I've never been especially adept at building regular expressions, and I personally will take any help I can get.

MochiKit also has a nice assortment of synchronized and sortable Ajax data tables, as well as an unusual color module for element color support. One of the best aspects of MochiKit is a nice logging panel, though browsers such as IE and Firefox have logging, error, and debugging tools that work regardless of the toolkit.

The Yahoo! UI

There is nothing better for developers than when search engines compete for our eyes and interest. Google provides a Java-based Ajax/server environment called the Google Web Toolkit (GWT). Yahoo!, not to be outdone, has developed the Yahoo! UI (YUI). The YUI differs from the GWT in that it is more a library than a framework. It also doesn't put limitations on the server-side development language—GWT works only with Java.

 As GWT is really a Java environment that happens to produce Ajax applications, it's not covered in detail in this book.

The YUI is used in all of the Yahoo! online applications, and as you can imagine, it gets heavily tested. It's a large download consisting of several folders of JavaScript and HTML, as well as images. It has several high-level packaged effects, such as a calendar, logger (for logging messages), menu, slider, and so on. It also has more basic functionality, such as animation and an effect called *easing*—a bounce effect at the end of a horizontal resizing and sliding that gives a little "polish" to the effect.

We'll be seeing more of YUI in the chapters ahead. In the meantime, you can download the tools at *http://developer.yahoo.com/yui* and check out the demos for yourself. Note that the toolset also has extensive documentation.

mooTools and moo.fx

The mooTools and moo.fx libraries are smaller than many of the other Ajax libraries. They are meant to be extended with new effects rather than to serve as a be-all, end-all Ajax infrastructure. The mooTools library consists of several separate files, such as *Moo.js*, *Function.js*, *Array.js*, *String.js*, and so on, each providing its own JavaScript extensions and classes. Effects that build on these base libraries are called *plug-ins*, and while their dependencies differ, they all require the base mooTools class, *Moo.js*. You can download any of the classes from the main site at *http://mootools.net*.

Like too many other Ajax libraries, the documentation for the mooTools library is rather sketchy, consisting more of program docs than tutorials and actual "how-to" documentation. Luckily, others have stepped up to fill in the void, and you can find a good mooTools tutorial at *http://clientside.cnet.com/examples/mootools-primer*.

The moo.fx library is a mooTools plug-in that bills itself as a "…superlightweight, ultratiny, megasmall javascript effects library." Two separate interface implementations allow the library to work with either mooTools or Prototype. Because there are two implementations, double-check that you've installed the appropriate library. Both can be downloaded from *http://moofx.mad4milk.net*.

The Sarissa Library

The Sarissa library is a cross-browser ECMAScript library that wraps native XML APIs, providing for document loading and serialization. The library also simplifies Ajax service calls, but its strength lies in its XML serialization and XPath support in addition to providing for XSL transformations.

I'm not sure if this is a joke, but Ajax applications that utilize XML API libraries such as Sarissa are beginning to be referred to as uppercase *AJAX* applications, in contrast to *Ajax* libraries that don't quite get that far down to "the metal." As mentioned in Chapter 1, originally Ajax was defined as an acronym, utilizing XML and XSLT to process web service data. However, most Ajax development uses the DOM and increasingly JSON, probably because it's simpler than using XSLT if the developer is unfamiliar with the technology. The Sarissa library is a way of simplifying the use of XSLT (and XPath and XML processing), returning the AJAX to Ajax.

The Sarissa library and documentation can be found at *http://dev.abiss.gr/sarissa*.

WZ_jsGraphics and qForms

A fun library, and one that is nicely detailed, is WZ_jsGraphics, which provides functionality to draw geometrical figures such as lines, circles, squares, and so on. You can download this library from *http://www.walterzorn.com/jsgraphics/jsgraphics_e.htm*.

qForms is a forms API from PengoWorks.com, available at *http://pengoworks.com/index.cfm?action=get:qforms*. This is a useful, specialized library that focuses on forms, pure and simple.

And More

We could go on for another several pages; that's how many Ajax libraries are available. We'll be examining several of these in the examples in the chapters to come, though most of the work will be demonstrated with unpackaged JavaScript so that you can view the application without a lot of extraneous material.

Of course, the concept of "buyer beware" does apply with any of the libraries. For all the coolness of Ajax, it is powerful and if applied incorrectly, it can take down your site or your web page reader's computer. One time I accidentally used a `false` value when I should have used true, resulting in a complete system lockup for any Opera on Mac OS X users coming to my site.

For the most part, though, the worst that will happen is the Ajax effects just won't work, and you might have to tweak your code to get the libraries to work with it or with each other.

Now, let's create some Ajax.

CHAPTER 4

Interactive Effects

All Ajax effects are interactive; the whole point of Ajax is to make a page more responsive. Some effects, though, are more interactive than others—especially those associated with providing immediate information based on some event.

If you've used either Netflix or Blockbuster Online, you've seen pop-up windows that open with information about a movie when your mouse hovers over the movie link. This is typical of an Ajax interactive effect, where the application interprets your intent. In this case, you can find out more about the movie and possibly add it to your queue.

If you've provided commentary at a site and can preview your effort as you write or before final submission, you are seeing another interactive effect. It gives you a chance to review what you've written, correct misspellings or transposed letters, and clarify sentence structure. This type of functionality isn't a requirement for the application to run; rather, it's an interpretation of what your web page readers may want—in this case, a way to preview the text.

Online applications that provide feedback when you perform an action, such as a red flashing effect when data is deleted, or a yellow flash when an update has occurred, are also interactive effects. None is essential, but they provide the page reader reassurance that an action has happened.

Each of these effects provides a signal that the application is aware of your intentions as well as your actions. It's not the same as clicking a button and having a form submitted, or dragging an item to a shopping cart, both of which are expected and essential behaviors, notable only when they don't happen.

No, the Ajax effects covered in this chapter are the web application's way of saying, "I hear you, I see what you're doing, I think I know what you want." None of the effects are essential, but in the great tool chest that is Ajax, these can be the simplest effects to implement and have the strongest positive impact for readers using your applications.

The effects are all quite different: tooltips, Just-In-Time (JIT) form help, color fades, live previews. However, they all have one thing in common—they are all responses to events. Because of this dependence on events, I'll begin the chapter with a review of event handling, particularly event handling in an Ajax environment where multiple libraries may be combined into one application.

Ajax-Friendly Event Handling

Event handlers have been part of JavaScript from the beginning. Most follow the onclick or onload format, where the handler begins with the keyword on, followed by the event name. Typically, the event handlers are placed within the object to which they're connected:

```
<body onload="somefunction( )">
```

Inline event handlers are still viable approaches for managing event capturing, except for two limitations: maintenance and mashability.

Maintainable Event Handling

If event handlers are added directly to page elements, and later there's a change to the function name or parameters, the web developer has to hunt down every occurrence of the load handler text and modify it. This approach of adding event handling isn't efficient, and with today's more complex and dynamically generated web pages, it's infeasible.

 An exception to this premise is dynamically generated content, where the code to create the content is located in one file. Though the generated content can stretch across many pages, you still only have to make changes in one place.

Rather than adding event handlers to objects, a better approach is to assign event handler functions in a scripting block, either in a separate JavaScript file or as a block of code in the head section of a document. This is known as the DOM level 0 event handling approach:

```
<script type="text/javascript">
...
document.onclick=somefunction
</script>
```

This is also a viable solution, but another problem arises when you assign a function to an event handler. In the example just given, assigning someFunction to the onclick event handler for the document object overwrites whatever other assignment has been made before this script is run. If you're incorporating external Ajax libraries or merging multiple Ajax libraries into an application, you can't assume that you "own" the event handler. Your code has to play well with others, unless you want to restrict all code to your code and your code only.

Mashable Event Handling

Another approach, and a recommended one, is to use DOM Level 2 event handling. This technique "chains" event handlers so that when an event fires, all associated functions are run. An example of adding an event handler to the click event for the document is as follows:

```
document.addEventListener("click",eventHandlerFunction,false);
```

In the addEventListener method, the first parameter is the event (click) and the second is the event handler function. The third optional parameter determines whether the processing of the event begins in the outermost object, flowing to the inner in a set of nested objects (true), or from the innermost to the outer (false). The first is known as the *capturing* phase, and the second, the default, emulates the older DOM level 0 event processing by handling the event in the bubble up phase.

To demonstrate both, Example 4-1 shows a page with two div elements, one within the other. A generic event handler routine, manageEvent, is created to attach event handlers to objects, taking as parameters three objects: the target object, the event, and the event handler function.

The first event captured is for the window, in order to assign the click event handler to the two div elements after they're loaded. The window's load event handler then assigns the click event handlers of both div elements to the same function: clickHandler.

Example 4-1. An event handler method that plays well with others

```
<!DOCTYPE html PUBLIC "-//W3C//DTD XHTML 1.0 Strict//EN"
    "http://www.w3.org/TR/xhtml1/DTD/xhtml1-strict.dtd">
<html xmlns="http://www.w3.org/1999/xhtml" lang="en" xml:lang="en">
<head>
<meta http-equiv="Content-Type" content="text/html; charset=utf-8" />
<title>Event Listening</title>
<style type="text/css">
#inner { width: 400px; height: 100px; background-color: #00f;}
#outer { width: 400px; background-color: #ff0; padding: 10px; }
</style>

<script type="text/javascript">
//<![CDATA[

function manageEvent(evntObject,event,eventHandler) {
    evntObject.addEventListener(event,eventHandler,false);
}
```

```
manageEvent(window,"load",
            function () {
    manageEvent(document.getElementById('inner'),"click",clickHandler);
    manageEvent(document.getElementById('outer'),"click",clickHandler);
            });

function clickHandler() {
    alert(this.id);
}
//]]>
</script>

</head>
<body>
<div id="outer">
<div id="inner">
</div>
</div>
</body>
</html>
```

In the example page, clicking on the innermost div element results in an alert message box that displays the word "inner," followed by another alert message box that displays the word "outer." Setting the third parameter in the manageEvent function to true (setting event handling to capturing phase), clicking on the two div elements results in an alert box with outer, followed by another with the word, "inner."

Capturing the event in the wrong phase can have a significantly negative impact on your application. Since most event handlers are coordinated to work in a bubble up phase, unless you want to capture an event in the capturing phase for a specific reason, you'll usually set the third parameter to false.

Using addEventListener is great, except for one thing: Microsoft's Internet Explorer (6.x and 7) doesn't support it. This browser supports another function—attachEvent:

```
document.attachEvent("onclick",eventHandlerFunction);
```

There are two differences between attachEvent and addEventListener. The first is that in attachEvent, you pass the event handler name, not the event, as the first parameter (onclick as compared to click). The second is that attachEvent doesn't have a third parameter because it always handles events in the bubble up phase.

To ensure that event handling works with IE 6.x/7 and other browsers, you'll need to incorporate both types of event handler methods, the W3C DOM Level 2 method and Microsoft's. This means you'll have to test to see whether a specific event listener is supported, and code accordingly. Modifying the manageEvent function to work with IE as well as other browsers results in the following:

```
function manageEvent(eventObj, event, eventHandler) {
    if (eventObj.addEventListener) {
```

```
      eventObj.addEventListener(event, eventHandler,false);
   } else if (eventObj.attachEvent) {
      event = "on" + event;
      eventObj.attachEvent(event, eventHandler);
   }
}
```

The event object is tested to see whether addEventListener is a property associated with the object. If it is, it's used as the event handler dispatch method; otherwise, attachEvent is checked, and it's used if found.

If the user agent doesn't support addEventListener or attachEvent, the application can then fall back to the older DOM level 0 event handler, onclick. This isn't as critical a need anymore, as browsers that can't support some form of advanced event handling have fallen more or less out of use.

To stop listening to an event, use the comple mentary methods, removeEventListener and detachEvent:

```
function stopManagingEvent(eventObj,event,eventHandler) {
   if (eventObj.removeEventListener) {
      eventObj.removeEventListener(event,eventHandler,false);
   } else if (eventObj.detachEvent) {
      event = "on" + event;
      eventObj.detachEvent(event,eventHandler);
   }
}
```

In the cases where you want to cancel an event, you'll need to stop the event propagation for the Mozilla browsers, but cancel the bubble up for IE. In addition, you'll need to stop the default event handling, which you do by using preventDefault with Mozilla/W3C browsers, and by setting the returnValue to false for IE. The following cancelEvent method should take care of this:

```
function cancelEvent(event) {
   if (event.preventDefault) {
      event.preventDefault();
      event.stopPropagation();
   } else {
      event.returnValue = false;
      event.cancelBubble = true;
   }
}
```

Event management functions are used so frequently, you'll want to add them to whatever libraries you use. I added them to this book's Ajax library as aaManageEvent, aaStopEvent, and aaCancelEvent, prepending the functions with "aa" so they won't conflict with other libraries you might be using.

If you use external libraries in your Ajax applications, most of them provide event handling. The next section briefly introduces the event handling system from one of them, Dojo's Event System.

The Dojo Event System and the Target Object

Most Ajax libraries provide some form of event handling functionality. For instance, the Dojo library includes the Dojo Event System, which simplifies event handling considerably—simplifies and adds its own little tricks.

In Dojo, to support the same functionality as in our last section—that is, to attach an event listener to catch the window load event and the clicks for the two div elements—all you need to do is use the connect method for the dojo.event object:

```
dojo.event.connect(obj,"onclick",eventHandler);
```

It's similar to the function shown in Example 4-1, except that Dojo's event system goes beyond the simple manageEvent. For one thing, Dojo manages browser differences when it comes to passing the event object to the function. Though not demonstrated in Example 4-1, typically if you want to access the event object in an event handler, and do so in a cross-browser manner, you must use code similiar to the following in the first line of the event:

```
function eventHandler(evnt) {
    var event = evnt || window.event;
    ...
}
```

Or:

```
function eventHandler(evnt) {
    var event = evnt ? evnt : window.event;
    ...
}
```

If the event object passed to the evnt method exists, that object is assigned to the event variable; otherwise, you can get the event object from the window object. This is, again, a technique to make the functionality compatible with IE 6.x and 7, which doesn't pass the event object to the event handler function automatically.

With the Dojo event system, the library handles this for you, so you can assume you'll always have the event object as a parameter in the event handler. Example 4-2 shows a modified version of Example 4-1, using Dojo and the event object.

Example 4-2. Event handling à la Dojo

```
<!DOCTYPE html PUBLIC "-//W3C//DTD XHTML 1.0 Strict//EN"
    "http://www.w3.org/TR/xhtml1/DTD/xhtml1-strict.dtd">
<html xmlns="http://www.w3.org/1999/xhtml" lang="en" xml:lang="en">
<head>
<meta http-equiv="Content-Type" content="text/html; charset=utf-8" />
<title>Event Listening</title>
<style type="text/css">
#inner
{
    background-color: #00f;
    height: 100px;
```

Example 4-2. Event handling à la Dojo (continued)

```
    width: 400px;
}
#outer
{
    background-color: #ff0;
    padding: 10px;
    width: 400px;
}
</style>

<script type="text/javascript" src="dojo/dojo.js">
</script>

<script type="text/javascript">
//<![CDATA[

dojo.require("dojo.event.*");

dojo.event.connect(window,"onload",
                    function setUp( ) {
    dojo.event.connect(document.getElementById('inner'),"onclick",clickHandler);
    dojo.event.connect(document.getElementById('outer'),"onclick",clickHandler);
    });

function clickHandler(evnt) {
    alert(evnt.currentTarget.id);
}
//]]>
</script>

</head>
<body>
<div id="outer">
<div id="inner">
</div>
</div>
</body>
</html>
```

In this example, the identifier of the element is accessed through the event object rather than through the object context, represented by this. The advantage to this approach is that the use of the event object is cross-browser compatible. If you use this.id with a browser like IE 7, you'll get a value of undefined rather than the identifier for the object that was impacted by the event.

If you want to stop listening to an event, use dojo.event.disconnect, using the same parameters you used with connect.

Of course, including Dojo just to do simple event management is equivalent to using a machete to open a package of bologna: it's serious overkill. However, the example does demonstrate that when using an external Ajax library, you're going to want to look to see whether it has event handling, and if so, use it rather than your own library. The main reason is to ensure compatible event handling between the external library and your application code as much as possible.

There's another reason I picked Dojo to demonstrate using packaged event management. Dojo goes beyond just handling cross-browser differences with events—it also provides a way of extending the event system so that you can attach invocation event handlers to the functions themselves. These invocation event handler functions are called when their associated functions are processed.

The reason for such an extension is that Dojo, unlike many other Ajax libraries, has an infrastructure that is meant to be built upon via plug-ins, all of which coexist with the library. The other libraries are architectures on which applications are built. If a new Dojo plug-in has a function that has to be called whenever another Dojo function is called, it *subscribes* to that function.

The web page in Example 4-3 consists of the same two div elements in Examples 4-1 and 4-2. In Example 4-3, though, when the inner block gets a click event, the inner block's color is changed. When this happens, we also want to change the color of the outer block. In the application code, a new object is created with two methods, change1 and change2, which change the inner and outer blocks, respectively. The application uses the Dojo event system to register the first object method, change1, as an "event publisher," assigning it the topic name of "/example". The code then uses the dojo.event.topic.subscribe method to add a subscriber to this new topic publisher, so that when the first method, change1 fires, the second object method, change2, also fires.

Example 4-3. Exploring publisher/subscribe in the Dojo Event System

```
<!DOCTYPE html PUBLIC "-//W3C//DTD XHTML 1.0 Strict//EN"
    "http://www.w3.org/TR/xhtml1/DTD/xhtml1-strict.dtd">
<html xmlns="http://www.w3.org/1999/xhtml" lang="en" xml:lang="en">
<html>
<meta http-equiv="Content-Type" content="text/html; charset=utf-8" />
<title>Event Listening</title>
<style type="text/css">
#inner
{
    background-color: #00f;
    height: 100px;
    width: 400px;
}
#outer
{
    background-color: #ff0;
    padding: 10px;
    width: 400px;
}
</style>
```

```
<script type="text/javascript" src="dojo/dojo.js">
</script>

<script type="text/javascript">
//<![CDATA[

dojo.require("dojo.event.*");

var connObj = {
    change1 : function ( ) {
            document.getElementById('inner').style.backgroundColor="#ff0000";
        },
    change2 : function ( ) {
            document.getElementById('outer').style.backgroundColor="#ff00ff";
        }};

dojo.event.topic.registerPublisher("/example", connObj, "change1");

dojo.event.topic.subscribe("/example", connObj, "change2");

dojo.event.connect(window,"onload", function( ) {
    dojo.event.connect(document.getElementById('inner'),"onclick",connObj.change1);
    });

//]]>
</script>

</head>
<body>
<div id="outer">
<div id="inner">
</div>
</div>
</body>
</html>
```

When accessing the example page and clicking on the inner block, its color is changed from blue to red, as you would expect because of the event handler function assigned directly to the click event for the block. However, the outer block's color also changes from yellow to magenta because of the topic publisher/subscriber functionality added through the Dojo event system. It's a simple demonstration of a very powerful functionality—one that is created specifically for extending Dojo with custom widgets.

It's an intriguing infrastructure, and one to be aware of if using Dojo. Additionally, keep it in mind for your own libraries if you need this type of pluggable infrastructure.

Now, on with the Ajax interactive effects.

Just-In-Time Information

Pages are interactive when they're responsive to actions from the web page reader. The interaction could be clicking a button or link, dragging a div element, or filling in a form. Most of the time, the page context provides enough information for readers to figure out what to do, but not always. For example, web page form fields with labels such as "last name" may be easy to figure out, but others, such as "Enter fiduciary amount" may not.

Printing out detailed information within the page, however, can be messy, and forcing folks to go to another page is a pain. Opening new windows may help, but they separate the action from the object. That's where just-in-time (JIT) help comes in.

In JIT help, typically a box is displayed with text describing the item or providing additional instructions. The box could open at the point of focus or at a standard place on the page regardless of the element getting focus. The help is displayed based on actions, such as hovering the mouse over a form field.

Form Help

Form element labels can be self-explanatory, such as "first name" or "age," but every once in a while you come across one like "Post Slug" (from Wordpress, a blogging application) that leaves people scratching their heads as they check through the help documentation. Rather than sending people to a separate page, a better approach would be to add information into the page itself. Unfortunately, though, there may not be enough room. The Wordpress edit page is a good example of too many form elements and too little space.

The simplest help for forms is to capture the focus events for each form element and then display the appropriate description text block. Rather than guessing which elements might need help, assume they all do, and provide for each one. The information can be preloaded into the page or pulled up from a web service using an Ajax call.

Example 4-4 shows a simple application of JIT form help. Since the application is so small, I've combined the script, stylesheet, and web page elements into one file. The code for the page attaches an onfocus event handler for each form element, including the submit button. When the form element receives the focus event. Its name is sent as part of a web service query using XMLHttpRequest. The web service returns the element's definition, which is then displayed in a separate page element, a div element identified as "help" using the innerHTML property.

Example 4-4. JIT onfocus form help

```
<!DOCTYPE html PUBLIC "-//W3C//DTD XHTML 1.0 Strict//EN"
    "http://www.w3.org/TR/xhtml1/DTD/xhtml1-strict.dtd">
<html xmlns="http://www.w3.org/1999/xhtml" xml:lang="en" lang="en">
<head>
```

Example 4-4. JIT onfocus form help (continued)

```
<meta http-equiv="Content-Type" content="text/html; charset=utf-8" />
<title>Form Field Help</title>
<style type="text/css">
#help
{
    left: 300px;
    padding: 10px;
    position: absolute;
    top: 20px;
}
form
{
    margin: 20px;
}
input
{
    margin: 10px;
}
</style>
<script type="text/javascript" src="addingajax.js">
</script>
<script type="text/javascript">
//<![CDATA[

var xmlhttp;

aaManageEvent(window, 'load', function( ) {
   for (var i = 0; i < document.forms[0].elements.length; i++) {
      aaManageEvent(document.forms[0].elements[i],"focus",showHelp);
   }
});

function showHelp(evnt) {
  evnt = (evnt) ? evnt : window.event;
  if (!xmlhttp)  xmlhttp = getXmlHttpRequest( );
  if (!xmlhttp) return;
   var objId = (evnt.currentTarget) ? evnt.currentTarget.id : evnt.srcElement.id;
  var qry = "item=" + objId;
  var url = 'help.php?' + qry;
  xmlhttp.open('GET', url, true);
  xmlhttp.onreadystatechange = printHelp;
  xmlhttp.send(null);
}

function printHelp( ) {
   if(xmlhttp.readyState == 4 && xmlhttp.status == 200) {
      document.getElementById('help').innerHTML=xmlhttp.responseText;
   }
}

//]]>
</script>
```

Example 4-4. JIT onfocus form help (continued)

```
</head>
<body>
<form action="ch04-04.htm" method="post">
<fieldset>
<legend>Personal info</legend>
<label for="firstname">First Name:</label><br />
<input id="firstname" name="firstname" type="text" /><br />

<label for="lastname">Last Name:</label><br />
<input id="lastname" name="lastname" type="text" /><br />

<input type="submit" value="Save" />
</fieldset>
</form>
<div id="help">
</div>
</body>
</html>
```

This is a very simple approach to dynamically providing help. With just the two fields, neither of which really need additional explanation, you wouldn't normally use this approach, but the simplicity does provide a clear demonstration. The server component of the Ajax application is equally as simple:

```
<?php
//If no search string is passed, then we can't search
$item = $_REQUEST['item'];
if(empty($item)) {
    echo "";
} else {
    //Remove whitespace from beginning & end of passed search.
    $search = trim($item);
    switch($item) {
      case "firstname" :
          $result = "<p>Enter your first name</p>";
          break;
      case "lastname" :
          $result = "<p>Enter your last name</p>";
          break;
      default :
          $result = "";
          break;
      }

      echo $result;
}
?>
```

However, if you have several forms spread out over several pages, providing the same help system to all of the pages allows you to make modifications in the help text in one place instead of in each of several different pages. This approach then becomes

---

much more viable. Additionally, if the application caches the lookup information when it's retrieved the first time, the connections to the server are decreased:

```
function printHelp( ) {
    if(xmlhttp.readyState == 4 && xmlhttp.status == 200) {
        document.getElementById('help').innerHTML=xmlhttp.responseText;
        helpObj[helpItem] = xmlhttp.responseText;
    }
}
```

With the caching modification, the application tests for the existence of the help item in the associative array cache.

Another improvement is to make the help more "on-demand," rather than putting it up only when the page reader enters a field. One way to do this is to capture the click event for the labels rather than the focus event for the fields, and display help when the labels are clicked:

```
function setUp( ) {
    var items = document.getElementsByTagName('label');
    for (var i = 0; i < items.length; i++) {
        aaManageEvent(items[i],"click",showHelp);
    }
}
```

For this approach to work, the labels are given identifiers, rather than the form fields:

```
<form action="ch04-05.htm" method="post">
<label id="elem1">First Name:</label><br />
<input type="text" /><br />
<label id="elem2">Last Name:</label><br />
<input type="text" /><br />
<input type="submit" Value="Save" />
</form>
```

A problem with using the labels is there's no way to know that they're clickable. One way around this is to add a mouseover effect to the label, setting the mouse pointer to a question mark. Do this by adding a CSS stylesheet setting to change the mouse pointer to the help cursor (typically a question mark) whenever it is placed over a label:

```
label { cursor: help; }
```

Of course, you still have to know to move your mouse over the label to get the cursor. Plus, you have to be using a mouse to realize that the label has a different cursor, and you must have script enabled.

A more unobtrusive and intuitive approach would be to surround the labels with a hypertext link, set the target attribute to a new window name, and display the help based on the mouseover event rather than the click. If scripting is enabled, the mouseover displays the help. If scripting is not enabled, the hypertext link opens a separate window with the help information. This change makes the JIT help "keyboard-enabled" and more accessible for screen readers.

There are two problems with the link workaround. One is that XHTML 1.0 Strict does not support the target attribute. The other is that you need to warn folks using a screen reader or other assisting device that they will open a new window if they click the link.

You could avoid both of these problems by opening the help within the same page, but that is *not* a good solution for providing help in a form, especially a form that has been partially filled in. A popular approach to this problem is to attach a rel="external" key/value attribute pair to the links to open in new windows and use JavaScript to create a new window when the link is clicked. However, one of the primary reasons for having the help open in a new window is because scripting is disabled.

There are also people who will want to click the link anyway because they're using screen readers that may not pick up the help that's generated dynamically. Again, we don't want to overwrite their half-filled form. For them, we could either decide to blow off the XHTML 1.0 Strict validation (tempting), or create the JavaScript to intercept the click and open the new window.

I can't tell you which is the best option, as only you can determine what's important for your applications and your clients. For now, I've extended the *addingajax.js* file to add the link interception routine based on the rel="external" attribute, which at least gives us this option. Example 4-5 shows the new library entries, including the window onload event handler to process the links.

Example 4-5. New library entries to provide an XHTML variation of the anchor target attribute

```
function externalLinks( ) {
 var anchors = document.getElementsByTagName("a");
 for (var i=0; i<anchors.length; i++) {
   var anchor = anchors[i];
   if (anchor.getAttribute("href") &&
       anchor.getAttribute("rel") == "external")
     anchor.target = "_blank";
 }
}

aaManageEvent(window,'load',externalLinks);
```

 A third option to the XHTML Strict and target problem is to extend the XHTML by creating a custom DTD. For discussion of this, see Wayne Burkett's weblog post, "Extending XHTML: Target and Strict," at *http://dionidium.com/2004/05/xhtml-tests*.

Though the page's static contents now validate, this approach does add invalid markup dynamically. A second way to code this function, one that bypasses the validation issue completely, is to use the following with each anchor:

```
aaManageEvent(anchor,'click',function() {
    window.open(this.href);
    aaCancelEvent(event);
});
```

This code opens a new window without adding invalid markup statically or dynamically. This approach does require accessing the event object in order to process the cancel event method call.

While we're improving the application, we can add some frills to our help to make it seem a little more polished. We will change the background color and add a border. The stylesheet is moved into its own file, *jit.css*:

```css
#help
{
    background-color: #FFFF8F;
    border: 1px solid #82887e;
    left: 300px;
    padding: 10px;
    position: absolute;
    top: 20px;
    visibility: hidden;
}
form
{
    margin: 20px;
        width: 500px;
}
input
{
    margin: 10px;
}
label
{
    cursor: help;
}
a
{
    text-decoration: none;
}
```

The JavaScript is also pulled into a separate file, *jit.js*. The new script, shown in Example 4-6, adds caching and event management on the labels. The JavaScript to show the help is split out into a separate function and called from both the XMLHttpRequest processing function, as well as the showHelp function—if the element's help is cached.

Example 4-6. The Just-In-Time form help using Ajax

```javascript
var xmlhttp;
var helpItem;
var helpObj = new Object();
```

Example 4-6. The Just-In-Time form help using Ajax (continued)

```
aaManageEvent(window,"load", function( ) {
    var items = document.getElementsByTagName('label');
    for (var i = 0; i < items.length; i++) {
        aaManageEvent(items[i],"mouseover",showHelp);
        aaManageEvent(items[i],"mouseout",hideHelp);
    }
});

// retrieve the help info
function showHelp(evnt) {
    evnt = (evnt) ? evnt : window.event;
    // get XMLHttpRequest object if not set
    if (!xmlhttp) xmlhttp = aaGetXmlHttpRequest( );
    if (!xmlhttp) return;

    helpItem = (evnt.currentTarget) ? evnt.currentTarget.id : evnt.srcElement.id;
    var qry = "item=" + helpItem;

    // if cached item, print existing and return
    if (helpObj[helpItem]) {
        printHelp( );
        return;
    }

    // invoke help system
    var url = 'help.php?' + qry;
    xmlhttp.open('GET', url, true);
    xmlhttp.onreadystatechange = getHelp;
    xmlhttp.send(null);
}

// hide help field
function hideHelp( ) {
    document.getElementById('help').style.visibility="hidden";
}

// display help field with help
function getHelp( ) {
    if(xmlhttp.readyState == 4 && xmlhttp.status == 200) {
        helpObj[helpItem] = xmlhttp.responseText;
        printHelp( );
    }
}
function printHelp( ) {
    var help = document.getElementById('help');
    help.innerHTML = helpObj[helpItem];
    help.style.visibility="visible";
}
```

In the web page, the CSS and JavaScript files are linked in, and the form labels are wrapped in hypertext links with the individual help item attached to the URL for each, as shown in Example 4-7. The links also have an explicit title with clear information that clicking the links will open a second window, in addition to the rel="external" attribute/value.

Example 4-7. JIT help page—valid, accessible, and active

```
<!DOCTYPE html PUBLIC "-//W3C//DTD XHTML 1.0 Strict//EN"
    "http://www.w3.org/TR/xhtml1/DTD/xhtml1-strict.dtd">
<html xmlns="http://www.w3.org/1999/xhtml" lang="en" xml:lang="en">
<head>
<meta http-equiv="Content-Type" content="text/html; charset=utf-8" />
<title>Form Field Help</title>
<link rel="stylesheet" href="jit.css" type="text/css" media="screen" />
<script type="text/javascript" src="addingajax.js">
</script>
<script type="text/javascript" src="jit.js">
</script>
</head>
<body>

<form action="ch04-05.htm" method="post">
<fieldset>
<legend>Personal info
<a href="help.php?item=firstname" " title="opens help window for firstname field"
rel="external">
<label id="firstname" for="first">First Name:</label></a><br />
<input type="text" id="first" name="first" /><br />

<a href="help.php?item=lastname" accesskey="l" title="opens help window for lastname
field" rel="external">
<label id="lastname" for="last">Last Name:</label></a><br />
<input type="text" id="last" name="last" /><br />

<input type="submit" value="Save" />
</fieldset>
</form>

<div id="help">
</div>
</body>
</html>
```

Figure 4-1 shows the page with one of the help items displayed.

Lots of code for a simple effect, but the pieces are in place to make this into a library of JavaScript functions to provide JIT help for more than forms. JIT help is almost equivalent to another effect known as the *tooltip*. All that remains now is expanding the functionality to other objects and positioning the displayed material where the event occurs.

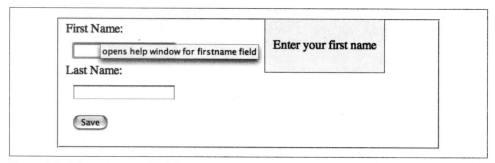

Figure 4-1. A form that uses JIT help

Tooltips

As I stated in the beginning of this chapter, if you've been out to the Netflix or Block-buster Online sites, you've seen how moving the mouse over a movie-related link or image pops up information about the movie, as well as a link to add the movie to the queue. This is probably one of the best uses of tooltips I've seen. It quickly provides more detailed information about an object rather than forcing users to go to another page. This is especially advantageous if the site user is browsing through many items. Tooltips can be used for anything: a shop, getting more detailed information about a row of data returned from a database, camera information associated with a photo, and so on—anytime you want to provide information about an object within a browsing context.

The only modifications required to convert the JIT application in the prevous section into a tooltip is to provide a bubble-like background for the text and position it so that it's close to where the mouseover event occurs. Sounds simple, but it begins to add to the amount of code.

The following web page fragment is very similar to that shown in Example 4-7, with the addition of two more page elements: an h1 header and a standalone link. These are added to demonstrate that any page element can get a tooltip, not just form elements:

```
<body>

<h1 id="header">Testing Tooltips</h1>

<form action="ch04-08.xhtml" method="post">
<fieldset>
<legend>Personal info</legend>
<a href="help.php?item=firstname" accesskey="f" title="opens help window for
firstname field" rel="external">
<label id="firstname" for="first">First Name:</label></a><br />
<input type="text" id="first" name="first" /><br />

<a href="help.php?item=lastname" accesskey="l" title="opens help window for lastname
field" rel="external">
<label id="lastname" for="last">Last Name:</label></a><br />
```

```
<input type="text" id="last" name="last" /><br />

<input type="submit" value="Save" />
</fieldset>
</form>
<p><a href="" id="link">Tooltip for a hypertext link</a></p>
<div id="help">
</div>
</body>
```

In the stylesheet, the tooltip help block is set to a bubble background:

```
#help
{
    background-image: url(back.png);
    background-repeat: no-repeat;
    height: 200px;
    padding: 10px 0 0 10px;
    position: absolute;
    visibility: hidden;
    width: 150px;
}
```

The most significant change to the new application is in the JavaScript. For each element that has a tooltip, the mouseover event is captured in order to display the tip. The mouseout event is captured to then hide it. When the mouseover event fires, the mouse cursor position is captured so that the help element can be moved to approximately the same page location. Its position is also modified relevant to the bubble size, to put the pointed part of the "bubble" as close to the cursor position as possible. The only variation is with the top element. Since it's at the top of the page, the vertical position of the tooltip is adjusted so that the tip's top won't go beyond the page top.

Example 4-8 shows the new JavaScript file.

Example 4-8. Providing tooltips for form and other elements

```
var xmlhttp;              // global XMLHttpRequest obj
var helpItem;             // current help item
var helpObj = new Object(); // cached help items
var posX; var posY;

// setup tooltip event
function addTooltip(ttObj) {
   aaManageEvent(ttObj,"mouseover",showHelp);
   aaManageEvent(ttObj,"mouseout",hideHelp);
}

// attach tooltip events to objects
aaManageEvent(window,"load",function() {
   var items = document.getElementsByTagName('label');
   for (var i = 0; i < items.length; i++) {
      addTooltip(items[i]);
   }
```

Example 4-8. Providing tooltips for form and other elements (continued)

```
    addTooltip(document.getElementById('title'));
    addTooltip(document.getElementById('link'));
});
// get help from the server
function showHelp(evnt) {
  evnt = (evnt) ? evnt : window.event;

  // get position
  posX = evnt.clientX;
  posY = evnt.clientY;

  // get XMLHttpRequest object if not set
  if (!xmlhttp) xmlhttp = aaGetXmlHttpRequest();
  if (!xmlhttp) return;

  helpItem = (evnt.currentTarget) ? evnt.currentTarget.id : evnt.srcElement.id;
  var qry = "item=" + helpItem;

  // if cached item, print existing and return
  if (helpObj[helpItem]) {
      printHelp();
      return;
  }

  // invoke help system
  var url = 'help.php?' + qry;
  xmlhttp.open('GET', url, true);
  xmlhttp.onreadystatechange = getHelp;
  xmlhttp.send(null);
}


// hide help bubble
function hideHelp() {
//I would suggest changing the class name instead of directly manipulating style
properties//
    document.getElementById('help').style.visibility="hidden";
}
// display help
function getHelp() {
    if(xmlhttp.readyState == 4 && xmlhttp.status == 200) {
      helpObj[helpItem] = xmlhttp.responseText;
      printHelp();
    }
}

//position tooltip
function printHelp() {
  var help = document.getElementById('help');
  help.innerHTML = helpObj[helpItem];
  y = posY - 130;
  if (y < 0) y = 10;
```

Example 4-8. Providing tooltips for form and other elements (continued)

```
    help.style.top = y + "px";
    help.style.left = (posX + 10) + "px";
    help.style.visibility="visible";
}
```

View the tooltips in action in Figure 4-2.

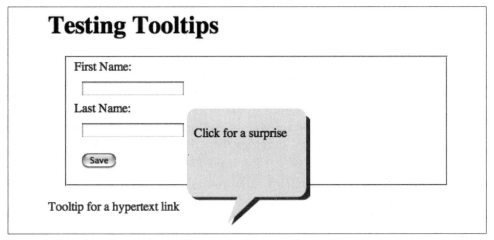

Figure 4-2. Tooltips in action, providing users with extra information

Again, it seems a lot of code to create a simple effect, but it's also code that can be easily repackaged for use in a separate library. All you have to do is provide a way to create the tooltip object, passing in the location and content, and the tooltip object takes care of the rest. You could package more of the functionality, passing in just an element, and the tooltip object can take care of the event handling, though you'll most likely need to provide the content unless you embed the contents as elements in the page rather than pulling it in from a web service.

 An even simpler approach is to use an existing tooltip library. One such library is *Tooltip.js*, which is based on Prototype and script. aculo.us. You can download the most recent version of the library at *http://tooltip.crtx.org*.

For effects such as those found on Netflix and Blockbuster, you'll need to provide an image that has a transparent background. The only way to do this is to use a transparent GIF or a PNG image, though the latter doesn't work that well with IE (not even with IE 7, which adds some odd color effects). You'll have to layer your effect, providing a header and footer image, and a separate body image that can repeat along the vertical axis so that it can be resized based on the length of the contents.

One other important item to remember when providing this type of functionality is that tooltips don't work if scripting is disabled. However, one workaround is to provide hypertext links around the element to open a separate page and use anchors for individual help items.

In-Page Previews

Sometimes the simplest technology can have the biggest impact. Of all the changes I've ever made at any of my sites, the one that people liked the best was also one of the simplest to implement: live preview.

Live preview echoes what a user writes as she types. It allows the user to see how the writing looks in the context in which it will be published, rather than within little windows in small forms. It does so before she submits the new or modified material. It's also quite easy to implement a nonscript and/or accessible alternative: you provide a preview page where a user can review the writing before it's permanently submitted. You can even provide both: live preview and a Preview button.

Where is live preview most useful? Anytime you ask for commentary from the web page reader. This includes email messages to be sent to customer service, comments on weblogs, feedback in product reviews—anyplace a user is writing more than a few words.

Live preview consists of listening for any activity in a form field, capturing the keys pressed, and echoing them to another page element. How you echo depends on how active you want the preview to be.

You can echo the letters as they're typed for a true "live" experience. You can also provide a Preview button, but rather than opening up a new page, it will display the comment directly in the page. This approach doesn't capture the keypress, and the data from the comment field is accessed only when the Preview button is activated.

Both approaches have good points and bad, which I'll get into as we look at each individual approach.

Live Echo Preview

A live, echoed preview is relatively simple to set up. You begin by capturing the keyup event in either a form textarea or input element, and take all of the text and reflect it in an associated div element through the innerHTML property.

In the code, you do need to adjust the text, replacing the hard carriage returns with a break element, br. This keeps the text more or less in sync with the input.

Example 4-9 includes a complete application that uses live preview. Since the example is so small, the stylesheet and script are both included within the web page. The previewed text isn't modified other than transforming the carriage break into a br. If you want to modify the text preview in other ways, such as stripping HTML tags to reflect what the comment will look like published, you'll need to adjust the script accordingly. Remember, though, to keep the preview simple—the function to live preview the input is called whenever a keyup event happens in the form element.

Example 4-9. Simple live preview

```
<!DOCTYPE html PUBLIC "-//W3C//DTD XHTML 1.0 Strict//EN"
    "http://www.w3.org/TR/xhtml1/DTD/xhtml1-strict.dtd">
<html xmlns="http://www.w3.org/1999/xhtml" lang="en" xml:lang="en">
<head>
<meta http-equiv="Content-Type" content="text/html; charset=utf-8" />
<title>Live Preview</title>
<style type="text/css">
#preview
{
    background-color: #ccc;
    margin: 20px;
    padding: 10px;
    width: 500px;
}
input
{
    margin-right: 10px;
}
</style>
<script type="text/javascript" src="addingajax.js">
</script>
<script type="text/javascript">
//<![CDATA[

manageEvent(window,"load",function() {
            aaManageEvent(document.getElementById('comment'),"keyup",echoPreview)});

// echo the keypresses
function echoPreview(evnt) {
    var commentText = document.getElementById("comment").value;
    modText = commentText.split(/\n/).join("<br />");
    var previewElem = document.getElementById("preview");
    previewElem.innerHTML = modText;
}
//]]>
</script>
</head>
<body>
<form action="preview.htm" method="post">
<div>
<textarea id="comment" cols=50 rows=10></textarea><br />
<input type="button" value="Preview" />
<input type="submit" value="Save" />
</div>
</form>
```

Example 4-9. Simple live preview (continued)

```
<div id="preview">
</div>
</body>
</html>
```

Whatever is typed into the `textarea` is reflected in the **preview** element.

The form also has Preview and Save buttons, both of which go to the *preview.php* page. From there, a user can save the comment or click the Back button to return to the form and continue editing. Neither requires script. Later on in this chapter, we'll see how we can submit the form and display the new comment, all without leaving the page.

There's one major problem with live preview, and that's what happens when the page is served with an XHTML MIME type. The way that browsers implement innerHTML differs among applications, though most do support some version of innerHTML. However, what happens during live preview if you begin to add an XHTML tag differs dramatically between browsers. In Firefox 2.x and up, the incomplete tag throws dozens of errors until it's completed, all of them saying the text is not well-formed XML. In Opera, however, the browser treats the incomplete tag as escaped content until the tag is closed, in which case, it then treats it as XHTML.

> A workaround is to escape HTML characters, <, >, and &, replacing the modText generation with the following:
>
> ```
> modText = commentText.replace(/&/g, '&amp;').replace(/>/g,
>     '&gt;').replace(/</g, '&lt;').split(/\n/).join("<br/>");
> ```
>
> This disables the links and other HTML. In nontrusted situations, you may want to consider completely stripping out all HTML.

The differences in behavior between browsers is significant enough that you'll probably want to use live preview only with pages served as HTML, at least until the new HTML 5.0 standard comes out, which should clarify how a document fragment is managed. In the meantime, if you want XHTML and an in-page preview, I'd suggest you use the "Ajax" version of comment preview.

> There are many implementations of live preview online, but I first saw it via a Wordpress plug-in created by Chris Davis at *http://www. chrisjdavis.org*.

Ajax Preview

The Ajax preview version of live preview doesn't echo the preview text as it occurs; rather, it takes all of the text when a Preview button is clicked, but instead of bringing up a separate preview page, the text is echoed in the preview area.

The advantage to this method is that the application isn't as CPU-intensive, since it doesn't have to catch all of the keyup events. It's also much friendlier from an XHTML perspective since the input can be formatted for proper XHTML handling before it's displayed. Live preview is just that: live. No real formatting can be done other than to strip out markup.

The page demonstrating Ajax preview is identical to that shown in Example 4-9 except for a few elements in the script and the addition of an identifier on the Preview button. Example 4-10 shows the page with these modifications highlighted.

Example 4-10. Using Ajax preview on comments

```
<!DOCTYPE html PUBLIC "-//W3C//DTD XHTML 1.0 Strict//EN"
    "http://www.w3.org/TR/xhtml1/DTD/xhtml1-strict.dtd">
<html xmlns="http://www.w3.org/1999/xhtml" lang="en" xml:lang="en">
<head>
<meta http-equiv="Content-Type" content="text/html; charset=utf-8" />
<title>Ajax Preview</title>
<style type="text/css">
#preview
{
        background-color: #ffc;
        margin: 20px;
        padding: 10px;
        width: 500px;
}
input
{
        margin-right: 5px;
}
form
{
        margin: 10px;
        width: 550px;
}
</style>
<script type="text/javascript" src="addingajax.js">
</script>
<script type="text/javascript">
//<![CDATA[

aaManageEvent(window,"load",function() {
    aaManageEvent(document.getElementById('previewbutton'),'click',showPreview)});

// echo keypress
function showPreview(evnt) {

    // cancel button's default click behavior
    evnt = evnt ? evnt : window.event;
    aaCancelEvent(evnt);

    // add preview
```

Example 4-10. Using Ajax preview on comments (continued)

```
    var commentText = document.getElementById("comment").value;
    modText = commentText.split(/\n/).join("<br />");
    var previewElem = document.getElementById("preview");
    previewElem.innerHTML = modText;
}
//]]>
</script>
</head>
<body>
<form action="preview.php" method="post">
<fieldset>
<legend>Comment</legend>
<label for="comment">Comment:</label><br />
<textarea id="comment" name="comment" cols="50" rows="10"></textarea><br />
<input type="submit" name="button" value="Preview" id="previewbutton" />
<input type="submit" name="button" value="Save" /> // Should these buttons not have
different values for name? //
</fieldset>
</form>
<div id="preview">
</div>
</body>
</html>
```

The event that triggers the preview now is a click of the Preview button. To prevent the default behavior, submitting the form, from occurring, the event is terminated within the event handler function.

With Ajax preview, embedding XHTML elements in the comment won't trigger an error while the text is in an incomplete state like it does with Firefox 2.x (at least, at the time of this writing).

However, if you put in "bad" XHTML and you're using a browser that checks the content with innerHTML, you will get JavaScript errors when you do assign the text to the innerHTML element. Throwing an error isn't a bad thing, but throwing a Java-Script error is.

A better approach would be to place the code setting the innerHTML element within a try...catch block and provide an error message meant for the web page reader, not the developer:

```
    modText = commentText.split(/\n/).join("<br />");
    var previewElem = document.getElementById("preview");
    try {
        previewElem.innerHTML = modText;
    } catch(err) {
        previewElem.innerHTML = "<p>An error occurred, please check your comment for
(X)HTML errors.</p>";
    }
```

Opera will just correct (or tolerate) the bad markup, as will Safari, IE, and Omni-Web, but Firefox and WebKit both trigger the error handling. Unfortunately, there's no way to pinpoint the error—not unless we want to attempt to create an XML document and then see what happens—a rather drastic approach, and one that goes way beyond the usefulness of this effect. A better technique is to avoid all errors by stripping out the markup and providing buttons to allow formatting of hypertext links and such.

 Again, if you don't want the risk of XHTML in the comments, either escape the HTML characters or strip tags out altogether.

Another nice effect you can use with commentary and the like, especially if all comments are listed in the page, is using Ajax to update the data store and then "refreshing" the list without having to refresh the page. Throw in a color fade, and you've got a nice bit of polish without too much code.

Color Fades for Success or Failure

One of the more popular Ajax effects is the color flash or *fade* (to differentiate the effect from the Adobe functionality) that signals some form of successful (or not) update. Usually these are associated with data updates, but they can be used for any activity where you want to signal to the application user to pay attention that something is happening.

A fade changes the background color of an element or group of elements, moving from a darker shade to a lighter, and typically back again. The fade can consist of variations of one color, such as flashing red to signal a deletion, or a yellow fade to create a highlight. Multiple colors can also be used, for instance, a blue to yellow fade to signal a positive outcome.

Regardless of the exact effect used, one thing all color fades require is the use of timers to create the necessary animation. Before getting into the code necessary to implement a fade, we'll do a quick refresher on timers and animation.

 If you're comfortable with your understanding of timers and animations, feel free to skip the next section.

Timers and Animations

JavaScript includes a couple of different ways of controlling animations. One is to use the `setTimeout` method, which is invoked once and has to be reset if multiple timer events are needed. The other is `setInterval`, which refires in consecutive intervals until canceled. However, setTimeout is used when different parameters are being passed to the timer function with each iteration, and as such, is the one most popularly used with animations such as a color fade.

The setTimetout method takes two parameters: a function or expression as the first, and the number of milliseconds before the timer function/expression is invoked for the second. The last parameter is relatively simple, but the first has undergone a significant metamorphosis through the generations of JavaScript, from simple uses in early DHTML applications to the more esoteric uses in Ajax.

Example 4-11 demonstrates one way that setTimeout was used in earlier iterations of JavaScript applications. The timer function does a countdown starting at 10 and ending when the count is set to zero. An element, item, is accessed with each iteration, and its innerHTML property is used to rewrite the page section. In the setTimeout call, the timer function and the count argument are given in the first parameter, the time interval, before next firing in the second. Straight, simple, and uncomplicated.

Example 4-11. Straight, simple, and uncomplicated timer function

```
<!DOCTYPE html PUBLIC "-//W3C//DTD XHTML 1.0 Strict//EN"
    "http://www.w3.org/TR/xhtml1/DTD/xhtml1-strict.dtd">
<html xmlns="http://www.w3.org/1999/xhtml" lang="en" xml:lang="en">
<head>
<meta http-equiv="Content-Type" content="text/html; charset=utf-8" />
<title>Old Timers</title>

<style type="text/css">
#item
{
        font-size: 72px;
        margin: 70px auto;
        width: 100px;
}
</style>
<script type="text/javascript" src="addingajax.js">
</script>
<script type="text/javascript">
//<![CDATA[

aaManageEvent(window,"load",function( ) {
    setTimeout('runTimer(10)',100);
});

function runTimer(count) {
    if (count == 0) return;
    document.getElementById('item').innerHTML=count;
    count--;
    setTimeout('runTimer(' + count + ')',1000);
}
```

Example 4-11. Straight, simple, and uncomplicated timer function (continued)

```
//]]>
</script>
</head>
<body>
<div id="item">
10
</div>
</body>
</html>
```

The approach is simple, but an issue with it is that using object methods rather than discrete functions means the timer doesn't have a way of passing the object's context along with the method, as the parameter to setTimeout.

With the increased interest in Ajax, and especially through the development of libraries such as Prototype, the look of setTimeout has changed significantly—enough to make it difficult to understand exactly what's happening. The next section looks at Prototype's use of setTimeout, and then implements the same functionality separate from the library to demonstrate the Ajaxian influence on timers and timer event handlers.

Ajaxian Timers

Prototype implements a method called bind, which is attached to the Function object through the JavaScript prototype property. A quick reminder: the prototype property is a way of attaching a new method or property to the basic implementation of an object in such a way that all instances of that object "inherit" the extension equally. In the case of Prototype's bind, this method returns a function that in turn calls the Function object's apply method, passing in a string of the outer function's arguments. The original code looks like the following:

```
Function.prototype.bind = function( ) {
  var __method = this, args = $A(arguments), object = args.shift( );
  return function( ) {
    return __method.apply(object, args.concat($A(arguments)));
  }
}
```

The JavaScript apply method lets us apply one object's method within the context of another object's method. It takes the external object's context, represented as an object (passed as the first parameter in the argument list), and passes it as the first parameter. The second parameter is an argument list, derived using Prototype's $A method, which returns an array of iterative objects (necessary when modifying the parameters of built-in objects, as Prototype does with objects like Function and Array).

How bind works with setTimeout is that the object's state is maintained with each call to setTimeout, including the value of the object's properties. Since the state is maintained, Ajax developers don't have to worry about passing function parameters with the timer or using a global variable.

This functionality will be necessary for other applications later in the book, so it is worthwhile to convert it into a function and add it to the *addingajax.js* library. It's not the same as Prototype's approach because this book's use differs, but it performs the same functionality of binding the object context to the method invoked as an event handler:

```
function aaBindEventListener(obj, method) {
   return function(event) { method.call(obj, event || window.event)};
}
```

Example 4-12 is a rewrite of Example 4-11, using objects and the new aaBindEventListener. Instead of passing a function directly into the setTimeout function call, the aaBindEventListener method is invoked, which returns a function. Doing this preserves the state of the object, including the countdown amount, which is now a property of the object.

Example 4-12. Taking a closer look at an Ajaxian timer

```
<!DOCTYPE html PUBLIC "-//W3C//DTD XHTML 1.0 Strict//EN"
    "http://www.w3.org/TR/xhtml1/DTD/xhtml1-strict.dtd">
<html xmlns="http://www.w3.org/1999/xhtml" lang="en" xml:lang="en">
<head>
<meta http-equiv="Content-Type" content="text/html; charset=utf-8" />
<title>New Timers</title>

<style type="text/css">
#item { font-size: 72px; margin: 70px auto;
        width: 100px;}
</style>

<script type="text/javascript" src="addingajax.js">
</script>
<script type="text/javascript">
//<![CDATA[

aaManageEvent(window,"load", function( ) {
   var theCounter = new Counter('item',10,0);
   theCounter.countDown( );
});

function Counter(id,start,finish) {
   this.count = this.start = start;
   this.finish = finish;
   this.id = id;
   this.countDown = function( ) {
      if (this.count == this.finish) {
         this.countDown=null;
```

Example 4-12. Taking a closer look at an Ajaxian timer (continued)

```
        return;
      }
    document.getElementById(this.id).innerHTML=this.count--;
    setTimeout(aaBindEventListener(this,this.countDown),1000);
  };

}
//]]>
</script>
</head>
<body>
<div id="item">
10
</div>
</script>
</body>
</html>
```

The reason that the Counter object sets its countDown method to null at the end is based on a memory leak in IE 6.x when using a recursive or function closure technique (function within function). This has been fixed in IE 7, but Ajax developers need to account for IE 6.x until clients are no longer using this browser.

The use of Function.call in managing timers is an interesting technique, if a bit difficult to wrap your mind around at first. It is a better approach than setting global values hither and yon, as it makes it much simpler to maintain values between timer calls.

The next section applies the timer functionality to creating a flashing notice fade.

Creating a Flashing Notice

I'm not sure why yellow became the color of choice for the Ajax fade technique. Come to think of it, I'm not sure why it's called a fade, other than because the color fades once flashed. The yellow fade was first pioneered at the 37signals site (at *http://www.37signals.com/svn/archives/000558.php*), and perhaps the color and the name were kept out of habit.

Yellow is a good choice, though, because yellow/blue color blindness is rare compared to red/green, which impacts up to eight percent of men (exact percentages are not known). Even with total color blindness, though, a fade is noticeable as a flash changing saturation rather than color.

The fade technique uses a timer and loops through a set of color variations, from bright to light shades of the same hue, changing the background color of an element with each iteration. There are now many variations, including ones that fade from one color to another rather than remaining limited to the yellow.

A fade technique is most likely not the most complex Ajax application you'll create, but it isn't trivial to implement unless you use a fixed array of color values. For a more generic fade, for each iteration of color shade, the application accesses the background color, parses out the two-character string for the hexadecimal value for the reds, the blues, and the greens, converts it to a numeric value, adjusts it for the next step, and then converts back to a string. Given beginning and ending values, the application has to calculate the change in each of the color tones between each step, maintain these values separately, and use them to adjust the value.

There is no real method to make a fade unobtrusive or accessible because it is a visual cue. However, a fade is more of a nicety than a necessity—other page effects should denote that some action has happened.

 Unfortunately, these secondary clues also don't tend to show up in screen readers. Chapter 7 covers some ways of working with screen readers for visual and dynamic effects.

We're going to combine examples from earlier in this chapter for our last application. The page has a comment form, with a textarea for a comment and two buttons, one for previewing and one for saving. If scripting is enabled, when the comment form is saved, rather than sending the contents through using the traditional post, an Ajax method is called to save the effects.

For this example, the called program doesn't do anything with the data except echo the comment if scripting is enabled and the Save button is clicked. If scripting is disabled or if the Preview button is clicked, the application prints the comment to the browser:

```
?php

$comment = $_POST['comment'];
$submit = $_POST['submitbutton'];

if (empty($submit)) {
   echo $comment;
} else {
   echo $submit . ':' . $comment;
}
?>
```

This example is simplified, but in your systems, you'll want to escape the content to ensure it's safe before updating your databases. Otherwise, you risk SQL injection errors.

The stylesheet isn't too complicated, but it does add some design and color to spice things up a bit:

```css
#list
{
        border: 1px solid #ccc;
        margin: 20px;
        padding: 10px;
        width: 600px;
}
.comment
{
        margin: 10px 0;
        width: 400px;
}
form, #preview
{
        border: 1px solid #cc0;
        margin: 20px;
        padding: 10px;
        width: 600px;
}
```

It's amazing how small a web page is when you split out the stylesheet and JavaScript:

```html
<!DOCTYPE html PUBLIC "-//W3C//DTD XHTML 1.0 Strict//EN"
    "http://www.w3.org/TR/xhtml1/DTD/xhtml1-strict.dtd">
<html xmlns="http://www.w3.org/1999/xhtml" lang="en" xml:lang="en">
<head>
<meta http-equiv="Content-Type" content="text/html; charset=utf-8" />
<title>Timers, Ajax, and Fade, oh my</title>
<link rel="stylesheet" href="events.css" type="text/css" media="screen" />
<script type="text/javascript" src="addingajax.js">
</script>
<script type="text/javascript" src="comments.js">
</script>
</head>
<body>
<div id="list">
<h1>Current Comments:</h1>
</div>
<form action="addcomment.php" id="commentform" method="post">
<fieldset>
<legend>Comments</legend>
<label for="comment">Comment:</label>
<textarea id="comment" name="comment" cols="65" rows="10"></textarea>
<br /><br />
<input type="submit" id="previewbutton" value="Preview" name="submitbutton" />
<input type="submit" id="save" value="Save" name="submitbutton" />
</fieldset>
</form>
<div id="preview">
</div>
</body>
</html>
```

Example 4-13 displays the content of the JavaScript file, *comments.js*. Since the data is being updated, the Ajax call is a POST rather than a GET. Once the comment is saved, it's reflected back in the comment list with a yellow fade to highlight that it has been added to the list. This example uses the traditional yellow, beginning with a value of #ffff00 and ending with white, #ffffff. In addition, it uses the Adding Ajax bind technique for managing the timer events.

Example 4-13. Combining comment preview, Ajax send method, and yellow flash

```
// global
var commentCount = 0;
var xmlhttp;

function yellowColor(val) {
    var r="ff";
    var g="ff";
    var b=val.toString(16);
    var newval = "#"+r+g+b;
    return newval;
}

aaManageEvent(window,"load", function() {
  aaManageEvent(document.getElementById('save'),"click",saveComment);

});

function saveComment(evnt) {

  // cancel event bubbling
  evnt = evnt ? evnt : window.event;
  aaCancelEvent(evnt);

  // create XHR object
  if (!xmlhttp) xmlhttp = aaGetXmlHttpRequest();
  if (!xmlhttp) return;

  // get comment
  var commentText = document.getElementById("comment").value;
  modText = commentText.split(/\n/).join("<br />");
  var param = "comment=" + modText;
  var url = 'addcomment.php?' + param;
  xmlhttp.open('POST', url, true);

  // send comment
  xmlhttp.onreadystatechange = addComment;
  xmlhttp.setRequestHeader('Content-Type',
    'application/x-www-form-urlencoded');
  xmlhttp.send(null);
  return false;
}
// add comment to existing list, with color flash
function addComment() {
```

```
  if(xmlhttp.readyState == 4 && xmlhttp.status==200) {
      var modText=xmlhttp.responseText;
      console.log(modText);
      var newDiv = document.createElement("div");
      commentCount++;
      newDiv.setAttribute("id","div"+commentCount);
      newDiv.setAttribute("class","comment");
      newDiv.innerHTML = modText;

      // add object to page
      document.getElementById("list").appendChild(newDiv);

      // start flash counter
      var ctrObj = new Counter("div"+commentCount,0,255);
      ctrObj.countDown();
  }
}

function Counter(id,start,finish) {
   this.count = this.start = start;
   this.finish = finish;
   this.id = id;
   this.countDown = function() {
      this.count+=25;
      if (this.count >= this.finish) {
         document.getElementById(this.id).style.background="transparent";
         this.countDown=null;
         return;
      }
      document.getElementById(this.id).style.backgroundColor=yellowColor(this.count);
      setTimeout(aaBindEventListener(this,this.countDown),100);
   }
}
aaManageEvent(window,"load",function() {
      aaManageEvent(document.getElementById('comment'),"keyup",echoPreview)});

function echoPreview(evnt) {
   var commentText = document.getElementById("comment").value;
   modText = commentText.split(/\n/).join("<br />");
   var previewElem = document.getElementById("preview");
   previewElem.innerHTML = modText;
}
```

From the top, when a comment is saved, the form submission is canceled because Ajax is being used to make the update. The comment is accessed and only simple processing is made on it before being POSTed through the XMLHttpRequest object. When the Ajax request is successfully processed, a new div element is created to host the comment, which is then appended to the existing list of comments. As the item is appended, the fade is flashed to highlight the addition.

The result of the final example is shown in Figure 4-3. Unfortunately, I'm not skilled enough with an image capture timer to catch the yellow fade, but the example is among those packaged for this book.

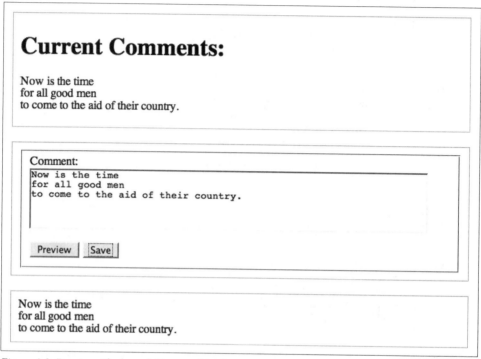

Figure 4-3. Preview, Flash, and Ajax combined

Of course, this is a simplified look at how live comments and live updates can coexist. However, it could be easily integrated into an existing application by calling whatever server-side functionality is used for comments, which should also ensure that the comment text is safe. Then the comment can either be fetched from the function or from the database to be returned for display in the field. To the user, all of this should take a fraction of a second, and the result looks instantaneous. Best of all, no page reload occurs to add distraction. Scripting disabled? No problem, regular comment management is still part of the page.

This application is, in a way, Ajax in a nutshell: a combination of user interaction, Ajax requests, objects, timers, and visual effects. Pat yourself on the back; you're an Ajax programmer now. However, I wouldn't skip the rest of the book.

CHAPTER 5

Space: The Final Frontier

Managing space on a modern web page works with four factors: the space reserved for each element, the elements' positions within the page's horizontal and vertical flow, their positions within the page layers, and whether the individual elements are currently displayed.

Before the advent of CSS and JavaScript, space in a web page was a static thing. You could use a flexible container such as an HTML table that adapted to the browser window size, but that was about it. If you had a web form with a lot of fields, you either put them all into one long page or you split the form up over many pages and updated the data in pieces. If the application user made an error, he wouldn't know until after the form was submitted to the server. Most likely he'd then be redirected to a page just to print out the error message.

Today, through a subset of the Ajax technologies, elements can be positioned and layered through the use of absolute positioning. Each element has its own internal characteristics such as width, height, padding, and margin, all of which can be adjusted. Elements also have a *clipping* region, which determines how much of the element is displayed and how much is "clipped" (not shown and also not influencing the flow around it).

If an element's `display` is set to `block` rather than `inline`, the setting incorporates line breaks before and after the element, forcing elements that follow to be pushed down the page. An element can also be removed completely from the page flow by setting its `display` to `none`.

Summarizing, through CSS and JavaScript we can:

- Change an element's height or width
- Change an element's borders, padding, or margin
- Alter the clipping region
- Layer the elements

- Move or hide the elements
- Alter an element's display characteristics such as making them inline, block, or even removing from display

Individually, these element manipulations are handy, but combined, they form the higher-level effects on which most Ajax applications are dependent. These effects include:

- The accordion, which expands or collapses based on user action
- The tabbed page, which displays a single page or panel at a time
- The overlay, which layers one element over all of the page's contents
- Pagination, which uses a combination of movement and clipping to "page" through content
- Fly-ins, which bring elements in from outside of the bounded area, such as the side of the page
- Drag and drop, which enables the application user to move things about

In this chapter, we'll look at three such effects—accordions, tabbed pages, and overlays—that manipulate both a page's space and elemental display. We'll also look at each effect's impact on accessibility and the approaches that can minimize the impact. In the process, we'll also explore how to package such higher-level effects into reusable libraries that can be used for more than one web page or application.

 The use of other space-conserving effects accomplished through the use of Ajax technologies, such as clipping, drag and drop, and pagination, are covered in later chapters.

Horizontal Spacing: The Accordion

One of my favorite Ajax space effects has been called the *accordion*, based on both the appearance and behavior of the effect. Two or more blocks of content, typically called *panels*, are stacked horizontally and hidden using one of three approaches:

- The display of each elements is set to none.
- The elements are clipped completely along the vertical axis.
- The height of each elements is set to zero.

When the accordion is first displayed, what typically shows for each panel is a title or label for each block with some visual icon indicating that the web page reader needs to click the title to expand (or collapse) the panel. From an implementation standpoint, the labels and panels are separate but associated elements that may or may not be embedded in a container, all of which can be combined and embedded in yet another container.

The accordion makes efficient use of space, especially when used with a long multi-part form. Additionally, it's a simple effect to work around if JavaScript is disabled. When scripting is turned off, all panels are expanded when the page is loaded.

Figure 5-1 shows a typical accordion with the first and third panel expanded, and the second collapsed. I'll demonstrate how to create this application in this section.

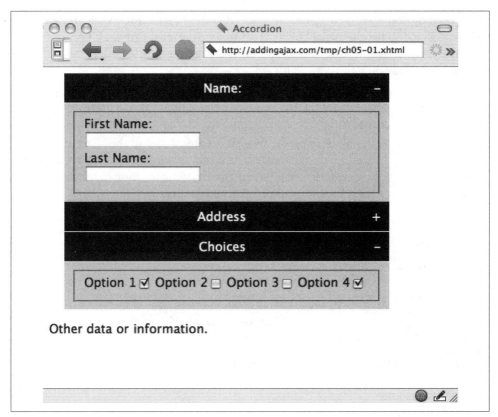

Figure 5-1. Accordion effect with three blocks

Creating the Effect

The simplest approach to managing the expansion of the panel is to use the CSS property display. Setting the display to block shows the panel and, incidentally, pushes the rest of the page contents down to make room for the object. Setting the panel's display to none removes the block from display and the elements below it move up to fill in the space.

An accordion may also have indicators within the title area for each block that signal an activity associated with clicking on the title bar. Most often, these include a plus sign (+) to indicate that hidden material can be expanded and a negative sign (–) to indicate that the material can be collapsed.

Some accordions don't use a visual indicator, relying on the web page readers to "intuitively" figure out that they can click directly on the accordion label to control the effect. Unless the context provides enough information, it's better to use some explicit indicator of hidden content.

An accordion starts with two or more stacked panel blocks, each with an associated title bar. The CSS for the panel blocks is set to `display:block` (default CSS setting for div elements), so if scripting is disabled for the page the blocks will display as completely expanded when the page loads.

Example 5-1 shows a web page consisting of three horizontal blocks, each with a subsection of a form. Each of the accordion expand/collapse indicators is surrounded by a hypertext link, and the `onclick` event handler for each is assigned to a function; the `id` for the block is passed as a parameter. Later in the chapter when the accordion code is packaged for easier reuse, these `onclick` event handlers are removed, leaving the page elements script-free. For now, though, their presence doesn't impact on accessibility or validity, just reusability.

Example 5-1. Web page with three accordion blocks

```
<!DOCTYPE html PUBLIC "-//W3C//DTD XHTML 1.0 Strict//EN"
    "http://www.w3.org/TR/xhtml1/DTD/xhtml1-strict.dtd">
<html xmlns="http://www.w3.org/1999/xhtml" lang="en" xml:lang="en">
<head>
<title>Accordion</title>
<meta http-equiv="Content-Type" content="text/html; charset=utf-8" />
<link rel="stylesheet" href="accordion.css" type="text/css" media="screen" />
<script type="text/javascript" src="addingajax.js">
</script>
<script type="text/javascript" src="accordion1.js">
</script>
</head>
<body>
<form action="" method="GET">
<div class="label" id="label1">
<div id="oneplus" class="control">
<a href="#name" onclick="expand('one');return false">+</a>
</div>
<div id="onenegative" class="control">
<a href="#name" onclick="collapse('one');return false">-</a>
</div>
<h3 class="name">
Name:
</h3>
</div>
<div class="elements" id="one">
<fieldset>
<legend>Names</legend>
```

Example 5-1. Web page with three accordion blocks (continued)

```
<label for="firstname">First Name:</label><br /><input type="text" name="firstname"
id="firstname"/>
<label for="lastname">Last Name:</label><br /><input type="text" name="lastname"
id="lastname" />
</fieldset>
</div>
<div class="label">
<div id="twoplus" class="control">
<a href="#name" onclick="expand('two');return false">+</a>
</div>
<div id="twonegative" class="control">
<a href="#name" onclick="collapse('two');return false">-</a>
</div>
<h3 class="name">
Address
</h3>
</div>
<div class="elements" id="two">
<fieldset>
<legend>Address</legend>
<label for="street">Street Address:</label><br /><input type="text" name="street"
id="street" />
<label for="city">City:</label><br /><input type="text" name="city" id="city" />
<label for="state">State:</label><br /><input type="text" name="state" id="state" />
</fieldset>
</div>
<div class="label">
<div id="threeplus" class="control">
<a href="#name" onclick="expand('three');return false">+</a>
</div>
<div id="threenegative" class="control">
<a href="#name" onclick="collapse('three');return false">-</a>
</div>
<h3 class="name">
Options
</h3>
</div>
<div class="elements" id="three">
<fieldset>
<legend>Options</legend>
<label for="opt1">Option 1</label><input type="checkbox" name="opt1" id="opt1"
checked="checked" />
<label for="opt2">Option 2</label><input type="checkbox" name="opt2" id="opt2"  />
<label for="opt3">Option 3</label><input type="checkbox" name="opt3" id="opt3"  />
<label for="opt4">Option 4</label><input type="checkbox" name="opt4" id="opt4"
checked="checked" />
</fieldset>
</div>

</form>
```

Example 5-1. Web page with three accordion blocks (continued)

```
<p>Other data or information.</p>
</body>
</html>
```

Since the application is script-only, it's tempting to remove the hypertext link for the accordion tab controls and just attach the `onclick` event handler to the `div` elements. However, doing so can interfere with keyboard access to the accordion behavior.

 An additional element attribute that can assist accessibility is accesskey, or the newer XHTML 2.0 access. Both map a keyboard key directly to the linked item. With these, keyboard users can go directly to an item using Alt+*key* in Windows and Ctrl+*key* in the Mac. Unfortunately, these can conflict with browser, user, or even assistive device shortcuts.

The application modifies the panel element's CSS property `display` to either `block` or none based on whether the block is to be expanded or collapsed. The rest of the CSS stylesheet for Example 5-1 is shown in the code below. Note the use of the CSS2 selector (type="checkbox") to differentiate between the text input buttons and the checkboxes. Though this selector works for most of our target browsers, IE ignores it and the checkboxes will be displayed in the default block mode:

```
.name
{
        margin: 0;
        padding: 0;
}
.label
{
        background-color: #003;
        border-bottom: 1px solid #fff;
        border-right: 1px solid #fff;
        color: #fff;
        margin: 0 20px;
        padding: 10px;
        text-align: center;
        width: 400px;
}
.label a
{
        color: #fff;
        text-decoration: none;
}
.elements
{
        background-color: #CCD9FF;
        margin: 0 20px;
        padding: 0px;
        width: 420px
```

```
        overflow: hidden;
}
.control
{
        display: none;
        float: right;
}
legend
{
        display: none;
}
input
{
        display: block;
        margin-bottom: 5px;
}
input[type="checkbox"]
{
        display: inline;
}
```

In the initial stylesheet setting, the collapse/expand indicator elements are hidden and the blocks themselves are all displayed. The reason for this is that if a reader accessing the page has script turned off or is using a tool that doesn't support Java-Script, the indicators will be hidden and the form elements will be displayed by default.

The JavaScript to implement the accordion (*accordion1.js*) is quite simple. Since the application uses the onclick event handlers inline, all that's left is to change the display style attribute of both the indicator and the block:

```
aaManageEvent(window,"load", function( ) {
   document.getElementById('one').style.display='none';
   document.getElementById('two').style.display='none';
   document.getElementById('three').style.display='none';

   document.getElementById('oneplus').style.display='block';
   document.getElementById('twoplus').style.display='block';
   document.getElementById('threeplus').style.display='block';
});

// expand accordion block
function expand(newItem) {
   document.getElementById(newItem).style.display='block';
   document.getElementById(newItem + 'plus').style.display='none';
   document.getElementById(newItem + 'negative').style.display='block';
}

// collapse accordion block
function collapse(newItem) {
   document.getElementById(newItem).style.display='none';
   document.getElementById(newItem + 'plus').style.display='block';
   document.getElementById(newItem + 'negative').style.display='none';
}
```

The window load event handler is assigned an anonymous function to collapse all the blocks (set display to none), and display the expand indicators for each. Two additional functions, expand and collapse, do exactly as they're named: expand or collapse the block whose identifier is passed as a parameter to the function. In addition, the expand function also hides the expand indicator and displays the collapse indicator; conversely, the collapse function does the opposite.

Try the application out yourself, and I think you'll see why this is such a popular technique—enough so that there are multiple ways of implementing the effect, including a more animated one using the height CSS property, demonstrated next.

A Transitioning Accordion

Example 5-1 demonstrates an accordion without transitioning between a block being displayed and hidden. Another approach to an accordion is to provide a transition between "no display" and "full display." However, you can't use the display: none CSS setting to create this effect because an element is either displayed or it's not—there is no in-between. To create an animated transition, we need to use some other CSS property, such as height or clipping, or even a combination of clipping and movement (unclipping the element as you "move" it down into place). For the accordion, adjusting the height style attribute is the simplest option.

To create an accordion effect with height, the application can set a height for each panel and then increment and decrement the height identically for every block. Or the application can find the height of the elements just before setting their heights to zero when the page is first loaded. I prefer the latter approach because the accordions can then be as long as necessary without running up against height limitations. However, getting an element's height can be tricky.

Getting an element's height and width

Finding the height of a element when its initial height is set within an inline style attribute is simple: just access the style.height property for the element, directly or using the W3C preferred method, getProperty:

```
var height = elem.style.height;
var height = elem.style.getProperty('height');
```

Since we're avoiding inline styles, another approach is to access the element's computed height via the computed style property set.

One approach to getting the computed style in a cross-browser friendly manner can be found in the Prototype Ajax library. The Prototype library Element object's getStyle method is a rather involved function that has to account for cross-browser variations in specific styles. It has to deal with including floats and returned values like auto, not to mention what happens with some browsers and fixed positioning compared to relative or absolute, or probably the worst style setting, opacity:

```
Element.Methods = {
  ...
  getStyle: function(element, style) {
    element = $(element);
    if (['float','cssFloat'].include(style))
      style = (typeof element.style.styleFloat != 'undefined' ? 'styleFloat' :
'cssFloat');
    style = style.camelize();
    var value = element.style[style];
    if (!value) {
      if (document.defaultView && document.defaultView.getComputedStyle) {
        var css = document.defaultView.getComputedStyle(element, null);
        value = css ? css[style] : null;
      } else if (element.currentStyle) {
        value = element.currentStyle[style];
      }
    }

    if((value == 'auto') && ['width','height'].include(style) && (element.
getStyle('display') != 'none'))
      value = element['offset'+style.capitalize()] + 'px';

    if (window.opera && ['left', 'top', 'right', 'bottom'].include(style))
      if (Element.getStyle(element, 'position') == 'static') value = 'auto';
    if(style == 'opacity') {
      if(value) return parseFloat(value);
      if(value = (element.getStyle('filter') || '').match(/alpha\(opacity=(.*)\)/))
        if(value[1]) return parseFloat(value[1]) / 100;
      return 1.0;
    }
    return value == 'auto' ? null : value;
  },
  ...
};
```

We don't need anything so complicated for the current example.

To find the element height, we can use either the clientHeight or the offsetHeight property. Unfortunately, the downside to using these properties is that neither is a W3C standard; nor is either based on any form of technical recommendation (they both originated from Internet Explorer). In addition, both can return different values depending on the browser, CSS settings for an element, and whether a browser is running in standards mode or quirks mode.

The clientHeight of the element should contain the height of the element *minus* the margin and border, which are external to the element. The offsetHeight should contain the height of the element, including the margin and border. Unfortunately, one specific problem that we'll see later is that when we access an element using something like getElementsByTagName rather than accessing each individual element by element identifier), the clientHeight property returns zero. However, offsetHeight still works, returning the individual element's offsetHeight. Add this to the fact that we

want to get the entire offset height of an element, and it makes sense to use
offsetHeight. Since this property is supported by the book's target browsers, that's
what we'll use.

 Most people recommend a library like Prototype to simplify the Ajax
requests; I find that the way the libraries handle the cross-browser
DOM methods and page effects is what justifies their use. The Ajax
service request method is quite simple in comparison with managing
the DOM.

Finishing the transition

The page elements in the transitioned accordion don't change, other than the Java-
Script source file, *accordion2.js*:

```
<script type="text/javascript" src="accordion2.js">
</script>
```

The stylesheet also needs no modification. The only component of the application to
change significantly is the JavaScript, shown in Example 5-2. The window load event
handler function calls another function, setHeight, to get the computed height of
each block and assign it, by block name, to an associative array. The function then
sets the initial height of the element to zero.

Example 5-2. JavaScript source for transitioning accordion effect

```
// global heightObjs for computed heights
var heightObjs = new Array( );

// find computed height and set all to zero
function setHeight(objName) {
    var obj = document.getElementById(objName);
    var height = aaGetStyle(objName,'height');
    heightObjs[objName] = Math.round(parseFloat(height.substr(0,height.length-2)));
    obj.style.height="0";
}

// set up panels
aaManageEvent(window,"load", function( ) {

    setHeight('one');
    setHeight('two');
    setHeight('three');

    document.getElementById('oneplus').style.display='block';
    document.getElementById('twoplus').style.display='block';
    document.getElementById('threeplus').style.display='block';
});

// transitionally expand the item
function expand(newItem) {
```

Example 5-2. JavaScript source for transitioning accordion effect (continued)

```
   document.getElementById(newItem + 'plus').style.display='none';
   document.getElementById(newItem + 'negative').style.display='block';
   var currentItem = document.getElementById(newItem);

   // find increment based on computed height divided by loop count of 20
   var incr = heightObjs[newItem] / 20;
   for (var i=0; i < 20; i++) {
      var val = (i+1) * incr;
      var func = "adjustItem("+val+",'"+newItem+"')";
      setTimeout(func,(i+1)*30);
   }
}
// transitionally collapse the item
function collapse(newItem) {
   document.getElementById(newItem + 'plus').style.display='block';
   document.getElementById(newItem + 'negative').style.display='none';
   var currentItem = document.getElementById(newItem);

   // find decrement based on computed height divided by a loop count of 20
   var decr = heightObjs[newItem] / 20;
   for (var i=0; i<20; i++) {
      var val = heightObjs[newItem]-(decr*(i+1));
      var func = "adjustItem("+val+",'"+newItem+"')";
      setTimeout(func,(i+1)*30);
   }
}

// individual adjustment
function adjustItem(val, newItem) {
    document.getElementById(newItem).style.height=val + "px";
}
```

The expand and collapse functions still expand and collapse the panels, but now each uses a loop to either increment or decrement the height to control how much is displayed. The amount of adjustment is determined by dividing the element's computed height (when fully displayed) by the number of loops—in this case, 20. A separate function, adjustHeight, makes the actual adjustment.

The incremental modifications to the height are managed with JavaScript timers to create an animated effect. Since this example doesn't have to maintain the context of an object within an event handler function, as the animations described in Chapter 4 did, the application doesn't have to use the specialized aaBindEventListener in the *addingajax.js* library. It can just use a computed string with the function name and the calculated parameters concatenated together.

The actual height is found by parsing out the numeric value of the height (without the px unit). This is then passed to the parseFloat function, which ensures it's treated as a numeric. Finally, it's rounded to the nearest whole number.

Once implemented, clicking on the expand/collapse indicator results in an animated open and closing event, providing a little more polish, though it doesn't necessarily add to the overall efficiency of the effect.

Now that we've looked at examples using a "homegrown" accordion effect, let's look and see how other developers implement the same functionality.

Using Prepackaged Accordions

Rather than cook your own accordion code, another approach is to use a prepackaged effect in an external Ajax library. One such library is the Accordion that comes with Rico, introduced in Chapter 3.

The Rico Accordion differs from the homegrown one in that it doesn't provide expand and collapse indicators. In addition, the panels in a Rico accordion cannot use borders or padding. If padding is needed, we have to use a nested div element or something such as the fieldset element used in the previous two examples. The elements' relationship with each other must also meet a certain page layout pattern, with content areas nested within an overall container.

To create a Rico accordion, you have to include both the Rico and the Prototype libraries in the web page. Use the following syntax to create a basic Rico Accordion with no options:

```
new Rico.Accordion( $('accordionDiv'));
```

There are options that can be passed as an object in the second parameter. The following comes from the library's code:

```
this.options = {
    expandedBg          : '#63699c',
    hoverBg             : '#63699c',
    collapsedBg         : '#6b79a5',
    expandedTextColor   : '#ffffff',
    expandedFontWeight  : 'bold',
    hoverTextColor      : '#ffffff',
    collapsedTextColor  : '#ced7ef',
    collapsedFontWeight : 'normal',
    hoverTextColor      : '#ffffff',
    borderColor         : '#1f669b',
    panelHeight         : 200,
    onHideTab           : null,
    onShowTab           : null,
    onLoadShowTab       : 0
}
```

Each of these default options can be overridden. The most common option to override is the panelHeight, as it's essential that the panels be tall enough to accommodate the panel contents (you don't want a vertical scrollbar).

To match the existing panel as much as possible, a height of 200px should be enough, and the background color of the name header has to be passed to the object. Though the Rico defaults are a shade of blue, they aren't the blue I've been using. In addition, the font weight and color also have to be customized to match the previous example:

```
new Rico.Accordion( $('accordionDiv'),
                    {expandedBg : '#003',
                     collapsedBg : '#003',
                     expandedFontWeight: 'normal',
                     collapsedTextColor: '#fff'
                    });
```

To match the new element structure, we have to adjust the CSS stylesheet:

```
#accordionDiv
{
        margin: 0 20px;
        width: 400px;
}
.name
{
        padding: 10px 0;
        text-align: center;
}
.elements
{
        background-color: #CCD9FF;
}
input
{
        display: block;
        margin-bottom: 5px;
}
input[type="checkbox"]
{
        display: inline;
}
```

Since Prototype provides event handling, the application doesn't require any other library for creating the accordion when the page is loaded. Example 5-3 contains the complete web page, including the JavaScript to create the accordion, and using the Prototype event handling.

Example 5-3. Using Rico for an accordion effect

```
<!DOCTYPE html PUBLIC "-//W3C//DTD HTML 4.01//EN"
"http://www.w3.org/TR/1999/REC-html401-19991224/strict.dtd">
<html lang="en">
<head>
<title>Accordion</title>
<link rel="stylesheet" href="accordion2.css" type="text/css" media="screen" />
<meta http-equiv="Content-Type" content="text/html; charset=utf-8" />
```

Example 5-3. Using Rico for an accordion effect (continued)

```
<script type="text/javascript" src="prototype.js">
</script>
<script type="text/javascript" src="rico.js">
</script>

<script type="text/javascript">
//<![CDATA[

Event.observe(window, 'load', function () {
        new Rico.Accordion( $('accordionDiv'),
                            {expandedBg : '#003',
                             collapsedBg : '#003',
                             expandedFontWeight: 'normal',
                             collapsedTextColor: '#fff'
                             });
        }, false);

//]]>
</script>
</head>
<body>
<form action="GET">

<div id="accordionDiv">

<div id="onePanel">
<div class="name">
Name:
</div>
<div class="elements" id="one">
<fieldset>
<legend>Name</legend>
<label for="firstname">First Name:</label><br /><input type="text" name="firstname"
id="firstname"/>
<label for="lastname">Last Name:</label><br /><input type="text" name="lastname"
id="lastname" />
</fieldset>
</div>
</div>

<div id="twoPanel">
<div class="name">
Address
</div>
<div class="elements" id="two">
<fieldset>
<legend>Address</legend>
<label for="street">Street Address:</label><br /><input type="text" name="street"
id="street" />
<label for="city">City:</label><br /><input type="text" name="city" id="city" />
<label for="state">State:</label><br /><input type="text" name="state" id="state" />
</fieldset>
```

Example 5-3. Using Rico for an accordion effect (continued)

```
</div>
</div>

<div id="threePanel">
<div class="name">
Options
</div>
<div class="elements" id="three">
<fieldset>
<legend>Options</legend>
<label for="opt1">Option 1</label><input type="checkbox" name="opt1" id="opt1"
checked="checked" />
<label for="opt2">Option 2</label><input type="checkbox" name="opt2" id="opt2"  />
<label for="opt3">Option 3</label><input type="checkbox" name="opt3" id="opt3"  />
<label for="opt4">Option 4</label><input type="checkbox" name="opt4" id="opt4"
checked="checked" />
</fieldset>
</div>
</div>
</div>
</form>

<p>Other data or information.</p>
</body>
</html>
```

The Rico Accordion displays with one already-opened content area. The library implements its accordion effect by opening another panel as one is closing, rather than operating the panels independently of each other. Clicking on the titlebar for another panel closes the open panel and then opens the new one.

Example 5-3 definitely demonstrates a decrease in the amount of code, which is welcome. There is a price for this convenience, though—you have to accept the behavior of the packaged effect, including the initial exposed panel, as well the open/close behavior. It also doesn't allow for independent panel heights.

If you want to continue using your own accordion effect but have the ease of use that comes with using a prepackaged external library, you might want to look at packaging your own code, covered next.

 One other major difference between the applications is that the Prototype/Rico effect would not work if the page were served up as XHTML. The DOCTYPE for the page is changed to HTML 4.01 Strict, and the page served up as HTML.

Packaging the Accordion Code

The accordion is popular for another reason outside of its efficient space management and simplicity: it's easy to package into reusable code. First, though, we'll review the existing applications and search for areas of improvement.

One of the first changes to make to the code is the expand/collapse indicator. Instead of a plus or minus character, we'll use a triangle image, facing down when a panel is expanded, and to the right when it's collapsed. This more closely matches what most people are familiar with from desktop applications. If most of the accordions are using darker header colors, white triangles with transparent backgrounds make the most sense. The images are in GIF format; IE 6.x doesn't support PNG transparency.

The structure of the effect also has to change. Rico's grouping makes much more sense than trying to tie pieces together based on identifier names. The relevant pieces of an accordion are the overall container and the panels, each of which consists of the panel label to receive the events and the panel content, which is expanded or collapsed.

Like Rico, the Adding Ajax accordion's structure consists of an overall accordion container for each panel, itself containing a panel label and the panel content. Clicking on the label expands or collapses the container using the animated method demonstrated earlier.

To find the elements, one popular approach is to programmatically pinpoint elements using the class attribute—not only to provide visual formatting, but also to "mark" which page elements are participating in one effect or another. We'll take it a step further: adding CSS label classes for the accordion bars. The bars will differ only based on whether the panel is collapsed or expanded—each is the same except that the background image differs, as highlighted in the following:

```
#accordionDiv
{
        margin: 0 20px;
        width: 400px;
}
.nameExpanded, .nameCollapsed
{
        background-position: center right;
        background-repeat: no-repeat;
        background-color: #003;
        border-bottom: 1px solid #fff;
        color: #fff;
        padding: 10px 0;
        text-align: center;
        background-image: url('expanded.gif');
}
.nameCollapsed
```

```
{
        background-image: url('collapsed.gif');
        cursor: pointer;
}
.nameExpanded
{
        background-image: url('expanded.gif');
        cursor: pointer;
}
.elements
{
        background-color: #CCD9FF;
        overflow: hidden;
}
input
{
        display: block;
        margin-bottom: 5px;
}
input[type="checkbox"]
{
        display: inline;
}
```

This page is similar to that used with the Rico example, except it has an XHTML DOCTYPE and can be served as XHTML. The Rico example isn't dependent on class use like the Adding Ajax library is:

```
<!DOCTYPE html PUBLIC "-//W3C//DTD XHTML 1.0 Strict//EN"
    "http://www.w3.org/TR/xhtml1/DTD/xhtml1-strict.dtd">
<html xmlns="http://www.w3.org/1999/xhtml" lang="en" xml:lang="en">
<head>
<title>Accordion</title>
<meta http-equiv="Content-Type" content="text/html; charset=utf-8" />
<link rel="stylesheet" href="accordion3.css" type="text/css" media="screen" />
<script type="text/javascript" src="addingajax.js">
</script>
<script type="text/javascript" src="accordionobj.js">
</script>
</head>
<body>

<form action="GET">

<div id="accordionDiv">

<div class="panel">
<div class="nameCollapsed">
Name:
</div>
<div class="elements">
<fieldset>
```

```
<legend>Name</legend>
<label for="firstname">First Name:</label><br /><input type="text" name="firstname"
id="firstname"/>
<label for="lastname">Last Name:</label><br /><input type="text" name="lastname"
id="lastname" />
</fieldset>
</div>
</div>

<div class="panel">
<div class="nameCollapsed">
Address
</div>
<div class="elements">
<fieldset>
<legend>Address</legend>
<label for="street">Street Address:</label><br /><input type="text" name="street"
id="street" />
<label for="city">City:</label><br /><input type="text" name="city" id="city" />
<label for="state">State:</label><br /><input type="text" name="state" id="state" />
</fieldset>
</div>
</div>

<div class="panel">
<div class="nameCollapsed">
Options
</div>
<div class="elements">
<fieldset>
<legend>Options</legend>
<label for="opt1">Option 1</label><input type="checkbox" name="opt1" id="opt1"
checked="checked" />
<label for="opt2">Option 2</label><input type="checkbox" name="opt2" id="opt2"  />
<label for="opt3">Option 3</label><input type="checkbox" name="opt3" id="opt3"  />
<label for="opt4">Option 4</label><input type="checkbox" name="opt4" id="opt4"
checked="checked" />
</fieldset>
</div>
</div>

</div>
</form>
<p>Other data or information.</p>
</body>
</html>
```

When the page is first loaded, the default class setting for the panel label is
nameCollapsed, and the panels are all collapsed.

Example 5-4 is the JavaScript to manage the packaged accordion. The Rico example also isn't dependent on the use of the class attribute, unlike the functionality used for the Adding Ajax accordion library.

Example 5-4. JavaScript with accordion elements using specialized class names

```
// setup accordion elements
aaManageEvent(window,"load", function( ) {
    var divs = document.getElementsByTagName('div');

    for (var i = 0; i < divs.length; i++) {

        // setup click for name bar
        if (divs[i].className == 'nameCollapsed') {
            aaManageEvent(divs[i],'click',Accordion.expandOrCollapse);

        // assign height as custom property to element and then collapse
        } else if (divs[i].className == 'elements') {

            // IE6.x handles elements returned from getElementsByTagName differently
            // and clientHeight doesn't work; using offsetHeight, instead
            var height = divs[i].offsetHeight;
            divs[i].height = height;
            if (divs[i].id == "") divs[i].id = "div" + i;
            divs[i].style.height = "0";
        }
    }
});
// manage the accordion
var Accordion = {

    // adjust height
    adjustItem  : function(val, newItem) {
            aaElem(newItem).style.height=val + "px";
    },

    // check if expand or collapse
    expandOrCollapse : function (evnt) {
            evnt = evnt ? evnt : window.event;
            var target = evnt.target ? evnt.target : evnt.srcElement;
            if (target.className == 'nameCollapsed')
                Accordion.expand(target);
            else
                Accordion.collapse(target);
    },

    // expand panel
    expand : function(target) {
            target.className = 'nameExpanded';
            // find panel
            var children = target.parentNode.childNodes;
            var panel;
```

Example 5-4. JavaScript with accordion elements using specialized class names (continued)

```
        for (var i = 0; i < children.length; i++) {
            if (children[i].className == 'elements') {
                panel = children[i];
                break;
            }
        }
        var height = panel.height;

        // find increment based on computed height divided by loop count of 20
        var incr = height / 20;
        for (var i=0; i < 20; i++) {
            var val = (i+1) * incr;
            var func = "Accordion.adjustItem("+val+",'"+ panel.id +"')";
            setTimeout(func,(i+1)*30);
        }

    },
    // collapse panel
    collapse : function (target) {
            target.className = 'nameCollapsed';
            // find panel
            var children = target.parentNode.childNodes;
            var panel;
            for (var i = 0; i < children.length; i++) {
                if (children[i].className == 'elements') {
                    panel = children[i];
                    break;
                }
            }
            var height = panel.height;

            // find increment based on computed height divided by loop count of 20
            var decr = height / 20;
            for (var i=0; i < 20; i++) {
                var val = height-(decr*(i+1));;
                var func = "Accordion.adjustItem("+val+",'"+ panel.id +"')";
                setTimeout(func,(i+1)*30);
            }
    }

};
```

Walking through the code from the top, each element with a class of nameCollapsed is assigned a click event handler function, the Accordion object's expandOrCollapse method. In addition, when the page is loaded, the panel element's height setting is calculated from the actual height of the element just before setting it to zero to collapse it. This value is then assigned to a custom property, height. Typically in Ajax, the height property would either be part of the object class specification or be appended through the use of the prototype object. However, it's perfectly acceptable to assign a custom property directly to an individual object in JavaScript. The only risk is that there's a possibility that one instance of an object has the property while another doesn't. That doesn't happen in this application.

 Assigning a custom property directly to an instance can have a negative impact on processing time. Scripting engines look for a property first in the object's original definition, then in the object's prototype collection, then finally in the individual object instance.

In the `Accordion` object, the `expandOrCollapse` method accesses the `target` element of the `click` event, and if the `class` for the element is `nameCollapsed`, the expand method is invoked; otherwise, the `collapse` method is invoked. In these methods, the `class` for the label is altered so that the background "arrow" reflects the state of the panel.

The parent for the accordion label element is accessed, and its children are traversed until one with the `elements` class is discovered. This is the panel that's then incrementally expanded or collapsed. The panel expands vertically only enough to encompass the panel's contents.

Through this new accordion library, elements with the proper classes are packaged into an accordion appearance and behavior after the page loads—with no work on the part of the person creating the web page. Well, other than using the class names on the elements themselves. However, they don't have to touch the JavaScript.

Summarizing the steps:

1. A single `Accordion` object contains all relevant functions.
2. When the page loads, all `div` elements with a `className` of `nameCollapsed` are assigned an `onclick` event handler that controls the accordion movement.
3. All panels are fully expanded when the page loads so that all the information is available if scripting is disabled, and so that the panel element's height can be determined.
4. Once the panel's height is determined, this value is assigned to the object representing the element.
5. Each of the panels is then collapsed.
6. When a panel's label is clicked, its class name is altered so that its appearance reflects the state of its panel.
7. Within the parent container for the clicked label, all `div` elements are traversed until the one with the class name of `elements` is found. This element is the actual panel.
8. Once the panel is found, it's expanded or collapsed accordingly.

There is risk with using class names as part of a scripting effect—if you have a new designer who is not familiar with the scripting dependency on the specific class names, he could innocently modify the classes and break the effect.

Good communication between designer and web page developer is essential when using complex Ajax effects. Documentation is also important for maintaining that communication over time.

We could merge the two separate JavaScript files, *addingajax.js* and *accordion.js*; however, you usually want to keep your basic JavaScript files as small as possible and bring in the higher-level effects as separate files. The file *addingajax.js* contains event handler and Ajax functions, both of which will be used frequently—more frequently than the accordion effect.

Speaking of separate libraries, what happens if we want to mix custom behaviors with external libraries? For instance, the examples to this point have static content within the accordion panels—what if we want to dynamically bring in the panel contents, but still use an external Ajax library, such as Rico's?

Expand and Request: Mixing Accordions and Ajax Calls

Accordions can be a terrific way of implementing data querying on demand. Rather than displaying several rows of data and providing next and previous page indicators for navigating through the results, you can split the data along meaningful parameters and then place the data into separate sections of an accordion. To prevent longer initial page load times, you can also load the data on demand, when the accordion panel is first expanded.

There are several approaches to creating these associated effects, but each has a limitation: when adding event-enabled functionality to a "canned" effect such as the accordion, we may not be able to use a preexisting library. Why? Because many of the libraries don't necessarily expose the events they capture or the underlying object implementations so that we can insert and merge them in our own code.

In the case of Rico's accordion, we can make some modifications when we create the object. For instance, we can adjust the colors and other visual parameters. However, there's nothing in the documentation about which events to capture in order to make the Ajax request, or how Rico manages the objects in order to add the results to the panel object. The only way to find this out is to drill into the code or to implement the effects—on-demand Ajax request and accordion expansion—separately, and see how our customized effects and Rico's packaged effects work together.

The application implemented in this section uses this hybrid approach—implementing the functionality to get the data from the server when a block expands using local code, while block expansion is managed by Rico. The multilibrary example combines the Drinks application from earlier chapters, with the Rico-enabled application demonstrated earlier in this chapter. Since Rico is dependent on the Prototype library, the example application also adds some direct access to this library.

With the modifications, clicking on a panel label loads the associated drink recipe. If the recipe hasn't been loaded into the panel previously, it's requested from the server and then published into the panel. If the recipe had already been requested, all that's needed is to expand the panel.

Another change in this application is how the functions to access the drink recipe are managed. Rather than using global functions and variables, we'll borrow some functionality from the underlying Prototype library to help maintain a Drink object. In particular, the application is using two specific pieces of Prototype functionality: the Class.create method, which calls an initialize method on the object when the object is created, and the bindAsEventListener method to associate a context with each method.

In Chapter 4, I created my own bind method, associating an object context with a setTimeout method to ensure that the object properties were accessible with each timer event. In this example, we'll use Prototype's bindAsEventListener, as it provides a similar service for the different methods of the Drink object.

Example 5-5 shows the web page. Note that the tab panels don't have content other than "working...," which is displayed in the panel until the recipe is loaded.

Example 5-5. Web page for the mixed library, accordion, and Ajax application web page

```
<!DOCTYPE html PUBLIC "-//W3C//DTD XHTML 1.0 Strict//EN"
    "http://www.w3.org/TR/xhtml1/DTD/xhtml1-strict.dtd">
<html xmlns="http://www.w3.org/1999/xhtml" lang="en" xml:lang="en">
<head>
<meta http-equiv="Content-Type" content="text/html; charset=utf-8" />
<title>Accordion Drink</title>
<style type="text/css">
#accordionDiv
{
        margin: 0 20px;
}
.name
{
        background-color: #003;
        border-bottom: 1px solid #fff;
        border-left: 1px solid #003;
        border-right: 1px solid #003;
        color: #fff;
        padding-bottom: 10px;
        padding-top: 10px;
        text-align: center;
        width: 400px;
}
.elements
{
        background-color: #CCD9FF;
        height: 300px;
```

Example 5-5. Web page for the mixed library, accordion, and Ajax application web page (continued)

```
          overflow: hidden;
          width: 400px;
}
.content
{
          padding: 20px;
}
</style>
<script type="text/javascript" src="addingajax.js">
</script>
<script type="text/javascript" src="prototype.js">
</script>
<script type="text/javascript" src="rico.js">
</script>
<script type="text/javascript" src="accordionrico.js">
</script>
</head>
<body>
    <form action="GET">
      <div id="accordionDiv">
        <div>
          <div class="name" id="tea">
            Hot Tea:
          </div>

          <div class="elements">
            <div class="content" id="tea-area">
              working...
            </div>
          </div>
        </div>

        <div>
          <div class="name" id="margarita">
            Margarita
          </div>

          <div class="elements">
            <div class="content" id="margarita-area">
              working...
            </div>
          </div>
        </div>

        <div>
          <div class="name" id="lemon">
            Lemon Drop
          </div>

          <div class="elements">
            <div class="content" id="lemon-area">
              working...
            </div>
          </div>
```

```
    </div>

    <div>
      <div class="name" id="nonchmp">
        Non-Alcoholic Champagne
      </div>

      <div class="elements">
        <div class="content" id="nonchmp-area">
          working...
        </div>
      </div>
    </div>
  </div>
</form>

<p>Other data or information.</p>
</body>
</html>
```

Notice the links to all of the script file libraries: Prototype, Rico, the Adding Ajax library, and the new application specific file, *accordionrico.js*. That's a lot of libraries.

The application's JavaScript is shown in Example 5-6 and consists of a mix of Prototype event handling through the Event object and event bind function, Rico's accordion, Adding Ajax's Ajax object, and the new application-specific Drink object. For each drink accordion panel, a new Drink object is created, drink-specific information is stored, and an event listener is created when Rico's label element is clicked. When the element is clicked, the drink name is used with the Ajax call to get the drink recipe, which is then used to replace the panel content.

Example 5-6. Mix of Ajax call and accordion effect

```
var xmlhttp;

// Using Prototype's event handler
Event.observe(window,"load",  function() {
   new Rico.Accordion( $('accordionDiv'), {panelHeight: 200} );
   setUp( );
});

// set page display
function setUp( ) {
   var divs = document.getElementsByTagName('div');
   for (var i = 0; i < divs.length; i++) {
     if (divs[i].className == 'name') {
        var drink = new Drink(divs[i]);
        if (drink.drink.id == 'tea') drink.getRecipe( );
     }
   }
```

Example 5-6. Mix of Ajax call and accordion effect (continued)

```
}

// Prototype's Class object is used to
// create the Drink object
Drink = Class.create();

// The Drink object's methods are added
// via the prototype object
Drink.prototype = {

  // initialize is automatically called first when
  // an object is created using Prototype's Class.create
  initialize: function(drink) {
    this.drink = drink;
    this._attachBehaviors();
    this.state = 'notloaded';
  },
  _attachBehaviors: function() {
    Event.observe(this.drink,"click",this.getRecipe.bindAsEventListener(this));
  },
  getRecipe : function() {
    if (this.state=='loaded') return;
    if (!xmlhttp) xmlhttp = aaGetXmlHttpRequest();
    var drink = this.drink.id;
    var qry = "drink=" + drink;
    var url = 'recipe5.php?' + qry;
    xmlhttp.open('GET', url, true);
    xmlhttp.onreadystatechange = this.printRecipe.bindAsEventListener(this);
    xmlhttp.send(null);
  },
  printRecipe : function () {
    if(xmlhttp.readyState == 4 && xmlhttp.status == 200) {

      // set state
      this.state = 'loaded';

      // access recipe element and clear
      var recipe = document.getElementById(this.drink.id + "-area");
      recipe.innerHTML = "";

      // add title
      var title = xmlhttp.responseXML.getElementsByTagName('title')[0].firstChild.
nodeValue;
      var titleNode = document.createElement('div');
      titleNode.className='title';
      titleNode.appendChild(document.createTextNode(title));
      recipe.appendChild(titleNode);

      // add ingredients
      var ingredients = xmlhttp.responseXML.getElementsByTagName('ingredient');
      for (var i = 0; i < ingredients.length; i++) {
        var x = document.createElement('div');
        x.className = 'ingredient';
        x.appendChild(document.createTextNode(ingredients[i].firstChild.nodeValue));
```

Example 5-6. Mix of Ajax call and accordion effect (continued)

```
        recipe.appendChild(x);
    }

    // add instruction
    var instr = xmlhttp.responseXML.getElementsByTagName('instruction')[0].firstChild.
nodeValue;
    var instrNode = document.createElement('div');
    instrNode.className='instruction';
    instrNode.appendChild(document.createTextNode(instr));
    recipe.appendChild(instrNode);
    }

}};
```

The Prototype Class.create method is used to create the Drink class. The Drink object has four methods: initialize, _attachBehaviors, getRecipe, and printRecipe. To ensure that each method has the context of the parent object, the bindAsEventListener method is called for each, passing in this, or the parent object.

Drilling into the Prototype code, the important line in the code is:

```
    return __method.call(object, event || window.event);
```

The JavaScript call method allows us to share objects across multiple methods—in this case, the object context (accessible by using this within the method). This allows all of the Drink object's methods to access each other, as well as to access the properties drink and state, the former being the name of the drink associated with the object and the latter being an indicator of whether the recipe has already been loaded.

The different drink objects are created when the page is loaded based on whether the element has a class of name or not. Since each named element is given an identifier of a drink name, this is extracted for use in the web service request. The actual request occurs in the getRecipe method.

When the Drink object associated with the first drink, "tea," is created, it's immediately loaded because this accordion panel is already displayed.

Figure 5-2 shows the application with one of the drink panels displayed.

Though the example is simple, it could be easily extended to other business uses: a list of people or companies and addresses, code samples for a tutorial site, store locations, or production information.

That's about enough on accordions, code packaging, and managing multiple libraries: time to check out other creative manipulations of page space, including the very popular tabbed pages. First, though, a note on a limitation with the example in this section: loading page content on demand is never going to be a fully accessible technique.

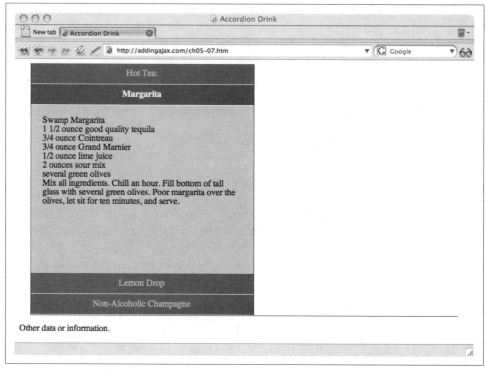

Figure 5-2. A mix and mash combining the accordion effect and the Drinks recipe application

An accordion can be accessible because all of the panels can be open when the page is loaded. However, if the data is not present when the page is loaded, and scripting is disabled, the only way to work around disabled scripting is to load the content using the server application or to provide links to pages with the panel open in each, and the data loaded by the server. Chapter 9 has a demonstration of this approach.

Tabbed Pages

While writing this book, Yahoo! came out with a redesigned web site for its popular Yahoo! TV. My, wasn't the redesign an unpopular decision among regular users.

One of the bigger complaints I heard about the new site was the use of Ajax pagination, which I'll briefly discuss later. Additionally, the use of tabbed pages in the full TV listing was roundly criticized because it was slow and had unnecessary Ajax effects. For instance, if you clicked a day to see the listings for that date, the tab indicator would slowly move over to that day and then the listings would be displayed. This was not typical behavior for tabbed pages, and I think the unfamiliar use of animation caused at least some of the pushback.

Tabbed pages have a very strong behavioral identity; data or content is split between different "pages," each of which is displayed when the page tab is clicked. What's contained within the page can differ—it could be pieces of a long form, different types of content for a portal, television listings by day, even coordinated data—each page reflecting what's chosen on the page proceeding. One thing they all have in common, though, is click the tab, display the page. Compared to the accordion, it's actually the easier effect to implement.

A Straightforward Look at Tabbed Content

"Tabbed pages" is a bit of a misnomer, as they don't have to be page-size; they can be tabbed content fitted into a small corner, or on a larger scale, even a page of tabbed content with each page based on a different topic or subtopic.

The content in tabbed pages can be static or dynamic. If it's dynamic, the content can be generated by the server or by an Ajax request when a tab is clicked.

The tabs can use graphic elements, CSS, or a combination of both. You do need a way to indicate which tab belongs to which panel, such as removing the bottom border of the tab when it's clicked, so that it blends in with the content page. Otherwise, your web page readers might not know which tab is currently open.

To demonstrated tabbed pages, I'm going to borrow the form used earlier in the chapter, except that instead of being stacked vertically, each form section will be split across tab pages.

The page contents are relatively simple: each tabbed page has a tab label, defined by the class name, and the page contents are identified by the class elements:

```
<div class="tab">
<div class="name">
Name:
</div>
<div class="elements" id="one">
<div class="content">
<label for="firstname">First Name:</label><br /><input type="text" id="firstname"
name="firstname" /><br /><br />
<label for="lastname">Last Name:</label><br /><input type="text" id="lastname"
name="lastname" /><br /><br />
</div>
</div>
</div>
```

The objects within the tabbed page are surrounded by another div element with a class of content. This is for styling only and has no impact on the code. In addition, all of the tabbed pages are contained within a "container" element, again for styling purposes only.

Notice the similarity between tabbed page markup and accordion? In reality, there are only so many ways you can manage page content. Once you've figured out one technique, it becomes quite easy to try out others.

The individual tabbed pages are also surrounded by a div element with a class of tab. Rather than using identifiers to access individual elements, as in the previous examples, we're going to be using the actual structure of the elements to create a connection between the tab that's clicked and the page that's displayed. This is how many of the external Ajax libraries create their effects because it's simpler for people to set up the examples (they don't have to worry about using different identifiers). It's also easier to generate dynamically from a server application.

During the design stage, all the panel pages are visible, making it easier to check the layout. At this time, it might be a good idea to hold off on putting in any content or anything more than a simple paragraph until we are finished with the layout and building the mechanics. Figure 5-3 shows the page at this point, with one tab element highlighted using the Firebug inspector.

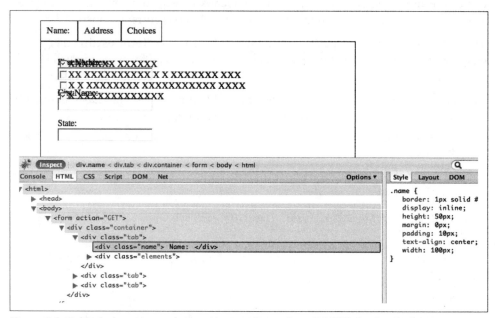

Figure 5-3. Tabbed pages as a work in progress with one element highlighted in Firebug

When the page is loaded, the application JavaScript looks for all div elements with the tab class. When found, it accesses the children of the particular element node. The first child is the actual tab and the second is the tab page. The application associates a click event handler function to the tab that displays the page when the tab is clicked.

We can create an overall object to hold arrays of tabs and pages and the current page. During the application load, each tab/panel pair is given an "index" relative to the page. This index is used to load each item into its associate array in the proper position, ensuring that the tab at array element 3 is paired with the page at page array element 3:

```
function setUp( ) {
    var divs = document.getElementsByTagName('div');
    var tabCount = 0;
    for (var i = 0; i < divs.length; i++) {
        if (divs[i].className == 'name') {
                tabs.addTab(divs[i]);
          } else if (divs[i].className == 'content') {
                tabs.addPanel(divs[i]);
        }
    }
    tabs.showPanel(0);
}
```

When the tab/panel pair is added, the tab element's click event handler is assigned a method, showPanel, which passes in the index of the tab that was clicked. When the tab is clicked, the following actions occur:

- The tab background color of the clicked tab changes to show the active color.
- The previously selected tab's background color is set to the inactive color.
- The current panel is hidden.
- The active tab's panel is displayed.

Example 5-7 shows the contents of the web page linked to the style sheet, the application-specific JavaScript, and the *addingajax.js* library.

Example 5-7. A simple tabbed page application

```
<!DOCTYPE html PUBLIC "-//W3C//DTD XHTML 1.0 Strict//EN"
    "http://www.w3.org/TR/xhtml1/DTD/xhtml1-strict.dtd">
<html xmlns="http://www.w3.org/1999/xhtml" lang="en" xml:lang="en">
<head>
<title>Tabbed Content</title>
<meta http-equiv="Content-Type" content="text/html; charset=utf-8" />
<link rel="stylesheet" href="tabbed.css" type="text/css" media="screen" />
<script type="text/javascript" src="addingajax.js">
</script>
<script type="text/javascript" src="tabbed.js">
</script>
</head>
<body>
    <form action="" method="get">
      <div class="container">
        <div class="tab">
          <div class="name">
            Name:
          </div>
```

Example 5-7. A simple tabbed page application (continued)

```
          <div class="name">
            Address:
          </div>

          <div class="name">
            Choice:
          </div>
        </div>

        <div class="elements">
          <div class="content" id="one">
            <fieldset>
              <legend>Name</legend> <label for="firstname">First Name:</label><br />
              <input type="text" name="firstname" id="firstname" /> <label
              for="lastname">Last Name:</label><br />
              <input type="text" name="lastname" id="lastname" />
            </fieldset>
          </div>

          <div class="content" id="two">
            <fieldset>
              <legend>Address</legend> <label for="street">Street Address:</label><br />
              <input type="text" name="street" id="street" /> <label
              for="city">City:</label><br />
              <input type="text" name="city" id="city" /> <label
              for="state">State:</label><br />
              <input type="text" name="state" id="state" />
            </fieldset>
          </div>

          <div class="content" id="three">
            <fieldset>
              <legend>Options</legend> <label for="opt1">Option 1</label><input
              type="checkbox" name="opt1" id="opt1" checked="checked" /> <label
              for="opt2">Option 2</label><input type="checkbox" name="opt2" id="opt2" />
              <label for="opt3">Option 3</label><input type="checkbox" name="opt3"
              id="opt3" /> <label for="opt4">Option 4</label><input type="checkbox"
              name="opt4" id="opt4" checked="checked" />
            </fieldset>
          </div>
        </div>
      </div>
    </form>
</body>
</html>
```

The JavaScript to manage the tabbed pages isn't too complicated and is shown in
Example 5-8. When the page is loaded, all the tabs and panels are accessed through
their class names and are added to the appropriate array, panel or tab. Since the
order between tab elements and panel elements is the same, even though they are

physically separated in the page, their order is the same when accessing the elements through the DOM. Clicking on the tab with the tab element's array index passed to the function displays the panel associated with that array index.

Example 5-8. Tabbed page JavaScript

```
aaManageEvent(window,"load",setUp);

function Tabs ( ) {
    current=0;
    tab = new Array( );
    panels = new Array( );
    this.addTab = function (tabItem) {
                        var index = tab.length;
                        tab[tab.length] = tabItem;
                        aaManageEvent(tabItem,"click",function( ) {
                                tabs.showPanel(index);});
                    };
    this.addPanel = function (panel) {
                        panels[panels.length] = panel;
                    };
    this.showPanel = function (index) {
                        panels[current].style.display="none";
                        tab[current].style.backgroundColor="#fff";
                        tab[index].style.backgroundColor="#ffc";
                        panels[index].style.display="block";
                        current = index;
                    };
}

tabs = new Tabs( );

function setUp( ) {
    var divs = document.getElementsByTagName('div');
    var tabCount = 0;
    for (var i = 0; i < divs.length; i++) {
        if (divs[i].className == 'name') {
            tabs.addTab(divs[i]);
        } else if (divs[i].className == 'content') {
            tabs.addPanel(divs[i]);
        }
    }
    tabs.showPanel(0);
}
```

The stylesheet layers the panels one on top of the other, and each is set to be invisible when the page is first opened. The background color of the tabs will change to reflect which tab is active:

```
    .container
    {
        margin: 30px;
```

```css
        padding: 10px;
}
.name
{
        border: 1px solid #000;
        display: inline;
        margin: 0;
        padding: 10px;
        text-align: center;
}
.elements
{
        background-color: #ffc;
        border: 1px solid #000;
        height: 200px;
        margin-top: 10px;
        width: 400px;
}
fieldset
{
        border: none;
        margin: 1px;
}
legend
{
         display: none;
}
.content
{
        display: none;
        margin: 10px;
}
.tab
{
        display: inline;
        margin: 0;
        padding: 0;
}
.footer
{
        clear: both;
}
input
{
        display: block;
        margin-bottom: 5px;
}
input[type="checkbox"]
{
        display: inline;
}
```

Figure 5-4 shows this new tabbed page effect.

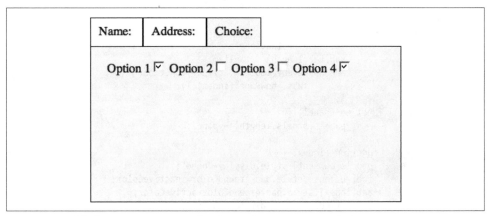

Figure 5-4. Tabbed page content created with JavaScript

To add server integration, the event handler for the tab `click` event could also pull in the data necessary to build the panel contents in a manner very similar to that demonstrated with the hybrid accordion example (Example 5-7) in the previous section. Chapter 9 uses tabbed pages to manage mashups and to demonstrate how to integrate the visual effect and the Ajax request.

To add more tabs to the application, just add more tab groupings within the page—the code doesn't have to change and can be packaged as-is and pulled into a second effect library, *tabs.js*, discussed in the next section.

Packaging Revisited: Creating Generic Tabs

As with the accordion, the tab portion of the application is generic enough that it can also be pulled out into a separate JavaScript library. The actual code, as shown in Example 5-9, could be used as-is in any application. The only requirement is that the page structure must reflect that demonstrated in Example 5-7. The CSS style settings also have to be maintained with the library and should be separated out into a new CSS file, but we'll leave it as-is for now.

We also don't have to use the background colors coded directly into the script. Instead, when the Tabs object is instantiated, the active and inactive background colors can be passed and stored as private members. Example 5-9 shows our *tabs.js* library in its entirety.

Example 5-9. Complete code for tabs.js

```
function Tabs (active,inactive) {
    current=0;
    tab = new Array();
    panels = new Array();
```

Example 5-9. Complete code for tabs.js (continued)

```
        activeColor = active;
        inactiveColor = inactive;
        this.addTab = function (tabItem) {
                        var index = tab.length;
                        tab[tab.length] = tabItem;
                        aaManageEvent(tabItem,"click",function( ) {
                                tabs.showPanel(index);});
                        };
        this.addPanel = function (panel) {
                        panels[panels.length] = panel;
                        };
        this.showPanel = function (index) {
                        panels[current].style.display="none";
                        tab[current].style.backgroundColor=inactiveColor;
                        tab[index].style.backgroundColor=activeColor;
                        panels[index].style.display="block";
                        current = index;
                        };
    }


function setUpTabs( ) {
    var divs = document.getElementsByTagName('div');
    var tabCount = 0;
    for (var i = 0; i < divs.length; i++) {
        if (divs[i].className == 'name') {
            tabs.addTab(divs[i]);
        } else if (divs[i].className == 'content') {
            tabs.addPanel(divs[i]);
        }
    }
    tabs.showPanel(0);
}
```

 In JavaScript, *object private members* are properties that are accessible only to methods of the object and not to code outside of the object. The presence or absence of this is what makes a member public or private.

To use the Tabs library, add a script element with a reference to the new library, create the page markup using the previously demonstrated structure, and instantiate the Tabs object:

```
    var tabs = new Tabs("#ccf","#fff");
```

That's it. You can adjust colors, style the fonts, change the size of the content blocks, and so on, and create as many tabbed pages as you like.

To interface Tabs with the Prototype library, the code can be modified to use Class.create to create the object and the bindAsEventListener to ensure the object context is passed to any event. You can also use a packaged library such as the Yahoo! UI for this effect instead of creating your own.

Using the YUI TabView

We haven't looked at the details of the Yahoo! UI library yet, and its TabView seems like a good introduction to one of its many higher-level effects.

 Download YUI, see examples, and read documentation at *http:// developer.yahoo.com/yui*.

Like other libraries, the YUI TabView uses list item (li) elements for the tabs, and typically uses div elements for the content. One advantage of this is that you don't have to access all of the page's div elements in order to discover the tabs:

```
<ul class="yui-nav">
  <li class="selected"><a href="#tab1">Name:</a></li>
  <li><a href="#tab2">Address:</a></li>
  <li><a href="#tab3">Choices:</a></li>
</ul>
```

Following is another div element with the individual panel entries, each included within its own div element. It's important to keep the panel elements in sync with the tabs because no identifiers are used; the elements are physically separated from each other, and they don't share a unique parent element.

Special classes are used to delimit the overall container (yui-navset), the navigation list (yui-nav), and the elements (yui-content). In addition, the overall container element is given an identifier. When the tabbed page is created, this identifier is passed to the function call to create the effect:

```
var myTabs = new YAHOO.widget.TabView("tabview");
```

Example 5-10 shows the entire page. As you can see, again we're looking at having to provide a lot less code when using a packaged higher-level effect. The YUI is also relatively well-documented, including where to add functionality to integrate web service requests and other behaviors into the effect.

Example 5-10. YUI-based TabView tabbed page content

```
<!DOCTYPE html PUBLIC "-//W3C//DTD XHTML 1.0 Strict//EN"
    "http://www.w3.org/TR/xhtml1/DTD/xhtml1-strict.dtd">
<html xmlns="http://www.w3.org/1999/xhtml" lang="en" xml:lang="en">
<head>
<title>Tabbed Content</title>
<meta http-equiv="Content-Type" content="text/html; charset=utf-8" />
```

Example 5-10. YUI-based TabView tabbed page content (continued)

```
<link rel="stylesheet" href="yui/build/tabview/assets/tabs.css" type="text/css" />
<link rel="stylesheet" href="yui/build/tabview/assets/border_tabs.css" type="text/css" />

<script type="text/javascript" src="yui/build/yahoo/yahoo.js">
</script>
<script type="text/javascript" src="yui/build/dom/dom.js">
</script>
<script type="text/javascript" src="yui/build/event/event.js">
</script>

<script type="text/javascript" src="yui/build/tabview/tabview.js">
</script>

<script type="text/javascript">
//<![CDATA[

var myTabs = new YAHOO.widget.TabView("tabview");

//]]>
</script>
</head>
<body>
<form action="GET">
<div id="tabview" class="yui-navset">
<ul class="yui-nav">
  <li class="selected"><a href="#tab1">Name:</a></li>
  <li><a href="#tab2">Address:</a></li>
  <li><a href="#tab3">Choices:</a></li>
</ul>
<div class="yui-content">
<div>
<label for="firstname">First Name:</label><br /><input type="text" id="firstname"
name="firstname" /><br /><br />
<label for="lastname">Last Name:</label><br /><input type="text" id="lastname"
name="lastname" /><br /><br />
</div>

<div>
<label for="street">Street Address:</label><br /><input type="text" id="street"
name="street" /><br /><br />
<label for="city">City:</label><br /><input type="text" id="city" name="city" /><br /><br
/>
<label for="state">State:</label><br /><input type="text" id="state" name="state" /><br />
<br />
</div>
```

Example 5-10. YUI-based TabView tabbed page content (continued)

```
<div>
<input type="checkbox" id="opt1" name="opt1" checked="checked" /><label for="opt1">
XXXXXXX</label><br />
<input type="checkbox" id="opt2" name="opt2"  /><label for="opt2">XX XXXXXX</label><br />
<input type="checkbox" id="opt3" name="opt3"  /><label for="opt3">X X XXXXX</label><br />
<input type="checkbox" id="opt4" name="opt4" checked="checked" /><label for="opt4">X
XXXXX</label><br />
</div>

</div>
</div>
</form>
</body>
</html>
```

The only thing I don't care for with the YUI TabView *widget*, as its developers call the effect, is that it doesn't look that great straight out of the box. Figure 5-5 shows a page using the YUI widget.

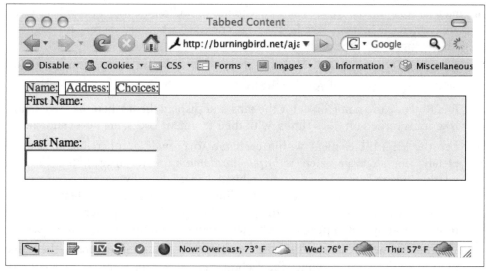

Figure 5-5. Tabbed content created using the YUI TabView widget

Of course, this can all be modified in the CSS, since classes are used to mark each of the components of the tabbed content.

I tend to call packaged behaviors "effects," but others call them "widgets" based on Apple's and other companies' reference to bits of packaged code and visual elements that can be "plugged" into an environment. However, widgets are also used to denote a complete object that can be included as-is in a web page and usually requests data from a remote resource. In fact, "widget" is becoming a fairly universal term in Ajax development.

That's why I don't like to use the term "widget"—it has too many connotations, and I'm concerned about the confusion surrounding the term. When I say "Ajax effect," it's unique to this particular environment. However, to each their own. Just be aware that when many Ajax developers use "widget," it's equivalent to the "Ajax effect" used in this book.

Tabbed Content and Accessibility

In Example 5-10, the YUI tabbed content features hypertext links around the tab names, each of which calls a URL fragment, such as *#tab1*. By using the link, the tabs are made accessible to keyboard action. The use of the fragment just provides a clean response when the link is clicked—the page stays as-is, because there is no fragment in with the specified name in the page.

For those who have JavaScript turned off, though, the use of tabbed page content should degrade gracefully if you use the following nonscript workaround:

1. Initially hide the name links for the tabs and display them when the page loads. If script is turned off, these links, with their fragment URLs, are never shown.

2. Use the NOSCRIPT element within each tab to provide another link to a completely separate page, such as *http://somedomain.com/formpage2.htm*. Clicking on the link will then display the tabbed "page" literally as a separate page. Another approach could be to add the link into the content and then use JavaScript to remove the link when the page is loaded. This is a preferable approach from the standpoint of progressive enhancement, but it does require more script.

3. For this example, there will be three pages. The first page will have the name portion of the form showing, the second page will display the address component, and the third page will display the choices. Store each interim component of the form in an interim data store on the server when the reader leaves the page to go to another page. If the form contents aren't all provided over a certain period of time, discard the contents after an interval.

4. A simpler approach—and simpler is good, we want simpler—could be to just display the entire contents of the form in the page when the page is opened, and use script to completely rearrange the page layout.

The pages that are displayed for each link in the workaround don't have to be static if your content management system uses some form of redirects based on URL.

Regardless of whether these new pages are generated or static, or if you just display the entire form in one page, the approach just given allows those who have script turned off to access all of the form components.

Overlays

Overlay effects load new content over the page based on some action. I, and others, use the term "overlay" because the new content is removed from the page flow completely, being positioned on top of the page through the use of absolute positioning. The overlays can stretch to cover the entire page, or can appear as a small box that is either inserted in or moving across the page.

Yes, these are also known as *pop-ups* and we're not fond of these. However, the functionality can be used for more than just creating a pop-up (and even a traditional pop-up can be useful if used more to help your web page readers than hide content from them). The overlay that is opened on top of the page can include a warning message, a form to fill in, the results of a query, or even, as demonstrated in this section, a larger size picture when the page reader clicks a thumbnail image.

In my web site, I use an image library to open up a larger image from a smaller thumbnail. It first overlays the page with an element that has an opaque filter so that the page contents don't distract from the picture.

When the page is first loaded, a JavaScript setup function grabs the page contents and wraps them, whatever they are, within a div element. It also adds a second div element containing an img element that is located outside of this wrapper element:

```
function setUp( ) {
   // add page container and image container
   var oldBody = document.body.innerHTML;
   document.body.innerHTML = "<div id='mtwCover'>" + oldBody +
                             "</div>" +
                             "<div id='mtwPicture'>" +
                             "<img id='mtwPictureimage' src='" + workingImage + "'
alt='' /></div>";


   var elem = elementClass = null;
   for (i = 0; i < document.images.length; i++) {
      elem = document.images[i];
      elementClass = elem.getAttribute("class");
      elementClass = elementClass ? elementClass : elem.getAttribute("className");
      if (elementClass == 'thumb') {
         elem.onclick=expandPic;
      }
   }

   // add event handler for image
   document.getElementById('mtwPicture').onclick=restore;

}
```

To provide a clue that the images can be expanded, CSS is used to provide a background "magnifier" image, and the img element is padded on the bottom to allow this magnifier icon to show. This class, .thumb, must be given to each thumbnail image:

```
.thumb
{
    background-image: url(magnify.gif);
    background-position: right bottom;
    background-repeat: no-repeat;
    border: 1px solid #000;
    margin: 0;
    padding-bottom: 25px;
}
```

I like this approach because no script is necessary to mark an image as expandable—it's all handled through class names.

Figure 5-6 shows a page with several thumbnails from one of my web sites, each using the thumb class.

Figure 5-6. Initial page with several thumbnail images, each using the thumb class

When a web page reader clicks a thumbnail image, the wrapper element's opacity is set to make it semitransparent, obscuring but not completely hiding the page contents. The src attribute of the img element is set to the image to be loaded, and it is resized to the size of the new image. In addition, the current scrolled position of the page is computed so that when the new image is opened, it's opened within the correct spot—the web page reader doesn't once have to scroll the page to see the expanded photo or to return to his original position:

```
// find photo position
var pos = 0;
if (window.pageYOffset) {
   pos = window.pageYOffset;
} else if (document.documentElement && document.documentElement.scrollTop) {
   pos = document.documentElement.scrollTop
} else if (document.body) {
   pos = document.body.scrollTop;
}
```

When the web page reader clicks an expanded photo, the photo is hidden, the overlay element is set to be completely transparent, and the page is returned to normal. The expanded photo has a "close box" image at the top, using the same approach used to add the magnifier to the thumbnail—CSS sets the background of the image to the close box, and padding at the top exposes this image.

The JavaScript file that managed the photo overlay is shown in Example 5-11. It's dependent on the *addingajax.js* library for event management. Note that it uses an animated GIF, which is set at the top of the file. This is what's loaded into the img element when it's first opened for display as the other image is being loaded. It provides a working animation that, again, doesn't require any JavaScript. You can set this image to any animated image (or no image) that you prefer.

Example 5-11. The img.js file that provides for an expanded photo overlay in the page

```
// global values, you may change these
var workingImage = "cogs04.gif";

aaManageEvent(window,'load',setUp);

// cross-browser adjust opacity function
function setOpacity(obj,val) {
  obj.style.opacity = val;
  obj.style.MozOpacity=val;
  obj.style.KhtmlOpacity=val;
  val*=100;
  obj.style.filter = "alpha(opacity="+val+")";
}

//
// Gets keycode. If 'x' is pressed then it hides the larger image.
//
function getKey(evnt){
    evnt = (evnt) ? evnt : ((window.event) ? window.event : "");
    var keycode = (evnt.which) ? evnt.which : evnt.keyCode;
    var key = String.fromCharCode(keycode).toLowerCase( );
    if(key == 'x'){ restore( ); }
}
```

```
// Adds 'wrapper' element to page contents
// Finds all images on the page with 'thumb' class
// adds click event handlers for each
// adds click event handler for the expanded picture element
//   added as part of the setup process
function setUp( ) {
    // add page container and image container
    var oldBody = document.body.innerHTML;
    document.body.innerHTML = "<div id='mtwCover'>" + oldBody +
                              "</div>" +
                              "<div id='mtwPicture'>" +
                              "<img id='mtwPictureimage' src='" + workingImage + "' alt=''
/></div>";
    var elem = elementClass = null;
    for (i = 0; i < document.images.length; i++) {
        elem = document.images[i];
        elementClass = elem.getAttribute("class");
        elementClass = elementClass ? elementClass : elem.getAttribute("className");
        if (elementClass == 'thumb') {
            elem.onclick=expandPic;
        }
    }

    // add event handler for image
    document.getElementById('mtwPicture').onclick=restore;

}

// expand the photo
//     adds keypress event handling for keyboard management
//     opaques the page 'wrapper' to obscure the page contents
//     determines the scrolled position of the clicked image
//     sets the expanded picture frame to this position
//     sets the image to the new image
function expandPic(evnt) {

    aaManageEvent(document,'keypress',getKey);

    evnt = (evnt) ? evnt : ((window.event) ? window.event : "");
    // find photo position
    var pos = 0;
    if (window.pageYOffset) {
        pos = window.pageYOffset;
    } else if (document.documentElement && document.documentElement.scrollTop) {
        pos = document.documentElement.scrollTop
    } else if (document.body) {
        pos = document.body.scrollTop;
    }

    var evntTarget = (evnt.target) ? evnt.target : evnt.srcElement;
```

```
    // discover image src name
    var oParent = evntTarget.parentNode;

    document.images['mtwPictureimage'].src=oParent;
  // fade background, display expanded image
    var obj = document.getElementById('mtwPicture');
    obj.style.top = pos + "px";
    var cover = document.getElementById('mtwCover');
    setOpacity(cover,.1);
    obj.style.visibility='visible';

    // end event bubbling
    return false;
}


// restore
// stops listening for keypress for this application
// sets wrapper element to be completely transparent
// resets picture frame image back to the 'working' image
// hides the picture frame element
function restore() {

    aaStopEvent(document,'keypress',getKey);

    // restore opacity
    var cover = document.getElementById('mtwCover');
    setOpacity(cover,1.0);
    cover.style.backgroundColor="transparent";
    var obj = document.getElementById('mtwPicture');

    // unhide image and clear img
    obj.style.visibility='hidden';
    document.images['mtwPictureimage'].src=workingImage;
}
```

To make the example keyboard accessible, a hypertext link to the larger image is placed around the thumbnail. We can also add in keyboard access so that when the web page reader clicks the x button on the expanded photo, the photo is hidden, and the page returns to normal:

```
    //
    // Gets keycode. If 'x' is pressed then it hides the larger image.
    //
    function getKey(evnt){
        evnt = evnt ? evnt : window.event;
        var keycode = evnt.which ? evnt.which : evnt.keyCode;
        var key = String.fromCharCode(keycode).toLowerCase();
        if(key == 'x'){ restore(); }
    }
```

```
// listens for keypress event
//
function listenKey () {

    if (document.addEventListener) {
       document.addEventListener("keypress",getKey,false);
    } else if (document.attachEvent) {
       document.attachEvent("onkeypress",getKey);
    } else {
       document.onkeypress = getKey;
    }
}

// stops listening for keypress event
//
function stopListenKey() {
    if (document.removeEventListener) {
       document.removeEventListener("keypress",getKey,false);
    } else if (document.detachEvent) {
       document.detachEvent("onkeypress",getKey);
    } else {
       document.onkeypress = '';
    }
}
```

Also note that the expansion and restoration procedures are assigned directly to the
onclick property:

```
document.getElementById('mtwPicture').onclick=restore;
```

The reason we're not using the more "mash"-friendly event handling is that we don't
want to have other applications doing their own thing when users click on the image.
This image expansion works best when it works alone. Ajax effects don't have to
work in conjunction with others; as long as the web page developer is aware of what
the effect is doing, it doesn't have to play well with other code.

To add the photo expansion functionality, all we have to do is add the following to
the page:

```
<link type="text/css" rel="stylesheet" href="img.css" />

<script type="text/javascript" src="addingajax.js">
</script>
<script type="text/javascript" src="img.js">
</script>
```

To make an image eligible for expansion, just add the thumb class:

```
<a href="robin1.jpg"><img src="robin1thumb.jpg" alt="robin in tree" class="thumb" />
</a>
```

This is a very unobtrusive effect, requiring little work on the part of the person adding it to her applications. In addition, it validates as XHTML and CSS, and is 100 percent accessible, and that's the way we want our Ajax applications to work.

There hasn't been a great deal of what is thought to be "Ajax" in this chapter—only one of the examples actually makes a web service request. However, web service requests are only part of the equation; processing the request is the other part, and that includes providing a place for the results and a way to manage lots of data in small spaces.

CHAPTER 6
Dynamic Data

Ajax has had a significant impact on traditional web approaches to data retrieval and updates. You realize this the first time you edit information on a web page "in-place" or delete a row of data without the page reloading. Implementing dynamic data updates and queries through Ajax can have the greatest positive impact on your web applications.

Among the different categories of Ajax-enabled dynamic data effects are:

- In-place editing
- Instant reflection of new or newly updated data
- Autocompletion in text fields
- Context-specific selection lists
- Immediate removal of deleted data

The data update effects such as in-place editing and instant deletions are also easy to manage when scripting is disabled, just by providing links to forms for doing more traditional updates. These links can be added in NOSCRIPT elements, but a better approach is to provide these nonscripting solutions as an option for every user, script-enabled or not. Providing more than one way to update data is actually seen as a customer service, so in this instance, Ajax and accessibility go hand in hand.

In addition to data updates, Ajax can also be used to enhance data querying and display through the use of autocompletion of search terms or by providing the ability to sort data using drag-and-drop functionality. Visual effects can be used to specifically highlight certain aspects of the data, though you have to be careful to ensure that important information doesn't depend solely on a visual effect.

Although there is no limit to what you can do with Ajax and a database, there are performance issues associated with any database application, particularly with the number of connections between any individual and the server, and between the application and the database. As we explore the different Ajax effects in this chapter, we'll look at some of these performance issues and at some of the tricks we can use to make sure our applications don't bog down, such as using multiple domains and caching.

We'll also look at security issues as we progress through the sections. Your web site's most vulnerable point is through database access via a public web page, regardless of whether the access is through a traditional web form or via Ajax calls. However, a bit of common sense in addition to your other database protection techniques is typically all you'll need.

In-Place Editing

My favorite Ajax dynamic data update technique is in-place editing. This technique gives web page readers with editing permissions the ability to "live edit" a page's modifiable fields without having to go to a separate web page or form.

I first saw this used with Flickr, a photo-sharing site at *http://flickr.com*, and I still think it's one of the better implementations. To edit a photo title, you click on the title and it immediately turns into a text box, complete with Save and Cancel buttons underneath. The same goes for modifying the description and adding tags. You are informed that this in-place editing option is available when you move your mouse over the description area—text is displayed with information about clicking the area to edit or add a description. Moving the mouse cursor over the title changes the background color of the title. There is a permanent visible label with "Add a tag" for the tags.

What makes all of this accessible, though, is the link to a more traditional web form. By providing both, in-place editing and a traditional web form, users with scripting enabled can choose how they want to edit their data. It might be preferable to use in-place editing to correct a title, but to use the web form to make modifications to several fields.

That's the key to truly successful in-place editing: provide a link to traditional editing and make the in-place editing unobtrusive.

Adding an Editable Field

Making a field into one that can be edited isn't particularly difficult, especially since you can layer context, and hide and display the different layers based on a mouse event or other action. I prefer to use the CSS display attribute rather than visibility, as content that follows in the vertical page flow moves up or down depending on whether the editable form fields are displayed or not.

What's critical in this type of Ajax effect is ensuring that only the users with editing permissions can edit the data. If the in-place editing takes place in a protected page, this isn't an issue. Typically, though, in-place editing occurs in a page that can be accessed by both users with edit permissions and users with read-only permissions. Web cookies offer a way to make sure the right users (and only the right users) are editing.

Most web applications that have an administrative component use web cookies to store the application user's login information and state. Persisting the client information makes it simpler to access the edit features—the application user doesn't have to continually log in every time he wants to make an edit. These same cookies can be used to determine if the field or fields can be made editable directly within the page.

After the fields have been made editable, and the user has made his edits, the next step in adding Ajax in-place editing is to process the change using an Ajax service request, and then return the page to its pre-edit state. This typically means that the server component of the application also has to be altered, to allow for web edit requests in addition to its traditional form processing.

To demonstrate this technique, and the others in this chapter, we'll be using a real database with real data—the database that manages my weblog, built on the Word-Press weblogging system—after making a copy of the database first, of course, so that we can test the data editing with impunity. When you're trying these examples on your own, you can use whatever database you have handy, ensuring that you first make a copy so that you don't accidentally hurt your real data. You'll just need to change the backend portion of the examples demonstrated here to fit whatever data you have.

 There is no sample database provided here, but if you have access to a web server with PHP enabled, WordPress is a simple application to install. Once installed, you can quickly create some example weblog posts in order to try out the examples shown in this chapter and in the subsequent chapters. You can download WordPress from *http://wordpress.org*.

There has to be a good level of cooperation between the server and the client for in-place editing to function properly. The server part of the application verifies that the user has edit permissions on the fields, information that is used to provide some indication to the client side to add the appropriate event handling.

On the client side, when there is an indication that the user has edit capability, the easiest approach to adding in-place editing is to make whatever is to be edited sensitive to whatever event triggers this process. Sometimes this can be a mouseover event, which changes the background color of the item, but more often, clicking on the item in question will open the editable interface.

In-place editing requires a fair bit of code, and you can't get around that. You can package up most of it into a library—in fact you should for reusability, but expect to put some time into coding this particular effect. I do think it's worth it, though.

First, before we get directly into the code, we're going to revisit the Ajax library in development, *addingajax.js*. In previous chapters, we added functions to create an XMLHttpRequest object and to manage events. Now, we'll add the aaElem function, which simplifies the process of accessing a specific element from the document given an element identifier:

```
function aaElem(identifier) {
    return document.getElementById(identifier);
}
```

The applications don't require this function—we're not adding custom properties or methods (though we could at some later point). After a while, though, as you'll see in the next example, you can get tired of writing out document.getElementById(id). All the aaElem function does, for now, is simplify the code.

Diving into the Client

In our example, the application loads the title and content for a given post. The identifier for the post is accessed through a traditional form, and the resulting title and content are printed on the page. Both the title and the content can be edited in place if the user accessing the page is currently signed into the weblog as the owner of the post and a if cookie with the user's username and password has been stored on the client.

Figure 6-1 shows the page with a newly loaded post. It appears the same whether you have editing capability or not.

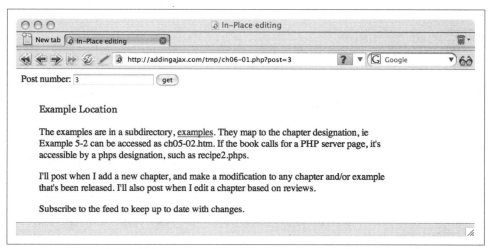

Figure 6-1. Page with data before in-place editing is activated

The web page is a mixture of server-side code and HTML (or in this example, XHTML), as is common for most web applications. The server-side code, in this case

PHP, provides the filler for the page content. In most framework applications, the integration between server and client can occur either through template tags or actual code. In Example 6-1, it's the actual code. The database query is processed before the page markup, and PHP embedded throughout the markup displays the actual data.

Example 6-1. Web page with PHP server-side code, and XHTML markup

```php
<?php

// connect to database and query for post, if post is given
mysql_connect('localhost','username','password');
mysql_select_db('database');

$post = $_REQUEST['post'];
$rows = mysql_query("select post_title, comment_status, ping_status,
post_content from wp_posts where ID='$post'");

?>
<!DOCTYPE html PUBLIC "-//W3C//DTD XHTML 1.0 Strict//EN"
    "http://www.w3.org/TR/xhtml1/DTD/xhtml1-strict.dtd">
<html xmlns="http://www.w3.org/1999/xhtml" lang="en" xml:lang="en">
<head>
<meta http-equiv="Content-Type" content="text/html; charset=utf-8" />
<title>In-Place editing</title>
<link rel="stylesheet" href="data.css" type="text/css" media="screen" />

<script type="text/javascript">
//<![CDATA[
<?php

require_once('./perms.php');

?>
//]]>
</script>
<script type="text/javascript" src="addingajax.js">
</script>
<script type="text/javascript" src="data1.js">
</script>

</head>
<body>
<form action="ch06-01.php">
<div>
<label for="post">Post number:</label> <input type="text" name="post" id="post"
value="<?php echo $post; ?>" />
<input type="submit" value="get" />
</div>
</form>

<div id="wrapper">
<div id="title">
```

Example 6-1. Web page with PHP server-side code, and XHTML markup (continued)

```
<label for="titleinput">Title:</label><input type="text" id="titleinput" /><br /><br />
<span class="button" id="savetitle" >Save</span><span class="button" id="canceltitle">
Cancel</span>
</div>
<?php

    if(($rows) && mysql_num_rows($rows) > 0) {
        while($row = mysql_fetch_row($rows)) {
?>
<div id="printtitle"><?php echo $row[0]; ?></div>
<div id="printcontent"><?php echo $row[3]; ?></div>
<?php
        }
    } else {
?>
<div id="printtitle"></div>
<div id="printcontent"></div>
<?php } ?>
<div id="content">
<textarea cols="80" rows="10" id="contenttext"></textarea><br /><br />
<span class="button" id="savecontent">Save</span><span class="button" id="cancelcontent">
Cancel</span>
</div>
</div>
<div id="message">
</div>
</body>
</html>

</body>
</html>
```

The only other PHP code in the page is a reference to another PHP application file, *perms.php*, which is discussed more fully in the next section. For now, know that all this application does is check if the person is the owner of the data, and if they are, sets a JavaScript variable, canedit to true.

> Many framework applications, such as WordPress, have a variable already set flagging whether the user is the owner or can edit a post, and you won't have to do all this work. Again, you'll want to incorporate the in-place editing features within your framework's existing functionality.

In the web page in Example 6-1, the form elements to enable in-place editing are included in the page directly following the actual printed text of either the title or the content. In the stylesheet, *data.css*, these are initially not displayed:

```
#title
{
        display: none;
        margin-bottom: 20px;
        width: 400px;
}
#wrapper
{
        background-color: #fff;
        margin: 20px;
        padding: 10px;
        width: 600px;
}
#printtitle
{
        font-family: Georgia, Verdana;
        margin-bottom: 20px;
}
#printcontent, content
{
        line-height: 120%;
}
#content
{
        display: none;
}
#title input, textarea
{
        background-color: #ffffd3;
        color: #000;
}
.button
{
        background-color: #ccccff;
        border: 1px solid #009;
        padding: 5px;
}
```

In the application's JavaScript, if the canedit variable is set to true, event handlers are assigned to capture events to certain elements, including ones to use a change the background color when the mouse cursor hovers over the elements containing data that can be edited, and to capture the click event for these elements. When in-place editing is enabled, each field will be accompanied by Save and Cancel buttons that will allow users to save an edit or cancel the edit and return the page to normal appearance, respectively. Summarizing the activity:

1. The server sets a canedit variable to true if the user can edit the fields.

2. A mouseover event handler is used for each field to change the background color of the field when the mouse cursor hovers over it.

3. A click event handler is assigned to each field.

4. When the user clicks a field, it's converted into an editable field, complete with Save and Cancel buttons. When users clicking the Save button, the application will update the database and print a message to the owner that the update has occurred. Conversely, when users click the Cancel button, the application returns to the page to its normal nonedit view.

Example 6-2 shows the application-specific JavaScript file, *data1.js*.

Example 6-2. In-place editing of two fields, title and content

```javascript
var xmlhttp;

// setup the request to update the data
function sendChange(params) {
  if (!xmlhttp) xmlhttp = aaGetXmlHttpRequest();
  var url = 'http://addingajax.com/tmp/process.php';
  xmlhttp.open('POST', url, true);
  xmlhttp.onreadystatechange = processResponse;
  xmlhttp.setRequestHeader('Content-Type',
    'application/x-www-form-urlencoded');
  xmlhttp.send(params);
}

// process response
function processResponse() {
  if(xmlhttp.readyState == 4 && xmlhttp.status==200) {
      var resp=xmlhttp.responseText;
      var txt = document.createTextNode(resp);
      aaElem("message").appendChild(txt);
  }
}

// add click events to all the relevant div elements
aaManageEvent(window,'load', function () {
          if (canedit) {
            aaManageEvent(aaElem('printtitle'),'click',setTitleEdit);
            aaManageEvent(aaElem('printcontent'),'click',setContentEdit);
            aaManageEvent(aaElem('printtitle'),'mouseover',setHover);
            aaManageEvent(aaElem('printcontent'),'mouseover',setHover);
            aaManageEvent(aaElem('printtitle'),'mouseout',setHoverOff);
            aaManageEvent(aaElem('printcontent'),'mouseout',setHoverOff);
            aaManageEvent(aaElem('savetitle'),'click',saveTitle);
            aaManageEvent(aaElem('canceltitle'),'click',cancelTitle);
            aaManageEvent(aaElem('savecontent'),'click',saveContent);
            aaManageEvent(aaElem('cancelcontent'),'click',cancelContent);
          }
      });

// setup title in-place edit
function setTitleEdit() {
```

Example 6-2. In-place editing of two fields, title and content (continued)

```
    // set text
    var obj = aaElem("printtitle");
    var txt = obj.firstChild.nodeValue;
    aaElem("titleinput").value = txt;

    // switch displays
    obj.style.display="none";
    aaElem("title").style.display="block";
}

// setup content for in-place edit
function setContentEdit( ) {

    // set text
    var obj = aaElem("printcontent");
    var txt = obj.innerHTML;
    aaElem("contenttext").value=txt;

    // switch displays
    obj.style.display="none";
    aaElem("content").style.display="block";
}

function setHover(evnt) {
    evnt = evnt ? evnt : window.event;
    var eventTarget = evnt.target ? evnt.target : evnt.srcElement;

    eventTarget.style.backgroundColor="#ccffff";
}

function setHoverOff(evnt) {
    evnt = evnt ? evnt : window.event;
    var eventTarget = evnt.target ? evnt.target : evnt.srcElement;

    eventTarget.style.backgroundColor="#ffffff";
}
// cancel title in-place editing
function cancelTitle( ) {
    aaElem("title").style.display="none";
    aaElem("printtitle").style.display="block";
}

// save the title changes
function saveTitle( ) {

    var post = aaElem('post').value;
    var title = aaElem('titleinput').value;
    var params = "post=" + post + "&title=" + encodeURI(title) + "&changetype=title";

    sendChange(params);

    aaElem("printtitle").firstChild.nodeValue=title;
```

Example 6-2. In-place editing of two fields, title and content (continued)

```
        aaElem("printtitle").style.display="block";
        aaElem("title").style.display="none";
}

// cancel content in-place editing
function cancelContent( ) {
        aaElem("content").style.display="none";
        aaElem("printcontent").style.display="block";
}

// save the content changes
function saveContent( ) {

        var post = aaElem('post').value;
        var content = aaElem('contenttext').value;
        var params = "post=" + post + "&content=" + encodeURI(content) + "&changetype=content";

        sendChange(params);

        aaElem("content").style.display="none";
        aaElem("printcontent").style.display="block";
        aaElem("printcontent").innerHTML=aaElem("contenttext").value;

}
```

One minor modification to the code could be to use CSS classes instead of setting the style property directly, but that's more a matter of style than necessity.

The code hopefully demonstrates that there's nothing inherently difficult about in-place editing, it's just a little tedious, as there are lots of little bits of functionality. The sendChange function manages the Ajax call to update either the title or the content. The parameters are sent through to this function by the process that manages the title and content editing. Since this is a data update, the request is sent as a POST. Post-request processing prints out either an update message or an error, if there is one.

For the in-place editing, the text of the printed area is accessed and the in-place editing form elements are set to the corresponding text. The title is a simple text string, and the DOM is used to pull in this value, but innerHTML is used with the content area. This is a bit of a shortcut in this code, and for a true XHTML application, you should iterate through all of the childnodes of the object, concatenating the result because the content area will stretch across more than one node, especially if there's a link or image or such in the text.

Another approach to pulling the data from the display is to fill the input elements when the page is loaded, using the same PHP that fills in the page. However, the content or title could be edited more than once in a session, and by filling in the value from the display, the in-place editing is using the most current text. Figure 6-2 shows the web page with in-place editing in effect.

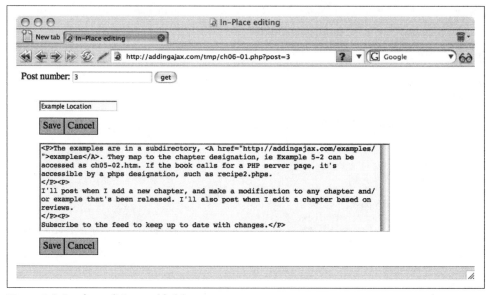

Figure 6-2. In-place editing enabled for a page

When the in-place editing is canceled, it's a simple matter to just hide the in-place form elements and show the printed text. If the title or content edits are saved, the new text is accessed and the function is called to perform an Ajax update.

The application prints out a message that an update (or error) has occurred. Although this is not a requirement, it's good to provide some notice that the update has happened. A yellow color fade could signal success, and a red fade could signal failure. Again, none of this ever shows up on the page for users who don't have permission to edit.

Though not as important for understanding the Ajax client component, the next section provides a look at the behind-the-scenes PHP processing. However, your own application will have its own unique quirks about checking for edit privileges and accessing data (as well as incorporating these items into whatever templates you might be using for your site). The next section includes the server code for completeness, but you could skip the section and continue on with the remainder of the chapter, where we discuss performance, security, and accessibility.

The Server Side of the Application

The server side of this application is based on a WordPress application, so I used the WordPress cookies in order to test the validity of the user. WordPress uses an encryption of the site directory to ensure that the username and password are unique, so we have to do the same for our own application. The password also uses a double encryption; when we pull the password from the database, we have to use the

MD5 encryption function on it before comparing it to the one pulled in from the cookie. Example 6-3 includes the *checkperms.php* function.

Example 6-3. The checkperms.php reader permission check function

```php
<?php

function getPermission( ) {
  $canedit = false;
  $cookiehash = md5('http://addingajax.com');
  define('COOKIEHASH', $cookiehash);

  if ( !defined('USER_COOKIE') )
      define('USER_COOKIE', 'wordpressuser_'. COOKIEHASH);
  if ( !defined('PASS_COOKIE') )
      define('PASS_COOKIE', 'wordpresspass_'. COOKIEHASH);

  if (isset($_COOKIE[USER_COOKIE])) {
      $user =  $_COOKIE[USER_COOKIE];
  }

  if (isset($_COOKIE[PASS_COOKIE])) {
      $pass = $_COOKIE[PASS_COOKIE];
  }

  $conn = mysql_connect('localhost','username','password');
  mysql_select_db('database');

  if ($user && $pass) {
      $result = mysql_query("select ID, user_login, user_pass from wp_users where user_
login = '$user'");

      if($result) {
        while($row = mysql_fetch_row($result)) {

          if ($pass == md5($row[2])) {
              $canedit = true;
          }
        }
      }
    }
  mysql_close($conn);
  return $canedit;
  }
}
?>
```

The *perms.php* application just calls this function and then prints out whether the user can edit it or not:

```php
<?php

require_once("./checkperms.php");

$canedit = getPermission( );
```

```
    if ($canedit) {
        echo "var canedit = true";
    } else {
        echo "var canedit = false";
    }
    ?>
```

The PHP program that processes the requests is pretty simple: pull in the posted data, make the update, and provide the feedback, as shown in Example 6-4.

Example 6-4. Process the Ajax requests

```
<?php

$post = $_POST['post'];
$content = $_POST['content'];
$title = $_POST['title'];
$change = $_POST['changetype'];

mysql_connect('localhost','username','password');
mysql_select_db('database');

if ($change == 'title') {
    $str = "update wp_posts set post_title = '$title' where ID = '$post'";
} else if ($change == 'content') {
    $str="update wp_posts set post_content = '$content' where ID = '$post'";
}

$result = mysql_query($str);

if ($result) {
    printf("Number of rows updated: %d\n",mysql_affected_rows());
} else {
    echo mysql_error();
}
?>
```

Of course, with your application, you'll probably want to provide friendlier error messages and put tighter controls on the security of the data used in the update, but that's the type of thing you need to do with any web application, Ajax or not. Again, the thing that's important to remember is to use POST rather than GET to get the data with the Ajax request. Otherwise, your application is pretty vulnerable. We'll discuss vulnerability, security, and accessibility next.

In-Place Editing: Performance, Security, and Accessibility

Anytime you add editing capability to the page, you run the risk of opening your application to unwanted access. However, with most applications, the framework is such that you can protect the in-place editing as much as you can any other editing.

The only thing you can't do is to protect the page itself. At least, not if you're adding in-place editing to a page that other people can access.

Example 6-3 used WordPress cookies, and the in-place editing is going to be as secure as WordPress editing is generally. That's good. Now, where it can be especially vulnerable is in the edit processing. The fact that we're using a POST helps, but we could add another level of security by again testing the validity of the user making the edit before saving it. Though not featured in the application, you'll also want to check to ensure that no SQL has been appended to the data, to prevent any form of SQL injection hack.

Preventing SQL Injection

Most of an application's vulnerabilities exist regardless of whether you're using Ajax or not. However, as you use Ajax, such vulnerabilities may become more apparent. One is the SQL injection.

An SQL injection occurs when nefarious users attach a bit of SQL at the end of the text or in place of the text within a form input field. However, as you begin to incorporate Ajax more and more into the application, such vulnerabilities may become more acute. One such vulnerability is known as SQL injections.

```
x' where ID = '1'; DROP TABLE wp_users; update wp_posts set post_title='x
```

Now, when this is used in the PHP program shown in Example 6-3, if you just plop in the passed value without any additional effort, what you end up with is a SQL statement like the following:

```
update wp_posts set post_title = 'x' where ID = '1'; DROP TABLE wp_users; update wp_
posts set post_title = 'x' where ID = '$post'
```

Since the SQL is concatenated and multiple SQL statements can be processed through one mysql_query, ouch!—you've just lost your user table.

Of course, in situations like this, your user should be a validated user anyway, and we can't necessarily see a validated owner of the data doing this, but cookies have been cracked in the past and will be cracked in the future.

Instead of processing the text sent to the web request as is, run it through whatever application function typically used to strip away possibly harmful material like what what was just shown. Most of the functions associated with your web application or framework that work for traditional web updates can also work with Ajax requests.

Performance and Accessibility

The use of in-place editing can actually be better for overall performance than having to pull up the regular editing form. A traditional form probably pulls in a lot more information and resources than we need for a simple one-field edit. For instance, with a weblog, it's easier and requires less resources to correct small typos in the title or content in the displayed page than it would be to go to the weblog's formal edit page. Conversely, you'd be better going with the full application for any detailed changes or rewrites, or when you're making changes to both the title and the description, as well as other fields.

It's important to remember that you do have to process the updates through the framework's own functions if you want post-edit functionality, such as formatting the data in special ways.

If you use your application framework's own database caching, there's no real additional draw on the system to check the validity of the user accessing the page—most applications do this anyway. In Example 6-3, this functionality is already a part of WordPress, and many weblogs use a special function to put an "Edit this post" link with the post to open it immediately in the edit page. It's just an additional small step to add in-place editing.

As for accessibility, the link to edit the post within the more formal environment is also available, which means that the effect should be completely accessible—at least as accessible as the regular edit form. This could be hidden in a NOSCRIPT element, but I wouldn't recommend it; in-place editing is an addition to more formal editing, and the latter should be available regardless of whether scripting is enabled or what type of user agent is used to access the page.

Improvements

You can easily make in-place editing available in more than one page, by packaging the code for reusability. The photo expansion application shown in Chapter 5 demonstrated how to use a specific class for all editable fields, such as inplaceinput for input fields, or inplacetextarea for textarea fields. To provide the information for the application processing the update, give the field the same name as the table/field:

```
<div id="wp_posts-post_content" class="inplacetextarea">...</div>
```

When the element is processed, information about the table and field can be consistent with the newly generated in-place editing element to ensure that the application can be used for any web page and field:

```
var divs = document.getElementsByTagName('div');
for (var i = 0; i < divs.length: i++) {

   // if editable field and using input element
   if (div.className && div.className == 'inplaceinput') {
      var id = divs[i].id.split("-");
      var table = id[0]; var field = id[1];
      ...
}
```

The combination of class name and table/field names can be used to generate the appropriate in-place editing content by attaching the table and field as identifiers (transposed) and inserting them after the original element:

```
var divs = document.getElementsByTagName('div');
for (var i = 0; i < divs.length; i++) {

    // if editable and input element item
    if (divs[i].className && divs[i].className == 'inplaceinput') {
        var id = divs[i].id.split("-");
        var table = id[0]; var field = id[1];

        // create new edit input item and populate
        var newDiv = document.createElement('div');
        newDiv.className="edit";
        var input = document.createElement('input');
        input.type = 'text'; input.id = field + '-' + table;
        input.value = divs[i].firstChild.nodeValue;

        // append printed text, append to parent, set event
        newDiv.appendChild(input);
        divs[i].parentNode.appendChild(newDiv);
        aaManageEvent(divs[i],'click',setEdit);
    }
}
```

The application finds these when the page loads and creates associated in-place edit fields, which are then appended into the document. When using this approach, all that's required is to drop in the JavaScript file and add the class setting to the element that can be edited, associating the class name with a variable that specifies whether the edit is being made in a text input field or textarea.

Another advantage to using the packaged technique is that the editing fields and form elements aren't embedded in the page when the page is loaded. If a user does not own the post and/or doesn't have scripting enabled, but is using a screen reader to access the page, the contents of the "hidden" form fields could be described and/or read just as easily as the "visible" fields. We don't want this.

This is very much how Dojo's in-place editing (or *inline editing*, as the creators behind Dojo refer to it) works. To incorporate Dojo's techniques into your own application, include the required Dojo source files—*dojo.js*, *dojo.widget*, and *dojo.event*—and use the class name inlineEditBox. What differs between the approach outlined previously in the chapter and Dojo's approach is that Dojo makes extensive use of declarative HTML, with an attribute named mode to differentiate between the different mode types. However, the page won't validate with the declarative HTML and could have potential problems when used with documents served as XHTML. It also uses a complete form with form buttons, while we used input fields outside of a form and div classes to manage the save and cancel actions.

Another problem with declarative HTML is that without namespaces, combining multiple libraries can cause conflicts, but providing namespaces can cause some quirky behavior in some browsers. See Dave Johnson's weblog post, "Declarative Ajax Components and XML Namespaces" at *http://blogs.nitobi.com/dave/?p=131*, for a discussion on these issues.

Highlighting Changes

Highlighting data changes or updates is another Ajax effect that can add considerable polish to an application. In Chapter 4, we saw this demonstrated when new comments were added and a yellow fade was used to highlight the new comment after it was saved.

This type of "fade and update the page" effect can also be used when an item is deleted. Rather than a yellow fade, a red fade could be used to differentiate this type of modification, or any color, really, as long as it differs from the "positive" or "additive" change.

Signaling a Deletion

Most deletions involve removing an item from a list. The item may be singular, such as a city in a list of cities. Or it can be a grouped item, such as a record from a database. Two components of the Ajax deletion are the fade, which signals the change, and the update, which shows the page with the item removed.

Sites such as Netflix and Blockbuster provide an ability to delete an item from a list, but with Netflix you have to check the item and then do a form update. Blockbuster provides a little garbage can that you can click, which triggers a delete and page update.

In applications like WordPress, you can delete a post by clicking a Delete link, which then triggers the deletion of the post and all associated records. Flickr also has a Delete link, which removes a photo.

A deletion should never be accomplished with a GET request; at a minimum you'll use the POST HTTP request if you can't use DELETE. It's not unusual to have a message pop up asking whether you're sure about your action, depending on the seriousness of this potentially destructive activity. Removing a movie from a queue isn't very serious and is easily reversed, so an "Are you sure?" confirmation is not needed. However, removing a weblog post or a customer record or an item from an order is serious enough to warrant a little extra check.

To demonstrate how to implement an Ajax delete, several rows have been selected from the demonstration database mentioned earlier. They're organized in an HTML table, each with a "Delete Now!" button added to the row using JavaScript. Rather than coding an update or a delete fade effect, we'll use Adam Michela's Fade Any-thing Technique (FAT) library, a special-purpose library that provides the ability to create a fade in any color, duration, and smoothness (number of frames per change).

 The Fade Anything Technique (FAT) library can be found at *http://www.axentric.com/posts/default/7*. The library does assign the onload event handler directly, which could override assignments in other libraries. Since the library's onload event handling isn't required for the effect demonstrated in this section, you may want to delete it from the bottom of the library.

We'll use an HTML table for this effect, since the forte of HTML tables is to display rows of data. In addition, the DOM provides specialized methods to add and remove table rows.

Example 6-5 shows the code for the client side of the application, including the PHP used to display the table rows and to assign the appropriate classes and identifiers. Notice in the page that the first column contains the post identifier, which is also assigned as a value to the delete checkbox and is used to derive the table row identifier for all but the first row. The use of the post identifier in this way maintains a physical connection between the actual database, the checkbox, and the row. As we'll see later, this is also used for the "Delete Now!" button so that when the button is clicked, the post identifier is pulled from the first cell to delete the appropriate database record and the HTML table row.

Example 6-5. Web page with table containing data rows

```php
<?php

// connect to database and query for post, if post is given
mysql_connect('localhost','username','password');
mysql_select_db('shelleyp_addingajax');

$qry = "select ID, post_date_gmt, post_title, cat_name, post_status, " .
       "comment_count from wp_posts, wp_post2cat, wp_categories where " .
       "post_id = ID and cat_ID = category_id order by ID limit 20";
$rows = mysql_query($qry);

?>
<!DOCTYPE html PUBLIC "-//W3C//DTD XHTML 1.0 Strict//EN"
"http://www.w3.org/TR/xhtml1/DTD/xhtml1-strict.dtd">
<html xmlns="http://www.w3.org/1999/xhtml" lang="en">
<head>
<meta http-equiv="Content-Type" content="text/html; charset=utf-8" />
<title>In-Place Deleting</title>
<style type="text/css">
t<style type="text/css">
table
{
```

Example 6-5. Web page with table containing data rows (continued)

```
        width: 800px;
}
.delete
{
        background-color: #f00;
        color: #fff;
        font-weight: bold;
        padding: 2px;
}
td
{
        border: 1px solid #ccc;
        margin: 5px;
        padding: 10px;
}
</style>
<script type="text/javascript" src="fat.js">
</script>
<script type="text/javascript" src="addingajax.js">
</script>
<script type="text/javascript" src="data2.js">
</script>
</head>
<body>

<form method="post" action="process2.php">
<table>
<tr><th scope="col">ID</th><th scope="col">Date</th><th scope="col">Title</th><th
scope="col">Category</th>
    <th scope="col">status</th><th scope="col">Comment<br /> count</th><th scope="col">
Delete</th></tr>
<?php

    if(($rows) && mysql_num_rows($rows) > 0) {
        while($row = mysql_fetch_row($rows)) {
?>
<tr id="tr<?php echo $row[0]; ?>">
    <td><?php echo $row[0]; ?></td>
    <td><?php echo $row[1]; ?></td>
    <td><?php echo $row[2]; ?></td>
    <td><?php echo $row[3]; ?></td>
    <td><?php echo $row[4]; ?></td>
    <td><?php echo $row[5]; ?></td>
    <td><input type="checkbox" name="delete[]" value="<?php echo $row[0]; ?>" /></td>
</tr>
<?php }
    }
?>

</table>
<div>
<input type="submit" value="Delete Checked" />
```

Example 6-5. Web page with table containing data rows (continued)

```
</div>
</form>
</body>
</html>
```

Again, within an application framework, we'd use whatever template functionality the framework provided rather than manually displaying the data using straight PHP. Figure 6-3 shows the table populated with data with scripting disabled. There is no "Delete Now!" button; to delete rows, the web page reader enables the delete checkboxes and clicks the Submit button.

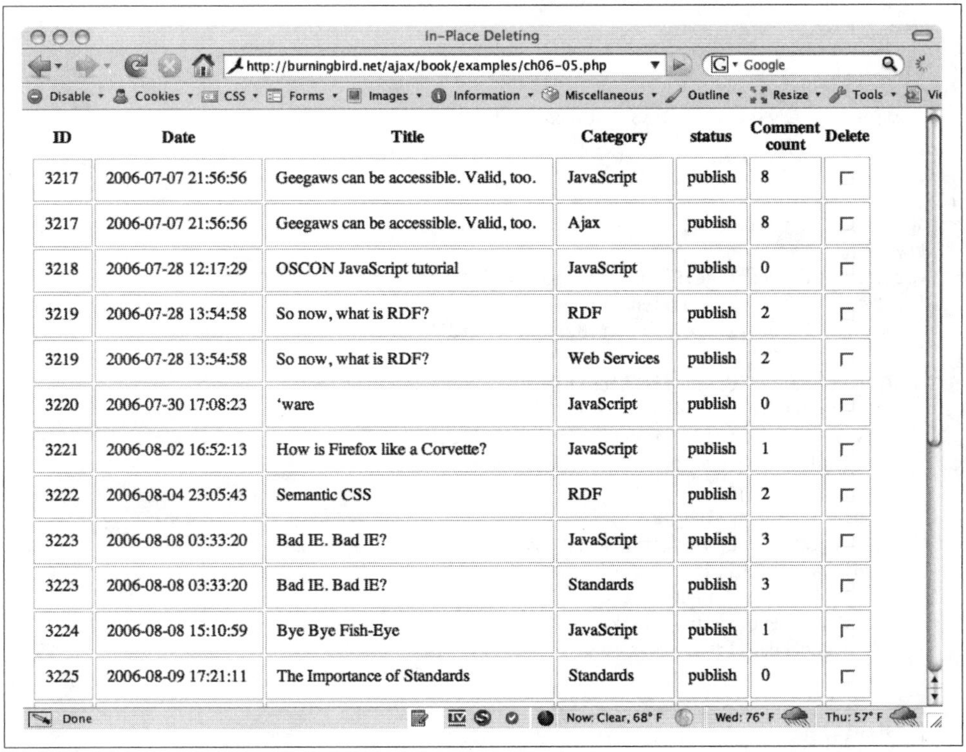

Figure 6-3. Delete row application with scripting disabled

If scripting is enabled, when the page is loaded, the application accesses each table row and appends a new table column, consisting of a div element containing the words "Delete Now!", and given an identifier consisting, in part, of the post identifier. An onClick event handler is assigned this div element. Example 6-6 includes the complete JavaScript for the application, included in the file *data2.js*.

Example 6-6. Delete Now! in-page application JavaScript

```javascript
var xmlhttp;
var currentId;

// setup the request to update the data
function sendChange(params) {
  if (!xmlhttp) xmlhttp = aaGetXmlHttpRequest();
  var url = 'process2.php';
  xmlhttp.open('POST', url, true);
  xmlhttp.onreadystatechange = processResponse;
  xmlhttp.setRequestHeader('Content-Type',
    'application/x-www-form-urlencoded');
  xmlhttp.send(params);
}

// process response
function processResponse() {
  if(xmlhttp.readyState == 4 && xmlhttp.status==200) {
      fadeRow();
  }
}
window.onload=function() {
   try {
   var rows = document.getElementsByTagName('tr');
   for (var i = 0; i < rows.length; i++) {
      var tds = rows[i].getElementsByTagName('td');

      // get identifier in first cell
      if (tds.length > 1) {
         var value = tds[0].firstChild.nodeValue;
         var div = document.createElement('div');
         div.className = 'delete';
         div.id = "item" + value;
         var txt = document.createTextNode("Delete Now!");
         div.appendChild(txt);
         var td = rows[i].insertCell(-1);
         aaManageEvent(div,'click',rowClick);
         td.appendChild(div);
      }
   }
   } catch(e) {
     alert(e);
   }
};

function rowClick(evnt) {
  evnt = (evnt) ? evnt : window.event;

  var item = (evnt.currentTarget) ? evnt.currentTarget : evnt.srcElement;
  currentId = item.id.split("item")[1];
  sendChange("id=" + currentId);
}
```

Example 6-6. Delete Now! in-page application JavaScript (continued)

```
function fadeRow( ){
  Fat.fade_element("tr" + currentId,null,800,"#ff0000");
  setTimeout('deleteRow("' + currentId + '")' , 802);
}
function deleteRow(id) {
  var item = aaElem("item" + id);
  var row = item.parentNode.parentNode;
  var table = row.parentNode;
  table.deleteRow(row.rowIndex);
}
```

When the "Delete Now!" div element is clicked, the database post identifier is derived from the element's identifier and is assigned to a global value. The database request to delete the row is made using a POST method, sending the post identifier as a parameter. A more RESTful solution would be to use the DELETE HTTP request. However, this is implemented so sparsely on both clients and servers that for now we need to restrict ourselves to GET and POST, which we know have universal support. Since the data is being updated, we're using a POST.

 One approach you can take when using DELETE and PUT is to use a POST and attach another parameter, _method, to the PUT or DELETE and process accordingly on the server.

The Ajax callback function calls the fadeRow function, which begins the fade on the table row associated with the data. The function also starts a timer to call the deleteRow function after the fade is finished. This final function uses the DOM and the document tree to find both the parent table row and the parent table, and uses the DOM deleteRow method on the table, passing in the table row's rowIndex value. We have to wait to physically remove the table row from the page until after the fade finishes, or not only will we end up with a rather bizarre visual effect, the FAT library will throw several errors because the item being faded no longer exists.

On the server side, the invoked web service would, in this case, delete the weblog post and all associated table rows, including comments and categories. However, you'd adjust the backend part of the application to specify whichever database you're using.

The application could run the fade in parallel with the Ajax service request, except that we really don't want to begin either the fade or the client-side table deletion until we know that the backend process has completed satisfactorily. If there's a chance that the data request to the server may suffer a noticeable delay, two effects could be used—one to mark that the click event happened and the row is being deleted, and one to appear after the deletion. Be aware, though, that you're not going to want to add any visual effects to the table row that could conflict with the fade. If you want a "working" effect, add it elsewhere in the page.

All of the fades and in-page or inline modification techniques presented so far have been responses to user events. However, in the next section, we'll look at the concept of polling for data changes and signaling updates.

Polling and Highlighting Updates

The online syndication feed aggregator, Bloglines (*http://bloglines.com*), provides a way to subscribe to several feeds. Once the site is set up, you can access it from any machine to see who has made updates, and you can access the new updates via their feeds.

The site uses frames, with the list of subscriptions in the left frame and a space to read the feed items on the right. The company also provides the administrative tasks to add and delete feeds, group feeds, and so on. It's what I've been using for some time.

Bloglines recently added a new effect to the site: polling and flashed updates. If you have your feed page currently loaded in a browser, every few minutes, Bloglines sends an Ajax request to the server to check for updates. If any are found, three things happen:

1. A semitransparent message is flashed to the bottom of the page in the left frame with the information that new feed items have been found, including the number of new items.

2. The count indicator for the feed containing the new items is updated, and the item is set to bold type if it didn't initially have unread items when Bloglines was opened.

3. The item is also quickly flashed in yellow, to make it stand out from the other feeds that may have unread items.

This is an impressive effect and not necessarily at a high cost in complexity. The most critical component is figuring out how often to send the Ajax request so that a server isn't unduly hammered by the addition of these new requests. Then it's just a matter of finding the item in the list (Bloglines uses ul and li elements), updating the text to reflect the update (and changing the style class to show bold text), flashing the item, and then flashing the message warning of updates.

To demonstrate polled updates, let's return to the comment application created in Chapter 4. When a new comment was created in this application, it was added directly to the page, and the item was highlighted with a fade to show that it was added. To make it more interactive, the application can be extended to add such polling.

The initial example didn't work with data directly from a database, so we can modify it to pull in comments from the WordPress database, giving it a specific post identifier. We can also modify the example to use the *addingajax.js* library, as well as the

FAT library used in previous examples. The live comment preview is removed to focus only on the updated comment list.

Example 6-7 shows just the new application, including the PHP to retrieve and display the comment text. One small portion of JavaScript is left in the page: the post identifier. By setting this locally in JavaScript, we could easily change the application to work with other posts.

Example 6-7. Web page setting up live comment updates

```php
<?php
$post = 3694;

// connect to database and query for post, if post is given
mysql_connect('localhost','username','password');
mysql_select_db('database');

$rows = mysql_query("select comment_ID, comment_author, comment_content from wp_comments
where comment_post_ID = '$post' AND comment_approved = '1' order by comment_ID");

?>
<!DOCTYPE html PUBLIC "-//W3C//DTD XHTML 1.0 Strict//EN"
"http://www.w3.org/TR/xhtml1/DTD/xhtml1-strict.dtd">
<html xmlns="http://www.w3.org/1999/xhtml" lang="en">
<head>
<meta http-equiv="Content-Type" content="text/html; charset=utf-8" />
<title>Polling and Updates</title>
<style type="text/css">
#list
{
        border: 1px solid #ccc;
        margin: 20px;
        padding: 10px;
        width: 600px;
}
.comment
{
        background-color: #ddd;
        font: 12px arial, sans-serif;
        margin: 10px 0;
        padding: 5px;
        width: 400px;
}
form, #preview
{
        border: 1px solid #cc0;
        margin: 20px;
        padding: 10px;
        width: 600px;
}
</style>
<script type="text/javascript" src="addingajax.js">
</script>
```

Example 6-7. Web page setting up live comment updates (continued)

```
<script type="text/javascript" src="fat.js">
</script>
<script type="text/javascript" src="getcomments.js">
</script>
<script type="text/javascript">
//<![CDATA[

// global
<?php echo "var post = '$post';"; ?>
</script>
</head>
<body>
<div id="list">
<h3>Current Comments:</h3>
<?php

    if(($rows) && mysql_num_rows($rows) > 0) {
        $ctr = 0;
        while($row = mysql_fetch_row($rows)) {
?>
        <div class="comment" id="div<?php echo $row[0]; ?>">
        <?php echo $row[2]; ?></div>
<?php }
    }
?>
</div>
<form action="addcomment.php" id="commentform">
<div>
<label for="comment">Comment:,/label><textarea id="comment" cols="65" rows="10"></
textarea>
<br /><br />
<input type="submit" value="save" />
</div>
</form>
</body>
</html>
```

There isn't anything particularly special about the page. The comments are retrieved from the database, and the PHP embedded in the page loops through the data, printing out the comments ordered by comment identifier.

In the *getcomments.js* file, a whole lot of work is happening. It still has the functionality to immediately see the comments reflected in the list. To ensure that it, or any other comment, doesn't repeat in the list through the Ajax comment update, we can use a little DOM trick to make sure it doesn't already exist in the page. Each comment div element is assigned a unique identifier based on the comment's identifier. If an element with the derived identifier doesn't exist, it's appended to the list.

The complete JavaScript file is shown in Example 6-8. Pay particular attention to the use of setInterval in the setUp function, as well as the checkNewName and updateComments methods. These manage the live updating of comments, polling for new comments from the database every 15 seconds, running through the comment list, checking to see whether a page element already exists by that name, and ignoring it if it does. If the page element doesn't already exist, the new comment is appended to the list using the new comment functionality, appendComment.

Example 6-8. The comments management JavaScript code

```
// global
var xmlhttp;

aaManageEvent(window,"load",setUp);

function setUp( ) {
  aaManageEvent(aaElem('commentform'),"submit",saveComment);
  setInterval(checkNewComment,15000);
}

function checkNewComment( ) {
  if (!xmlhttp) xmlhttp = aaGetXmlHttpRequest( );
  if (!xmlhttp) return;
  xmlhttp.open('GET', 'getcomments.php?post=' + post, true);
  xmlhttp.onreadystatechange = updateComments;
  xmlhttp.send(null);
}

function updateComments( ) {
  if(xmlhttp.readyState == 4 && xmlhttp.status==200) {
    eval("var polled = " + xmlhttp.responseText);
    for (var i = 0; i < polled.length; i++) {
      var polledId = "div" + polled[i].id;
      var elem = aaElem(polledId);
      if (!elem) {
        appendComment(polled[i]);
      }
    }
  }
}

// Save new comment
function saveComment(evnt) {
  evnt = (evnt) ? evnt : window.event;
  aaCancelEvent(evnt);
  if (!xmlhttp) xmlhttp = aaGetXmlHttpRequest( );
  var commentText = document.getElementById("comment").value;
  modText = commentText.split(/\n/).join("<br />");
  var param = "comment=" + modText;
  xmlhttp.open('POST', 'addComment.php', true);
  xmlhttp.onreadystatechange = addComment;
  xmlhttp.setRequestHeader('Content-Type',
    'application/x-www-form-urlencoded');
  xmlhttp.send(param);
  return false;
}
```

Example 6-8. The comments management JavaScript code (continued)

```
function addComment( ) {
  if(xmlhttp.readyState == 4 && xmlhttp.status==200) {
      eval("var newComment = " + xmlhttp.responseText);
      appendComment(newComment);
  }
}

function appendComment(comment) {
    var newDiv = document.createElement("div");
    var newName = "div"+comment.id;
    newDiv.setAttribute("id",newName);
    newDiv.setAttribute("class","comment");
    newDiv.innerHTML = comment.content;
    aaElem("list").appendChild(newDiv);
    Fat.fade_element(newName,null,800,"#ffff00","#eeeeee");
}
```

The yellow fade to signal a new comment finishes with a paler gray than the other comments in order to subtly set them apart. The new comments are appended to the list even if they're out of sync because they were moderated and have only been recently approved. This ensures that a user reading the comments doesn't have her reading disrupted by comments being inserted into the list, which would otherwise push the existing comments down as they're being read. This becomes more complicated, though, if threaded comments are used (this is way beyond the scope of what we will cover in this chapter). However, it's important to see what's happening in the server-side application when the updated comments are accessed. Example 6-9 contains the code.

Example 6-9. The PHP web service that accesses updated comments

```
<?php

$post = trim($_GET['post']);

if ($post) {

    mysql_connect('localhost','username','password');
    mysql_select_db('database');

    $rows = mysql_query("SELECT comment_ID,comment_author,comment_content from wp_comments
                where  comment_post_ID = '$post' and comment_approved = '1' order by
comment_ID");
    if ($rows && mysql_num_rows($rows) > 0) {
        $str = "[";
        while($row = mysql_fetch_row($rows)) {
            if ($str != '[') $str.=",";
            $str.= "{ id : '$row[0]', author : '$row[1]', content : \"$row[2]\" }";
        }
        $str.="]";
    }
```

Example 6-9. The PHP web service that accesses updated comments (continued)

```
    echo $str;
} else {
    echo "no post";
}
?>
```

The application uses JSON for the formatting, returning an array of comment objects. The application that saves the new comment must also be adjusted to return the same type of object because the same function, appendComment, is used to append new comments to the page, and it expects a comment object. Figure 6-4 shows the application in mid-update.

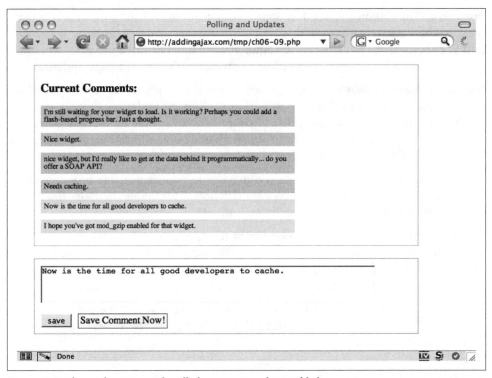

Figure 6-4. The applications with polled comment updates added

This example demonstrates how many moving parts an effect like a live update of new data can have. At the same time, though, there isn't anything overly complicated about the process—it's just a lot of code. However, much of it can be converted into libraries, providing live updates on prices of items, number of items still available, number of people who have signed up, and so on—basically, any time you have different users responding on one specific item, and each user's response impacts the others.

Of course, from a performance viewpoint, you're going to want to minimize your database access. For instance, you could cache the most recent comments for any one post every 5 or 10 seconds, and then each individual web page's Ajax request could go to this cache. You can also adjust the timing to fit both the demand and your resources. Frankly, if you have a monstrously busy site, I wouldn't recommend live updates unless they form a critical component of your application's functionality.

However, if you can handle the extra load on your system, live updates can be a terrific option. They're also an accessible one, as we'll get into in the next section.

Revisiting In-Page Update Accessibility One More Time

For the polled comments, the fact that screen readers and screen magnifiers don't pick up the updates isn't really that much of an issue, as users can refresh the page and get the updates. This is the traditional functionality for applications of these types, so there is no loss of functionality by providing dynamic in-page updates.

For the in-page edit shown in Example 6-1, the row deletion in Example 6-5, and the add comment feature in Example 6-7, though, in-page updates can be a problem because a screen reader would most likely not discover that the update has taken place. The only way for the user to know that data modification was successful would be to reload the page and check the data—not an acceptable solution.

One way to work around this issue could be to provide a message box that opens and makes a comment about a successful deletion. This spoils the fade, though, as the message box and the fade are really redundant.

Another approach is to provide an option in the application that specifies how users are notified that a change has taken place. One option would be a message box with the information and another would be using the fade and deleting the row in place. These choices could then be stored in cookies, and the program altered accordingly.

What happens, though, if scripting is turned off? That's where the concept of progressive enhancement comes in: create the application to be nonscript-enabled at first, and then modify it.

Revisiting the In-Page Deletion

When creating an "accessible" Ajax application, our first inclination might be to either make heavy use of NOSCRIPT to provide accessible workarounds, or even create completely separate pages that are displayed if a user has signaled that he is restricted to keyboard use, using a screen reader, or has scripting disabled.

However, let's return to an earlier example, Example 6-1, where options are provided to edit the data in-place, or to click a link that takes the data owner to a separate page form. Both are provided if scripting is enabled, the latter if scripting is disabled. In other words, the in-place editing is an additional option, complementary to the more traditional form page.

The same goes for the Delete Now! example. Previously, I showed the page in Figure 6-4 with scripting disabled. Figure 6-5 shows the same page, this time with scripting enabled. The options that were available when scripting was disabled are still given. It's just now, there's an additional way to delete the data using the Delete Now! functionality.

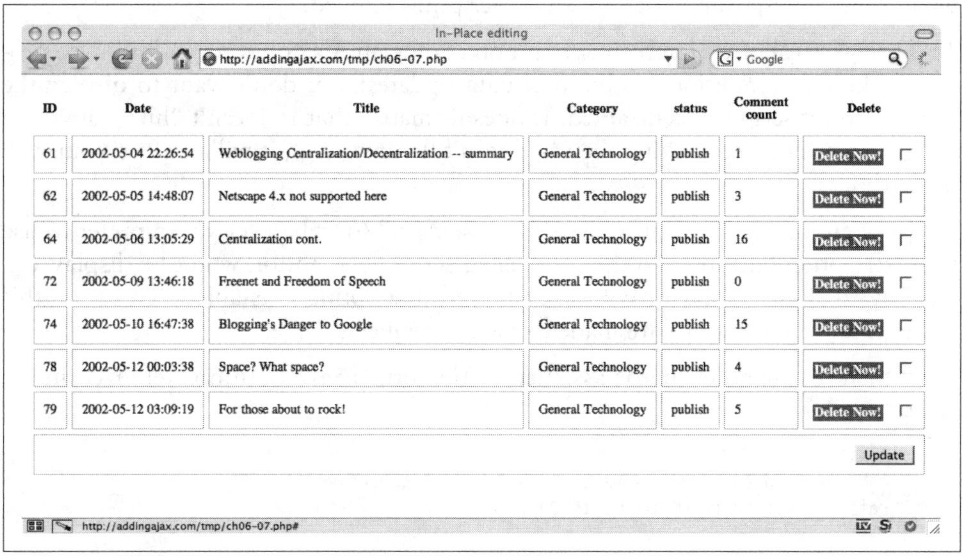

Figure 6-5. The application, now with in-page deletion enabled

Without script, the way to delete items is to either provide a Delete button for the form page for an individual item or to provide a checkbox for each item in a list. In the version shown in Figure 6-4, the application displayed a checkbox to delete the item. In this case, the web page reader can go down the list, enabling the checkbox of the items to be deleted, then delete all of the selected items at once. Submitting the page calls a traditional server-side application that processes the form, deletes the items, and redisplays the page with a message about how many items were deleted (or updated, or added, and so on).

The use of the checkbox would also provide additional accessibility for keyboard access, rather than restricting the page to mouse access. A person using the keyboard to navigate the page could tab between the different checkboxes, selecting the items to be deleted.

Revisiting In-Place Additions

Making an in-place addition application, such as the comments application shown in Example 6-7, is by its very nature accessible. Anytime you refresh the page, all current comments are displayed. The only change required to support the addition of comments if scripting is disabled is to reset the form's Submit button to process the comment in the traditional manner. We can then add an "Add Comment Now!" div element, just like the "Delete Now!" ones covered in Chapter 5 to support users who want to use the Ajax approach and have scripting enabled.

This brings up another interesting point on adding an Ajax option in addition to providing the more traditional submitted data updates: you don't want to display the Ajax option if scripting is disabled. It doesn't matter that it doesn't "hurt" anything to display it (because clicking the div doesn't do anything), it will confuse your web page readers.

The way around this is to insert the "choose Ajax" (or whatever you'd prefer to use for text) option buttons into the page using script. The button won't be displayed if scripting is disabled, but it will be displayed if scripting is enabled. To create this effect, three modifications are made to the *getcomments.js* file.

First, the event handler that is assigned to the form's Save button is removed in the setUp function:

```
function setUp() {
  aaManageEvent(aaElem('commentform'),"submit",saveComment);
  setInterval(checkNewComment,15000);
}
```

Since we're dealing with the form button's built-in event handling, the cancel event bubbling no longer needed, so it is removed from the saveComment function:

```
// Save new comment
function saveComment(evnt) {
  evnt = (evnt) ? evnt : window.event;
  aaCancelEvent(evnt);
  if (!xmlhttp) xmlhttp = aaGetXmlHttpRequest();
  var commentText = document.getElementById("comment").value;
  modText = commentText.split(/\n/).join("<br />");
  var param = "comment=" + modText;
  xmlhttp.open('POST', 'addComment.php', true);
  xmlhttp.onreadystatechange = addComment;
  xmlhttp.setRequestHeader('Content-Type',
    'application/x-www-form-urlencoded');
  xmlhttp.send(param);
  return false;
}
```

A new function is created and kicked off when the window is loaded to create the new "choose Ajax" button:

```
aaManageEvent(window,"load",function( ) {
  var elem = document.createElement('div');
  elem.id = 'saveajax';
  elem.className = 'saveajax';
  var txt = document.createTextNode("Save Comment Now!");
  elem.appendChild(txt);
  aaManageEvent(elem,"click", saveComment);
  aaElem("save").parentNode.insertBefore(elem,aaElem("save").nextSibling);
});
```

That's it to make the page accessible, even if scripting is disabled.

Live Validation

There's nothing that irritates me more than signing up for an account on a site that asks for a username and then responds with, "That username has been taken. Please choose another," usually with some lame variation of the username as a suggestion. The process is made worse when you have to submit a form and have it rejected because of the username or some other value that doesn't validate. If the application is decent, it will have preserved the data, but still, it adds to the overall awkwardness of the sign-up process, and if it's annoying enough, I won't even finish.

This is another area where Ajax can be added unobtrusively. It can provide live validation of entered data as soon as the user tabs away from the field or clicks a button to submit the form, but before the form is actually submitted. It's not the same as typical client-side validation, which would check to ensure that a field was filled in or that the email address entered in a field had proper syntax. No, it uses Ajax to validate a value against a database, returning whatever error is provided by the service, all within the same page.

> I say unobtrusive because if scripting is disabled, the errors will be found when the page goes through the regular form submission. The scripting is an enhancement, not a requirement.

In WordPress, a user can register for an account if the WordPress weblog owner allows it. When a user registers, he provides a preferred username and email address, and a password is emailed to him. Once the user has access to the system, he can log in and provide a first and last name, web URL, display name, and so on. We'll skip through all of that and provide a form that allows a user to provide a username, email address, first and last name, and display name. Of the fields, the username is the one that gets live validation.

Example 6-10 includes a web page with a simple web form containing several fields, including the targeted username field. Aside from the links to scripting files in the application, there's nothing to mark this page as different from a billion or so other web page forms that exist today.

Example 6-10. Simple web page form

```
<!DOCTYPE html PUBLIC "-//W3C//DTD XHTML 1.0 Strict//EN"
"http://www.w3.org/TR/xhtml1/DTD/xhtml1-strict.dtd">
<html xmlns="http://www.w3.org/1999/xhtml" lang="en">
<head>
<title>Live Validation</title>
<meta http-equiv="Content-Type" content="text/html; charset=utf-8" />
<style type="text/css">
input
{
        display: block;
        margin-bottom: 10px;
}
input[type="text"]
{
        width: 450px
}
form
{
        width: 500px;
        margin: 50px;
        background-color: #ffc;
}
fieldset
{
        border: 1px groove #ccc;
}
.error
{
        color: #f00;
        font: italic small-caps 900 14px arial;
        margin: 10px;
}
</style>
<script type="text/javascript" src="addingajax.js">
</script>
<script type="text/javascript" src="validation.js">
</script>
</head>
<body>
<form action="something" method="POST">
<fieldset id="myform">
<legend>Registration</legend>
<label for="username">Preferred Username:</label><input type="text" name="username"
id="username" />
<label for="email">Email:</label><input type="text" name="email" id="email" />
<label for="firstname">First Name:</label><input type="text" name="firstname"
id="firstname"/>
<label for="lastname">Last Name:</label><input type="text" name="lastname" id="lastname" /
>
<label for="displayname">Display Name:</label><input type="text" name="displayname"
id="displayname" />
```

Example 6-10. Simple web page form (continued)

```
<input type="submit" value="Register" />
</fieldset>

</form>

</body>
</html>
```

The page validates across the board: XHTML, CSS, and accessibility. However, if scripting is enabled and a user types an existing username into the username field, such as **admin** an error message will appear stating that the username is not unique (Figure 6-6). This message remains until either the form is submitted or a unique username is entered.

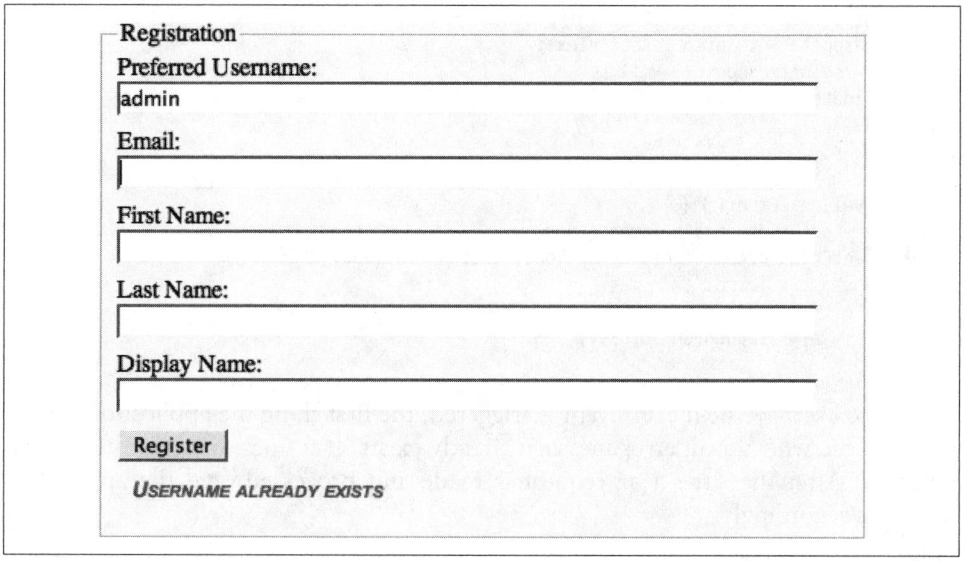

Figure 6-6. Demonstrating live validation of a username field

The code to implement this validation, *validation.js*, is given in Example 6-11. It's relatively simple: attach a blur event to the target field, username, and when the event is triggered, grab the value in the field and make an Ajax request to verify its existence. If the count of names that match it is 1, throw an error message.

Example 6-11. Live validation JavaScript

```
aaManageEvent(window,"load", function( ) {
    aaManageEvent(aaElem("username"),"blur", validate);
    });

function validate( ) {
```

Example 6-11. Live validation JavaScript (continued)

```
    // erase any existing message
    var error = aaElem('errorMessage');
    if (error)
       error.parentNode.removeChild(error);

    if (!xmlhttp) xmlhttp = aaGetXmlHttpRequest();
    if (!xmlhttp) return;
    var username = aaElem("username").value;
    xmlhttp.open('GET', 'validate.php?username=' + username, true);
    xmlhttp.onreadystatechange = processValidation;
    xmlhttp.send(null);
}

function processValidation() {
  if(xmlhttp.readyState == 4 && xmlhttp.status==200) {
    var response = xmlhttp.responseText;
    if (parseInt(response) == 1)
      validateError();
  }
}

function validateError() {
  var div = document.createElement('div')
  div.appendChild(document.createTextNode("Username already exists"));
  div.className = "error";
  div.id="errorMessage";
  aaElem('myform').appendChild(div);
}
```

When the username field blur event is triggered, the first thing the application does is check to see whether an error message already exists. If it does, the error message is removed. After that, the Ajax request is made and processed, and the application responds accordingly.

Live validation works really well, especially for a field like username, which can result in a lot of tries before a valid value is returned. What about performance problems associated with this type of action? The next section discusses issues with performance and two-phase commits, as well as other items related to database access with an Ajax frontend.

Performance and Two-Phase Commits

The resources that need the most protection in a web application are Input/Output (I/O)-specific: file writes and database connections. Both typically have a limited number of "threads"—parallel paths of execution—and if you're adding hundreds of new Ajax requests that result in either of these I/O activities, you could be running into blocking problems; Ajax requests waiting for a response from the server, which is blocking on the request because a resource is not available. In particular, a database update frequently results in both types of action—a database connection and a file write. Based on this, you're going to want to evaluate each use of Ajax against the number of concurrent users who might be using the Ajax service at a time, and how many concurrent database connections your system supports.

Ajax That Plays Well with Others

In-page deletion, discussed previously in this chapter, can add to the burden of a web application. Using the traditional approach where each item to be deleted is checked, one database connection is made for all of the deletions, and it is managed as one transaction that establishes a connection, begins the delete transaction, deletes all the items, ends the transaction, then ends the connection.

The Ajax deletion method does require a separate connection for each deletion. The burden of having to open a connection for each Ajax delete request is offset by how simple and fast the request is, and how quickly the database resources are released.

Still, the deletion request is also running against other Ajax database accesses, each of which contends for valuable connections, all without necessarily seeming that burdensome.

Live validation is another one of those database accesses that is seemingly innocuous at first, but if you start adding live validation for every field and every form, your web application will quickly become bogged down from the demand for database connections.

When creating an Ajax application that uses a limited resource, such as a database connection, examine the trade-offs between ease of use the effect provides and costs of the resources needed. In addition, package such effects whenever possible, so that, for instance, one database connection can be used for several effects. In the application demonstrated in Example 6-11, validating on the username makes sense because it can be difficult to find a unique username in a system with many users. It's one area where a person could easily get frustrated by having to submit an entire form only to find out that a single field is not valid (in this case, the username was not unique). This method can also enhance the application's performance because rather than having to process an entire form, the server only has to respond to a simple Ajax request for one field.

For live validation of several fields, though, a better approach would be to provide a separate validation button that initiates live validation all of the fields in one Ajax request, perhaps combined with any in-page, non-Ajax request-dependent validations, such as checking email formats. The application could then list all of the errors at once, letting the user make the necessary corrections before the form is actually submitted.

These are all good examples of how Ajax can be used to enhance a site, while still keeping it accessible. One last area of concern includes database transactions and concepts such as row locking and two-phase commits.

Ajax, Caching, and Database Transactions

In Example 6-11's use of live validation, when the reader tabs away from the username field, no message is given as long as that username isn't currently being used. However, what happens if someone else comes along at the same time and takes that same username before the first user actually submits the form?

In a database application, when a user is making a change to a table row, the database typically locks the row from changes made by other users. This prevents concurrent changes to the same data, which could otherwise leave the data out of sync for different users and in an unstable condition. In Ajax, especially when validating form entries, if multiple users are making changes to the same database table or even the same table row, there is no database locking to prevent users from working on data that is already out of date because of the changes made by other users.

Your first thought might be to emulate a form of database locking. No, no! Don't do that! Even if we can get around bending the rules of the Web with Ajax, we can't get around the rules of safe database transactions, and we shouldn't even try.

What comes to our rescue, oddly enough, is the accessibility of the application. In the example with the username, if a value validates successfully, the rest of the form still has to be submitted. By providing the formal form submission, at that point in time, the data is updated or added, and if any database rule is violated, such as a nonunique username, then a message is returned and the user handles the problem as she would have before Ajax was ever on the scene. It might be an annoyance, but chances are that it is less of an annoyance than going through the form submission and having the name fail each time. There's a very good chance that if the name validates, the form submission will succeed.

We could attempt to cache the username based on the validation request, thereby preventing others from using that username until the form is actually submitted. However, what happens if the user never finishes or submits the form? When the form is submitted, if the username or other validated data has been altered in such a way that the data no longer validates, the form submission will fail and the a message about the cause of the failure returned to the user.

In most cases, if the use of Ajax is unobtrusive, then its use is backed up by normal web operations, and that includes normal database actions. Trying to be clever and routing around this is going to add considerably to the complexity of your application without bringing in any real benefit.

If the concept of emulated row-level locking isn't feasible from a validation perspective, how about something like two-phase commits—committing a complete update all at once where Ajax has enabled updates on individual pieces of the whole?

A good example of this is a form implemented as tabbed pages, where as each user completes one section, it's validated and/or stored. It's tempting to store what's completed into the production database to preserve it, but that's a mistake. If the data is never completed, you end up with a lot of junk in your production system, which can only impact negatively on the overall performance.

If the multicomponent form doesn't have to persist beyond the session, the data can be validated with Ajax but stored locally in memory until it's all finished, and then non-Ajaxian form submission is applied and the production database is updated.

If the form does have to persist beyond the session, cookies can be used to store much of the data, or you can use interim tables that age the data, cleaning out incomplete submissions if they're not completed by a certain time or date. When the user accesses the form again, the stored data is used to populate the form and is cleaned out the temporary store. Eventually, when the user is finished, the data can be processed as it normally would be if scripting wasn't enabled.

The point of all of this is that just because Ajax is being used and page requests are being made within the page rather than requiring a complete page reload, it doesn't mean that we should rearchitect our backend, adding in all sorts of faux locking and Ajax 2-Phase Kommits with cool apple-green coloring. In fact, redesigning the back-end based on a frontend change has long been considered bad design practice, and Ajax doesn't redefine the rules of good software design practices.

Let's finish out the chapter by looking at some external libraries that provide packaged data effects for some of the more popular Ajax/data effects.

External Library Data Effects

Incorporating Ajax effects into an application isn't all that difficult, and as long as the page is created using traditional web functionality first and then has scripting and Ajax requests added, it is also accessible and unobtrusive. Many of the Ajax effects don't even require a great deal of coding if an external library is used. In this final section, we'll explore some of the more popular Ajax/data effects using different Ajax libraries, both to demonstrate the effect and to introduce more libraries for your consideration.

Building and Maintaining Forms

Though Ajax requests have lessened the need for traditional forms, most transactions will continue to be managed through forms. Unfortunately, forms are a lot of work to set up. The qForms API is a specialized API that provides all manner of form validations and constraints. Unlike many other Ajax libraries, it also has excellent documentation (*http://pengoworks.com/qforms/docs*).

There are also some Ajax-based form-building sites that would be worth examining, just to see how the Ajax is implemented, if no other reason. One is WuFoo, at *http://wufoo.com*. Others are jotForm at *http://www.jotform.com*, and BlueForm at *http://www.theblueform.com*. All three of these sites require registration, and you'll want to check other terms first before using them. None of the sites provides the software for downloading and hosting in your own development environment.

Drag-and-Drop Sorting with script.aculo.us

I must admit that I'm underwhelmed by drag-and-drop sorting. Actually, outside of its use in an application like Google Maps, I'm not fond of drag-and-drop at all. It requires considerable script to maintain and adds a great deal of overhead to the page. Most importantly, it's not an unobtrusive and accessible technique, and it doesn't provide functionality important or central enough to justify its use.

It is popular, though, if the support for the functionality in many Ajax libraries is any indication. We'll look at the script.aculo.us library's use of drag-and-drop sorting and then explore what we possibly could do with the concept to make it friendlier, if not unobtrusive.

Creating a sortable list using script.aculo.us is a piece of cake. Example 6-12 shows the page, including the PHP to pull the data, in this case a post title, and print it out in an unordered list. The script.aculo.us script, all one line of it, is shown in bold.

Example 6-12. A sortable column with script.aculo.us

```
<!DOCTYPE html PUBLIC "-//W3C//DTD XHTML 1.0 Strict//EN"
"http://www.w3.org/TR/xhtml1/DTD/xhtml1-strict.dtd">
<html xmlns="http://www.w3.org/1999/xhtml">
<head>
<meta http-equiv="Content-Type" content="text/html; charset=utf-8" />
<title>script.aculo.us sorting</title>
<style type="text/css">
li { margin-bottom: 10px; padding: 3px; list-style-type: none; background-color: #fcc; }
ul { width: 600px; }
</style>
<?php

// connect to database and query for post, if post is given
mysql_connect('localhost','username','password');
mysql_select_db('database');

$qry = "select ID,  post_title from wp_posts limit 20";
$rows = mysql_query($qry);

?>
<script type="text/javascript" src="prototype.js">
</script>
<script type="text/javascript" src="scriptaculous.js">
</script>
```

Example 6-12. A sortable column with script.aculo.us (continued)

```
<script type="text/javascript">
//<![CDATA[

window.onload=function( ) {
Sortable.create("firstlist",
    {dropOnEmpty:true,containment:["firstlist"],constraint:false});
}

//]]>
</script>
</head>
<body>

<ul id="firstlist">
<?php

   if(($rows) && mysql_num_rows($rows) > 0) {
      while($row = mysql_fetch_row($rows)) {
?>
   <li><?php echo $row[1]; ?></li>
<?php }
      }
?>
</ul>
</body>
</html>
```

The script.aculo.us code creates a Sortable object, tying it to the firstlist unordered list. The options provided in the code state that what can be dragged can also receive a drop, and it provides the array of elements that can be sorted.

The application lists the titles out in a column. Clicking on any one and dragging it up or down causes the other titles to shift as the dragged title moves over them. When you're at the spot where you want the title placed, release the mouse button.

The example could be persisted back to the database by accessing the elements in the list in their current order and then resorting the values in the database. Or the sort order could be maintained in cookies, and then the list items displayed in this order when the page is next accessed.

To make the sort more accessible, we could also associate text fields with each item that allow you to type in a number that represents where you want the item listed, and then add an Update button to alter the item permanently in the list and refresh the page. This is how sites like Netflix work.

Adobe Spry's Validation

Adobe has entered into the Ajax field with its own framework, which we'll examine in more detail in Chapter 10. Among some of its effects is a nice set of libraries that enable custom and standardized form validation. This isn't the Ajax call type of validation; this is more like the in-page JavaScript validation.

From the forms validation demonstration included with the framework (currently in beta), you add the spry namespace to the page, along with the XHTML namespace:

```
<html xmlns="http://www.w3.org/1999/xhtml" xmlns:spry="http://ns.adobe.com/spry">
```

Depending on what kind of validations you need, you add in the appropriate libraries. There's a considerable number of libraries, which has the benefit of ensuring that you're not loading huge amounts of unneeded JavaScript if you only need one form of validation:

```
<script type="text/javascript" src="../../widgets/textfieldvalidation/
SpryValidationTextField.js"></script>
<script type="text/javascript" src="../../widgets/selectvalidation/
SpryValidationSelect.js"></script>
<script type="text/javascript" src="../../widgets/textareavalidation/
SpryValidationTextarea.js"></script>
<script type="text/javascript" src="../../widgets/checkboxvalidation/
SpryValidationCheckbox.js"></script>
```

As well as adding your regular form elements, add script to attach a spry validation to a specific field. The following validates a date field:

```
var theDate = new Spry.Widget.ValidationTextField("theDate", "date",
{useCharacterMasking:true, format:"mm/dd/yyyy", hint:"mm/dd/yyyy", validateOn:
["change"]});
```

The following validates that only three options are picked with a checkbox field:

```
var checkboxes = new Spry.Widget.ValidationCheckbox("checkboxes", {validateOn:
["change"], maxSelections:3});
```

It's a nice concept, though Adobe isn't the only one that provides packaged forms validation behavior. Other libraries, such as jQuery, also provide such behavior.

Other Library Data Effects

Rico's LiveGrid API connects an Ajax data query directly to an HTML table, providing "live" scrolling of the data. You can see an example of this effect at *http://openrico.org/demos/livegrid*, and you can read a tutorial on how to use this API at *http://openrico.org/docs/RicoLiveGrid.pdf*.

MochiKit has a "sortables" tutorial and example application that can be used as a template for creating HTML tables that allow one-click column sorts in either descending or ascending order: *http://mochikit.com/examples/sortable_tables/index.html*.

The mooTools framework also has a sortables capability in the form of a plug-in, which is described at *http://docs.mootools.net/files/Plugins/Sortables-js*.

The Yahoo! UI Library (YUI) has several data-related objects and functionalities including autocomplete—a script that captures key movements within fields, queries the data source, and provides suggestions or even completes the value when only one match is made. The YUI also has a complete calendar UI that allows users to pick dates from a calendar to fill in search or form fields.

Using Dojo is a real commitment due to the fact that it's a largish infrastructure, but there are numerous widgets that can be used within this infrastructure that make it attractive. It has widgets like SortableTable, FilterTable, and date pickers for forms. The only difficulty with Dojo is finding all these items—the Dojo documentation isn't linked from the main Dojo page and there is no real list of widgets. You have to dig around to find all the Dojo goodies.

Whether its worthwhile to use an external library for a data effect is really dependent on how much time it saves you compared with how much the library might constrain your existing environment (many of the libraries don't support XHTML), and how much bandwidth the library takes.

Another option, especially for the open source libraries, is to copy the specific functions you need and incorporate them into your own library. If you do this, make sure you attribute the code, and make sure you're not violating licensing or copyright restrictions on the code.

CHAPTER 7

History, Navigation, and Place with Single-Page Applications

Ajax tends to operate outside the normal web viewing experience. Usually, you click a link to a page, your browser opens another page, you click another link to another page, it's loaded into the browser, and so on. If you wanted to return to the original page, you would click the Back button, navigating back through all the pages visited in the current session. If you wanted to bookmark a page or create a link to the page, you would just copy the URL that's loaded in the browser's navigation bar.

When web applications are created as *single-page applications*, where all content is managed and loaded on demand via JavaScript, the Back button is useless, as is the concept of a page URL; there is no sense of place when Ajax is used to load and unload page content. As Alex Bosworth wrote in May 2005 (at *http://sourcelabs.com/ ajb/archives/2005/05/ajax_mistakes.html*):

> The back button is a great feature of standard web site user interfaces. Unfortunately, the back button doesn't mesh very well with JavaScript. Keeping back button functionality is a major reason not to go with a pure JavaScript web app.

Lack of real web paging is also a big issue for much of a site's advertising. Before Ajax, ad costs were based on the number of page views for a site. Now, if content can be loaded willy-nilly into any page that opens, page views no longer reflect what's really going on with a site.

Search engine optimization also takes a hit when using Ajax for content management. If a search engine web bot tries to follow a link, but the link exists only to trigger an application, you've defeated the primary purpose of a link, which is go somewhere. Links also provide information to screen readers, telling the web page users that this is something clickable and, again, assumed to be going somewhere.

Conversely, constructing menus using Ajax and disregarding the use of links tells Google and those with scripting turned off that this is a dead-end page. Yet the page could have hundreds of options ready for a user to access—just follow the Ajax-enabled menus in the side there (or at the top of the page, the bottom of the page, or popping up, hither and yon).

Even functionality as basic to the Web as caching can be impacted when Ajax is used to retrieve data from a web server. Whether bypassing caching protocols at the server or the browser, using Ajax adds additional caching challenges, forcing us to rely less on the web environment and more on our own diligence and innovation. At the same time, though, Ajax can also facilitate caching, not to mention allay bandwidth and other resource concerns.

These are all issues having to do with basic web functionality. They include navigation, place, and history. These are areas where the built-in web and browser functionality we've had for over a decade is routed around through the use of Ajax. The question is, once we introduce Ajax to a site, do any of these matter as once they did? If they do—and think hard on this, because this type of functionality should be discarded only after great consideration—how can we make sure they're properly taken care of as we whiz madly about tossing up any old content in any old place at any old time?

Introducing the Challenger: Paged Content

For the first 10 years of the web's existence, a measure of a site's worth was based on the number of page views it received. That all changed, though, when the concept of a "page" began to lose its meaning. If clicking the button refreshes a single page's content without actually leaving the page, one user can then view 100 pages worth of content while registering only one page view.

At this early stage of the web, it was also simple to backtrack, to retrace the steps taken when going from web page to web page. Again, though, the Back button is directly related to pages loaded, not changes in content. If you load 100 pages of content within one page and you hit the Back button once, the history of visiting all 100 pages of content is gone. You have no way of returning to, say, page 23 or 89.

You also have no way of creating a permanent link to page 23 or 89 if you want to add them to your browser bookmarks or create a link to them from another page. All you can do is tell people to go to the page that serves as the launching point for the virtual tour, and to click the Next button (or whatever navigational device) 23 times to get to the content you want them to see. Not many people will do this. I know I won't.

Single-paged content breaks the Web. Literally. If a site is based on JavaScript-loaded content, it's going to end up taking three times as much effort to maintain for the same functionality you get for free if you just use the Web's and the browsers' concepts of document. (Document, in this case, being a complete page worth of content that can be accessed via a specific URL—since so much content nowadays is dynamically created.)

At the same time, though, single-paged content helps us circumvent some of the limitations of the Web. If I have to click through 100 complete page reloads to go through a show or presentation, with all the additional overhead that comes with loading a brand new page (and it can be considerable if the periphery around the content is loaded with images and whatnot), I'm going to get irritated.

The key is to minimize the breakage and maximize the usefulness of Ajax applications—single-page applications.

What kind of content can be served up in a single-page application? Anything, really. At the time of this writing, a web site was released that consisted of a single web page, and all links loaded content on demand; there were no permanent links to any of the site's subpages, nor was any history maintained of the site navigation. Needless to say, it received a considerable amount of criticism.

For the most part, single-page applications typically consist of either an application, such as an email program or online Word document, or it could consist of presentational material, where there's some connection between the pages. A slideshow is a popular example of this latter type of paged content, and it has been around since the advent of DHTML and Flash. Now it's being created more and more with Ajax technologies.

The architectural principle behind the slideshow is a frame surrounding content that is static, while the content itself changes based on some event. Though the concept originated with images and photos, individual pages can contain any manner of material, from bullets for a presentation to database records, and yes, photos for an album.

In the next three sections, we'll examine three completely different types of slideshow based on three different types of content: photo, text, and data retrieval. As we progress through the examples, we'll focus just on creating the effect without worrying about the overall impact to the Web. Once we're finished "breaking the Web," so to speak, we'll look at how we can put the pieces back together again.

Creating the Slideshow Infrastructure

The infrastructure for all three slideshow examples is the same. It features previous and next navigational links, as well as a link for home—to return to the beginning. The content is set off from the rest of the page using CSS styling, and the page is designed from the ground up to be XHTML Strict. The page *template* features two content components: the main content, and then an associated metacontent area for title, photo information, or whatever is appropriate for the content.

The basic page template is very simple. It consists of a slideshow container and a content container, which itself contains "main" and "meta" content containers. Below the content is the navigational area, which consists of text links rather than buttons. Future innovations can modify the application, adding in graphics for more polish. For now, though, we'll focus on only the necessary components.

Example 7-1 shows the complete XHTML web page.

Example 7-1. Basic slideshow XHTML

```
<!DOCTYPE html PUBLIC "-//W3C//DTD XHTML 1.0 Strict//EN"
  "http://www.w3.org/TR/xhtml1/DTD/xhtml1-strict.dtd">
<html xmlns="http://www.w3.org/1999/xhtml" lang="en">
<head>
<meta http-equiv="Content-Type" content="text/html; charset=utf-8" />
<title>Slideshow</title>
<link rel="stylesheet" type="text/css" href="slideshow.css" />
</head>
<body>
<div id="slideshow">

<div id="content">
<div id="main">
</div>
<div id="meta">
</div>
</div>

<div id="navigation">
<span class="navlink"><a href="">Previous</a></span>
<span class="navlink"><a href="">Home</a></span>
<span class="navlink"><a href="">Next</a></span>
</div>

</div>
</body>
</html>
```

The basic stylesheet is shown in Example 7-2. It resets several elements to eliminate built-in styles so we can have greater control over presentation.

Example 7-2. Preliminary stylesheet settings

```
ul
{
        list-style-type: none;
        margin: 0;
        padding: 0px;
}
body
{
        font: 12px Verdana, arial, sans-serif;
}
#slideshow
{
        margin: 0 auto;
        width: 800px;
}
#content
{
```

Example 7-2. Preliminary stylesheet settings (continued)

```
        margin: 20px;
}
#main
{
        margin: 10px;
}
#meta
{
        margin: 10px;
}
#navigation
{
        text-align: center;
}
.navlink,.displaynavlink,.hiddennavlink
{
        background-color: #fcc;
        display: inline;
        border: 1px outset #ccc;
}
.navlink a
{
        line-height: 140%;
        padding-left: 10px;
        padding-right: 10px;
}
```

We could be extremely rigorous with design and reset all default presentation values, including setting all headers to one height, eliminating all margins and padding for all objects, and so on:

```
* { padding: 0; margin: 0; border: 0}
```

However, the slideshow CSS is a good start.

Regardless of the content—photo, text, or data—page navigation is more or less the same. You start at page one, where clicking the Previous link doesn't result in any change, and go to the end, where clicking the Next link doesn't change the display. Home always returns to the beginning, which is page one. Because the navigation is the same, the code to manage it should be usable by all the application types.

We could use the quick and dirty approach of tracking the current page and incrementing or decrementing the value depending on the direction of the movement, but we'd like to be able to insert and remove pages and not to have to maintain a counter if we can avoid it. Another approach is to have a set of objects, each of which has two properties: a pointer to the previous page (if any) and a pointer to the next page (again, if any).

To insert a new item, or *node*, at a specific place, rather than appending it at the end of the list, we only need to adjust the pointers for the objects on either side of the new item. If we have an array of items where navigation is dependent on the array index, we'd have to reorder the entire array from the point of insertion. With our bidirectionally linked list, the application can add a page by adding a node at the end of the array and adjusting properties on the impacted nodes on either side.

In the slideshow application, each of the node objects has four other properties in addition to those for navigation: events that are fired when the page is loaded and unloaded, and a function to load the page. There won't be an unload function, as this happens automatically when another page is loaded. The final property is a unique identifier, which can be used to help link the navigational unit with whatever content is being shown. It could be a numeric value and even reflect an array index, but it's not used as an array entry, and is an identifier, nothing more.

Example 7-3 shows the new navigational library, *navigation.js*. In addition to the navigational node class, NavigationNode, the library contains a global object, Navigation, which manages the overall navigation between the nodes. It manages the nextPage and prevPage methods, which are assigned as event handlers to the overt slideshow navigation buttons or links. The setCurrentPage is used to go to a specific page (node), and setHome sets the home node, used whenever a "go home" request occurs; the returnHome method manages this latter event. Navigation is managed by adjustNavigation, which checks the current node to see whether there is a previous or next node set, and hides or shows the next and previous navigational links accordingly.

Example 7-3. The slideshow navigational library

```
// individual navigation node
function NavigationNode(identifier,prev,method) {
   this.identifier = identifier;
   this.previous = prev;
   this.showPage = aaBindObjMethod(this,method);
   this.next;
}
// global Navigation object to maintain page state
// and coordinate navigation
var Navigation = {
   setHome : function(node) {
      this.homeNode = node;
      },
   returnHome : function(evnt) {
      evnt = evnt ? evnt : window.event;
      aaCancelEvent(evnt);
      Navigation.setCurrentPage(Navigation.homeNode);
   },
   nextPage : function(evnt) {
      evnt = evnt ? evnt: window.event;
      aaCancelEvent(evnt);
      if (this.currentPage.next) {
         this.setCurrentPage(this.currentPage.next);
      }
```

Example 7-3. The slideshow navigational library (continued)

```
    },
    adjustNavigation : function( ) {

        var node = this.currentPage;

        // adjust next navigation
        if (!node.next) {
            aaElem('next').style.visibility="hidden";
        } else {
            aaElem('next').style.visibility="visible";
        }

        // adjust navigation
        if (!node.previous) {
            aaElem('previous').style.visibility="hidden";
        } else {
            aaElem('previous').style.visibility="visible";
        }
    },
    prevPage : function(evnt) {
        evnt = evnt ? evnt: window.event;
        aaCancelEvent(evnt);
        if(this.currentPage.previous) {
            this.setCurrentPage(this.currentPage.previous);
        }
    },
    setCurrentPage : function(current) {
        this.currentPage = current;
        this.adjustNavigation( );
        current.showPage( );
    },
    addNavigationNode : function(past,index,method) {
        var nav = new NavigationNode(index,past,method);
        if (past) past.next = nav;
        return nav;
    }
};
```

The Navigation object also has addNavigationNode to create a new node, passing in the node linked previous to the current node (if any), the unique identifier to be associated with the node, and a method that is assigned to the node's showPage property. Since the method passed has to operate within the context of the navigation node, in order to have access to the node identifier or other pertinent information, we can create a new function that uses the JavaScript apply method in order to apply an object's context to a method. This is very similar to what Prototype and other libraries use in their version of bind or similarly named functions. Since this is a universally useful function, it's added to the global *addingajax.js* file:

```
    function aaBindObjMethod(obj, method) {
        return function( ) { method.apply(obj, arguments); }
    }
```

The pieces are all present, and all we need now is a quick sample application to make sure they work. Example 7-4 shows a complete example page, with links to the base *slideshow.css* file, the in-progress *addingajax.js* file, and the new *navigation.js* script (displayed in bold type). These are in addition to modifications to the style settings and the script to run the test case, both embedded within the page to make the example easier to view.

Example 7-4. Test application

```
<!DOCTYPE html PUBLIC "-//W3C//DTD XHTML 1.0 Strict//EN"
  "http://www.w3.org/TR/xhtml1/DTD/xhtml1-strict.dtd">
<html xmlns="http://www.w3.org/1999/xhtml" lang="en">
<head>
<meta http-equiv="Content-Type" content="text/html; charset=utf-8" />
<title>Slideshow</title>
<link rel="stylesheet" type="text/css" href="slideshow.css" />
<style type="text/css">
#slideshow  { width: 600px; border:3px solid #cfc; }
#main       { border: 2px dashed #060; font-size: 18px; overflow: scroll; }
#navigation { margin-bottom: 20px; }
.navlink    { background-color: #fcc; display: inline; margin: 5px; padding: 3px; }
</style>
<script type="text/javascript" src="addingajax.js">
</script>
<script type="text/javascript" src="navigation.js">
</script>
<script type="text/javascript">
//<![CDATA[

// display current node's 'page'
function showPage( ) {
   var main = aaElem('main');
   var txt = document.createTextNode(this.identifier);
   main.appendChild(txt);
}

// create navigation nodes, assign navigation links event handlers
aaManageEvent(window,'load',function( ) {
   var past;
   var home;
   for (var i = 0; i < 20; i++) {
      var nav = Navigation.addNavigationNode(past,i,showPage);
      if (!past) {
        home = nav;
      }
      past = nav;
   }

   // set home and current page
   Navigation.setHome(home);
   Navigation.setCurrentPage(home);
```

Example 7-4. Test application (continued)

```
    // attach event handlers to navigation
    aaManageEvent(aaElem('next'),'click',aaBindObjMethod(Navigation,Navigation.nextPage));
    aaManageEvent(aaElem('previous'),'click',aaBindObjMethod(Navigation,Navigation.
prevPage));
    aaManageEvent(aaElem('home'),'click', Navigation.returnHome);
});

//]]>
</script>

</head>
<body>
<div id="slideshow">

<div id="content">
<div id="main">
</div>
<div id="meta">
</div>
</div>

<div id="navigation">
<div id="previous" class="navlink"><a href="">Previous</a></div>
<div id="home" class="navlink"><a href="">Home</a></div>
<div id="next" class="navlink"><a href="">Next</a></div>
</div>

<div id="footer">
</div>

</div>
</body>
</html>
```

The test case just attaches a function to output the node identifier to the main content section of the page whenever the Previous, Next, or Home links are clicked.

The application begins by setting the Navigation object's current page, as well as the home node to the first node. A loop is run 20 times to create 20 navigation nodes, each assigned the showPage function as its show page method, and the for loop counter as the identifier. In this application, all the showPage function does is print out this identifier whenever the page associated with the node is displayed.

The application uses the new aaBindObjMethod function to attach the Navigation object's context to its nextPage and prevPage methods; otherwise, the event overwrites the object context. We don't require the specific context association to attach the click event handler for the home link.

Figure 7-1 shows the test page in operation after all the navigational buttons and links have been clicked several times.

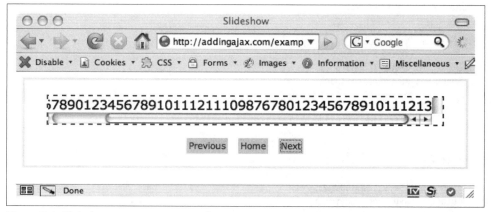

Figure 7-1. Slideshow component test application page

Now that the page templates and the generic navigation routine are finished, we'll create the first slideshow.

Creating a Photo Slideshow

The most typical slideshow, the photo album, is also the simplest—the navigation displays a new photo with each click. If only the photo changes, this type of application doesn't require XMLHttpRequest (XHR) to get the new content, as the application can load a new photo just by changing the src attribute of an existing img element. If, however, we want to display associated information with the image, we have to use XHR or dynamic scripting to get the information from somewhere. This includes getting information from the photo itself.

There's a lot of information stored in many JPEG files: EXIF (Exchangeable Image File Format), XMP (Extensible Metadata Platform), Adobe's IRB (Information Resource Block), and so on. In the next example, we're only interested in the EXIF data, which contains information about how the picture was taken, specifically the model, aperture, exposure time, date the picture was taken, and ISO.

There are libraries for getting this information from the photo, but in the example that follows, we'll use the built-in PHP function (it's built-in if PHP is compiled with --enable-exif), to get the EXIF data returned as an associative array. I also use the Services_JSON package by Michael Migurski, Matt Knapp, and Brett Stimmerman (a PEAR proposed package at *http://pear.php.net/pepr/pepr-proposal-show.php?id=198* that is installed locally to my server) to convert the array to JSON. The web service also takes a callback function to act as an endpoint for a dynamic scripting block. Example 7-5 has the complete server code.

Example 7-5. Photo slideshow web service

```php
<?php
require_once "json/JSON.php";

$filename = $_REQUEST['photo'];
$callback = $_REQUEST['callback'];

if (empty($filename)) {
 echo "This application requires a photo file  name.";
} else {

   $exif = exif_read_data($filename);

   $json = new Services_JSON( );
   $output = $json->encode($exif);

   if ($callback) {
      $output = $callback . "(" . $output . ")";
   }

   print($output);
}
?>
```

A new object is introduced into this application—the Photo. We can add style settings for this new object into an application-specific stylesheet called
photoslideshow.css, and also make other minor modifications, primarily setting the
height of the content area so that it doesn't move up and down as different-sized
photos are displayed:

```css
#slideshow
{
    border: 3px solid #cfc;
    width: 650px;
}
#content
{
    margin: 10px;
}
#main
{
    border: 2px dashed #060;
    font-size: 18px;
    height: 500px;
    overflow: scroll;
}
#navigation
{
    margin-bottom: 20px;
}
.navlink
{
    background-color: #fcc;
```

```
        display: inline;
        margin: 5px;
        padding: 3px;
    }
    #photo
    {
        padding: 10px;
    }
```

On the client side of the application, the web page doesn't change at all from that shown in Example 7-4, other than adding in the photo slideshow's own CSS file and the application-specific JavaScript, which is now pulled into a separate file, *photoslideshow.js*.

The JavaScript source in Example 7-4 is modified to display a photo and process the EXIF data returned by the web service whenever another photo is retrieved. An array of photo names is given in the setup procedure, and a navigation node is created for each, with the navigation node's identifier assigned the photo's filename.

If an existing image element is in the page when the photo node is shown, that existing element is removed. The filename is retrieved from the node's identifier and is used to create a new image element and to get the EXIF data as a complete JSON object. The callback function used in the dynamic scripting, printEXIF, pulls in the relevant information and creates an unordered list (ul) of all of the photo metainformation, inserting it into the metacontent area of the page.

The only components of the previous template objects that change are the CSS settings, displayed earlier, and the JavaScript for the application (located in *photoslideshow.js* and shown in Example 7-6).

Example 7-6. Code section for the photo slideshow with EXIF data

```
// show the node's page
function showPage( ) {
    getEXIF(this.photo);
    var main = aaElem('main');

    // clean up old content
    var current = aaElem('photo');
    if (current) main.removeChild(current);

    var img = document.createElement("img");
    img.src=this.photo;
    img.id='photo';
    main.appendChild(img);
}

// create endpoint dynamic scripting block to get the EXIF data for the photo
function getEXIF(photo) {
    var url = 'get_photo.php?photo=' + photo;
    var script = document.createElement('script');
    script.type = 'text/javascript';
```

Example 7-6. Code section for the photo slideshow with EXIF data (continued)

```
    script.src = url + '&callback=printEXIF';
    document.getElementsByTagName('head')[0].appendChild(script);
}

// create a list item given text and the UL
function createListItem(text,ul) {
    var li = document.createElement('li');
    var txt = document.createTextNode(text);
    li.appendChild(txt);
    ul.appendChild(li);
    return ul;
}
// display the EXIF data for the photo
function printEXIF(exifObj) {

    // access recipe element and clear
    var meta = aaElem('meta');
    var metacontent =aaElem('metacontent');
    if (metacontent) meta.removeChild(metacontent);

    var ul = document.createElement('ul');
    ul=createListItem(exifObj.Model,ul);
    ul=createListItem(exifObj.ISOSpeedRatings,ul);
    ul=createListItem(exifObj.ExposureTime,ul);
    ul=createListItem(exifObj.DateTimeOriginal,ul);
    ul=createListItem(exifObj.COMPUTED.ApertureFNumber,ul);
    ul.id="metacontent";
    meta.appendChild(ul);

}

// application setup
aaManageEvent(window,'load',function() {
    var photos = new Array();
    photos[0] = 'bollingerforestthumb.jpg';
    photos[1] = 'robin1thumb.jpg';
    photos[2] = 'silverthaw1thumb.jpg';
    photos[3] = 'robin2thumb.jpg';

    var past;
    var home;
    for (var i = 0; i < photos.length; i++) {
        var nav = Navigation.addNavigationNode(past,photos[i],showPage);
        if (!past) {
            home = nav;
        }
        past = nav;
    }

    // set home and first page
    Navigation.setHome(home);
    Navigation.setCurrentPage(home);
```

```
    // add navigation events
    aaManageEvent(aaElem('next'),'click',aaBindObjMethod(Navigation,Navigation.nextPage));
    aaManageEvent(aaElem('previous'),'click',aaBindObjMethod(Navigation,Navigation.
prevPage));
    aaManageEvent(aaElem('home'),'click', Navigation.returnHome);
});
```

The original web page isn't changed except for the addition of links to the new stylesheet and the application-specific JavaScript. Other than making sure the application works in our target browsers, we're not going to be concerned at the moment about efficiency or accessibility, or about the fact that we've effectively smashed the navigational, historical, and placement components of the web all to heck. For now, we'll enjoy the effect of the application, as shown in Figure 7-2, and then work on the next slideshow, featuring split text.

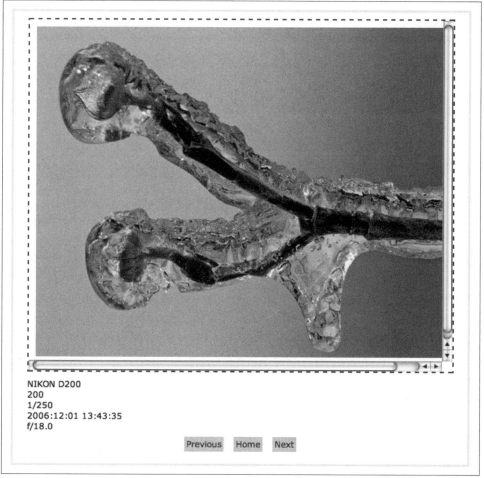

NIKON D200
200
1/250
2006:12:01 13:43:35
f/18.0

Previous Home Next

Figure 7-2. Sample "page" from the photo slideshow

Splitting Text

We don't often think of narrative text when we think of a "slideshow," but a slideshow is nothing more than a variation of a single-page web application, and on the Web, text is probably the most partitioned data there is. It's not unusual to find longer articles and essays split into different pages, not to mention that most web sites are really separate blocks of formatted text, split up into an organization and all connected via some form of navigation such as a menu.

For the next example, we will use an article that I wrote called the "Ten Basic Commands of Unix," splitting it into 11 separate sections consisting of the introduction and individual commands. We can organize the material into 11 separate, complete HTML fragments in 11 separate files. The PHP web service program is very simple, consisting of code to retrieve the GET request parameter, file_get_contents, for each fragment. The application uses this to load the entire file into a variable, which is then echoed:

```php
<?php
$page = $_GET['page'];

// safety check on the data would normally be performed here
if (empty($page)) {
  echo "You need to provide a page number.";
} else {
    $filename = $page . '.html';
    $content = file_get_contents($filename);
    echo $content;
}

?>
```

It takes about 10 minutes to create this version of the slideshow, including the time it takes to split the text into manageable portions. Once we have a good infrastructure for an effect, the hard part is finished, and the rest is pure fun and giggles.

We can modify the application CSS again to better suit this new content format by placing the navigation bar at the top, removing any height restrictions and box borders and moving the additional CSS into a file called *textslideshow.css*:

```css
#slideshow
{
        margin: 0 20px;
}
#content
{
        position: absolute;
        top: 40px;
        margin: 10px;
        width: 700px;
}
#navigation
```

```
        {
                margin-top: 20px;
                width: 300px;
        }
        .navlink
        {
                background-color: #ccc;
                display: inline;
                margin: 5px;
                padding: 3px;
        }
        #page
        {
                margin: 20px;
        }
```

All that's left is to modify the application-specific JavaScript. In this example, the application loops through a sequence of numbers from 1 through 11, creating the navigation node and setting its identifier to the HTML fragment filename, sans the extension. In the showPage method, the application uses this to kick off an Ajax request, which in turn invokes the server to load the page fragment from its file, and triggers the printPage function to process the results.

In printPage, we can load a new element from the document called page, creating it first if it doesn't already exist. The HTML fragment is loaded using the page element's innerHTML property. Example 7-7 shows the JavaScript, located in *textslideshow.js*, to create this "textshow."

Example 7-7. Creating a text-based slideshow with HTML fragments

```
function showPage( ) {
   getPage(this.identifier);
   var main = aaElem('main');
}

function getPage(page) {
        if (!Navigation.xmlhttp) Navigation.xmlhttp = aaGetXmlHttpRequest( );
        var qry = "page=" + page;
        var url = 'get_page.php?' + qry;
        Navigation.xmlhttp.open('GET', url, true);
        Navigation.xmlhttp.onreadystatechange = printPage;
        Navigation.xmlhttp.send(null);
}

function printPage( ) {
  if(Navigation.xmlhttp.readyState == 4
              && Navigation.xmlhttp.status == 200) {

   var content = aaElem('page');
   if (!content) {
      content = document.createElement('div');
      content.id = 'page';
```

Example 7-7. Creating a text-based slideshow with HTML fragments (continued)

```
      aaElem('main').appendChild(content);
    }
    content.innerHTML = Navigation.xmlhttp.responseText;
  }
}

aaManageEvent(window,'load',function( ) {
  var past;
  var home;
  var pageCount = 11;
  for (var i = 1; i <= pageCount; i++) {
    var id = 'part' + i;
    var nav = Navigation.addNavigationNode(past,id,showPage);
    if (!past) {
      home = nav;
    }
    past = nav;
  }

  // set home and first page
  Navigation.setHome(home);
  Navigation.setCurrentPage(home);

  aaManageEvent(aaElem('next'),'click',aaBindObjMethod(Navigation,Navigation.nextPage));
  aaManageEvent(aaElem('previous'),'click',aaBindObjMethod(Navigation,Navigation.
prevPage));
  aaManageEvent(aaElem('home'),'click', Navigation.returnHome);
});
```

A more proper approach would be to strip the markup from the fragment, splitting the text further into text strings. The whole thing would be put back together using the DOM before being inserted into the document. This would result in about four times the amount of code. It's true that you'd be guaranteed good markup using this approach, but at what cost?

Another issue is that innerHTML supposedly wouldn't work with a page served up or streamed as XML. All the examples in this chapter are created with the XHTML extension XHTML DOCTYPE, and served up as application/xhtml+xml. Thanks to the now-ubiquitous use of innerHTML, the page loads fine. As for streaming it as XML via another agent, well, that's another story. It's a tradeoff, but one that I'll take in this case.

Figure 7-3 shows this new application in action.

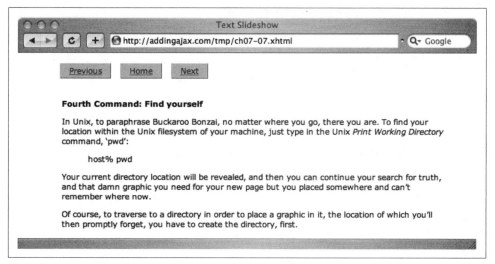

Figure 7-3. Text-based slideshow, turned to a page of a multipart article

Paging Through Data

One of the most common paging operations is browsing through the results of some form of search. Any time we use Google or Yahoo!, we're paging through the results. When we access our bank account records, search for an item at an online store, read through a weblog, peruse a set of restaurant recommendations, or check out a listing of music, we're paging through data returned as part of some query.

These paging applications break up the data, returning only so many rows in order to keep page loading times down. They provide a Next and Previous operation to allow us to go back and forth in the data. Through HTTP response codes, as well as application implementation, we can go back and forth in the results without another search taking place.

Paged data seems a natural candidate for our "paged" slideshow application. The next application uses the same Wordpress posts table used in Chapter 6, retrieving the post ID, title, and GUID (globally unique identifier). Since the application is MySQL, we can use the limit property on the query, starting at a different row each time and limiting the number of rows returned. In the example, the application retrieves 20 rows at a time, starting at the first row, and then updating the search to begin at positions in 20-row increments. The new server-side application is shown in Example 7-8, with the username and password modified, of course.

Example 7-8. Web service pulling in rows from the database

```php
<?php

$start = $_REQUEST['start'];
$limit = $_REQUEST['limit'];
$callback = $_REQUEST['callback'];

if (empty($start)) {
    $limitstr = "limit $limit";
} else {
    $limitstr = "limit $start,$limit";
}
mysql_connect('localhost','username','password');
mysql_select_db('database');

$rows = mysql_query("SELECT ID, post_title, guid, comment_count from wp_posts order by ID
$limitstr");
if ($rows && mysql_num_rows($rows) > 0) {
    $str = "[";
    while($row = mysql_fetch_row($rows)) {
        if ($str != '[') $str.=",";
        $str.= "{ id : '$row[0]', title : \"$row[1]\", guid : '$row[2]', comments: '$row[3]'
}";
    }
    $str.="]";
}
echo $callback . '(' . $str . ')';
?>
```

The service provides JSON formatting consisting of rows of objects, which is the logical structure for this type of application.

The stylesheet settings are similar to those in the other examples, except for some modifications for the data type and subtle differences in color and font. The navigation bar is pulled to the left of the data, and the buttons are vertically aligned. The modified stylesheet is named *dataslideshow.css*:

```css
#slideshow
{
        border: 3px groove #ccf;
        width: 760px;
}
#content
{
        margin: 10px;
        float: right;
        width: 640px;
}
#main
{
        border: 2px dotted #fcf;
        font-size: 14px;
}
```

```
#navigation
{
        margin-top: 50px;
        float: left;
        margin-left: 5px;


}
.navlink
{
        display: block;
        background-color: #fcf;
        margin: 5px;
}
#dataTable
{
        margin: 15px;
        width: 95%;
}
#footer
{
        clear: both;
}
```

In the client, the identifier this time is the starting position, beginning with 0 and incrementing by multiples of 20. This, the limit on the number of rows returned, and the callback function are passed in the dynamic script accessing the service end-point. In the printRows callback function, the DOM and script build an HTML table using a helper function to create a couple of table cells, but using innerHTML to manage the linked title. If we want to avoid using innerHTML, we'd also have to create a new hypertext element, append the GUID or URL to it, create a textNode for the title, and so on—it would add considerably to the code. Consider it a good exercise for future effort.

Example 7-9 displays the JavaScript, located in *dataslideshow.js*, for another slide-show data type. Again, most of your time will be spent writing the server code—the client is relatively simple other than the numerous DOM method calls for the table.

Example 7-9. Database-driven "slideshow"

```
function showPage( ) {
   getRows(this.identifier);
}

function getRows(start) {
   var url = 'getposts.php?start=' + start;
   var script = document.createElement('script');
   script.type = 'text/javascript';
   script.src = url + '&limit=20&callback=printRows';
   document.getElementsByTagName('head')[0].appendChild(script);
}

function createTableCell(value,tr) {
```

Example 7-9. Database-driven "slideshow" (continued)

```
    // creates a <td> element
    var cell = document.createElement("td");

    // creates a Text Node
    var text = document.createTextNode(value);

    // appends the Text Node we created into the cell <td>
    cell.appendChild(text);

    // appends the cell <td> into the row <tr>
    tr.appendChild(cell);

    return tr;
}
function printRows(rowsObj) {

    var main = aaElem('main');

    // clean up old content
    var oTable = aaElem('dataTable');
    if (oTable) main.removeChild(oTable);

    var table     = document.createElement("table");
    table.id = "dataTable";
    var tableBody = document.createElement("tbody");

    // table rows
    for(var i = 0; i < rowsObj.length; i++) {
        // creates a <tr> element
        var row = document.createElement("tr");

        row = createTableCell(rowsObj[i].id, row);

        // anchor and title
        var cell = document.createElement("td");
        cell.innerHTML = "<a href='" + rowsObj[i].guid + "'>" + rowsObj[i].title + "</a>";
        row.appendChild(cell);

        row = createTableCell(rowsObj[i].comments,row);

        tableBody.appendChild(row);
    }

    table.appendChild(tableBody);
    aaElem('main').appendChild(table);

}

// set up the application and navigation nodes
aaManageEvent(window,'load',function() {

    var past;
```

Example 7-9. Database-driven "slideshow" (continued)

```
var home;
for (var i = 0; i <= 10; i++) {
  var nav = Navigation.addNavigationNode(past,i*20,showPage);
  if (!past) {
    home = nav;
  }
  past = nav;
}

// set page
Navigation.setHome(home);
Navigation.setCurrentPage(home);

aaManageEvent(aaElem('next'),'click',aaBindObjMethod(Navigation,Navigation.nextPage));
aaManageEvent(aaElem('previous'),'click',aaBindObjMethod(Navigation,Navigation.
prevPage));
aaManageEvent(aaElem('home'),'click', Navigation.returnHome);
});
```

Figure 7-4 shows this newest incarnation of our handy slideshow, after a couple of clicks of the Next button.

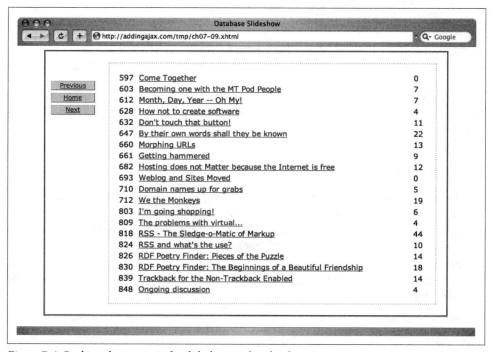

Figure 7-4. Pushing the concept of a slideshow with a database query

It's rather interesting to see what we can shove into a single-page application, or a slide for that matter, when we put our minds to it. We've also beaten the Web all to heck with the applications. There's nothing that provides a permanent link for a "page," enables the Back button to return to a specific place, or makes use of browser caching. Checking the browser history, it looks as if we haven't gone beyond the one page, which would be a tough position for ad views. Even the use of the links for navigation is such that both search engine web bots and screen readers are defeated by their use. If scripting is disabled or not supported, the page ends up with a lovely, minimalist view, and the user accessing the page has a strong sense that something is missing.

Now that we've broken the Web, let's see if it can be put back together again.

Remembering Place

In the last of the slideshows, which contains "pages" of links to existing weblog posts, clicking one of the links loads that story into the browser. Well and good, but if you click one of the links, another page opens in the browser. When you're ready to go back to the list, depending on the browser, the "place" where you had left the original slideshow is lost, and the first page is opened. If you open another page by typing in a new URL, using a search engine toolbar, or clicking a link in the bookmarks list, when you attempt to use the Back button to return to the slideshow application, again, you'll lose your "place."

A second problem is associated with trying to create a permanent link to a specific page in the slideshow, for instance, if you want to link to the fifth page in the text slideshow, or link to the third photo. The most you can do, with the way the application is currently coded, is tell users to go to the first page and then click the Next button so many times. This really isn't a workable option. What we need is a way to remember place.

Remembering Place and Page Fragments

Remembering place and persisting place are two problems with Ajax slideshows or any other single-page application. The way around both of these challenges is through the use of the window.location object, and the use of a page fragment, called the *hash*. A page hash is a value that's tacked on to the end of a URL when a page fragment is accessed within a page. Page fragments are created through the name anchor, but they can also be created dynamically, just by assigning a value to the location object's hash property:

```
window.location.hash = value;
```

This provides a specific location for the slideshow page that can be persisted, either for navigation using the Back button in your browser within one session, or as a permanent link embedded in another page.

I'm not sure who originated the idea of the page fragment, but I first read about it in Mike Stenhouse's "Fixing the Back Button and Enabling Bookmarking for Ajax Apps" (at *http://www.contentwithstyle. co.uk/Articles/38/fixing-the-back-button-and-enabling-bookmarking-for-ajax-apps*) and Brad Neuberg's onJava article, "Ajax: How to Handle Bookmarks and Back Buttons" (at *http://www.onjava.com/pub/a/ onjava/2005/10/26/ajax-handling-bookmarks-and-back-button.html*).

Returning now to the Navigation object. One of the items each navigation node has is an identifier. It's used to help load the relevant data, but it can also be used to mark place with the use of the location object and its hash property. Luckily, this doesn't require any change at all to the Navigation object, and requires only minor changes to each slideshow application's own specific code.

Working backward, Example 7-10 recreates Example 7-9, the database-driven content example, except this time using the page hash. Only minor modifications are needed for the code—adding to the location when a page is shown and pulling up a specific slideshow page when the page is first loaded. The changes are emphasized in bold in the code.

Example 7-10. Modified code to add paging to application code in Example 7-9

```
function showPage( ) {
  window.location.hash = this.identifier;
  getRows(this.identifier);
}
...
aaManageEvent(window,'load',function( ) {

    var past;
    var index;
    var current;
    var hash = window.location.hash;
    if (hash) {
        index = hash.split("#")[1];
    }

    for (var i = 0; i <= 10; i++) {
       var id = i*20;
       var nav = Navigation.addNavigationNode(past,id,showPage);
       if (!past) {
         home = nav;
         if (!index)
            current = nav;
       }
       past = nav;
    }

    Navigation.setHome(home);
```

Example 7-10. Modified code to add paging to application code in Example 7-9 (continued)

```
if (!index) {
   Navigation.setCurrentPage(home);
} else {
   Navigation.setCurrentPage(current);
}

   aaManageEvent(aaElem('next'),'click',aaBindObjMethod(Navigation,Navigation.nextPage));
   aaManageEvent(aaElem('previous'),'click',aaBindObjMethod(Navigation,Navigation.
prevPage));
   aaManageEvent(aaElem('home'),'click', Navigation.returnHome);

});
```

In the example, since the page identifier is used to drive out at which database row to begin the query, it's shown as a numeric value, increasing in increments of 20: 20, 40, 60, and so on. Once the application is loaded, the placing of the page is maintained when users click on one of the links, load another page, and then return to that page.

Example 7-11 recreates the text slideshow from Example 7-7. In this example, the paging is text-based rather than numeric, though the code to set the location hash is the same (assigned by the navigation node's identifier).

Example 7-11. Modified code to add paging to application code in Example 7-7

```
function showPage( ) {
   window.location.hash = this.identifier;
   getPage(this.identifier);
   var main = aaElem('main');
}
...
aaManageEvent(window,'load',function( ) {
   var past;
   var home;
   var current;

   var pageCount = 11;

   var index;
   var hash = window.location.hash;
   if (hash) {
      index = hash.split("#")[1];
   }

   for (var i = 1; i <= pageCount; i++) {
      var id = 'part' + i;
      var nav = Navigation.addNavigationNode(past,id,showPage);
      if (!past) {
         home = nav;
      }
      past = nav;
```

```
      if (index && id == index)
        current = nav;
   }

   Navigation.setHome(home);

   if (!current) {
      Navigation.setCurrentPage(home);
   } else {
      Navigation.setCurrentPage(current);
   }

   aaManageEvent(aaElem('next'),'click',aaBindObjMethod(Navigation,Navigation.nextPage));
   aaManageEvent(aaElem('previous'),'click',aaBindObjMethod(Navigation,Navigation.
prevPage));
   aaManageEvent(aaElem('home'),'click', Navigation.returnHome);
});
```

The reengineering for the photo slideshow is the same, except that the identifier in this case is the name of a photo thumbnail source file, as shown in Example 7-12.

Example 7-12. Modifications to enable Back button persistence in Example 7-6

```
aaManageEvent(window,'load',function( ) {
   var photos = new Array( );
   photos[0] = 'bollingerforestthumb.jpg';
   photos[1] = 'robin1thumb.jpg';
   photos[2] = 'silverthaw1thumb.jpg';
   photos[3] = 'robin2thumb.jpg';

   var index;
   var hash = window.location.hash;
   if (hash) {
      index = hash.split("#")[1];
   }

   var past;
   for (var i = 0; i < photos.length; i++) {
      var id = photos[i];
      var nav = Navigation.addNavigationNode(past,id,showPage);
      if (!past) {
        Navigation.setHome(nav);
        if (!index)
           Navigation.setCurrentPage(nav);
      }
      past = nav;
      if (id == index)
        Navigation.setCurrentPage(nav);
   }

   aaManageEvent(aaElem('next'),'click',aaBindObjMethod(Navigation,Navigation.nextPage));
```

Example 7-12. Modifications to enable Back button persistence in Example 7-6 (continued)

```
    aaManageEvent(aaElem('previous'),'click',aaBindObjMethod(Navigation,Navigation.
prevPage));
    aaManageEvent(aaElem('home'),'click', Navigation.returnHome);
});
```

We get two things from making this minor modification to each of the applications: maintaining state when the web page reader clicks away from the page and then returns, and a form of permanent link to return to a specific "page."

Unfortunately, though, the application doesn't work as planned for all browsers and all circumstances. In IE, setting the hash doesn't add the page to the history. In Firefox and other Mozilla browsers, as well as Opera, Safari, and WebKit, clicking the Back and Forward buttons will not reset the page contents.

Remembering Place in a Timely Manner

Firefox, Opera, and Safari are the closest to having a working application that can remember place, lacking only the ability to reflect change when the user clicks the Back or Forward buttons from within the actual slideshow. It would be a simple matter to fix this problem if only there were a way to capture Back and Forward button clicks, but no such functionality exists.

The only way to really determine that an action has occurred is to capture a snapshot of the URL the last time we changed the page contents, and compare this with what exists within the browser's location bar. If they don't match, update the page and recapture a snapshot of the new URL. The only way to get this to work is through the use of timers, which is simple enough, though it makes me cringe to do it.

Triggering a timer and reloading the page content leads to another difficulty that is related to the way the application is implemented: the navigation nodes are linked to each other rather than being linked via an array. Because of this, the only way to access a specific navigation node is to traverse the linked list and compare identifiers. If the identifier of the page to be loaded matches the node, load that particular navigation node.

We could avoid having to navigate the nodes by using an array of nodes rather than a linked list. I like the linked list, though, as it reflects the nature of this type of activity far better than an array of nodes does. We could have both—the linked list for navigation and an array of nodes as pointers—but it seems redundant, especially since the amount of processing to find the appropriate node is very small. For this example, we'll iterate through the nodes until we find the correct one.

Converting the database example to this new approach, Example 7-13 shows the application source with the changes highlighted so they stand out. The timer is set at 700 milliseconds, which seems to be a good time for this type of effect. The application captures the current "page" in a global value, which is compared with the `window.location.hash` property. If they're different, the node list is traversed until the page is found, and when found, it is passed to the `Navigation` object's `setCurrentPage` method.

Example 7-13. Faux backspace based on timer event

```
var currentLocation;

function showPage( ) {
  window.location.hash = this.identifier;
  currentLocation = this.identifier;
  getRows(this.identifier);
}

function getRows(start) {
    var url = 'getposts.php?start=' + start;
    var script = document.createElement('script');
    script.type = 'text/javascript';
    script.src = url + '&limit=20&callback=printRows';
    document.getElementsByTagName('head')[0].appendChild(script);
}

function createTableCell(value,tr) {

    // creates a <td> element
    var cell = document.createElement("td");

    // creates a Text Node
    var text = document.createTextNode(value);

    // appends the Text Node we created into the cell <td>
    cell.appendChild(text);

    // appends the cell <td> into the row <tr>
    tr.appendChild(cell);

    return tr;
}
function printRows(rowsObj) {

    var main = aaElem('main');

    // clean up old content
    var oTable = aaElem('dataTable');
    if (oTable) main.removeChild(oTable);

    var table     = document.createElement("table");
    table.id = "dataTable";
    var tableBody = document.createElement("tbody");

    // table rows
    for(var i = 0; i < rowsObj.length; i++) {
        // creates a <tr> element
        var row = document.createElement("tr");
```

Example 7-13. Faux backspace based on timer event (continued)

```
        row = createTableCell(rowsObj[i].id, row);

        // anchor and title
        var cell = document.createElement("td");
        cell.innerHTML = "<a href='" + rowsObj[i].guid + "'>" + rowsObj[i].title + "</a>";
        row.appendChild(cell);

        row = createTableCell(rowsObj[i].comments,row);

      tableBody.appendChild(row);
   }

   table.appendChild(tableBody);

   aaElem('main').appendChild(table);

}
function checkLocation( ) {
   var hash = window.location.hash;
   if (hash) {
     index = hash.split("#")[1];
     if (currentLocation != index) {
        var node = Navigation.homeNode;
        while (true) {
           if (node.identifier == index)
               break;
           node = node.next;
        }
        Navigation.setCurrentPage(node);
     }
   }
   setTimeout(checkLocation,700);
}

aaManageEvent(window,'load',function( ) {

   var past;
   var index;
   var hash = window.location.hash;
   if (hash) {
      index = hash.split("#")[1];
   }

   for (var i = 0; i <= 10; i++) {
      var id = i*20;
      var nav = Navigation.addNavigationNode(past,id,showPage);
      if (!past) {
        Navigation.setHome(nav);
        if (!index)
            Navigation.setCurrentPage(nav);
      }
      past = nav;
```

Example 7-13. Faux backspace based on timer event (continued)

```
    if (id == index)
      Navigation.setCurrentPage(nav);
  }
  aaManageEvent(aaElem('next'),'click',aaBindObjMethod(Navigation,Navigation.nextPage));
  aaManageEvent(aaElem('previous'),'click',aaBindObjMethod(Navigation,Navigation.
prevPage));
  aaManageEvent(aaElem('home'),'click', Navigation.returnHome);

  // set timer to check page location
  setTimeout(checkLocation,700);
});
```

Now we have a paged system that's integrated into the browser's own navigation system...for Firefox. It works haphazardly with Opera and Safari, and completely shuts down WebKit. The existing problem with IE also hasn't been fixed, in that IE doesn't add hash mark entries in the location bar to the history. To get around that, the solution is to embed an `iframe` into the page, use it to load an external page with a hash mark, and then adjust it to reflect the changing "pages" so that IE's history buffer is updated.

Of course, once that's fixed, there's still the problem with Safari...and with Opera... and...wait a sec, is this the path we want to take?

The Difference Between Clever and Smart

Some of the most significant pushback against Ajax derives from the fact that many people see a whole lot of code added to a site just to create "gewgaw" effects. The sad thing is that the effect that the developer slaved over for hours and days and weeks most likely won't impress folks as much as another effect that only took a couple of hours. Many of the more complex Ajax effects will impress another Ajax developer, but not necessarily the people who actually visit your web pages or use your web application.

There's a difference between being clever and being smart. The clever developer will spend the hours and days and weeks in order to make a web page or application work exactly the way she wants. As a developer, I appreciate such efforts because we can all learn from what they've done and add their efforts to our own. However, the smart developer will work for a certain length of time on an effect, and when she has reached a point of complexity, will stop and review what she's doing and think about the point in time at which further effort will no longer have any real returns. If our only audience is developers, then all efforts have a big return. However, if our audience is our bosses, our clients, and our web page readers and application users, then whatever we do in code has to be balanced against how maintainable an effect is, how much bandwidth it takes, and yes, how much it "breaks the Web."

At some point, we have to acknowledge that, yes, a single page application such as those demonstrated earlier does break the Web. When we start to add timer events and iframes and other odd bits of coding just to get an effect to sort of work, then we know we're either heading down a very complex path or we have to just acknowledge that, as the browsers exist today, there are times when we do break the Web, and there's not a lot we can do about it.

Even if we do derive a method to keep the application from breaking the Web, such as using the location hash as a way of returning to a specific page whenever we follow a link outside the page, it isn't effective if we use it as a permanent link to the page. Whoever clicks on this link elsewhere may not have scripting enabled. Then there's the issue of web bots not following code-enabled links, and all the pages not being scanned for inclusion in search engines—not to mention that page view problem.

At the same time, loading content on demand using Ajax and single-paged applications are techniques that can provide significantly better performance over a multipage application, or more importantly, allow us to add some sophistication and polish to the presentation. What we need is to compromise—keeping a little of the old and mixing in a little new.

Old and New Persistence: Side by Side

A photo slideshow is probably one of the single-page applications most acceptable as a pure Ajax solution. It's not the type of thing one would expect to interact with using the browser's Back and Forward buttons, and it's not likely to have persistent links to any photo. Still, if users access a photo slideshow and have a browser extension like NoScript enabled, they will be faced with a blank page and will have to turn scripting on just to see what they're missing. No matter how nice the fades or the description pop-ups in the bottom, users come away a little less impressed than if the slideshow creator had just created the show using a traditional multipage approach and then added in the Ajax stuff. Not only will users with scripting disabled not be faced with a blank page when accessing the slideshow, the latter method also provides a way of managing the persistence problem that Ajax can add to a project.

The first slideshow, the photo slideshow, has been around quite some time, though most photo galleries and slideshows are managed via server-side code, not through Ajax (this is changing, quickly).

Implemented in PHP, an application like this would be given a collection of photos (usually in a subdirectory, but names listed in an array can also work). You can specify which photo to display by adding it as a GET HTTP request parameter, and also add these GET parameters as part of the URL to specify the Previous, Home, and Next links. These also form the permanent links for the individual slide pages.

Example 7-14 is a reimplementation of the earlier application, except this time as a multipage application managed through the server, multipage in this regard being multiple URLs, not actual physical pages. There's no JavaScript involved at all.

Example 7-14. Traditional photo slideshow, implemented using server-side technologies

```php
<?php

require_once "photos.php";

function getExifData($filename) {

    if (empty($filename)) {
        echo "This application requires a photo file  name.";
    } else {
        $exif = exif_read_data($filename);
    }
return $exif;

}

    $index = $_GET['photo'];
    $uri = $_SERVER['SCRIPT_NAME'];

    if (empty($index)) {
        $index = 0;
    }

    $prev = $index - 1;

    if ($index < (count($photos) - 1)) {
      $next = $index + 1;
    }

    $exif = getExifData($photos[$index]);
?>
<!DOCTYPE html PUBLIC "-//W3C//DTD XHTML 1.0 Strict//EN"
  "http://www.w3.org/TR/xhtml1/DTD/xhtml1-strict.dtd">
<html xmlns="http://www.w3.org/1999/xhtml" lang="en">
<head>
<title>Slideshow</title>
<meta http-equiv="Content-Type" content="text/html; charset=utf-8" />
<link rel="stylesheet" type="text/css" href="slideshow.css" />
<link rel="stylesheet" type="text/css" href="photoslideshow.css" />
</head>
<body>
<div id="slideshow">

<div id="content">
<div id="main">
<img src="<?php echo $photos[$index]; ?>" id="photo" alt="" />
</div>
<div id="meta">
<ul id="metacontent">
<?php

echo "<li>" . $exif['Model'] . "</li>";
echo "<li>" . $exif['ISOSpeedRatings']. "</li>";
```

Example 7-14. Traditional photo slideshow, implemented using server-side technologies (continued)

```php
echo "<li>" . $exif['ExposureTime'] . "</li>";
echo "<li>" . $exif['DateTimeOriginal'] . "</li>";
echo "<li>" . $exif['Computed']['ApertureFNumber'] . "</li>";
?>
</div>
</div>

<div id="navigation">
<?php if ($prev >= 0) : ?><div id="previous" class="navlink"><a href="<?php echo
"$uri?photo=$prev"; ?>">Previous</a></div><?php endif; ?>
<div id="home" class="navlink"><a href="<?php echo $uri ?>?photo=0">Home</a></div>
<?php if (!empty($next)) : ?><div id="next" class="navlink"><a href="<?php echo
"$uri?photo=$next"; ?>">Next</a></div><?php endif; ?>
</div>

<div id="footer">
</div>
</div>
</body>
</html>
```

Nothing fancy. If the first photo in the series is showing, the Previous button isn't displayed, and if the last photo is being shown, the Next button isn't displayed. To bookmark to link to a specific photo, just copy the URL in the location bar. It's straightforward and there seems to be little reason to add Ajax.

However, if you want to jazz up the display—add in a fade from/to effect to handle the transitions between the photos, pop up a semitransparent panel at the bottom with the EXIF data, or add a feature that uses a single click to expand the photo—you'll need to handle this as a single-page Ajax application using XHR. The solution is to use both server and client technologies in a cooperative venture to ensure the application degrades. However, when a web page reader is using a capable browser and has scripting enabled, he will get the full show, nice visual effects and all.

Example 7-15 is the same web application just described, but now we've added the Ajax functionality. The only differences in the web page, highlighted in the example, is the addition of the necessary JavaScript libraries and an array of photos to be traversed in the photo slideshow. The photo array is created using server-side functionality so that the photos and their order remains the same with the nonscript, server-enabled application, as well as the Ajax-client-enabled application. The function to get the EXIF data is also packaged now as a function, accessible via a server-side application or Ajax-enabled web service.

Example 7-15. Photo slideshow packaged as a PHP/Ajax parallel application

```php
<?php

    require_once "getphotoexif.php";
    require_once "photos.php";
```

Example 7-15. Photo slideshow packaged as a PHP/Ajax parallel application (continued)

```php
    $index = $_GET['photo'];
    $uri = $_SERVER['SCRIPT_NAME'];

    if (empty($index))
       $index = 0;

    $prev = $index - 1;

    if ($index < (count($photos) - 1)) {
      $next = $index + 1;
    }

    $exif = getExifData($photos[$index]);

?>
<!DOCTYPE html PUBLIC "-//W3C//DTD XHTML 1.0 Strict//EN"
  "http://www.w3.org/TR/xhtml1/DTD/xhtml1-strict.dtd">
<html xmlns="http://www.w3.org/1999/xhtml" lang="en">
<head>
<title>Slideshow</title>
<meta http-equiv="Content-Type" content="text/html; charset=utf-8" />
<link rel="stylesheet" type="text/css" href="slideshow.css" />
<link rel="stylesheet" type="text/css" href="photoslideshow.css" />
<script type="text/javascript" src="mootools.js">
</script>
<script type="text/javascript" src="addingajax.js">
</script>
<script type="text/javascript" src="navigation2.js">
</script>
<script type="text/javascript" src="photoslideshow3.js">
</script>
<script type="text/javascript">
//<![CDATA[

var photos = [];
<?php

for ($i = 0; $i < count($photos); $i++) {
   echo "photos[$i] = '" . $photos[$i] . "';\n";
}

?>
//]]>
</script>
</head>
<body>
<div id="slideshow">

<div id="content">
<div id="main">
<img src="<?php echo $photos[$index]; ?>" id="photo" alt="" />
</div>
```

Example 7-15. Photo slideshow packaged as a PHP/Ajax parallel application (continued)

```
<div id="meta">
<p id="permalink">
<a href="<?php echo $uri + "?photo=$index"; ?>">Permanent Link to this page</a>
</p>
<ul id="metacontent">
<?php

echo "<li>" . $exif['Model'] . "</li>";
echo "<li>" . $exif['ISOSpeedRatings']. "</li>";
echo "<li>" . $exif['ExposureTime'] . "</li>";
echo "<li>" . $exif['DateTimeOriginal'] . "</li>";
echo "<li>" . $exif['COMPUTED']['ApertureFNumber'] . "</li>";

?>
</div>
</div>

<div id="navigation">
<div id="previous" class="<?php if ($prev >= 0) echo 'displaynavlink'; else echo
'hiddennavlink'; ?>">
<a href="<?php echo "$uri?photo=$prev"; ?>">Previous</a></div>
<div id="home" class="displaynavlink"><a href="<?php echo $uri ?>?photo=1">Home</a></div>
<div id="next" class="<?php if (!empty($next)) echo 'displaynavlink'; else echo
'hiddennavlink'; ?>">
<a href="<?php echo "$uri?photo=$next"; ?>">Next</a></div>
</div>

<div id="footer">
</div>
</div>
</body>
</html>
```

Another related issue is the addition of a permanent link to the metadata area of the page area. This permanent link contains the PHP-based URL, which retrieves the current photo via a photo query argument. Hopefully this will encourage users to use the link if they want to directly access the application. The EXIF data for the PHP application is the same as that printed out using the Ajax application.

When the application originally loads, one of the first things the Ajax application does is assign click event handlers for the three navigational buttons. These override the action normally taken when the links are clicked, loading the "pages" through Ajax. However, if scripting is disabled, the PHP-generated pages are loaded when the links are clicked, which should also be sufficient for web bots in addition to those turning off scripting.

There are only minor modifications to the CSS file. There are two different classes for the buttons now: one where the button is visible and one where it is not. At the beginning of the slideshow, the Previous button is hidden, and at the end of the slideshow, the Next button is hidden:

```css
#slideshow
{
        border: 3px solid #cfc;
        width: 650px;
}
#content
{
        margin: 10px;
}
#main
{
        border: 2px dashed #060;
        font-size: 18px;
        height: 500px;
        overflow: scroll;
}
#navigation
{
        margin-bottom: 20px;
}
.navlink, .hiddennavlink, .displaynavlink
{
        background-color: #fcc;
        display: inline;
        margin: 5px;
        padding: 5px;
}
.hiddennavlink
{
        visibility: hidden;
}
.displaynavlink
{
        visibility: visible;
}
#photo
{
        padding: 10px;
}
```

There are some variations to the navigation JavaScript in order to manage the hiding and showing of the buttons:

```javascript
adjustNavigation : function( ) {

    var node = this.currentPage;

    // adjust next navigation
    var next = aaElem('next');
    if (!node.next) {
        next.className='hiddennavlink';
    } else {
        next.className = 'displaynavlink';
    }
```

```
      var previous = aaElem('previous');
      if (!node.previous) {
         previous.className = 'hiddennavlink';
      } else {
         previous.className = 'displaynavlink';
      }

   },
```

The main functional change is to the application-specific JavaScript. Example 7-16 shows this in its entirety. Note that the application now adds a little transitional visual effect, using the moo.fx library from mooTools (*http://mootools.net*). The photo area is transitioned to almost completely transparent just before the picture is swapped, then it is brought back completely after the photo is swapped. The amount of code to create this bit of polish is quite small.

Example 7-16. Ajax application for the new parallel Ajax/PHP application

```
function showPage( ) {
   window.location.hash = this.identifier;
   var photo = photos[this.identifier];

   var func = "removeOld('" + photo + "')";
   setTimeout(func, 500);
   new Fx.Style('main', 'opacity').custom(1,0.3);
}

function removeOld(photo) {
   getEXIF(photo);
   var main = aaElem('main');

   // clean up old content
   var current = aaElem('photo');
   if (current) main.removeChild(current);

   var img = document.createElement("img");
   img.src=photo;
   img.id='photo';
   main.appendChild(img);

   new Fx.Style('main', 'opacity').custom(0.3,1);
}
function getEXIF(photo) {

   // delete old data
   if (aaElem('exifid')) {
      document.getElementsByTagName('head')[0].removeChild(aaElem('exifid'));
   }

   var url = 'get_photo.php?photo=' + photo;

   var script = document.createElement('script');
   script.type = 'text/javascript';
```

Example 7-16. Ajax application for the new parallel Ajax/PHP application (continued)

```
    script.src = url + '&callback=printEXIF';
    script.id = 'exifid';
    document.getElementsByTagName('head')[0].appendChild(script);
}

function createListItem(text,ul) {
    var li = document.createElement('li');
    var txt = document.createTextNode(text);
    li.appendChild(txt);
    ul.appendChild(li);
    return ul;
}

function printEXIF(exifObj) {

    // access recipe element and clear
    var index;
    var hash = window.location.hash;
    if (hash) {
        index = hash.split("#")[1];
    }

    var meta = aaElem('meta');
    var metacontent =aaElem('metacontent');
    var permalink = aaElem('permalink');
    if (metacontent) meta.removeChild(metacontent);
    if (permalink) meta.removeChild(permalink);

    var p = document.createElement('p');
    p.id = 'permalink';
    var a = document.createElement('a');
    var href = window.location.pathname + "?photo=" + index;
    a.setAttribute('href', href);
    a.appendChild(document.createTextNode('Permanent Link to this page'));
    p.appendChild(a);
    meta.appendChild(p);

    var ul = document.createElement('ul');
    ul=createListItem(exifObj.Model,ul);
    ul=createListItem(exifObj.ISOSpeedRatings,ul);
    ul=createListItem(exifObj.ExposureTime,ul);
    ul=createListItem(exifObj.DateTimeOriginal,ul);
    ul=createListItem(exifObj.COMPUTED.ApertureFNumber,ul);
    ul.id="metacontent";
    meta.appendChild(ul);

}


aaManageEvent(window,'load',function() {
    var home;
    var current;
```

Example 7-16. Ajax application for the new parallel Ajax/PHP application (continued)

```
var index;
var past;

var hash = window.location.hash;

// get hash value
if (hash) {
    index = hash.split("#")[1];
}

// create navigation nodes
for (var id = 0; id < photos.length; id++) {
    var nav = Navigation.addNavigationNode(past,id,showPage);
    if (!past) {
        home = nav;
    }
    past = nav;
    if (index && id == index)
        current = nav;
}

// set home and current page
Navigation.setHome(home);
if (!current) {
    Navigation.setCurrentPage(home);
} else {
    Navigation.setCurrentPage(current);
}

// add slideshow button events
aaManageEvent(aaElem('next'),'click',aaBindObjMethod(Navigation,Navigation.nextPage));
aaManageEvent(aaElem('previous'),'click',aaBindObjMethod(Navigation,Navigation.
prevPage));
aaManageEvent(aaElem('home'),'click', Navigation.returnHome);
});
```

When the page is first accessed, the request is processed through the PHP application, but it's immediately overridden by the Ajax application. The version used here for the Ajax application maintains the hash marks in the URL in case a user navigates away from the page and then back again.

The Back button itself isn't supported, though, within the application; the use of a timer solely for this activity is an overhead that I didn't want to build into the application. If we provide very clear inner-application navigation and permanent links that aren't script-dependent, and then manage the application for those cases when a person clicks a link away from the page or opens another page in the browser, we have touched all the bases, in a cross-browser manner, with a minimum of extraordinary tweaking. The only thing missing is keyboard access, but that can be added in using a variation of the "click X to close" example associated with overlays in Chapter 5.

This approach could also be used for the database paging, except that in that case, the query parameters are passed to the PHP application or stored as part of the hash. Both of these applications suit the "load on demand" functionality created in this example. However, there is another approach we can take for a paged application when the data is small enough to preload as soon as the application is accessed. We'll explore that in the next section.

The New Page View

Eric Meyer, well-known CSS expert and author, created a standards-based, accessible slideshow/presentation code framework called S5: a Simple Standards-Based Slide Show System (hence the 5 in the S5 name). The premise behind the application is to load each page, or presentation slide, into the document and give each a specific class name. When the page is opened, if scripting is enabled, these class names are processed using the DOM and are then "layered" into pages that can be traversed using a navigational aid. S5 also has good keyboard support.

Read more about S5, see examples, and download code at *http:// meyerweb.com/eric/tools/s5*.

This concept is good because if scripting is disabled, all the pages are displayed, one after another; users can vertically scroll down the page, reading each section in turn. No server-side code is necessary, and the code to manage the dynamic presentation doesn't have to be very complicated.

This isn't technically an Ajax application because we're not using an Ajax call. However, Ajax has broadened to include most dynamic JavaScript functionality, so we'll call the application "Ajax" by marriage.

After pulling apart the Unix command article, we can put it back together again for this next application. The slideshow elements are left as-is, and each of the pages are added below them, each with its own unique identifier and a shared "section" class. The entire page is not duplicated here, as that would be quite large; enough is shown so that you can get a feel for how the page works (the complete example is part of the book examples, which can be downloaded from here: *http://www.oreilly.com/ catalog/9780596529369*). Example 7-17 contains the web page fragment, which is almost identical to the other examples except for the addition of the text fragments as pages.

Example 7-17. Text pages or presentation based on the concepts derived with S5

```
<!DOCTYPE html PUBLIC "-//W3C//DTD XHTML 1.0 Strict//EN"
  "http://www.w3.org/TR/xhtml1/DTD/xhtml1-strict.dtd">
<html xmlns="http://www.w3.org/1999/xhtml" lang="en">
```

Example 7-17. Text pages or presentation based on the concepts derived with S5 (continued)

```html
<head>
<title>Text Slideshow</title>
<meta http-equiv="Content-Type" content="text/html; charset=utf-8" />
<link rel="stylesheet" type="text/css" href="slideshow.css" />
<link rel="stylesheet" type="text/css" href="textslideshow2.css" />
<script type="text/javascript" src="addingajax.js">
</script>
<script type="text/javascript" src="navigation.js">
</script>
<script type="text/javascript" src="textslideshow3.js">
</script>

</head>
<body>
<div id="slideshow">

<div id="content">
<div id="main">
</div>
<div id="meta">
</div>
</div>

<div id="navigation">
<div id="previous" class="navlink"><a href="">Previous</a></div>
<div id="home" class="navlink"><a href="">Home</a></div>
<div id="next" class="navlink"><a href="">Next</a></div>
</div>

<div id="footer">
</div>
</div>
<div id="section1" class="section">
...
</div>
<div id="section2" class="section">
...
</div>
...
</body>
</html>
```

When the page is loaded, if scripting is disabled, the slideshow portion is removed from the page layout via the overall slideshow element's display property of none. The slideshow won't interfere with access to the page fragments, which are styled simply with a dashed border and spacing between the elements.

However, if scripting is enabled, the slideshow elements, buttons and frame, are displayed, and the sections are not displayed.

The JavaScript to control this simple pages/presentation application is much simpler than previous examples, as shown in Example 7-18. In the setup function, the sections are found, hidden, and their identifiers used to build navigation nodes. When each page is displayed, the innerHTML property of the main page is set to the contents of the hidden section. This is a shortcut, and if bullets or such are used, a better approach could be to use the DOM to copy the material into the show.

Example 7-18. Application code for the text presentation/slideshow

```
function showPage( ) {
    window.location.hash = this.identifier;
    var content = aaElem('page');
    if (!content) {
        content = document.createElement('div');
        content.id = 'page';
        aaElem('main').appendChild(content);
        aaElem('slideshow').style.display = 'block';
    }
    content.innerHTML = aaElem(this.identifier).innerHTML;
}
aaManageEvent(window,'load',function( ) {
    var past;
    var home;
    var current;

    var pageCount = 11;

    var index;
    var hash = window.location.hash;
    if (hash) {
        index = hash.split("#")[1];
    }

    var elems = document.getElementsByTagName('div');
    var pages = [];
    for (var j = 0; j < elems.length; j++)
        if (elems[j].className == 'section') {
            elems[j].style.display = 'none';
            pages[pages.length] = elems[j];
        }

    for (var i = 0; i < pages.length; i++) {
        var id = pages[i].id;
        var nav = Navigation.addNavigationNode(past,id,showPage);
        if (!past) {
            home = nav;
        }
        past = nav;
        if (index && id == index)
            current = nav;
    }
```

Example 7-18. Application code for the text presentation/slideshow (continued)

```
    Navigation.setHome(home);

    if (!current) {
       Navigation.setCurrentPage(home);
    } else {
       Navigation.setCurrentPage(current);
    }

    aaManageEvent(aaElem('next'),'click',aaBindObjMethod(Navigation,Navigation.nextPage));
    aaManageEvent(aaElem('previous'),'click',aaBindObjMethod(Navigation,Navigation.
prevPage));
    aaManageEvent(aaElem('home'),'click', Navigation.returnHome);
});
```

The appearance of the application is the exact same as Example 7-7 earlier in the chapter, where each page fragment is loaded through an external application and Ajax call. The use of the hash, too, actually works whether scripting is enabled or not, just by adding named anchors at the top of each section.

Having the content in the page creates a form of page caching. It's not effective if the page contains a lot of material, larger images, or other multimedia. It is effective for presentations or longer articles.

Post-Mortem

Not all applications will have an accessible, gracefully degradable, unobtrusive solution. Some of the more complex Ajax applications that emulate a word processor or spreadsheet, email application, and such would require huge amounts of code to even attempt to add back basic web functionality, or to make them accessible.

Even the later examples demonstrated in this chapter will fail with most screen readers—all but the last example, which contains all the data when the page loads.

For applications that can be run in parallel with server-side functionality or run with some other unobtrusive implementation, trying to "recover" all web functionality isn't necessarily a good use of time or effort. It's more effective to build in a prominent internal navigation system than to emulate true Back button behavior. Any use of timers just to create this type of behavior should be avoided, as they can add to erratic side effects.

However, it is advisable to provide a script-based temporary URL that can enable recovery of a page's state if a user follows a link external to the application or accesses another web site through her bookmarks. It shouldn't be treated as a permanent link to the page, though.

The examples in this chapter are all loosely based on the concept of a slideshow, but the same approaches can be used for all forms of paged content. This includes tabbed pages, as we will examine in Chapter 9.

CHAPTER 8

Adding Advanced Visual Effects

Ajax doesn't require sophisticated visual effects. The only effects necessary are those that have been demonstrated in previous chapters: the ability to add, alter, or remove page contents; hide or show new data; highlight changes in some way. All of these effects make use of relatively simple and widespread technologies, such as HTML and CSS. At the opposite spectrum of Ajax applications are the Rich Internet Applications (RIAs)—applications that seek to recreate traditional desktop applications in web browsers using Ajax technologies. Among the applications you can create are word processing applications, spreadsheets, email programs, and even graphics programs, such as those like Paint, GIMP (GNU Image Manipulation Program), or Photoshop.

The RIA applications make greater demands on the browser's graphics capability—a demand not met by CSS, or only by simpler implementations of CSS. Though creating such applications is far outside the scope of this book, the visual tools that the RIA developers use are not. Or at least, not so far out that we can't take one chapter to have a little fun and spend some time exploring the possibilities of what they can add to our in-place edits and polled updates.

There are two approaches we can take to add advanced visual effects to web applications. The first is the one commonly accessible to all web browsers—the effects that can be managed through CSS. These include transparency, sizing, clipping, and so on.

The second approach uses specialized objects or specifications, and in this we're both lucky and not because we're given multiple graphics libraries, objects, and technologies from which to choose. Choice is good, and choice in web application development is a good thing, as long as the choice is viable across all of your target browsers. That's the twist associated with the visual effects specifications available to Ajax developers—there's support for advanced visual effects built into all the most commonly used browsers. However, each browser supports only a subset of the techniques, and no technique is supported universally across all major browsers.

Other companies promoted another graphics specification, Scalable Vector Graphics (SVG). SVG is currently implemented in Gecko-based browsers (such as Firefox), Opera, and in the version of Safari (WebKit) currently under development.

Other companies promoted another graphics specifications. Scalable Vector Graphics (SVG) is currently implemented in Gecko engine-based browsers (Mozilla, Camino, and Firefox), Opera, and in the version of Safari (WebKit) currently under development. There are plug-ins available that provide SVG support for other browsers, including IE. SVG is also the specification that the W3C has approved, and will most likely become the de facto standard over time.

Apple came out with a WebKit extension called Canvas, which provides the underlying graphics implementation for Dashboard widgets and Safari. It provides access to the Cocoa 2D API from within JavaScript, which of course is only meaningful in the Mac OS X. Still, the canvas element has made its way into the WhatWG's Web Applications 1.0 HTML, commonly referred to as the HTML 5 specification. For this reason, the Gecko browsers, Opera, and Safari also support this element.

Since support for VML is limited, we won't cover it in this chapter other than to point out any libraries that provide VML/SVG cross-browser libraries. Instead, we'll focus on the canvas element and SVG and take a more advanced look at CSS.

 The WhatWG/HTML5 effort has joined forces with the W3C to create a new, updated version of HTML. This effort is focused on providing an updated, standardized markup option for site developers who aren't quite ready to transition to XHTML. Read more on the WhatWG HTML5 specification at *http://www.whatwg.org/specs/webapps/current-work* and at the W3C at *http://www.w3.org/html/wg*.

Advanced CSS Tricks

I've always felt that the visual effects demonstrated earlier in the book—effects such as making objects transparent, hiding or showing elements, or moving them on demand—is pretty advanced. However, there are other CSS tricks used in Ajax application in addition to the ones already demonstrated.

Are any of the tricks I'm going to show you necessary? I don't think any visual effect is absolutely necessary—and shouldn't be if one of our goals is to ensure that our use of Ajax is unobtrusive. However, they can add polish to a web page, which can be just as important as making sure the page is accessible. Best of all, if the effects are already built into a library, that saves us the work.

Rounded Corners

Ajax and rounded corners go together like pastrami on rye. Most of the time, the effect is made by using images of round corners, used as background for multiple layers, thereby creating a "box" that can size vertically or horizontally.

Other approaches use PNG elements with transparency to "build" the rounded corner a few pixels at a time. I don't favor this approach much, largely due to IE's poor support for PNG's alpha transparency.

Several of the Ajax libraries we've looked at in this book provide rounded corners created via JavaScript. Rico's library is simple to use and provides options for blending and specifying one corner only, such as tl (rounded on top-left edge):

```
Rico.Corner.round('div1'); // give element's identifier
Rico.Corner.round('div', {corners: "tl"});
```

Simple, but Rico's rounding has a peculiar side effect: if you use padding or make an element's height greater than the content, you'll get a cinched-in looking block, as shown in Figure 8-1.

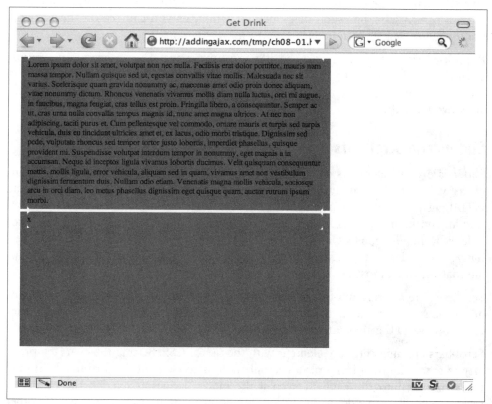

Figure 8-1. An oddly interesting rounded-corner effect

The way to avoid the "waist" is to not use padding and not set the height. If you want internal padding, use an inner block and set its margins to whatever value you wish. Do this, and Rico's corners work nicely. You can see more Rico rounding at *http://openrico.org/demos/?demo=corner*.

MochiKit also has rounded corner support in its Visual library. It has the ability to round the blocks of an entire class of elements, not just one at a time:

```
roundClass('div');
```

This is a nice option. To use it, though, you'll need to include several libraries:

```
MochiKit/Base.js
MochiKit/Iter.js
MochiKit/DOM.js
MochiKit/Color.js
MochiKit/Visual.js
```

However, MochiKit is a complete Ajax library, as well as an infrastructure. If you're using the other components for other efforts, make use of the Visuals for rounding; otherwise, you might want to forgo the curves. MochiKit, like Rico, also suffers the "waist" effect, and you'll need to use inner elements with a margin if you want padding. MochiKit also has such nice documentation, as you can see on the Visual.js library at *http://mochikit.com/doc/html/MochiKit/Visual.html*.

Rounded corners can add a polished effect to a web page. The decision to use multiple images or JavaScript to create the effect depends on whether you're already using a library. One thing to remember is that if you use JavaScript and scripting is disabled, you lose the effect.

Sliders and Scrollbars

Sliders are visual elements consisting of a thumb, two endpoints, and a thin rectangle as wide as the thumb and capped by the endpoints. Some of the earliest dynamic HTML visual component packages had built-in support for scrollbars, and you can find an enormous number in JavaScript or specialized Ajax libraries. All should provide event handling, as well as some form of keyboard access and a text-based alternative if scripting is disabled. Well, they should, but many don't provide a nonscript alternative; you'll most likely have to provide that yourself.

Scrollbars are a variation of sliders, in that they are located to the right or bottom of an element and are used to scroll vertically or horizontally through content that extends beyond the element rectangle's border.

Scrollbars are built into any element with the use of CSS. Setting the overflow property to scroll automatically places scrollbars into an element. Unfortunately, it puts the scrollbars into the element even if the material doesn't overlap the element's region, but this can add a dimension to the element if used effectively. Another approach is to use a specific height on the element and set the overflow to auto, in which case the scrollbar is only displayed when the content actually exceeds the space.

Scrollbars in an Ajax sense tend to be associated with the concept of Ajax pagination, though sliders by themselves can be used for a variety of things, including color sliders to adjust object colors or other sliders to extend the width of an element.

There are so many good libraries for creating sliders and scrollbars that I can't imagine you needing to create any yourself. The Yahoo! UI has a built-in slider, and there's a nice implementation included in Mike Foster's X Library (available and documented at *http://cross-browser.com*). Dojo has a slider component, as does script.aculo.us. In fact if you search the Web for the word "slider," you'll most likely either find a slider component, documentation for using a built-in slider, or examples of how to implement a slider. And that's just on the Ajax side—search for "javascript" and "slider," and you'll find even more advanced versions of sliders that exist independent of any Ajax library.

As I've said in previous chapters, I'm overly fond of pagination. I think navigating through content that's layered in something such as a tabbed page or slideshow works nicely. Still, when returning results from a query, if the returned data is simple, pagination could provide an interesting effect. It definitely provides a good example of the use of a slider or scrollbar.

In the next example, we will create a paginated example using the data query service created in Chapter 7 for the database single-page application/slideshow. The backend service requires absolutely no change. The frontend consists of a slider and a page element containing an HTML table to which rows are incremented as the slider is thumbed down. The table also scrolls up and down based on the slider's thumb movement so that recently retrieved and older data can be viewed.

The web page is very simple, containing the slider and the elements to contain the HTML table (Example 8-1).

Example 8-1. Slider/pagination example web page

```
<!DOCTYPE html PUBLIC "-//W3C//DTD XHTML 1.0 Strict//EN"
  "http://www.w3.org/TR/xhtml1/DTD/xhtml1-strict.dtd">
<html xmlns="http://www.w3.org/1999/xhtml" xml:lang="en" lang="en">
<head>
<meta http-equiv="Content-Type" content="text/html; charset=utf-8" />
<title>Slider</title>
<link rel="stylesheet" type="text/css" href="pagination.css" />
<!-- Namespace source file -->
  <script src = "yui/yahoo/yahoo.js" ></script>

  <!-- Dependency source files -->
  <script type="text/javascript" src = "yui/dom/dom.js" ></script>
  <script type="text/javascript" src = "yui/event/event.js" ></script>
  <script type="text/javascript" src = "yui/dragdrop/dragdrop.js" ></script>

  <!-- Slider source file -->
  <script type="text/javascript" src = "yui/slider/slider.js" ></script>
```

Example 8-1. Slider/pagination example web page (continued)

```
<!-- Application specific -->
<script type="text/javascript" src="addingajax.js">
</script>
<script type="text/javascript" src="paginate.js">
</script>

</head>
<body>
<div id="container">
<div id="sliderbg">
  <div id="sliderthumb"><img src="yui/slider/vertSlider.png" alt="slider thumb" /></div>
</div>
<div id="main">
<div id="inner">
</div>
</div>
</div>
</body>
</html>
```

The thumbnail image is from the YUI example, though you can use any image. The CSS file for the example is also simple. The most important component is to float the vertical slider to the left, the table area to the right, and set the underlying main element of the table to hide overflow in order to create the "scroll" effect when the data is moved based on the slider actions:

```
#container
{
        margin: 20px auto;
        width: 700px;
        height: 440px;
}
#sliderbg
{
        background-color: #ccc;
        border: 1px outset #333;
        float: left;
        height: 420px;
        width: 10px;
}
#main
{
        position: absolute;
        background-color: #ccc;
        border: 1px outset #333;
        height: 420px;
        margin-left: 20px;
        overflow: hidden;
        width: 600px;
}
```

```
#inner
{
        margin: 5px;
        top: 10px;
}
tr
{
        margin-bottom: 3px;
        margin-top: 3px;
}
td
{
        margin: 2px;
}
table
{
        width: 98%;
}
```

The application JavaScript, shown in Example 8-2, is a modification of the code from Example 7-9 from Chapter 7. The only difference is that when the page loads, a table with an associated slider is created, and the data loaded is added to this table.

When the thumb is moved, the table area's top CSS setting is set to the negative value of the thumb's offset (the amount it's moved from the top). Doing this, the table always scrolls up as the thumb moves down and down as the thumb moves up. Only 40 rows are retrieved in the beginning, and a global cache object is used to determine how many rows have been retrieved (based on whether the thumb's offset is higher than a value set the last time the cache was updated). A 400-pixel scrollbar equals about five trips to the database.

Example 8-2. JavaScript to maintain the slider/pagination examples

```
var cache = {
    offset : 80,
    fetch : 40
};

aaManageEvent(window,"load", function( ) {
  var slider = YAHOO.widget.Slider.getVertSlider("sliderbg",
          "sliderthumb", 0, 400);
  slider.setValue(0,true);
  slider.subscribe("change",adjustPage);

  // adjust positioning based on IE quirks
  createTable( );
  getRows(0);
  aaElem('inner').style.position='relative';
});

// adjust table container based on offset
// determine if database cache needs to be
// incremented
```

Example 8-2. JavaScript to maintain the slider/pagination examples (continued)

```
function adjustPage(offset) {

    var inner = aaElem('inner');
    var newTop = -offset;
    inner.style.top = newTop + "px";

    // if offset is greater than
    // cached offset, fetch rows, update cache
    if (offset > cache.offset) {
        getRows(cache.fetch);
        cache.offset+=80;
        cache.fetch+=40;
    }
}
// retrieve next set of rows
function getRows(start) {
    var url = 'getposts.php?start=' + start;
    var script = document.createElement('script');
    script.type = 'text/javascript';
    script.src = url + '&limit=40&callback=printRows';
    document.getElementsByTagName('head')[0].appendChild(script);
}

// create and append a table cell
function createTableCell(value,tr) {

    // creates a <td> element
    var cell = document.createElement("td");

    // creates a Text Node
    var text = document.createTextNode(value);

    // appends the Text Node we created into the cell <td>
    cell.appendChild(text);

    // appends the cell <td> into the row <tr>
    tr.appendChild(cell);

    return tr;
}

// create empty table and add to page
// set container's top position
function createTable( ) {
    var inner = aaElem('inner');

    var table = document.createElement('table');
    table.id = 'dataTable';
    var tableBody = document.createElement("tbody");
    tableBody.id = "dataTableBody";
    table.appendChild(tableBody);
```

```
    inner.appendChild(table);
    inner.style.top = "0px";
}
// append newly fetched rows as table rows
function printRows(rowsObj) {

    // clean up old content
    var tableBody = aaElem('dataTableBody');

    // table rows
    for(var i = 0; i < rowsObj.length; i++) {
        // creates a <tr> element
        var row = document.createElement("tr");

        row = createTableCell(rowsObj[i].id, row);

        // anchor and title
        var cell = document.createElement("td");
        cell.innerHTML = "<a href='" + rowsObj[i].guid + "'>" + rowsObj[i].title + "</a>";
        row.appendChild(cell);

        row = createTableCell(rowsObj[i].comments,row);

        tableBody.appendChild(row);
        tableBody.style.overflow="hidden";
    }
}
```

Positioning is static by default, and in order to get the clipping to work correctly, the inner element that contains the table has to be set to relative positioning while the outer element is set to absolute positioning. However, due to a quirk with IE, the inner element can't be set to relative positioning until after the HTML table is created. Otherwise, the table would scroll, but it wouldn't clip at the borders of the other, main container.

Again, this is the use of a slider at its simplest, but it does work. To make sure that the application remains accessible, the page could be implemented as those in Chapter 7, where server-side functionality retrieves the data and creates the table with the first set of rows, providing links to get each next set, and is overridden by the Ajax application if the page is accessed by a script-enabled browser. Both applications could use the same web service to retrieve the rows.

The slider has a lot of moving parts, including a great deal of drag-and-drop processing, which is why I take it easy on myself and use an external library, YUI.

This use of pagination isn't very common as an Ajax effect. More common is the use of dynamic menus, discussed next.

Web-Friendly Menus

Menus slide in from the side, drop down from the top, float around the page, expand, collapse, and sometimes they stay perfectly still. Menus are the area where we also have to be the most careful, because if we create a menu based purely in JavaScript, users with scripting disabled have absolutely no way to navigate our sites or our applications.

Menus can be made of buttons and div elements, but again, when we don't use hypertext links, we deny navigation to those not using a mouse.

We can have scalable, layered, and dynamic menus, and still have accessible navigation, not to mention a semantically accurate menu, by using a type of menu popularized by A List Apart (*http://alistapart.com/articles/dropdowns*), and known as the Suckerfish menu. This menu uses an unordered list, the CSS :hover pseudo attribute, and a little JavaScript to make it work for IE 6.x, which doesn't support the :hover pseudo attribute for anything but anchor tags (a).

This was later extended to Son of Suckerfish, which allows us to have more than two levels of menu, and fixes some quirks in other browsers (*http://www.htmldog.com/ articles/suckerfish/dropdowns*). It's a little cumbersome with multiple levels of menus and having to battle the CSS cascade effect. In the original Suckerfish menu, if there were more than one menu level, all additional levels would open if the first level opened. To counter this behavior, we have to add CSS to turn off the display for additional levels when the menu displays the first level. A more recent version is (Son-of-)Suckerfish with IE 7: *http://de.siteof.de/extended-menu-faq-suckerfish-ie7.html*. Technology comes and goes, but Suckerfish lives on.

Still, it is accessible, it works if scripting is disabled, and it allows us a drill-down navigational system for a complex site.

 Suckerfish is really only semiaccessible because it requires a lot of tabbing for a keyboard user.

Unfortunately, most Ajax library menu systems are dependent on scripting being enabled. A navigation system is one area where you just can't compromise when it comes to adding DHTML or Ajax effects to a site. For this reason, I can't recommend any DHTML menu, unless it's for part of an application that is completely dependent on scripting, in which case the enabling or disabling of scripting is moot.

Draggable Container

I'm going to borrow this discussion from my JavaScript book, *Learning JavaScript* (O'Reilly). I'm not a real fan of drag-and-drop because most uses of it are counterintuitive to what people expect. When you go buy an item at an online store, you don't expect to drag it into a shopping cart: you expect to click a button, and the item is popped into the cart for you. As for dragging page elements around so that users can customize their page environment, chances are that users will end up dragging elements on top of other elements that might not be initially visible.

Still, it's not a bad idea to see how drag-and-drop works because there are good cases for this technique. One is Google Maps, where you can drag a map within the map container and see the map location above or to the side, or below the container edge. This ability to drag "within" a container to see what's not showing is a decent alternative to having to deal with scrollbars, or overflow, or such.

Example 8-3 includes the contents of the web page with the stylesheet embedded for simplicity's sake. Notice that all that the page contains is an img element contained within a div element. The picture used for the example is much larger than that of the block's view port, and the overflow is hidden.

Example 8-3. Drag-and-drop view port

```
<!DOCTYPE html PUBLIC "-//W3C//DTD XHTML 1.0 Strict//EN"
  "http://www.w3.org/TR/xhtml1/DTD/xhtml1-strict.dtd">
<html xmlns="http://www.w3.org/1999/xhtml" lang="en">
<head>
<title>GoogleMapEffect</title>
<meta http-equiv="Content-Type" content="text/html; charset=utf-8" />
<style type="text/css">
#div1
{
        border: 5px solid #000;
        height: 200px;
        left: 100px;
        overflow: hidden;
        position: absolute;
        top: 100px;
        width: 400px;
}
img
{
        border: 1px solid #000;
}
</style>
<script type="text/javascript" src="addingajax.js">
</script>
<script type="text/javascript" src="draggable.js">
</script>
</head>
<body>
<div id="div1" >
<img id="img1" src="robin1.jpg" alt="large picture of curious American robin" />
</div>
</body>
</html>
```

The code for the effect is shown in Example 8-4. Though this is for the element contained within the container, any of this code could be used for any element—just make it draggable by calling the makeDraggable function and passing in the identifier for the element you want to be able to drag.

Example 8-4. JavaScript to support the container-based drag-and-drop

```
// global variables
var dragObject;
var mouseOffset;

// capture mouse events
aaManageEvent(document,'mouseup',mouseUp);
aaManageEvent(document,'mousemove',mouseMove);
aaManageEvent(window,'load', function() {
   makeDraggable('img1');
});

// create a mouse point
function mousePoint(x,y) {
   this.x = x;
   this.y = y;
}

// find mouse position
function mousePosition(evnt){
  var x = parseInt(evnt.clientX);
  var y = parseInt(evnt.clientY);
  return new mousePoint(x,y);
}

// get element's offset position within page
function getMouseOffset(target, evnt){
   evnt = evnt ? evnt : window.event;
   var mousePos  = mousePosition(evnt);
   var x = mousePos.x - target.offsetLeft;
   var y = mousePos.y - target.offsetTop;
   return new mousePoint(x,y);
}

// turn off dragging
function mouseUp(evnt){
   dragObject = null;
}
// capture mouse move, only if dragging
function mouseMove(evnt){
   if (!dragObject) return;
   evnt = evnt ? evnt : window.event;
   var mousePos = mousePosition(evnt);

   // if draggable, set new absolute position
   if(dragObject){
```

Example 8-4. JavaScript to support the container-based drag-and-drop (continued)

```
    dragObject.style.position = 'absolute';

    dragObject.style.top    = mousePos.y - mouseOffset.y + "px";
    dragObject.style.left   = mousePos.x - mouseOffset.x + "px";
    return false;
  }
}

// make object draggable
function makeDraggable(item){
  if (item) {
    item = aaElem(item);
    item.onmousedown = function(evnt) {
                    dragObject  = this;
                    mouseOffset = getMouseOffset(this, evnt);
                    return false; };
  }
}
```

Chances are, if you've been working with JavaScript, you've been exposed to drag-and-drop, and I won't get into the details of how it works. A good online tutorial can be found at Web Reference: *http://www.webreference.com/programming/javascript/mk/column2/index.html*.

This container-driven drag-and-drop application could be paired with the paginating effect created previously to drag the table up, much like you would grab a piece of paper from a file and move it up to read the bottom. Drag-and-drop is also popular with sorting, as I mentioned previously in the book, though I would recommend using a packaged library for that effect.

We've seen other CSS effects throughout this book, including flashes, pop-ups, and floats. There are also effects to make things poof, pop, and slide. Most Ajax libraries have an effects or fx extension, sublibrary, or plug-in that provides this functionality. At this point, we'll jump out of the CSS world and into SVG.

Scalable Vector Graphics

According to the W3C's web site on SVG, it is a "…language for describing two-dimensional graphics and graphical applications in XML" (*http://www.w3.org/Graphics/SVG*). The latest released version of the specification is 1.1, but a draft copy of 1.2 is currently being reviewed, and there are both print and mobile versions of the specification.

Currently, Opera and Firefox support SVG, Safari has plans to add support (and support is showing up in nightly builds), and there is a viewer provided by Adobe for viewing SVG in IE.

The Adobe SVG Viewer for IE can be accessed at the Adobe site at *http://www.adobe.com/svg/viewer/install/main.html*. Be aware, though, that Adobe is dropping support for the Viewer beginning January 1, 2008.

SVG is XML-based, consisting of a basic set of XML elements, each with attributes that determine how the element is drawn. There are two ways to incorporate SVG. The first is to create SVG markup as a separate document, and then embed it into the page. The second is to use inline SVG.

Embedding SVG

To use an embedding approach, you create a separate SVG file and then use an embed, object, or iframe element to include the SVG within a web page.

The preferred approach is to use the newer, standard object element. An example of using object with an SVG file is the following:

```
<object type="image/svg+xml" data="./some.svg" width="200" height="150" ></object>
```

If you want to provide alternative content for browsers that don't support SVG, you can include HTML within the object opening and closing tags:

```
<object type="image/svg+xml" data="./some.svg" width="200" height="150" >
<img src="some.jpg" alt="alternative image" />
</object>
```

The embed element, unfortunately, is the only one that older browsers (and I mean older, such as Netscape 2 and 3) support, and the one that Adobe supports with its SVG Viewer. If you want the SVG to be viewable via this plug-in, you'll want to use embed:

```
<embed src="some.svg" width="200" height="150" />
```

The only problem with the embed element is that it isn't a part of the HTML specifications, and as such, the document won't validate either as HTML or XHTML. In addition, IE won't support the use of embed and insists on the newer object.

There is a trick provided at the SVG wiki (*http://wiki.svg.org/SVG_and_HTML*) to work around the validation issue—adding the data definitions to define the embedded element and attributes to the web page.

A third approach to work around these issues is to use an iframe. This element is supported in all of our browsers of interest, and also has opening and closing tags in order to insert alternative content if SVG isn't supported.

Example 8-5 is a small SVG page that has a red ellipse with a black border. We'll get into the SVG elements later in the chapter, but for now, if you run this SVG through the XML validator (*http://validator.w3.org*), it validates as SVG 1.1. Note the inclusion of the SVG DTD, as well as the use of the default namespace for the SVG elements.

Example 8-5. Simple SVG file with one ellipse

```
<?xml version="1.0" standalone="no"?>
<!DOCTYPE svg PUBLIC "-//W3C//DTD SVG 1.1//EN"
"http://www.w3.org/Graphics/SVG/1.1/DTD/svg11.dtd">

<svg width="100%" height="100%" version="1.1"
xmlns="http://www.w3.org/2000/svg">

<ellipse cx="210" cy="90" rx="200" ry="80"
style="fill:rgb(255,0,0);
stroke:rgb(0,0,0);stroke-width:2"/>

</svg>
```

As long as your web server is set to serve XML documents, you could actually open this file directly in an SVG-compatible browser and the ellipse will be displayed. However, in Example 8-6, the web page uses each of the three possible techniques to open the SVG file: object, embed, and iframe.

Example 8-6. Page that loads the SVG file using three techniques

```
<!DOCTYPE html PUBLIC "-//W3C//DTD XHTML 1.0 Strict//EN"
  "http://www.w3.org/TR/xhtml1/DTD/xhtml1-strict.dtd">
<html xmlns="http://www.w3.org/1999/xhtml" lang="en">
<head>
<title>Embedded SVG</title>
<meta http-equiv="Content-Type" content="text/html; charset=utf-8" />
<body>
<h3>Embed</h3>
<embed src="test.svg" type="image/svg+xml" width="600" height="180" />
<h3>Object</h3>
<object type="image/svg+xml" data="test.svg" width="600" height="180">
<p>No SVG support</p>
</object>
<h3>iFrame</h3>
<iframe src="test.svg" width="600" height="180" frameborder="0">
<p>No SVG support</p>
</iframe>
</body>
</html>
```

We can test this page in various browsers. In Firefox 2.0, three red ellipses are displayed. This is expected behavior, as this version of Firefox (and the underlying Gecko engine) supports most of SVG 1.1. The three ellipses are also shown when the page is opened in Opera 9+.

However, when you open the page with Safari, you will receive an error about SVG not being supported. Downloading and installing the Adobe SVG Viewer enables Safari to view the SVG, and all three ellipses are displayed. The three ellipses are also displayed when the page is opened in WebKit, which signals that eventually Safari will have native support for SVG.

Moving over to the PC side of things, we can test the page with IE 6.x on Windows 2000. Again, the SVG doesn't display without the Adobe plug-in, but even with it, it only works within the object and iframe elements. The same holds true with IE 7 on Windows XP. Since the iframe is a valid transitional (not strict) XHTML element, we'll stick with iframes for embedded SVG.

 There's a specialized plug-in for the Konquerer browser, KSVG, part of the KDE. See the support page at *http://svg.kde.org*.

Adding Script

You can do quite a bit with SVG in a separate file that's eventually embedded into a page. Since XHTML is valid XML, it can be used in combination with SVG, which means you can add JavaScript within a script element to manipulate the SVG objects. The SVG objects become as much a part of the DOM as every other element within the page.

You can add a script element directly to the svg element, but you'll want to surround the script with a CDATA section or set the src attribute to an external JavaScript file. You'll also be more dependent on the DOM Level 2 methods, as you won't have access to many of the XHTML shortcut methods you might be familiar with.

 This is where the use of something like Firebug in Firefox really comes in handy. By using the script and DOM options, you can easily examine each object in the code and see which properties and methods are available. It works for any XML document, including SVG.

Example 8-7 contains an SVG document similar to that shown earlier, except that a script block is added to the svg element. This JavaScript modifies the cx attribute (the horizontal position) of the element, as well as one of the style settings. When the object is first clicked, it moves to the right and turns blue. When clicked again, it's returned to the original state.

Example 8-7. SVG document with script

```
<?xml version="1.0" standalone="no"?>
<!DOCTYPE svg PUBLIC "-//W3C//DTD SVG 1.1//EN"
"http://www.w3.org/Graphics/SVG/1.1/DTD/svg11.dtd">
<svg width="100%" height="100%" version="1.1"
```

Example 8-7. SVG document with script (continued)

```
xmlns="http://www.w3.org/2000/svg">
<ellipse id="ellipse1" cx="210" cy="90" rx="200" ry="80"
style="fill:rgb(255,0,0);
stroke:rgb(0,0,0);stroke-width:2"/>
<script type="text/javascript">
<![CDATA[
document.getElementById('ellipse1').onclick=changeColor;

function changeColor() {
  var svgObj = document.getElementById('ellipse1');
  var attr = svgObj.attributes.getNamedItem('cx').value;
  if (parseInt(attr) == 210) {
     svgObj.setAttribute('cx',400);
     svgObj.style.setProperty('fill','#0000ff',null);
  } else {
     svgObj.setAttribute('cx',210);
     svgObj.style.setProperty('fill','#ff0000',null);
  }
}
]]>
</script>
</svg>
```

No additional namespace is needed for the script element, as script is a part of the SVG 1.1 full specification. When the SVG document is opened in the previous XHTML test document, clicking any of the three ellipses causes the transformation for that specific element, depending, of course, on which browser you're using.

 If you haven't worked much with page dimensions, anything related to *y* is associated with the vertical axis, *x* is associated with the horizontal axis, and *z* with the perpendicular. In other words, *y* is the side and *x* is the bottom, while *z* sticks in your face.

Firefox and the Mozilla family support the full SVG 1.1 specification (or most of it), as does Opera and WebKit, which means that the example works as expected with these browsers. However, the Adobe SVG plug-in supports only *SVG 1.1 tiny*, which is a smaller subset of the specification that doesn't support the script element.

The example added script within an SVG document. What about combining SVG within an XHTML document, and then using script to work with the graphics?

SVG Inline

It's nice that we can load SVG into an object, but we really want the SVG to be part of the page, so we can mix and mash it with other document elements. Creating inline SVG is both easy and complicated, and again, it's because of browser differences.

The SVG wiki has a great page on inline SVG at *http://wiki.svg.org/index.php?title=Inline_SVG*, but I'll try to give a working synopsis. When the web page is created as XHTML and treated as XML within a Firefox or Opera browser, inline SVG is processed correctly. However, IE doesn't interpret XML in this way, and just prints out the syntax rather than processing it. Or, I should say, having the Adobe plug-in process it.

If the web page is treated as HTML, IE interprets the SVG as another form of HTML, which means the plug-in processes the SVG correctly. However, Firefox (and other Gecko-engined browsers) uses a separate parser for HTML and XML, so it does not process the SVG correctly.

What this means is that if you use an htm/html file extension or HTML MIME type, the SVG is processed correctly in IE, but not Firefox/Mozilla/Camino, Opera, or the Safari WebKit. If you use xml/xhtml, it works with all browsers but IE.

The SVG wiki provides a workaround so that you can serve pages with inline SVG that work in all browsers, and it's the same workaround we use to get XHTML to process correctly in all browsers (covered previously in Chapter 1). The workaround is to create a *.htaccess* file for the site directory and add the following directives, which provide instructions as to how the web pages are served. If the user agent supports XHTML, the pages are served as XHTML; otherwise, the pages are served as HTML:

```
AddType text/html .xhtml
RewriteEngine on
RewriteBase /
RewriteCond %{HTTP_ACCEPT} application/xhtml\+xml
RewriteCond %{HTTP_ACCEPT} !application/xhtml\+xml\s*;\s*q=0
RewriteCond %{REQUEST_URI} \.xhtml$
RewriteCond %{THE_REQUEST} HTTP/1\.1
RewriteRule .* - [T=application/xhtml+xml]
```

Using this approach, you should then be able to use SVG inline and have it work with the most commonly used browsers.

The rest of the SVG examples in the chapter use the inline approach to make the examples easier to follow. Now it's time to take a closer look at exactly what kind of effects we can create with SVG.

SVG Quick View

A comprehensive discussion of SVG would require an entire book, so here I'm going to be touching on various common elements and actions, enough to get you started. We've seen in the last few sections that the svg element itself acts like a container in which to add other objects. It can be given a width and a height, given a version number, or hold the SVG namespace, and if contained within other svg elements, it can have an *x* and *y* to mark its position:

```
<svg xmlns="http://www.w3.org/2000/svg" width="300" height="200">
...
</svg>
```

 I'm covering SVG only briefly in this chapter. For more detailed coverage of SVG I recommend the following web sites: the SVG Basics
Tutorial at *http://www.svgbasics.com*, the *http://svg.org* community
site, and the SVG wiki at *http://wiki.svg.org*.

Basic Shapes and Attributes

There are several basic shapes provided in svg: ellipse, circle, rect, line, polyline,
and polygon. Each has a given way of specifying a height and width, as well as location, rounding for corners, fill, border stroke, opacity, clipping, and so on—depending on what the element is, of course. All elements also have the style attribute to
apply CSS styling as well as the SVG specialized attributes.

Example 8-8 demonstrates each of the basic SVG shapes using some of the more
common attributes for the specific shape. It's using inline SVG, and the example is
given an xhtml extension, accessed from a folder where the *.htaccess* modifications
have been made. In addition, this document is also designed to validate with the XHTML
1.1 plus MathML 2.0 plus SVG 1.1 DOCTYPE, given at the beginning of the document.

Example 8-8. Valid XHTML document with SVG elements

```
<!DOCTYPE html PUBLIC "-//W3C//DTD XHTML 1.1 plus MathML 2.0 plus SVG 1.1//EN"
"http://www.w3.org/2002/04/xhtml-math-svg/xhtml-math-svg-flat.dtd">
<html xmlns="http://www.w3.org/1999/xhtml">
<head>
  <title>SVG embedded inline in XHTML</title>
  <meta http-equiv="Content-Type" content="text/html; charset=utf-8" />
</head>
<body>
  <h1>SVG embedded inline in XHTML</h1>

  <svg:svg xmlns:svg="http://www.w3.org/2000/svg" width="800" height="600" >

    <svg:polyline points="20,20 30,10 50,10 150,100 70,300 200,200" fill="none"
    stroke="#0f0" stroke-width="2" />

    <svg:circle cx="150" cy="100" r="50" fill="#ffcccc" stroke="#ccc" stroke-width="3"
    opacity=".8" />

    <svg:line y1="0" x1="300" y2="400" x2="300" stroke="#ff0" stroke-width="4" />

    <svg:polygon points="460,0 520,0 580,60 580,120 520,180 460,180 400,120 400,60"
    fill="#f00"
            style="stroke: #000; stroke-width: 1"/>

    <svg:rect x="150" y="250" rx="20" ry="20" width="300" height="100"
          opacity=".5" fill="purple" stroke="black" stroke-width="1"/>
```

Example 8-8. Valid XHTML document with SVG elements (continued)

```
      <svg:ellipse  cx="710" cy="290" rx="200" ry="80"
            style="fill:rgb(0,0,255);
            stroke:yellow;stroke-width:2"/>

    </svg:svg>

  </body>
</html>
```

The DOCTYPE is a mouthful, but it allows XHTML elements, as well as SVG and MathML, if you want to toss that in for grins and giggles. Among the page elements, the polyline draws a line based on a set of paired points, shown in this example as separated from each other by commas, though spaces would also work. Following the polyline is the circle, with its center placed at the given cx and cy (horizontal and vertical) position, and a radius of 50. The line takes start and stop end points, while the polygon is like the polyline, following given points, but joined into a solid figure.

The rectangle is given with rounded corners, represented by the rx and ry attributes. Both it and the ellipse, like the circle, are placed in the svg element based on x and y and cx and cy values. All the figures have fill values and stroke (border), and the rectangle and circle are partially transparent (determined by an opacity of less than 1.0).

Figure 8-2 shows the output of the page using WebKit. The artwork isn't anything special, but it does show how everything works in relation to the containing svg element. Note that the ellipse, which is over to the right and toward the bottom, is clipped because it exceeds the dimensions of this container. Also note that the zig-zaggy polyline appears through the circle because of the opacity of the circle element. You can also see the straight line through the semitransparent rectangle.

This example demonstrates the various ways of adjusting the elements, including the use of style and the SVG attributes. In addition, notice that some named colors are used in the example, though this is typically frowned on. A better approach would be to use the RGB setting (also demonstrated) or hexadecimal value (the #ff0000 you typically find with CSS stylesheets).

Defs, Gradients, Filters, and Effects

In addition to shapes, SVG also provides a fairly rich set of visual effects that can be applied to SVG objects. Many are included within def elements, which are a way of predefining objects and effects to be used later in the document. These are restricted to an SVG document rather than used inline, but can be included in a web document using the techniques described earlier.

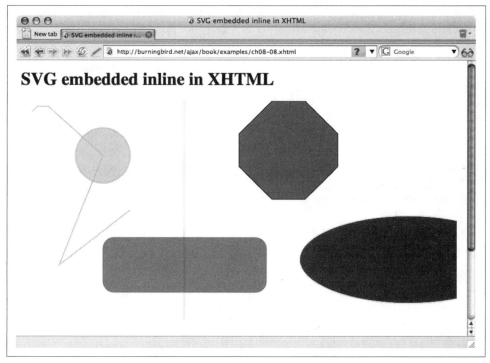

Figure 8-2. SVG sampler in a validating XHTML document

Predefined objects and effects are enclosed within opening and closing def tags, and the objects are drawn with the use of the appropriately named use element. Example 8-9 is an example of an SVG document consisting of a circle that's filled with a gradient that begins red, blends to yellow, and then finishes at a dark gold. The circle has also been outlined with the same gold.

Example 8-9. Circle with tricolor gradient fill

```
<?xml version="1.0" standalone="no"?>
<svg viewBox="0 0 1100 400"
xmlns="http://www.w3.org/2000/svg" version="1.1"
xmlns:xlink="http://www.w3.org/1999/xlink">
    <defs>
        <circle id = "s1" cx = "200" cy = "200" r = "200" stroke = "#F5B800" stroke-width
= "1"/>
        <radialGradient id = "g1" cx = "50%" cy = "50%" r = "50%">
            <stop stop-color = "#f00" offset = "0%"/>
            <stop stop-color = "#ff0" offset = "75%"/>
            <stop stop-color = "#f5b800" offset = "100%"/>
        </radialGradient>
    </defs>
    <use x = "100" y = "50" xlink:href = "#s1" fill="url(#g1)"/>
</svg>
```

For a few lines of XML, the example is rather impressive, as shown in Figure 8-3. Remember, this is created via XML and not a graphics program.

The SVG vocabulary is what we've been missing in web development from the very beginning—a built-in, cross-browser, sophisticated graphics vocabulary that allows us to create wonderful effects without having to depend on Flash or loading the page down with images. More importantly, since we can manipulate the elements with script, we can also merge our Ajax effects with these graphics to create impressive presentations.

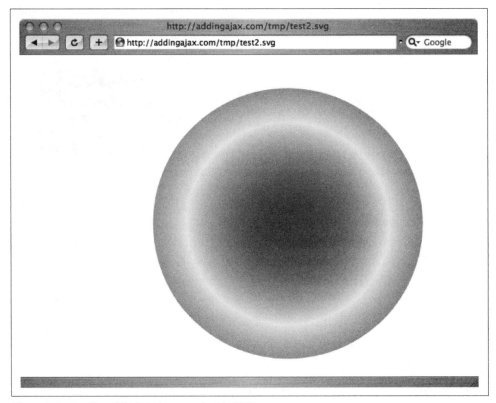

Figure 8-3. Gradient-filled circle created with SVG

Some of the SVG options aren't supported in several browsers, including the filters. Firefox 2.x doesn't support SVG filters at the time of this writing, but the plan is to eventually incorporate them. Firefox does support the ability to provide a clipping path and masks, but I'll leave that for your own explorations.

Though it's a bit tricky laying out the SVG elements using code and trying to work it through your mind, there are editors that allow us to manipulate objects and then generate SVG. One is Inkscape, available at *http://www.inkscape.org* with versions for Mac OS X, Windows, and Linux. There are other tools and the SVGI page (*http://www.svgi.org*) lists several.

Next up, we'll mix SVG and Ajax.

Mixer: SVG and Ajax

The implementation of SVG within browsers is still very young, but the commitment is there, and as new versions of browsers are rolled out, we have stronger integration between SVG elements and regular web elements. This is my way of saying that the examples mixing SVG and Ajax are limited primarily to Firefox and Opera, WebKit (mostly), and rarely, IE. I've avoided working within such limitations in the book, but we're due for a little fun. For your own production needs, you can use embedded SVG and script, and if you use an `iframe`, you can communicate between the two environments. You might want to restrict the use for nonessentials.

In Example 8-10, we will take the paginated example from Example 8-1 and add a "popularity bubble." A small SVG circle is embedded below the pagination table. Moving the mouse over the table highlights rows as it goes, setting the row background to red, and then back to gray after the mouse passes. The number of comments for each post, located in the last cell of the table row, is accessed, and its value is used to determine how big the SVG `circle` is, from no size at all for zero comments, to larger for more commented posts.

The additions to the JavaScript from Example 8-2 would be quite small except for the problem of having to deal with browser differences. Inline SVG isn't supported in enough browsers, so the SVG is created in a separate file and then loaded into a web object. When the page is loaded, depending on whether the browser is IE, the SVG object is either loaded into an embed element or an object:

```
aaManageEvent(window,"load", function( ) {
  var slider = YAHOO.widget.Slider.getVertSlider("sliderbg",
        "sliderthumb", 0, 400);
  slider.setValue(0,true);
  slider.subscribe("change",adjustPage);

  // find IE and use embed
  if (document.all && !window.opera) {
    var embed = document.createElement('embed');
    embed.src = 'bubble.svg';
    embed.type = 'image/svg+xml';
    embed.width='100%';
    embed.height = '300';
    aaElem('obj').appendChild(embed);

  } else {
    var obj= document.createElement('object');
```

```
        obj.type = 'image/svg+xml';
        obj.id = 'svgDoc';
        obj.data = 'bubble.svg';
        obj.width = '100%';
        obj.height = '300';
        aaElem('obj').appendChild(obj);
    }

    createTable();
    getRows(0);

    aaElem('inner').style.position="relative";
});
```

As the rows are entered, mouseover and mouseout events are assigned event handlers:

```
        aaManageEvent(row,'mouseover',showBubble);
        aaManageEvent(row,'mouseout',restoreRow);
```

When the mouseover event fires, showBubble is called and the background color of the table row is changed to red. In addition, the column count is accessed and used to resize the SVG bubble:

```
function showBubble(evnt) {
    var row = this;
    var val = parseInt(row.lastChild.firstChild.nodeValue);
    val = val * 5;
    row.style.backgroundColor = "#ff0000";

    // get for IE
    if (document.all && !window.opera) {
        var svgDocument = document.embeds[0].getSVGDocument();
        var svgObject = svgDocument.getElementById('circle1');

    // get for rest
    } else {
        var svgDocument = document.getElementById("svgDoc").contentDocument;
        var svgObject = svgDocument.getElementById('circle1');
    }

    // set for both
    svgObject.setAttribute("r",val);
}
```

When the mouseout event fires, the background color of the table row is set back to gray:

```
function restoreRow(evnt) {
    var row = this;
    row.style.backgroundColor="#ccc";
}
```

The web page, with the new SVG element, is shown in Example 8-10. Again, adding SVG into an XHTML document is quite trivial—as long as the browser supports it.

Example 8-10. Pagination example integrated with SVG

```
<!DOCTYPE html PUBLIC "-//W3C//DTD XHTML 1.1 plus MathML 2.0 plus SVG 1.1//EN"
"http://www.w3.org/2002/04/xhtml-math-svg/xhtml-math-svg-flat.dtd">
<html xmlns="http://www.w3.org/1999/xhtml" lang="en">
<head>
<title>bubble</title>
<meta http-equiv="Content-Type" content="text/html; charset=utf-8" />

<link rel="stylesheet" type="text/css" href="pagination.css" />
  <!-- Namespace source file -->
  <script src = "yui/yahoo/yahoo.js" ></script>

  <!-- Dependency source files -->
  <script type="text/javascript" src = "yui/dom/dom.js" ></script>
  <script type="text/javascript" src = "yui/event/event.js" ></script>
  <script type="text/javascript" src = "yui/dragdrop/dragdrop.js" ></script>

  <!-- Slider source file -->
  <script type="text/javascript" src = "yui/slider/slider.js" ></script>

  <!-- Application specific -->
  <script type="text/javascript" src="addingajax.js">
  </script>
  <script type="text/javascript" src="paginate2.js">
  </script>

</head>
<body>
<div id="container">
<div id="sliderbg">
  <div id="sliderthumb"><img src="yui/slider/vertSlider.png" alt="slider thumb" /></div>
</div>
<div id="main">
<div id="inner">
</div>
</div>
</div>
<div id="obj">
</div>
</body>
</html>
```

Figure 8-4 shows the example in Opera. This is a fairly simple example, but it does represent how easy it can be to integrate these two technologies.

There is some support for SVG in the Ajax libraries. Dojo offers preliminary support with dojo.gfx, but the library is not in production yet. It works across browsers and includes support for Windows, most likely through VML. There is a chart and graphing kit for MochiKit, called PlotKit SVG, that supports HTML Canvas (discussed next), and SVG.

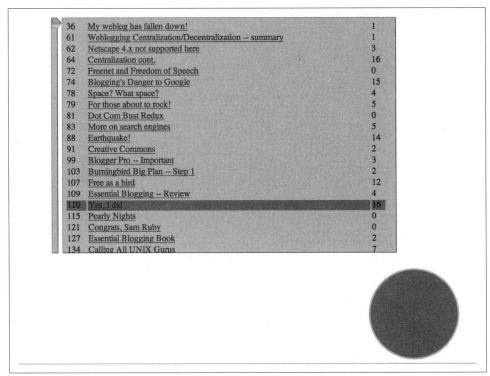

36	My weblog has fallen down!	1
61	Weblogging Centralization/Decentralization -- summary	1
62	Netscape 4.x not supported here	3
64	Centralization cont.	16
72	Freenet and Freedom of Speech	0
74	Blogging's Danger to Google	15
78	Space? What space?	4
79	For those about to rock!	5
81	Dot Com Bust Redux	0
83	More on search engines	5
88	Earthquake!	14
91	Creative Commons	2
99	Blogger Pro -- Important	3
103	Burningbird Big Plan -- Step 1	2
107	Free as a bird	12
109	Essential Blogging -- Review	4
110	Yes, I did	16
115	Pearly Nights	0
121	Congrats, Sam Ruby	0
127	Essential Blogging Book	2
134	Calling All UNIX Gurus	7

Figure 8-4. Ajax integrated with SVG

Google Maps uses SVG for plot lines, falling back on VML for IE. Google also provides an SVG widget for its GWT (Google Web Toolkit). The biggest limiting factor on support for SVG is Microsoft's lack of support for SVG in IE. Hopefully over time, the near-universal support for SVG in all other browsers will encourage Microsoft to do the same for IE. At a minimum, there are libraries that translate SVG into VML for use in IE in addition to the Adobe plug-in. Among these libraries are SVG-VML-3D (*www.lutanho.net/svgvml3d/index.html*), JsVectorGraphics (*www.walterzorn.com/jsgraphics/jsgraphics_e.htm*), and RichDraw (*http://starkravingfinkle.org/blog/2006/04/richdraw-simple-vmlsvg-editor*). You can search on the Web for the terms "SVG VML JavaScript Libraries" to find additional resources.

HTML5 Canvas

Apple originated the Canvas element, not just for its Safari browser, but also for use in the Mac OS X Dashboard. It ended up being picked up by the WhatWG group, and has made its way into the future implementation of HTML 5.0, the next version of HTML. The Gecko-based browsers support it, such as Firefox, Safari (of course), and Opera. IE doesn't, but there has been some effort to provide cross-browser objects (Google currently has such a project).

Unlike SVG, which is a formal XML vocabulary, the canvas element is just that: an element. In most cases, you access the canvas element's context via the DOM and use it to create some sophisticated effects. Unlike SVG, though, you do have to use JavaScript to create these effects.

 Mozilla has a good tutorial on working with the Canvas object at *http://developer.mozilla.org/en/docs/Canvas_tutorial*; Apple does as well at *http://developer.apple.com/documentation/AppleApplications/ Conceptual/SafariJSProgTopics/Tasks/Canvas.html*.

The Canvas object is rather easy to use. To start, all you need to do is add a canvas element to the web page:

```
<canvas id="graph" width="100%" height="300"></canvas>
```

To create the graphics, you'll access the Canvas context using an object-specific DOM method, getContext, testing first to ensure that the browser supports the object:

```
var canvas = aaElem('graph');
if (canvas.getContext) {
    var ctx = canvas.getContext('2d');
    ...
}
```

Once you have the canvas object, you can perform a number of graphical operations: create figures, draw paths, make arcs, manipulate images (added to the Canvas object in the XHTML page), create quadratic curves, and such. Once objects are created, just like with SVG, you can add effects such as color, fills, transparencies, and even create patterns as a stamp. You can also create gradients, as well as miter line joins, which are rather unique.

As with SVG, you can manage the canvas effects with Ajax. Returning to the pagination example, we can replace the svg element in the page with a canvas element:

```
<canvas id="graph" width="1000" height="150"></canvas>
```

In the new version of the code, the application retrieves the number of comments as the rows are being added and uses this number to plot a line of comment frequency at the bottom of the page, using the Canvas moveTo and lineTo methods. As the data is paged, the line is extended until it eventually fills in the bottom of the page. The JavaScript is shown in Example 8-11.

Example 8-11. Plotting frequency of comments using Canvas

```
var startx = 20;
var starty = 150;

var cache = {
   offset : 80,
   fetch : 40
```

Example 8-11. Plotting frequency of comments using Canvas (continued)

```
};

aaManageEvent(window,"load", function( ) {
  var slider = YAHOO.widget.Slider.getVertSlider("sliderbg",
          "sliderthumb", 0, 400);
  slider.setValue(0,true);
  slider.subscribe("change",adjustPage);

  createTable( );
  getRows(0);

  aaElem('inner').style.position='relative';
});

// adjust table container based on offset
// determine if database cache needs to be
// incremented
function adjustPage(offset) {

    var inner = aaElem('inner');
    var newTop = -offset;
    inner.style.top = newTop + "px";

    // if offset is greater than
    // cached offset, fetch rows, update cache
    if (offset > cache.offset) {
        getRows(cache.fetch);
        cache.offset+=80;
        cache.fetch+=40;
    }
}
// create and append a table cell
function createTableCell(value,tr) {

    // creates a <td> element
    var cell = document.createElement("td");

    // creates a Text Node
    var text = document.createTextNode(value);

    // appends the Text Node we created into the cell <td>
    cell.appendChild(text);

    // appends the cell <td> into the row <tr>
    tr.appendChild(cell);

    return tr;
}

// create empty table and add to page
// set container's top position
function createTable( ) {
```

Example 8-11. Plotting frequency of comments using Canvas (continued)

```
    var inner = aaElem('inner');

    var table = document.createElement('table');
    table.id = 'dataTable';
    var tableBody = document.createElement("tbody");
    tableBody.id = "dataTableBody";
    table.appendChild(tableBody);
    inner.appendChild(table);
    inner.style.top = "0px";
}
// append newly fetched rows as table rows
function printRows(rowsObj) {

    // clean up old content
    var tableBody = aaElem('dataTableBody');

    // table rows
    for(var i = 0; i < rowsObj.length; i++) {
        // creates a <tr> element
        var row = document.createElement("tr");
        row = createTableCell(rowsObj[i].id, row);

        // anchor and title
        var cell = document.createElement("td");
        cell.innerHTML = "<a href='" + rowsObj[i].guid + "'>" + rowsObj[i].title + "</a>";
        row.appendChild(cell);

        row = createTableCell(rowsObj[i].comments,row);

        tableBody.appendChild(row);
    }
    var canvas = aaElem('graph');
    if (canvas.getContext) {
        var ctx = canvas.getContext('2d');
        for (var j = 0; j < rowsObj.length; j++) {
            ctx.moveTo(startx,starty);
            startx+=5;
            starty = 150 - (parseInt(rowsObj[j].comments) * 5);
            ctx.lineTo(startx, starty);
        }
        ctx.stroke();
    }
}
```

The changed elements of the code are highlighted, which demonstrates how simple it is to use the canvas object. Figure 8-5 shows a snapshot of the example in action in Safari, since the browser supports Canvas, though it doesn't yet support SVG.

This isn't much beyond a quick introduction. Follow the Mozilla tutorial for an excellent introduction to all of the Canvas capabilities.

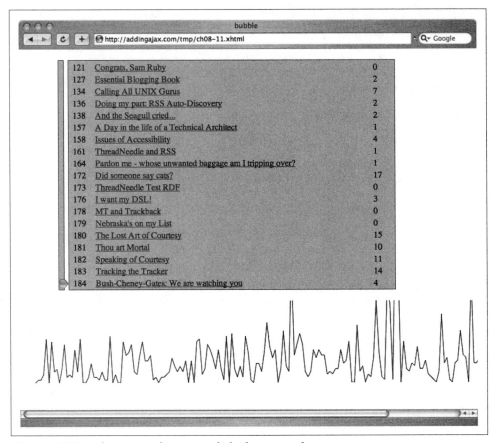

Figure 8-5. Using the Canvas object to track the frequency of comments

The Future of Graphics

Graphics are the last frontier of the web page, and thankfully, we're seeing considerable progress in what we can do as web developers. All browsers support at least a significant subset of CSS, and all browsers support at least one of the extended graphical libraries/objects. Unfortunately, not all browsers support all libraries. Firefox and Opera are the browsers with the most support, though WebKit promises much for Safari, and Microsoft has been making moves to bring IE more in line with the rest of the world.

Thanks to the inventiveness of folks, there is cross-browser library support for most of the graphics demonstrated in this chapter—support for effects beyond these relatively uncomplicated examples.

There are issues associated with using any of the graphics, not the least of which is that they're all "visual" elements and thus will be a not a useful addition to your site for those with some sight impairment. However, as demonstrated in the examples here, they could be fun and interesting additions to your existing applications, especially as visual charts of data that you're already providing in a text format. Most use is dependent on script, but again, if script is disabled, the effect isn't displayed and no functionality is lost.

As for the cross-browser differences, like those in the last example, if a browser doesn't implement the canvas object, nothing will show. However, the table with the text data will be present.

When used as a fun addition, any of the advanced visual effects and objects described in this chapter can add a lot of sizzle without costing you the steak.

CHAPTER 9
Mashup Your Site

Adding Ajax to your site opens your site opens it up to a world of services, applications, and assorted and sundry widgets. Both Yahoo! and Google provide mapping services, Amazon external storage, imagery with Flickr, syndication feeds with Newsgator, and a host of metadata made available through XML, microformats, and the Resource Description Framework (RDF).

You could get carried away and end up with a site that tries to load the entire Internet into your sidebar, but if used wisely, these external services can be a real bonus for your web applications.

You can also, in turn, provide services from your site to other sites by providing widgets created specifically to take advantage of your services or data. Why would you want to? For the same reasons other sites provide their widgets for your use: to get your services in front of others, to sell or to share.

How much you can integrate with other services really depends on the service provider. Google manages all aspects of its mapping service, but provides a decent API that lets you show map locations, plot routes, and define the viewpoint window. However, it is a Google viewpoint window, and if the company decides to insert ads one day, you won't have any say in the matter.

Other services, such as the del.icio.us tag API, provide access to limited raw data, but may impose restrictions on how you use the data—or how often, since several services only allow you to call an API using the same license so many times a day.

There's also a risk with combining data like this in *mashups*: a service may go away, become suddenly restricted, or undergo a change in API. If you build a dependency on an external service, you're putting your effort at risk. However, if you build an application, widget, or product from data provided at several sources, or as a fun new interface to an existing service, your effort brings reward, even if it's just having something new and interesting to provide to your site readers or people who use your code. In other words, don't bank on external services—you'll only get bitten if you do.

I'm not going to get into detailed overviews of most of the APIs in this chapter because each has its own excellent documentation, which I'll point you to. Instead, I'm going to focus on how to begin pulling together multiple services and APIs and how to look for new opportunities for web mashups for your own efforts.

Mapping with Google

Google Maps, more than any other application, sparked interest in Ajax. Consider that through this service you can post a map (with associated satellite and hybrid views) on your site, providing directions and other annotations, all easily managed through a relatively simple-to-use JavaScript API. This was Google's most powerful offering.

 See examples and detailed documentation and get a Google Maps API key at *http://www.google.com/apis/maps*.

Google has stated that it currently has no advertising in its Google Maps API, and promises to notify API users 90 days in advance if advertising will be offered. In addition, each map key may be used to access the mapping service 50,000 times a day. The terms of use state that the service you provide should be made freely available. In other words, you can't charge folks for the use of your modification of Google Maps. The service also has a lengthy "Appropriate Conduct and Prohibited Uses" section in the terms of use that you might want to review first.

Once you have your Google Maps key, note that the key is specific to a subdirectory and that you can use the key only from that subdirectory.

Google Maps: Quick and Easy

Using Google Maps is relatively simple. You'll create an element, usually a div element, in your page where the map will be placed, passing the identifier for this element to the API when constructing the map. To see whether you have the minimum requirements for a Google map, you can use the following JavaScript to ensure that the browser is Google Maps-capable. This JavaScript then creates a map, placing it into the div element identified as map, and centers it at a given longitude and latitude:

```
if (GBrowserIsCompatible( )) {
  var map = new GMap2(document.getElementById("map"));
  map.setCenter(new GLatLng(38.627952, -90.1843880), 13);
}
```

That's about all you need just to put in a map and position it. With this, you also have the ability to pan the map using drag-and-drop, which is built into the map object. Typically, though, you'll also want to provide more control over the map so that a user can zoom in and out to see more or less of the map details. The map object's addControl is used to provide a basic map control to the map:

```
if (GBrowserIsCompatible( )) {
  var map = new GMap2(document.getElementById("map"));
  map.addControl(new GSmallMapControl( ));
  map.setCenter(new GLatLng(38.627952, -90.1843880), 13);
}
```

This creates a small control on the left side of the map with a plus sign (+) to zoom in, a minus (–) to zoom out, and arrows for click scrolling.

This is sufficient, but why stop here? Since Google Maps provides three different view types—map, satellite, and hybrid—it seems a shame not to provide a view option. The addControl method is used again, but this time creating a Google Maps type control:

```
if (GBrowserIsCompatible( )) {
  var map = new GMap2(document.getElementById("map"));
  map.addControl(new GSmallMapControl( ));
  map.addControl(new GMapTypeControl( ));
  map.setCenter(new GLatLng(38.627952, -90.1843880), 13);
}
```

This is more or less how the Google Maps API works: it provides a set of objects with methods where you can pass objects or other values as parameters, all of which combine to create an effect on a single map. Put it all together with a window onload event, and you can see from Example 9-1 exactly how easy it is to add Google Maps functionality to your site.

This example creates a map centered on the St. Louis Arch, with a small navigational control, as well as the type switcher. I recommend you try this with the satellite view and zoom in on the Arch; it makes a great effect.

Example 9-1. Google Maps, quick and easy

```
<!DOCTYPE html PUBLIC "-//W3C//DTD XHTML 1.0 Strict//EN"
    "http://www.w3.org/TR/xhtml1/DTD/xhtml1-strict.dtd">
<html xmlns="http://www.w3.org/1999/xhtml" lang="en" xml:lang="en">
  <head>
    <meta name="generator"
    content="HTML Tidy for Linux/x86 (vers 1st November 2002), see www.w3.org" />
    <meta http-equiv="content-type" content="text/html; charset=utf-8" />
    <title>Google Maps First Look</title>
    <style type="text/css">
    /*<![CDATA[*/
#map  { width: 600px; height: 400px; border: 1px solid #ccc;
      margin: 20px;}
    /*]]>*/
    </style>
    <script src="addingajax.js" type="text/javascript">
    </script>
```

Example 9-1. Google Maps, quick and easy (continued)

```
    <script
    src="http://maps.google.com/maps?file=api&amp;v=2&amp;key=yourkey" type="text/
javascript">
    </script>
    <script type="text/javascript">
//<![CDATA[
aaManageEvent(window,"load",setUp);
aaManageEvent(window,"onunload",GUnload);
function setUp( ) {
  if (GBrowserIsCompatible( )) {
    var map = new GMap2(document.getElementById("map"));
    map.addControl(new GSmallMapControl( ));
    map.addControl(new GMapTypeControl( ));
    map.setCenter(new GLatLng(38.627952, -90.1843880), 13);
  }
}
//]]>
    </script>
  </head>
  <body>
    <div id="map">
    </div>
  </body>
</html>
```

Of course, to create this example yourself, you'll need your key, but these are simple
to get. Go to the Google Maps API site, type in a URL, provide a Google username,
agree to the terms, and you're off.

One other thing worth pointing out in Example 9-1, before we move on to the
"mashing" part of this mashup, is the use of the window onunload event. Since Google Maps does use function closure (an anonymous function within another function), the API provides a "cleanup" routine to prevent memory leaks that can occur
with Internet Explorer 6.x when these types of JavaScript constructs are used.
Regardless of which functions and objects you use, you'll want to include this in
your application.

The map that opens on the page can be dragged to scroll it to the right, left, top, or
bottom. You can also zoom in and out with the controls to the left, or switch the
view with the controls along the top. All of this can be enabled with a few function
calls, but there's more—you can also integrate Google Maps with your own data.
This is the first mashup we'll cover in this chapter.

> The examples in this chapter use an XHTML DOCTYPE, but the pages
> are served up as HTML. The reason for this is that Google's Map
> application does not work when the page is processed as XHTML.

Get There from Here

If all you're doing is providing a Google Map to show the general location of your office, home, or other pertinent location, you're more or less set and can stop at this point. However, there is a whole lot more that you can do with this API.

You can add graphics to each Google map through an overlay layer. For instance, you can place a marker at a specific location to make it more visible in the code:

```
var point = new GlatLng(lat, long);
var marker = new GMarker(point);
map.addOverlay(map);
```

Now when the map is displayed, an icon is placed at the given point. If no icon is provided, the default is used, which is a reddish balloon with a centered black dot.

You can also trace a route on the map by providing an array of points in the order that you want the trace to display:

```
for (var i = 0; i < points.length; i++) {
  var point = new GLatLng(parseFloat(markers[i].getAttribute("lat")),
                          parseFloat(markers[i].getAttribute("lng")));
  var mark = new GMarker(point);
  map.addOverlay(mark);
  points.push(point);
}
map.addOverlay(new GPolyline(points));
```

In our example, an array of elements containing latitude and longitude points is given, a marker is created for each, and the points are pushed onto an array, which is eventually used to add another overlay, this time a `polyline` connecting the points.

You can also annotate a marker by providing an *info window*, which is a bubble that's attached to the marker and which provides whatever information you want to provide:

```
marker.openInfoWindowHtml(text);
```

Where do the points for the markers and `polyline` trace? And where does the text in the marker information windows come from? Well, this is where we bring Ajax into the mix.

The Google Maps API provides a `GdownloadUrl` function that can load external data on demand from a provided URL and invoke a callback function to process the data. The external data is an XML file, usually containing latitude and longitude points, but you can include other data. The one restriction is that the method is using `XMLHttpRequest`, so the URL provided for the data must be local to the domain of the web page.

Example 9-2 pulls this all together—data provided locally and the Google maps API— creating an application that loads and centers a map, and provides the zoom and type controls. In addition, a div element acts as a button that users can click to

---

load external data. The data file has four points containing longitude and latitude, as well as information to put in the info window. When users click the div element that reads "Load Data," the data is loaded and the markers and route are drawn. Clicking one of the markers opens an info window bubble above the marker, repositioning the map if the bubble would otherwise be cut off via the map boundaries.

Note the emphasized sections in Example 9-2. These add in Vector Markup Language specifications necessary for the polyline function to work with IE. Google Maps uses SVG for route marking for those browsers that support SVG, but also provides VML for IE. Be aware, though, that this page will not validate with these additions.

Example 9-2. Google Maps API with markers and route polyline and info windows

```
<!DOCTYPE html PUBLIC "-//W3C//DTD XHTML 1.0 Strict//EN"
        "http://www.w3.org/TR/xhtml1/DTD/xhtml1-strict.dtd">
<html xmlns="http://www.w3.org/1999/xhtml" xmlns:v='urn:schemas-microsoft-com:vml'
        lang="en" xml:lang="en">
<head>
<meta http-equiv="content-type" content="text/html; charset=utf-8">
<title>Google Maps First Look</title>

<style type="text/css">
#map
{
    border: 1px solid #ccc;
    height: 400px;
    margin: 20px;
    width: 600px;
}
#loader
{
    background-color: #ccf;
    margin: 20px;
    padding: 5px;
    text-align: center;
    width: 150px;
}
v\:*
{
    behavior:url(#default#VML);
 }
</style>
<script src=
   "http://maps.google.com/maps?file=api&amp;v=2&amp;key=your-own-key"
   type="text/javascript">
</script>
<script src="addingajax.js" type="text/javascript">
</script>
<script type="text/javascript">
//<![CDATA[
var map;
```

Example 9-2. Google Maps API with markers and route polyline and info windows (continued)

```
aaManageEvent(window,"load",setUp);
aaManageEvent(window,"unload",GUnload);

// Creates a marker at the given point with the given label
function createMarker(point, text) {
  var marker = new GMarker(point);
  GEvent.addListener(marker, "click", function() {
    var txt = text + '<br />' + point.toString();
    marker.openInfoWindowHtml(txt);
  });
  return marker;
}

function loadData(evnt) {
    evnt = evnt ? evnt : window.event;
    aaCancelEvent(evnt);
    GDownloadUrl("points.xml",function(data,responseCode) {
        var xml = GXml.parse(data);
        var markers = xml.documentElement.getElementsByTagName("marker");
        var points = [];
        for (var i = 0; i < markers.length; i++) {
            var point = new GLatLng(parseFloat(markers[i].getAttribute("lat")),
                                    parseFloat(markers[i].getAttribute("lng")));
            var mark = createMarker(point,markers[i].getAttribute("title"));
            map.addOverlay(mark);
            points.push(point);
        }
        map.addOverlay(new GPolyline(points));
        });
    return false;
}

function setUp() {
  if (GBrowserIsCompatible()) {
    map = new GMap2(document.getElementById("map"));
    map.addControl(new GSmallMapControl());
    map.addControl(new GMapTypeControl());
    map.setCenter(new GLatLng(38.627952, -90.1843880), 13);
  }

  aaManageEvent(document.getElementById("loader"),"click",loadData);
}

//]]>
</script>
</head>
<body>
<div id="loader"><a href="">Load Data</a></div>
<div id="map"></div>
</body>
</html>
```

Figure 9-1 shows the Google map loaded into Safari, just after the external data has been loaded and one of the markers clicked, and with information window displayed.

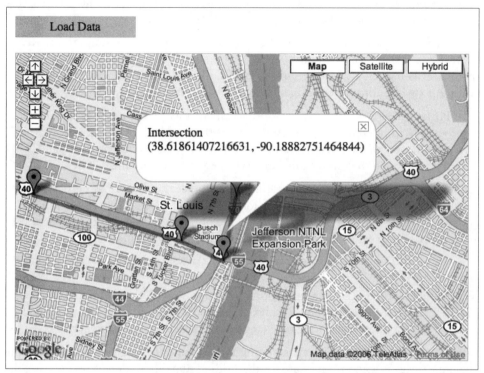

Figure 9-1. A Google map with markers, route, and info window displayed after loading external data

If you're using Firefox with Firebug installed, open the tool before making the request. The file request is displayed in the Console, and we can see both the data and the response headers.

This is an example of mashing together local data and the Google Map API, but a real mashup occurs when we start combining two or more external services, with or without our own data.

A Second Service: Flickr

Flickr has achieved prominence as a socially oriented photo site. Not only can members post their photos (as well as tag, categorize, annotate, and share them), but they can also comment on each others' work, join forums, and integrate Flickr services with other third-party applications. You can get a free Flickr account with limitations on how much bandwidth you can use to upload photos every month, or you can buy virtually unlimited bandwidth and storage with a "pro" account.

Flickr was bought by Yahoo! and can be accessed at *http://flickr.com*. The Flickr API, which we'll be looking at in this section, can be found at *http://www.flickr.com/ services/api*, which also includes a link to the page to sign up for a Flickr key. Using the API requires a unique key, but there's no charge for its use.

Flickr's web services are some of the most complete, offering support for REST, XML-RPC, SOAP, a PHP library (since PHP is so ubiquitous), and recently, JSON. The latter is particularly important because it allows us to make direct service calls using Ajax without running up against the browser sandbox.

The Flickr API is split into classes of objects, such as photos, people, groups, and photosets. Within each class is a set of services that can be requested. The Flickr API site provides excellent documentation about what each service provides and what has to be passed to the service call. All service requests require the API key.

In the examples in this section, we'll use Ajax to get the data cross-domain, which means using the REST approach and formatting the request as a URL. We'll also pass in a format value of json to get back JSON-formatted data and provide a call-back function. An example request would look like the following:

```
http://api.flickr.com/services/rest/?method=flickr.photos.geo.getLocation&photo_id="
+ photo.id + "&api_key=your-keya&format=json&jsoncallback=placeMarker
```

When used as the URL for a new script element's source, the data is returned as a JSON-formatted object within the callback function's parameters. The result is used to dynamically create a scripting block, as demonstrated in previous chapters.

Since we plan on using dynamic scripting more than once, the process to build the dynamic script is a good candidate for the Adding Ajax library, *addingajax.js*. It's the same code used each time, with only the URL of the web service endpoint differing between each use. The new function, aaAddScript, follows:

```
// add script
function aaAddScript(url) {
   var script = document.createElement('script');
   script.type = 'text/javascript';
   script.src = url;
   document.getElementsByTagName('head')[0].appendChild(script);
}
```

The service request to Flickr shown previously retrieves the geographical location for the given photo identifier. It's through the location data that the Google Maps and Flickr API web services are mashed together.

Creating the Mashup

In the next application a Flickr search request is made, returning photos for a specific user identifier. The default limit for an unconstrained request is usually 100 photos. We can create a mini slideshow of the photos on the righthand side of the page, while the placeholder for the Google Map is on the left. As each photo is opened, a marker is placed in the map to mark the spot where the photo was taken.

We can split the JavaScript out into a separate file, leaving the HTML page shown in Example 9-3. Once the JavaScript is removed, there's very little left in a page—a few placeholder elements and the stylesheet.

Example 9-3. XHTML page including script tags

```html
<!DOCTYPE html PUBLIC "-//W3C//DTD HTML 4.01//EN"
"http://www.w3.org/TR/1999/REC-html401-19991224/strict.dtd">
<html>
<head>
<meta http-equiv="content-type" content="text/html; charset=utf-8">
<title>Google/Flickr Mashup</title>

<style type="text/css">
#map
{
        border: 1px solid #ccc;
        float: left;
        height: 300px;
        margin: 20px;
        width: 400px;
}
#loader
{
        background-color: #ccf;
        margin: 20px;
        margin-bottom: 0;
        padding: 5px;
        text-align: center;
        width: 150px;
}
#image
{
        margin-top: 20px;
}
#button
{
        background-color: #fff;
        border: 1px solid #000;
        font: 12px arial;
        left: 460px;
        padding: 2px;
        position: absolute;
        text-align: center;
        top: 35px;
        width: 50px;
}
</style>

<script type="text/javascript" src="addingajax.js">
</script>
```

Example 9-3. XHTML page including script tags (continued)

```
<script src="http://maps.google.com/maps?file=api&amp;v=2&amp;key="your_key"
   type="text/javascript">
</script>
<script type="text/javascript" src="googleflickr.js">
</script>
</head>
<body>
<div id="button"><a href="">Next</a></div>
<div id="map"></div>
<div><img id="image" src="" alt="slideshow"></div>
</body>
</html>
```

The div that serves as the button is placed first, so that keyboard users are served the button link first, rather than having to tab through all the other page links, including those put in by Google. Since it's absolutely positioned anyway, placing it first doesn't impact the page layout.

The real power of the application is found in the JavaScript file, *googleflickr.js*, shown in Example 9-4. Summarizing the application processes:

1. When the page is loaded, Google Maps is set to the default center position.
2. The location is checked for a hash and, if found, the page is reset to the given photo.
3. The first Flickr service call is made to get an array of photos for a specific user identifier.
4. The first photo (or hashed photo) is displayed and another Flickr service call is made to get the photo's geographical location.
5. The Flickr location is used to derive a marker placed on the Google map, any previously existing marker is removed, and the map is repositioned.

Whenever the user clicks Next, the next photo is pulled from the Photos array, the location is retrieved, and the map marker is placed. The globals variables are at the top of the file to cache the list of photos returned by Flickr, as well as to maintain a counter for the photo currently being displayed. The Google Maps marker is also maintained globally because we want to be able to clear the current marker before creating a new one based on the next photo.

Example 9-4. Google/Flickr mashup JavaScript

```
// globals
var map;
var photos;
var currentPhoto=0;
var marker;

// setup load and uload
```

Example 9-4. Google/Flickr mashup JavaScript (continued)

```
aaManageEvent(window,"load",setUp);
aaManageEvent(window,"unload",GUnload);

// if map compatible, create map and retrieve photos for user id
// use default settings: info for 100 photos
function setUp() {

  // check for hash on location and reset application accordingly
  var hash = window.location.hash;
  if (hash) {
    var subLoc = hash.split("#")[1];
    currentPhoto = parseInt(subLoc);
  }

  // create map
  if (GBrowserIsCompatible()) {
    map = new GMap2(document.getElementById("map"));
    map.addControl(new GSmallMapControl());
    map.addControl(new GMapTypeControl());
    map.setCenter(new GLatLng(38.627952, -90.1843880), 13);
    aaManageEvent(document.getElementById('button'),'click',loadPhoto);
    addScript("http://api.flickr.com/services/rest/?method=flickr.photos.search&user_
id=69562477@N00&
api_key=your-key&format=json&jsoncallback=processPhotos");
  }
}

// assign photos globally, call first to loadfunction processPhotos(obj) {
  photos = obj.photos.photo;
  getPhoto();
}

function loadPhoto(evnt) {
  evnt = evnt ? evnt : window.event;
  aaCancelEvent(evnt);
  getPhoto();
  return false;
}

// derive photo url
// get geolocation of photo
function getPhoto() {
  var photo = photos[currentPhoto];
  var pic = "http://farm" + photo.farm + ".static.flickr.com/" +
            photo.server + "/" + photo.id + "_" + photo.secret + ".jpg";

  // set 'location'
  window.location.hash = currentPhoto;

  aaElem("image").src=pic;
  aaAddScript("http://api.flickr.com/services/rest/?method=flickr.photos.geo.
getLocation&photo_id="
```

Example 9-4. Google/Flickr mashup JavaScript (continued)

```
+ photo.id + "&api_key=your-key&format=json&jsoncallback=placeMarker");

  // update photo counter, reset if over length of photo array
  currentPhoto++;
  if (currentPhoto == photos.length) currentPhoto = 0;
}

// clear existing marker, and place new one
function placeMarker(obj) {
  var point = new GLatLng(parseFloat(obj.photo.location.latitude),
                          parseFloat(obj.photo.location.longitude));
  if (marker) map.removeOverlay(marker);
  marker = new GMarker(point);
  map.addOverlay(marker);
  map.setCenter(point, 13);
}
```

The first function, setUp, creates the Google map, as demonstrated in the previous two examples. It also makes the first Flickr services call, using the new aaAddScript function added to the *addingajax.js* library previously. The web service call uses the REST method, passing in the user-id for the Flickr account and the developer key (you'll need to get your own developer key, but the user-id account is valid). At the end of the service call is the request for the JSON-formatted data, as well as the callback function name. Flickr expects the callback parameter to be named jsoncallback.

The next function in the example code is the processPhotos callback function, which extracts the photo array from the returned object and assigns it to a global variable. It also calls getPhoto to load the first photo. The photo URL is derived from several parameters returned for each photo. The method for deriving these photo URLs is described at the Flickr developer site, but the code used here should work for all future efforts. The function also sets the location object's hash to provide a level of persistence if the page is reloaded, as described in Chapter 7.

Once the photo is loaded, another Flickr service request is made, this time for the location for the photo. In the placeMarker callback function for this service, the location is extracted from the returned object and used to create a new Google map marker, first clearing any existing previous marker.

Figure 9-2 shows the example page. As you click through the slideshow, the geographical coordinates for the photo are used to pinpoint the location of the marker, and the map is recentered on this point.

This is a fairly simple mashup, though useful. One lack of efficiency is in the request for the location. If the application is making the same call multiple times to a service for the same data, it's better to store the data locally in memory.

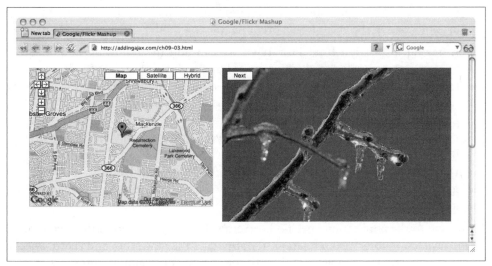

Figure 9-2. Mashup between Flickr and Google Maps

Creating Photo Objects and Revisiting Prototype Versus Localized Functions

A solution for maintaining data directly with the photo would be to create an object for each photo with the location and photo URL as members. Then the URL could be set when the object is created, but the location is set only when the photo is displayed:

```
var photo = function(url) {
    this.url = url;
    this.longitude = null;
    this.latitude = null;
    this.setLocation(lon,lat) {
        this.longitude = lon;
        this.latitude = lat;
    }
}
```

To create and maintain an array of these photo objects, we can first create a single global object, Photo, which consists of an array of photo objects and a member to hold the current photo index. Using a framework such as Prototype, we could use its functionality to create and manage the object. For now, though, we'll hack together our own and move all the photo-relevant methods to it.

One piece of functionality the Photo object requires is a way of binding an event to an object in such a way that the process doesn't redefine the context. However, we still have to access to the event and don't want it stripped out. In Chapter 7, we added aaBindObjMethod to the *addingajax.js* library to associate an object's context with a function. Now we need to extend the library to add something similar—maintaining context and passing the event for an event handler method.

Again, taking inspiration from Prototype, we can add the following new method, aaBindEventListener, to the *addingajax.js* library. Instead of apply, it uses the Function.call method, allowing us to pass in multiple arguments. The new library function passes in the event argument, as well as the object:

```
function aaBindEventListener(obj, method) {
  return function(event) { method.call(obj, event || window.event)};
}
```

With this new function, we can use object methods as event handlers, knowing the method will get the event object and also knowing that the object context is still maintained.

Returning to the application-specific JavaScript, Example 9-5 shows the new rebuild of the JavaScript library from Example 9-4, but uses the new photo and Photo objects. There is only one Photo object, and all of the methods pertaining to the photo processing are moved to it.

Example 9-5. A remake of the Google/Flickr JavaScript library

```
// object function for each
// individual photo element
function photo(id, url) {
    this.id = id;
    this.url = url;
    this.longitude = null;
    this.latitude = null;
    this.setLocation = function(lon,lat) {
        this.longitude = lon;
        this.latitude = lat;
    }
}


// global Photo object
// to manage all photo Ajax calls
// and process all photo data
var Photo = {

    // extract array of photos and set photo URLS
    processPhotos : function(obj) {
        this.currentPhoto = -1;
        this.photos = new Array(obj.photos.photo.length);
        for (var i = 0; i < obj.photos.photo.length; i++) {
            var pic = obj.photos.photo[i];
            var url = "http://farm" + pic.farm + ".static.flickr.com/" +
                pic.server + "/" + pic.id + "_" + pic.secret + ".jpg";
            this.photos[i] = new photo(pic.id, url);
        }
        aaManageEvent(aaElem('button'),'click',this.loadPhoto.bindAsEventListener(this));
```

Example 9-5. A remake of the Google/Flickr JavaScript library (continued)

```
      this.getPhoto( );
   },

   // event handler for getting next photo
   loadPhoto   : function(evnt) {
      evnt = evnt: ? evnt : window.event;
      aaCancelEvent(evnt);
      getPhoto( );
      return false;
   },

   // process next photo request and get location
   // if location not already present in photo object
   getPhoto      : function( ) {
       this.currentPhoto++;
       if (this.currentPhoto >= this.photos.length) this.currentPhoto = 0;
       var pic = this.photos[this.currentPhoto];
       aaElem("image").src=pic.url;
       if (!pic.latitude) {
          addScript("http://api.flickr.com/services/rest/?method=flickr.photos.geo.
getLocation&photo_id=" +
               pic.id + "&api_key=yourkey&format=json&jsoncallback=Photo.placeMarker");
       } else {
         var point = new GLatLng(pic.latitude,pic.longitude);
         map.setCenter(point,13);
       }
       window.location.hash = this.currentPhoto;
    },

   // place marker
    placeMarker   : function(obj) {
      var lat = parseFloat(obj.photo.location.latitude);
      var lon = parseFloat(obj.photo.location.longitude);
      this.photos[this.currentPhoto].setLocation(lon,lat);
      var point = new GLatLng(lat,lon);
      var marker = new GMarker(point);
      map.addOverlay(marker);
      map.setCenter(point, 13);
    }
};

// setup load and uload
aaManageEvent(window,"load",setUp);
aaManageEvent(window,"unload",GUnload);

// if map compatible, create map and retrieve photos for user id//
 use default settings: info for 100 photos
function setUp( ) {
  if (GBrowserIsCompatible( )) {
    map = new GMap2(document.getElementById("map"));
    map.addControl(new GSmallMapControl( ));
    map.addControl(new GMapTypeControl( ));
```

```
    map.setCenter(new GLatLng(38.627952, -90.1843880), 13);
    addScript("http://api.flickr.com/services/rest/?method=flickr.photos.search&user_
id=69562477
        @N00&api_key=yourkey&format=json&jsoncallback=gPic.processPhotos");
  }
    var hash = window.location.hash;
    if (hash) {
        var subLoc = hash.split("#")[1];
        Photo.currentPhoto = parseInt(subLoc) - 1;
    }
}
```

This recode of the library is a more efficient approach, and it does make it easier to keep functionality grouped by object. It also prevents a lot of global functions from floating around, possibly conflicting with functions in other libraries.

It would make sense to also take the map functions and these with the Map object. We could try to use the JavaScript prototype object with Google's Map API, but it's not a good idea to muck around overly much with other libraries, especially ones that do change.

Also note the slight effect that caching the data for the Flickr API calls has on the application when you make your first round through the photos. On the first go, you'll see calls to both Flickr and Google. After that, there are calls to Google only, other than the request to Flickr for the photo. Again, it would be nice to cache the map pieces so we don't have to call Google, but that functionality is out of our hands.

Of course, one of the risks with mashups is that you never know when the service you're using will change or become unavailable. While I was writing this chapter, the Flickr API had temporary problems and started returning the same callback function: jsonFlickrApi. The problem is made more challenging when you're dealing with more than one API from more than one service. Still, as long as you're working with a stable web service, problems should occur infrequently, and API modifications should be minimized.

Flickr provides more data than just the photo's location. We have access to metadata embedded with the photo, such as camera make and model, the date the photo was taken, and exposure settings. We also have access to data managed at the Flickr site, including title, description, comments, set membership, and any tags associated with the photo. A *tag* is a keyword associated with an object that provides a form of global categorization, making it easier for several users' efforts to gather about this tag as a focal point. A set of objects grouped together based on tag is called a *tag cloud*.

For the examples in this chapter, we're definitely interested in getting the tag information because we can use this to add other web services into the ongoing mashup. That's another useful feature of tags: many so-called "social" web services provide this type of functionality and usually expose it in their APIs.

If we're going to add more data to the mashup page, though, we need to organize the page better. Luckily we have the *tabs.js* tabular page API from Chapter 5, and setting the application up in tabbed pages makes a lot of sense. The first thing to do before adding the next mashup is to organize the Flickr/Google page using tabs. It's doing this conversion, though, that leads us to discover another challenge associated with mashups: the expectations of the external library developers.

Converting Flickr/Google to Tabbed Pages

Converting the application to tabbed pages should be relatively trivial. First, redefine the page layout to use the structure necessary for the *tabs.js* library including the tab name and the tab content. Next, create the tabs object and set its active and inactive colors. The rest should fall into place nicely. After all, both the Flickr and Google Map portions of the application simply require a specific element to place the content, and it shouldn't matter where that content is in the page.

It shouldn't, but it does. In this application, since the button to control the content is associated with the photo, it makes sense to put it as the first tabbed page and place the map second. However, when we do so, we find that the Google map isn't showing when we get to the second tabbed page. The framework is there, but not the map components.

What's happening within the Google Maps API is unknown and remains so, at least at a more than casual glance, with all the JS obfuscation applied to the API. We can guess, though, and my guess is that the API can't "draw" the map to a nondisplayed area because it uses the width and height of the area to determine how many map panels are necessary to create the map. Yet if we open the page with the map area displayed and then switch back to the photo, we create a distracting visual effect that tarnishes the smooth presentation of the effect.

The workaround is actually rather simple, and we can be thankful, again, for the power of the underlying DOM. Instead of creating the map directly within the tab page, we'll create it as a separate invisible element, and then once the map is created and loaded, we can use the DOM to append it to the content area of the panel where it will reside. Once the map elements are in place, this display challenge is no longer an issue because Google has what it needs to determine what to load—the size of the map element. It doesn't matter to the application whether the element is visible.

This workaround works for all the book's target browsers except IE 6.x and IE 7, both of which have their own versions of funky problems with Google Maps. See the section at the end of this section specifically for fixing IE-related problems with our mashup application. All the examples in this chapter work with Gecko-based browsers (Camino, Firefox), Opera, Safari (including WebKit), and OmniWeb.

Example 9-6 shows the new page with a reference to a new JavaScript library, *googflicobj.js*, in addition to the global Adding Ajax library, *addingajax.js*, and the *tabs.js* libraries. The page contents have been rearranged into the Tabs application required structure.

Example 9-6. Google/Flickr mashup in tabbed pages

```
<!DOCTYPE html PUBLIC "-//W3C//DTD XHTML 1.0 Strict//EN"
    "http://www.w3.org/TR/xhtml1/DTD/xhtml1-strict.dtd">
<html xmlns="http://www.w3.org/1999/xhtml" lang="en" xml:lang="en">
  <head>
    <meta http-equiv="content-type" content="text/html; charset=utf-8" />
    <title>Google/Flickr Mashup</title>
    <link rel="stylesheet" type="text/css" href="mashup.css" />
    <script type="text/javascript" src="addingajax.js">
    </script>
    <script type="text/javascript" src="tabs.js">
    </script>
    <script
    src="http://maps.google.com/maps?file=api&amp;v=2&amp;key=yourkey"
     type="text/javascript">
    </script>
    <script type="text/javascript" src="googflicobj.js">
    </script>
  </head>
  <body>
    <div class="container">
      <div class="tab">
        <div class="name">
          Photo:
        </div>
        <div class="name" id="maptab">
          Map:
        </div>
      </div>
      <div class="elements">
        <div class="content">
          <div id="button">
            <a href="">Next</a>
          </div>
          <img id="image" src="" alt="slideshow" />
        </div>
        <div class="content" id="mapcontent">
        </div>
      </div>
```

Example 9-6. Google/Flickr mashup in tabbed pages (continued)

```
    </div>
    <div id="map">
    </div>
  </body>
</html>
```

The stylesheet for the application has also been separated out into its own file, *mashup.css*:

```
map
{
        border: 1px solid #ccc;
        height: 335px;
        visibility: hidden;
        width: 500px;
}
#loader
{
        background-color: #ccf;
        margin: 20px;
        padding: 5px;
        text-align: center;
        width: 150px;
}

#button
{
        background-color: #fff;
        border: 1px solid #000;
        font: 12px arial;
        padding: 2px;
        text-align: center;
        width: 50px;
}
.name
{
        border: 1px solid #000;
        display: inline;
        padding: 10px;
        text-align: center;
}
.elements
{
        background-color: #ccf;
        border: 1px solid #000;
        height: 500px;
        margin-top: 10px;
        width: 600px;
}
.content
{
```

```
        display: none;
        margin: 10px;
}
.tab
{
        display: inline;
}
.footer
{
        clear: both;
}
.container
{
        margin: 30px;
}
```

The style setting for the map object in this new application page is set to be invisible, and the object is completely removed from the Tabs structure so its dimensions don't impact on the layout of the tabs. The tab elements are also added to the stylesheet, with the panel color set to a nice, soft blue.

We don't want to reproduce all of *googflicobj.js*, as most of it resembles that shown in Example 9-5. What we will reproduce is the SetUp routine, which now adds in the small bit of code to move the map object and reset its visibility after it's been loaded:

```
// if map compatible, create map and retrieve photos for user id
// use default settings: info for 100 photos
function setUp() {
  setUpTabs();

  if (GBrowserIsCompatible()) {
    map = new GMap2(aaElem("map"));
    map.addControl(new GSmallMapControl());
    map.addControl(new GMapTypeControl());
    map.setCenter(new GLatLng(38.627952, -90.1843880), 13);

    // associate map with page
    var cnt = aaElem("mapcontent");
    var mapObj = aaElem("map");
    cnt.appendChild(mapObj);
    mapObj.style.visibility="visible";

    var hash = window.location.hash;
    if (hash) {
      var subLoc = hash.split("#")[1];
      Photo.currentPhoto = parseInt(subLoc) - 1;
    }
    addScript("http://api.flickr.com/services/rest/?method=flickr.photos.search&user_
    id=69562477@N00&api_key=98dc95d53bbd454ad501591bbc53532a&format=json&jsoncallback
    =Photo.processPhotos");
  }
}
```

The only other line of code added to the JavaScript file is the line to create the tabs object:

```
var tabs = new Tabs("#ccf","#fff");
```

The new tabbed Google/Flickr mashup is shown in Figure 9-3, with the map tab page selected.

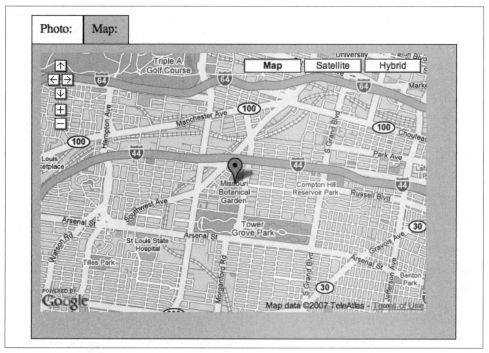

Figure 9-3. Google/Flickr mashup, tabbed

Now that we've got some room in which to add to the page, we'll fill it with more stuff.

Adding Technorati to Our Mashup

Technorati is a weblog search engine that tracks posts by tags, as well as other search criteria. Its main site is at *http://technorati.com*.

As mentioned earlier, a commonly shared functionality in many of today's web services is the support of tags. Flickr has them, and so does Technorati. Technorati provides a mashup of its own, pulling in tag-related photos from Flickr and videos from YouTube to annotate its tag pages.

Technorati's API is a RESTful interface, supports both GET and POST requests, and requires a free API key. The API service we're interested in, tag, returns weblog entries that have associated a given tag with its post. The request has the following format, including the two required parameters:

```
http://api.technorati.com/tag?key=[apikey]&tag=[tag]
```

Other optional parameters are:

format
    XML for XML, RSS for RSS 2.0

Limit
    Default of 20, maximum of 100 blog entries to return

start
    Used to provide paging, and if set to the limit amount plus one (limit+1), returns the next page of results

excerptsize
    Number of word characters returned, 100 by default

Topexcerptsize
    Number of word characters in first post returned, 150 by default

Technorati doesn't provide dynamic scripting and callback function support, which means we have to use a more formalized service request. Since the request is coming from another domain, we're going to have to create a proxy to make the service request on the server and pass the returned data back to the client.

PHP programs making REST service requests are quite simple to build, and Technorati is no exception. The format you select really depends on what you want to do with the results. In the next example, we're interested in the XML rather than the RSS-formatted return data.

Example 9-7 includes the code for the web service proxy, which uses the cURL functions to manage the actual request. When the data is returned, an XML header is attached to the response, and the XML is passed straight through to the client.

Example 9-7. Proxy application to manage the Technorati web service request

```php
<?php

$tag = $_GET['tag'];

function getTechnorati($tag) {

    // prepare request
    $base        = 'http://api.technorati.com/tag';
    $query_string = '';

    $params = array( 'key'   => 'yourkey',
                     'tag'   => $tag,
                     'limit' => '10'

    );
```

```
    foreach ($params as $key => $value) {
     $query_string .= "$key=" . urlencode($value) . "&";
    }

    $url = "$base?$query_string";

    // execute request using curl
    $c   = curl_init($url);
    curl_setopt($c, CURLOPT_RETURNTRANSFER, 1);
    $xml = curl_exec($c);
    curl_close($c);

    return $xml;
}

$xml = getTechnorati($tag);

// set header and echo response
header("Content-Type: text/xml; charset=utf-8");
echo $xml;
?>
```

The only changes to the web page itself are the addition of the new tabbed page names for the Flickr tags and the Technorati posts. Since data is being placed dynamically in these pages, we need a way to specifically access each:

```
...
<div class="name">
Flickr Tags:
</div>
<div id="techpostname" class="name">
Technorati Postings:
</div>
...
<div class="content" id="flickrtags">
</div>
<div class="content" id="techposts">
</div>
```

In this version of the mashup, a new tabbed page is opened to display the Flickr tags attached with a specific photo. Not all the tags, though. Flickr supports the concept of *machine tags*, which are machine-specific tags, similar in nature to RDF but without the format. They're interesting and can be used in yet other mashups, but for this one, we'll just grab the nonmachine tags.

The tags are annotated with a link to the Technorati tag page of the same name, though the application overrides this to pull in the most recent 10 posts related to this tag. The actual URL is used more to "identify" the link than to open a separate page. The use of a link makes the item keyboard accessible and identifies the element as clickable.

Clicking the link makes the request to the proxy server, which returns the most recent posts from Technorati for the tag. These are processed and the Technorati Posts tab element is populated with links to the stories. The tab name is also made invisible when no tag is selected, and is visible when posts for a tag are loaded into the page. Summarizing the processes involved:

1. When the page is loaded, the Google map is created and then moved to the maps tab. The location is used to mark which photo to display, if the hash exists.

2. The Flickr photos for a specific user are requested from Flickr.

3. The photos are used to build individual photo objects, all appended to the Photo object's photos array.

4. When each photo is retrieved from the array, the location is accessed from the object. If the location is not found, a request is made to Flickr to retrieve it.

5. In addition, when each photo is retrieved, the photo's Flickr tags are accessed from Flickr if they don't currently exist within the object.

6. The map is recentered based on the current photo.

7. The Flickr Tags page is populated based on the current photo.

8. If a Flickr tag is clicked in the Flickr Tag tabbed page, a request is made to the local web service to get the related weblog posts from Technorati.

9. These posts are used to populate a fourth tabbed page labeled "Technorati." This page is made visible only after it's been populated.

Example 9-8 includes the complete JavaScript for the application, with the additions enhanced to make them stand out.

Example 9-8. Complete JavaScript code, modified to add in Technorati web services

```
var tabs = new Tabs("#ccf","#fff");
var map;
var xmlhttp;

// object function for each
// individual photo element
function photo(id, url) {
   this.id = id;
   this.url = url;
   this.longitude = null;
   this.latitude = null;
   this.tags = [];
   this.setLocation = function(lon,lat) {
      this.longitude = lon;
      this.latitude = lat;
   }
}

// global Photo object
// to manage all photo Ajax calls
```

Example 9-8. Complete JavaScript code, modified to add in Technorati web services (continued)

```
// and process all photo data
var Photo = {

    // create array of photo objects retrieved from
    // Flickr for specific user
    processPhotos : function(obj) {
        this.currentPhoto = -1;
        this.photos = new Array(obj.photos.photo.length);
        for (var i = 0; i < obj.photos.photo.length; i++) {
            var pic = obj.photos.photo[i];
            var url = "http://farm" + pic.farm + ".static.flickr.com/" +
                pic.server + "/" + pic.id + "_" + pic.secret + ".jpg";
            this.photos[i] = new photo(pic.id, url);
        }
        aaManageEvent(aaElem('button'),'click',aaBindEventListener(this,this.loadPhoto));
        this.loadPhoto( );
    },
        this.getPhoto( );
    },

    // event handler for getting next photo
    loadPhoto   : function(evnt) {
        evnt = evnt ? evnt : window.event;
        aaCancelEvent(evnt);
        this.getPhoto( );
        return false;
    },

    // process next photo request and get location
    // if location not already present in photo object
    getPhoto    : function( ) {
        if (this.currentPhoto >= this.photos.length) this.currentPhoto = 0;
        var pic = this.photos[this.currentPhoto];
        aaElem("image").src=pic.url;

        // set map
        if (!pic.latitude) {
          addScript("http://api.flickr.com/services/rest/?method=flickr.photos.geo.
getLocation&photo_id=" +
                pic.id + "&api_key=your key&format=json&jsoncallback=Photo.placeMarker");
        } else {
          this.recenterMap( );
        }
        // set flickr tags
        if (pic.tags.length == 0) {
          addScript("http://api.flickr.com/services/rest/?method=flickr.tags.
         getListPhoto&photo_id=" +
                pic.id +
             "&api_key=your key&format=json&jsoncallback=Photo.createTagArray");
        } else {
          this.resetTags( );
        }
        window.location.hash = this.currentPhoto;
```

```
      this.currentPhoto++;
  },

  // recenter map and place marker
  placeMarker  : function(obj) {
    var lat = parseFloat(obj.photo.location.latitude);
    var lon = parseFloat(obj.photo.location.longitude);
    this.photos[this.currentPhoto].setLocation(lon,lat);
    var point = new GLatLng(lat,lon);
    var marker = new GMarker(point);
    map.addOverlay(marker);
    map.setCenter(point, 13);
  },

  // just recenter map, marker already present
  recenterMap  : function() {
      var pic = this.photos[this.currentPhoto];
      var point = new GLatLng(pic.latitude,pic.longitude);
      map.setCenter(point,13);
  },

  // attach array of tags to picture
  createTagArray : function(obj) {
      var pic = this.photos[this.currentPhoto];
      var tags = obj.photo.tags.tag;
      for (var i = 0; i < tags.length; i++) {
        if (tags[i].machine_tag != 1) {
            var tag = tags[i].raw;
            pic.tags[pic.tags.length] = tag;
        }
      }
      this.resetTags();
  },
  // reset tags tab to current photos tags
  resetTags : function() {
    var pic = this.photos[this.currentPhoto];
    aaElem('techpostname').style.visibility="hidden";
    var tagArea = aaElem('flickrtags');
    var ul = aaElem('tagUl');

    // reset display
    if (ul)
       tagArea.removeChild(ul);
    if (pic.tags.length > 0) {
       ul = document.createElement('ul');
       ul.id = 'tagUl';

       // add each tag
       for (var i = 0; i < pic.tags.length; i++) {
         var li = document.createElement('li');
         var a = document.createElement('a');
         a.setAttribute('href', 'http://technorati.com/tag/' + pic.tags[i]);
```

```
            a.appendChild(document.createTextNode(pic.tags[i]));
            li.appendChild(a);
            aaManageEvent(li,'click',aaBindEventListener(this,this.getTechPosts));
            ul.appendChild(li);
        }
        tagArea.appendChild(ul);
    }
  },
  // get technorati posts matching flickr tag
  getTechPosts : function(evnt) {
    evnt = evnt ? evnt : window.event;
    aaCancelEvent(evnt);
    var target = evnt.target ? evnt.target : evnt.srcElement;
    var tag = target.childNodes[0].nodeValue;

    // reset technorati post area
    var content = aaElem('techpostcontent');
    if (content)
       aaElem('techposts').removeChild(content);

    // get XHR, prep, and send request
    if (!xmlhttp) xmlhttp = aaGetXmlHttpRequest();
    var qry = "tag=" + tag;
    var url = 'technorati.php?' + qry;
    console.log(url);
    xmlhttp.open('GET', url, true);
    xmlhttp.onreadystatechange = this.processTechPosts;
    xmlhttp.send(null);

  },

  // process the tech posts
  processTechPosts : function( ) {
    if(xmlhttp.readyState == 4 && xmlhttp.status == 200) {
        var items = xmlhttp.responseXML.getElementsByTagName('item');
        var content = document.createElement('div');
        content.id = 'techpostcontent';

        // append links to posts
        if (items.length > 0) {
           for (var i = 0; i < items.length; i++) {
              var name = "";
              if (items[i].getElementsByTagName('name')[0].firstChild)
                 name = items[i].getElementsByTagName('name')[0].firstChild.nodeValue;
              var title = "No title";
              if (items[i].getElementsByTagName('title')[0].firstChild)
                 title = items[i].getElementsByTagName('title')[0].firstChild.nodeValue;
              var link = "";
              if (items[i].getElementsByTagName('permalink')[0].firstChild)
                 link = items[i].getElementsByTagName('permalink')[0].firstChild.
nodeValue;

              var a = document.createElement('a');
```

```
                  a.appendChild(document.createTextNode(title));
                  a.setAttribute('href',link);
                  var p = document.createElement('p');
                  p.appendChild(a);
                  p.appendChild(document.createTextNode(' by ' + name));
                  content.appendChild(p);
               }
            } else {
               content.appendChild(document.createTextNode('no technorati posts'));
            }
            aaElem('techposts').appendChild(content);
            aaElem('techpostname').style.visibility="visible";
         }
      }
};

// setup load and uload
aaManageEvent(window,"load",setUp);
aaManageEvent(window,"unload",GUnload);

// if map compatible, create map and retrieve photos for user id
// use default settings: info for 100 photos
function setUp() {
  setUpTabs();
  aaElem('techpostname').style.visibility="hidden";

  if (GBrowserIsCompatible()) {
    map = new GMap2(aaElem("map"));
    map.addControl(new GSmallMapControl());
    map.addControl(new GMapTypeControl());
    map.setCenter(new GLatLng(38.627952, -90.1843880), 13);

    // associate map with page
    var cnt = aaElem("mapcontent");
    var mapObj = aaElem("map");
    cnt.appendChild(mapObj);
    mapObj.style.visibility="visible";

    var hash = window.location.hash;
    if (hash) {
       var subLoc = hash.split("#")[1];
       Photo.currentPhoto = parseInt(subLoc);
    }

    addScript("http://api.flickr.com/services/rest/?method=flickr.photos.search&user_id=
    69562477@N00&api_key=your key&format=json&jsoncallback=Photo.processPhotos");
  }
}
```

A lot of code, eh? It is, but much of it is just the tedious creation and management of page display once the data is retrieved. Any of these aspects can be easily packaged into reusable higher-level functions or accessed through an external Ajax library. The code is not complicated as much as it is extensive. The new addition of Technorati to the mashup is shown in Figure 9-4.

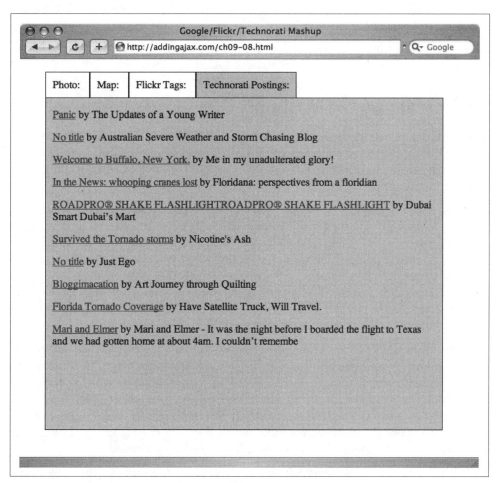

Figure 9-4. Mashup between Google Maps, Flickr, and Technorati

Now that there's a working prototype of a mashup between the data and/or services provided by three different companies, how can the application be improved? Typically with a mashup, the application is sketched in at a minimum, just to test the interaction between all the pieces of data. Once the prototype is working, it's reengineered to add in improvements in processing, security, and accessibility. As the application stands now, it's completely unworkable if scripting is turned off, and even with scripting on, it doesn't work correctly in IE.

Additionally, there are some security issues, most importantly the fact that the Flickr API key is exposed in the JavaScript for the application. The Google key is also exposed, but it's usable only for the specific subdirectory where the page is served.

The Flickr API, on the other hand, could be used anywhere. Though it, and its parent company, Yahoo!, aren't as concerned about the secrecy of the keys, it still isn't in our best interest to expose it for others to grab, in which case we risk having it overused and having our account cut off.

All of these are addressed in the next section of this chapter, where we have a chance to reengineer the application, making it more robust and more accessible.

Reengineering the Mashup

The most significant reengineering is for the tabs interface. In earlier chapters, we explored the ability to provide a nonscript interface that can then be converted into tabbed pages when scripting is enabled. We can do all of this using CSS and a minimum of JavaScript.

Once the tab conversion is finished, the next step is to provide a server-side interface to all of the services except for the Google Maps. We want the same application to provide services for a nonscript-based server-driven application and the JavaScript-based Ajax client. Google Maps is not something that will convert cleanly to a nonscript interface. What we can do with it is use the location to create a link to the Google Maps, and then the user accessing the page can decide whether he wants to turn on scripting for Google Maps. Or we could use the location to create a link to Google, Yahoo! maps, or even just print out the longitude and latitude.

Just like in previous chapters, the nonscript version will be generated by server-side processes, which also provide the permanent link for each "page." To make this work, the "on-demand" nature of the Flickr-to-Technorati tag connection either has to be completely supported for all Flickr tags, or just the link to Technorati provided, or the posts opened in a separate page. In this case, since we're doing a mashup, the application generates links for all posts by the Flickr tag. In the Ajax application, the on-demand nature of the application doesn't change.

As with the applications demonstrated in Chapter 7, the links to the server-side-generated pages are overridden in the Ajax application to provide client-side functionality. One major change with the client, though, is that the Flickr dynamic scripting is removed and replaced with a call to a web service that makes the request for the application. This effectively hides the Flickr key.

First up: transforming the tabbed pages into vertically organized page blocks.

Accessible Tabs

The current tab setup won't work for a changing layout presentation. The tab names must be associated with the tab bodies in physical proximity so that when the elements are layered as tabs, they naturally display horizontally: a title item goes with a content area.

The tabs layout consists of a container div, which holds a set of tab div elements, each followed immediately by the content div elements. Each of the content areas could have other elements, but that's the primary structure. The tabs are given a class name of name and the content areas are given a class name of content. These names are a requirement based on the CSS for the scripted and nonscripted displays. An example of a structure with three tabs is shown in the following markup snippet:

```
<div class="container">

<div class="name">
Photo:
</div>
<div class="content">
<p>Photo panel</p>
</div>

<div class="name" id="flickrtab">
Flickr Tags:
</div>
<div class="content" id="flickrtags">
<p>Flickr Tags</p>
</div>

<div id="techpostname" class="name">
Technorati Postings:
</div>
<div class="content" id="techposts">
<p>Technorati Posts</p>
</div>

</div>
```

The markup is what differentiates between the scripted and nonscripted displays. For the *scripted* display, the tabs of the panels are set to absolute positioning, which removes them from the page flow. The tabs themselves are then set to display inline, which lines them up from left to right along the top of the container:

```
.name
{
        border: 1px solid #000;
        display: inline;
        margin: 0;
        text-align: center;
        padding: 10px;
}
.content
{
        background-color: #ccf;
        border: 1px solid #000;
        height: 500px;
        width: 600px;
        position: absolute;
}
```

```
.container
{
        margin: 30px;
}
```

For the *nonscripted* display, the container is given automatic horizontal margins to center the content, and the tabs and panels line up as they occur in the page. The height restriction is removed since we're not concerned now if the content goes longer with one panel over another:

```
.name
{
        border: 1px solid #000;
        margin: 0;
        text-align: center;
        margin-bottom: 10px;
        padding: 10px;
        width: 580px;
}
.content
{
        background-color: #ccf;
        border: 1px solid #000;
        width: 600px;
        margin-bottom: 10px;
}
.container
{
        margin: 30px auto;
        width: 600px;
}
```

The Tabs JavaScript that manages which panel to display when the tab is clicked is identical to the script used in previous examples, except that each panel is set to display='none'. The panels layer on each other, and without this minor difference, the last panel would be on top even with the Tabs application managing the display based on tab clicks. This modification doesn't impact on the previous examples, and the adjustment is made to the overall *tabs.js* library:

```
function setUpTabs( ) {
    var divs = document.getElementsByTagName('div');
    var tabCount = 0;
    for (var i = 0; i < divs.length; i++) {
        if (divs[i].className == 'name') {
            tabs.addTab(divs[i]);
        } else if (divs[i].className == 'content') {
            tabs.addPanel(divs[i]);
            divs[i].style.display = 'none';

        }
    }
    tabs.showPanel(0);
}
```

One last browser-specific adjustment: Internet Explorer 6.x and 7 do not position correctly with the scripted stylesheet. To adjust for these Microsoft browsers, the top margin panel must be set to 30 pixels, and the left position set to 40 pixels

```
content
{
    margin-top: 30px;
    left: 40px;
}
```

This causes problems for all the other browsers, so these minor adjustments are added to an IE-only stylesheet, *iemashuphacks.css*, and an IE-specific condition is used to turn on the sheet only for IE:

```
<!--[if IE]>
<link rel="stylesheet" type="text/css" href="iemashuphacks.css" title="ie" />
<![endif]-->
```

We could spend more time working with the CSS and most likely create a stylesheet that works for all browsers. However, when working with Ajax, it's important to be aware of the ability to bring in an IE-specific stylesheet. Chances are you will need it at some point.

Script is used to disable other stylesheets and enable the scripted one. If scripting is disabled, the nonscripted stylesheet controls the display. The code is a variation of the stylesheet switcher used by many sites. Example 9-9 shows a Tabs test page with the script to turn on the scripting stylesheets.

Example 9-9. Tabs test page

```
!DOCTYPE html PUBLIC "-//W3C//DTD XHTML 1.0 Strict//EN"
  "http://www.w3.org/TR/xhtml1/DTD/xhtml1-strict.dtd">
<html xmlns="http://www.w3.org/1999/xhtml" xml:lang="en" lang="en">
<head>
<meta http-equiv="content-type" content="text/html; charset=utf-8" />
<title>Tabs Test</title>

<link rel="stylesheet" type="text/css" href="mashup3.css" title="not" />
<link rel="alternate stylesheet" type="text/css" href="mashup2.css" title="scripted" />
<!--[if IE]>
<link rel="stylesheet" type="text/css" href="iemashuphacks.css" title="ie" />
<![endif]-->

<script type="text/javascript" src="addingajax.js">
</script>
<script type="text/javascript" src="tabs.js">
</script>
<script type="text/javascript">
//<![CDATA[

var tabs = new Tabs("#ccf","#fff");

aaManageEvent(window,'load',function() {
```

Example 9-9. Tabs test page (continued)

```
    var links = document.getElementsByTagName('link');
    for (var i = 0; i < links.length; i++) {
      var a = links[i];
      a.disabled = true;
      if ((a.getAttribute("title") == "scripted") || (a.getAttribute("title") == "ie"))
        a.disabled = false;
    }
    setUpTabs( );
});

//]]>
</script>

</head>
  <body>
    <div class="container">
      <div class="name">
        Photo:
      </div>
      <div class="content">
        <p>Photo panel</p>
      </div>
      <div class="name" id="flickrtab">
        Flickr Tags:
      </div>
      <div class="content" id="flickrtags">
        <p>Flickr Tags</p>
      </div>
      <div id="techpostname" class="name">
        Technorati Postings:
      </div>
      <div class="content" id="techposts">
        <p>Technorati Posts</p>
      </div>
    </div>
  </body>
</html>
```

Trying the page out in several browsers, with scripting turned on and off, the stylesheet works and provides a decent presentation regardless of whether scripting is enabled. Now we're ready to adjust the mashup to work in both script-enabled and script-disabled environments. First, though, it's time to make a decision about Google Maps and the problem with IE.

An additional approach for providing nonscript-enabled tabbed pages is to use iframes for the content and then load the associated content into the one iframe based on the link. An iframe can take an entire page, and the page could be created by a single server-side application, altered to display each different type of content based on whatever parameters are passed to it. The page wouldn't require scripting, but the actual interface would "look" and "act" similar to the scripted interface.

Google Maps, IE, and Knowing When to Let Go

In earlier tabbed examples, having Google Maps open in an element that isn't displayed caused a great deal of unexpected work. That's one of the challenges when using widget applications that package presentation and functionality rather than providing an API and allowing us to manage our own presentations.

The examples shown so far in this chapter don't work with IE, and even with the other browsers there is a great deal of back-and-forth traffic between Google and the application. This results in load time problems and excessive network traffic.

Also, Google Maps does not work in a nonscripted environment and it doesn't degrade well. It can't be included in the nonscripting version of the application.

The Google Map was the first part of the mashup, but it's really not essential to the overall functionality, so it's dropped from the final application. Google provides a link structure where we can directly open a map to a specific zoom level, and that's as good as or better than including the map on a second tabbed page. Not only does this solve the browser problems, it also keeps the scripted and nonscripted applications in sync—both have access to the same data, merged from multiple sources.

The application still has to get the Flickr location information to create the related Google link, and the link is more or less the same as a REST request, so the concept of "mashup" still pertains—just more remotely. Best of all, we no longer have to worry about future ads intruding into the application or getting a Google Maps API key for every subdirectory.

Once the Google Maps beastie has been laid to rest, it's time to finish the rest of the application. We'll begin by making the web service requests accessible to both a server-side application and an Ajax client.

Another option could be to provide a scripting-enabled link to open an overlay on the page with the Google Maps, centered at the photo location, in addition to the link to the Google site.

Abstracting the Web Services

In the application in Example 9-8, the Flickr service requests were handled directly within the Ajax client using JSON callback endpoints. There are three problems with this approach.

First is the lack of security and reliability. We're accessing Flickr services directly in the client code, which means that if the services change, the client code has to change in all pages that use these services. We need a layer of abstraction between the raw web services request and the code to build the clients.

In addition, the service request contains the Flickr API key, clearly visible, which means it could be easily grabbed and used by other folks. Even if we were to obfuscate the code, something I don't like to do, it could be easily found among the gibberish. In fact, it would probably stand out among all the gibberish.

Finally, there are now two clients accessing the same set of web services: the nonscripting application, written in our unassuming PHP, and the Ajax client. The PHP will need the web services packaged as functions and the Ajax client packaged as a local web service call.

These issues are common to all Ajax applications and are worth highlighting a second time:

- Rather than working with a remote service's data directly in multiple clients, provide an abstraction layer to process the remote data, manipulating it into application-specific format. Have all clients then access this abstraction layer.

- When using API keys, hide the key by incorporating its use into server-side proxies. Don't use the key in JavaScript.

- When following the precepts of progressive enhancements, you'll invariably need to have all web services accessible by both a client Ajax application and a traditional web application. Provide services for both right from the start.

The Technorati web service call is already hosted locally, but it has to be packaged into a function that can be called by the PHP interface program for the Ajax client, and directly by the nonscripted application:

```php
<?php

function getTechnorati($tag) {

// prepare request
$base        = 'http://api.technorati.com/tag';
$query_string = '';

$params = array( 'key'   => 'yourkey',
                 'tag'   => $tag,
                 'limit' => '10'

);
```

```
foreach ($params as $key => $value) {
    $query_string .= "$key=" . urlencode($value) . "&";
}

$url = "$base?$query_string";

// execute request using curl
$c   = curl_init($url);
curl_setopt($c, CURLOPT_RETURNTRANSFER, 1);
$xml = curl_exec($c);
curl_close($c);

return $xml;
}
?>
```

The Ajax client really doesn't call the server-side function directly, and an interface layer is created to manage the interaction between the two:

```
?php

require_once "techno.php";

$tag = $_GET['tag'];

$xml = getTechnorati($tag);

// set header and echo response
header("Content-Type: text/xml; charset=utf-8");
echo $xml;
?>
```

The Ajax client doesn't change at all; it's already accessing the local web service, as we'll see later while exploring the modified application's JavaScript. Now, though, the Flickr services are available for the PHP application.

I hesitated about including all the PHP libraries and abstracted layers, as this is an Ajax book, which should be independent of the language used for the server-side portion of the applications. However, not showing all the pieces could be confusing, so forgive the "bonus" PHP. Example 9-10 shows the Flickr web services "wrapper."

Example 9-10. PHP Flickr web services wrapper

```
<?php

// wraps the Flickr get photo request
function getPhotos($callback,$format) {

    // prepare request
    $base         = 'http://api.flickr.com/services/rest/';
    $query_string = '';

    $params = array( 'method'    => 'flickr.photos.search',
```

Example 9-10. PHP Flickr web services wrapper (continued)

```php
                'api_key'   => 'your key',
                'user_id'   => '69562477@N00',
                'format'    => $format
    );

    foreach ($params as $key => $value) {
        $query_string .= "$key=" . urlencode($value) . "&";
    }

    $url = "$base?$query_string";

    if (!empty($callback))
      $url = $url . 'jsoncallback=' . $callback;

    $rsp = file_get_contents($url);

    if ($format == 'php_serial') {
        $output = unserialize($rsp);
    } else {
        $output = $rsp;
    }

    return $output;
}

// wraps request to get geo for photo
function getLocation($callback,$format,$photo) {

    // prepare request
    $base         = 'http://api.flickr.com/services/rest/';
    $query_string = '';

    $params = array( 'method'    => 'flickr.photos.geo.getLocation',
                'api_key'   => 'your key',
                'photo_id'  => $photo,
                'format'    => $format
    );

    foreach ($params as $key => $value) {
        $query_string .= "$key=" . urlencode($value) . "&";
    }

    $url = "$base?$query_string";

    if (!empty($callback))
      $url = $url . 'jsoncallback=' . $callback;

    $rsp = file_get_contents($url);

    if ($format == 'php_serial') {
        $output = unserialize($rsp);
    } else {
```

Example 9-10. PHP Flickr web services wrapper (continued)

```php
        $output = $rsp;
    }

    return $output;

}
// wraps request to get tags for photo
function getTags($callback, $format,$photo) {

    // prepare request
    $base        = 'http://api.flickr.com/services/rest/';
    $query_string = '';

    $params = array( 'method'    => 'flickr.tags.getListPhoto',
                    'api_key'   => 'your key',
                    'photo_id'  => $photo,
                    'format'    => $format,
                    'jsoncallback' => $callback
    );

    foreach ($params as $key => $value) {
        $query_string .= "$key=" . urlencode($value) . "&";
    }

    $url = "$base?$query_string";

    if (!empty($callback))
      $url = $url . 'jsoncallback=' . $callback;

    $rsp = file_get_contents($url);

    if ($format == 'php_serial') {
        $output = unserialize($rsp);
    } else {
        $output = $rsp;
    }

    return $output;

}
?>
```

This is just a quickly assembled application with lots of redundant code, but it's a start.

The Ajax client still handles the web service requests using the service endpoints and dynamic scripting. Now, though, the PHP application also has access to the remote data, except that it's not using JSON. Instead, it's using Flickr's newly supported php_serial format in addition to PHP's serialize and unserialize functions to push the data into a PHP associative array.

Now that the web services are wrapped and we've abstracted out the external dependencies from the local development, it's time to create the client. Which means more decisions.

The Reengineered Clients

The biggest decision at this point is whether to implement the server-side application and the Ajax client within the same pages. This was the approach used in Chapter 7, but it doesn't always provide the best value for an application.

There are times when a user may have scripting enabled, but would choose to work with the nonscript-enabled version of an application. People using screen readers would most likely prefer the nonscripted version, but may still have scripting turned on. After all, not all scripting pushes elements in the page around. Then there are folks using some oddball browser that does strange things to the page, or others who really aren't fond of Ajax (No! How can that be!), and it's nice to be able to give all these web page readers a choice.

The Script-Free Application

Both the scripting and nonscripting versions of the application are served from the same intro page, which uses PHP to list out all the links to the "static" photo pages (effectively caching the Flickr request to get the original set of photos), as well as providing a link to the slideshow. The links pass all the information necessary to populate the page in the server-side application, including the photo identifier and other identifying information for the image URL. Example 9-11 includes the code for this page.

Example 9-11. Nonscript-dependent introduction page

```
<!DOCTYPE html PUBLIC "-//W3C//DTD XHTML 1.0 Strict//EN"
   "http://www.w3.org/TR/xhtml1/DTD/xhtml1-strict.dtd">
<html xmlns="http://www.w3.org/1999/xhtml" lang="en">
<head>
<meta http-equiv="content-type" content="text/html; charset=utf-8" />
<title>Flickr/Technorati Mashup and Slideshow</title>
<link rel="stylesheet" type="text/css" href="mashup3.css" title="not" />
</head>
<body>
<div class="container">
<div class="name">
List of Photos
</div>
<div class="content">
<div id='menu'>

<ul>
<?php
```

Example 9-11. Nonscript-dependent introduction page (continued)

```
require_once('./flickr.php');

$obj = getPhotos('','php_serial');
for ($i = 0; $i < count($obj['photos']['photo']); $i++) {
   $photo = $obj['photos']['photo'][$i];
   $url = "slideshow.php?farm=" . $photo['farm'] . "&server=" . $photo['server'] .
          "&id=" . $photo['id'] . "&secret=" . $photo['secret'];
   $title = $photo['title'];
   echo "<li><a href='$url'>$title</a></li>";
}

?>
</ul>

<p>...or view Ajax driven <a href="slideshow.xhtml">Slideshow</a>--requires JavaScript and
modern browser</p>
</div>
</div>
</body>
</html>
```

One major difference between the nonscripted application and the Ajax client is that the nonscripted application does not have an event-driven connection between clicking on a Flickr tag to populate a window and retrieving the Technorati posts for that tag.

For the nonscripted application, each Flickr tag is used to process a Technorati request, and all the results are printed out, indented under each tag. This isn't a feasible approach if there are a lot of Flickr tags, though. A better approach would be to allow users to click a link associated with each Flickr tag and open the Technorati results in a separate page. However, for this example application, it's a single-page *slideshow.php*, as shown in Example 9-12.

The use of PHP serialization inserts the Flickr data into an associative array, and we can use the SimpleXMLElement to do the same with the Technorati data. Another approach we could take is to use XSLT to transform the XML, but the associative array works well enough with such a simple example.

Example 9-12. Alternative client for the mashup example with no scripting required

```
<?php
require_once('./flickr.php');
require_once('./techno.php');
$farm = $_GET['farm'];
$secret = $_GET['secret'];
$server = $_GET['server'];
$id = $_GET['id'];
$url = "http://farm$farm.static.flickr.com/$server/" . $id . "_$secret.jpg";
$obj = getTags(null,'php_serial',$id);
$tags = $obj['photo']['tags']['tag'];
?>
```

Example 9-12. Alternative client for the mashup example with no scripting required (continued)

```
<!DOCTYPE html PUBLIC "-//W3C//DTD XHTML 1.0 Strict//EN"
    "http://www.w3.org/TR/xhtml1/DTD/xhtml1-strict.dtd">
<html xmlns="http://www.w3.org/1999/xhtml" lang="en">
  <head>
    <meta name="generator"
    content="HTML Tidy for Linux/x86 (vers 1st November 2002), see www.w3.org" />
    <meta http-equiv="content-type" content="text/html; charset=utf-8" />
    <title>Google/Flickr/Technorati Mashup</title>
    <link rel="stylesheet" type="text/css" href="mashup3.css" title="not" />
  </head>
  <body>
    <div class="container">
      <div class="name">
        Photo:
      </div>
      <div class="content">
        <div id="innerphoto">
          <img id="image" src="<?php echo $url; ?>" alt="slideshow" />
          <div id="required">
          </div>
        </div>
      </div>
      <div class="name" id="flickrtab">
        Flickr Tags:
      </div>
      <div class="content" id="flickrtags">
        <div id="innertags">
          <ul>
            <?php
            foreach ($tags as $tag) {
               if ($tag['machine_tag'] != 1)
                 echo '<li>' . $tag['raw'] . '</li>';
            }
            ?>
          </ul>
        </div>
      </div>
      <div id="techpostname" class="name">
        Technorati Postings:
      </div>
      <div class="content" id="techposts">
        <div id="techpostcontent">
          <?php
          foreach ($tags as $tag) {
             if ($tag['machine_tag'] != 1) {
                 echo '<p><b>' . $tag['raw'] . '</b></p>';
                 echo '<ul>';
                 $xmlstr = getTechnorati($tag['raw']);
                 $xml = new SimpleXMLElement($xmlstr);
                 foreach ($xml->document->item as $item) {
                   echo '<li><a href="' . $item->permalink . '">' . $item->title . '</a></
                   li>';
                 }
```

```
                echo '</ul>';
            }
        }
        ?>
        </div>
      </div>
    </div>
  </body>
</html>
```

Though it's difficult to show how this application works via a figure, Figure 9-5 does show some of the overlapping areas of the page.

Figure 9-5. Snapshot of a partial page created using the script-free application

Not only does providing a script-free alternative give the readers a choice, it also frees up the Ajax developer to push the Ajax limits as much as possible (within the browser limits). Next up, the last piece—the Ajax client.

The New Ajax Client

The application will have three tabs instead of four, since we've dropped Google Maps. However, on the first page under the photo, the application now has an unordered list with three links: one to Flickr per their usage requirements, one to the nonscripted alternative static page for the photo as a permanent link, and one to Google maps, passing in the latitude and longitude so that the map opens to the exact location of the photo (see Figure 9-5).

This has become quite a large application now, too large to list out the application as a whole. Instead, we'll walk through each piece and examine what's happening.

 This application, as well as all the other example code, can be downloaded from *http://www.oreilly.com/catalog/9780596529369*.

The page loading function creates the Tabs interface and also implements the hash hack. The Google maps initialization code is no longer needed and has been removed, and the initial Flickr service call is now to the local service:

```
// setup load and uload
aaManageEvent(window,"load", function( ) {

    setUpTabs( );
    aaElem('techpostname').style.visibility="hidden";

    var hash = window.location.hash;
    if (hash) {
        var subLoc = hash.split("#")[1];
        Photo.currentPhoto = parseInt(subLoc) - 1;
    }

    addScript("flickrjs.php?service=getPhotos&format=json&callback=Photo.
processPhotos");

});
```

The Photo object's processPhotos function is more or less the same. It creates an instance of the application's photo objects for each photo object returned from the service request. One difference is that the original photo object obtained from Flickr is assigned to the application's own photo object as a way of persisting all of that URL-forming data without having to create several different properties. We need this for the changes to the web service:

```
processPhotos : function(obj) {
    this.photos = new Array(obj.photos.photo.length);
    for (var i = 0; i < obj.photos.photo.length; i++) {
        var pic = obj.photos.photo[i];
        var url = "http://farm" + pic.farm + ".static.flickr.com/" +
            pic.server + "/" + pic.id + "_" + pic.secret + ".jpg";
        this.photos[i] = new photo(pic.id, url);
        this.photos[i].origObject = obj.photos.photo[i];
    }
    aaManageEvent(aaElem('button'),'click',aaBindEventListener(this,this.
loadPhoto));
    this.getPhoto( );
},
```

Most of the nuts and bolts for the application are managed in the `Photo.getPhoto` method. In it, the photo is displayed, a Flickr service request is made for the geographical location data, a Flickr service request is made for the Flickr tags, and two of the three links on the first page—the required Flickr link and the permanent link to the static page—are created and loaded to a `div` element that is added to the photo panel. The following summarizes the steps in this method:

1. The current `photo` object is retrieved from the photos array.

2. The `src` is used to set the page image.

3. A link is created back to the original Flickr photo and is appended to the photo tabbed page.

4. A link is created to the nonscripted page for the photo as a form of permanent link and is added to the photo page.

5. If the Flickr tags for the photo haven't been retrieved yet, an Ajax request is made to get the Flickr tags.

6. A method is called as a callback to process the Flickr tags.

7. If the location for the photo hasn't been retrieved yet, an Ajax request is made to get this information.

8. A function is called as a callback to add the location link for Google Maps to the photo page.

Example 9-13 shows the getPhoto JavaScript.

Example 9-13. JavaScript for the getPhoto method

```
// load specific photo into display
// get relevant location, google maps, and tags if not already
// retrieved
getPhoto     : function( ) {

    // get next photo
    this.currentPhoto++;
    if (this.currentPhoto >= this.photos.length) this.currentPhoto = 0;
    var pic = this.photos[this.currentPhoto];
```

Example 9-13. JavaScript for the getPhoto method (continued)

```
      // set photo
      aaElem("image").src=pic.url;

      // required link to Flickr and photo page permalink
      if (aaElem('maplinks'))
          aaElem('required').removeChild(aaElem('maplinks'));
      var a = document.createElement('a');
      a.setAttribute('href','http://flickr.com/photos/69562477@N00/' + pic.id + '/');
      a.appendChild(document.createTextNode('Link to photo on Flickr'));
      var ul = document.createElement('ul');
      ul.setAttribute('id','maplinks');
      var li = document.createElement('li');
      li.appendChild(a);
      ul.appendChild(li);

      // set permalink to static photo page
      a = document.createElement('a');
      var url = "slideshow.php?farm=" + pic.origObject.farm +
              "&server=" + pic.origObject.server + "&id=" + pic.id +
              "&secret=" + pic.origObject.secret;
      a.setAttribute('href',url);
      a.appendChild(document.createTextNode('Permanent Link to static photo page'));
      li = document.createElement('li');
      li.appendChild(a);
      ul.appendChild(li);
      aaElem('required').appendChild(ul);
      // set flickr tags
      if (pic.tags.length == 0) {
        addScript("flickrjs.php?service=getTags&format=json&callback=Photo.
createTagArray&photo_id=" + pic.id);
      } else {
        this.resetTags();
      }

      //get location data
      if (!pic.latitude) {
        addScript("flickrjs.php?service=getLocation&format=json&callback=Photo.
placeLocation&photo_id=" + pic.id);
      }

      // remember current position
      window.location.hash = this.currentPhoto;
  }
```

Note the last line of the function. Here's where the window's location hash is set to help provide a way of restoring the page if the user clicks away from the page and then uses the History or the Back button to return.

Much of this code revolves around building the elements for the first page using the DOM. This is a good demonstration of the benefits of Ajax libraries, where much of the code for this application could be reduced.

Figure 9-6 shows the first page of the application. Notice how the Technorati Posts tab is not visible, and it won't be until a Flickr tag is picked.

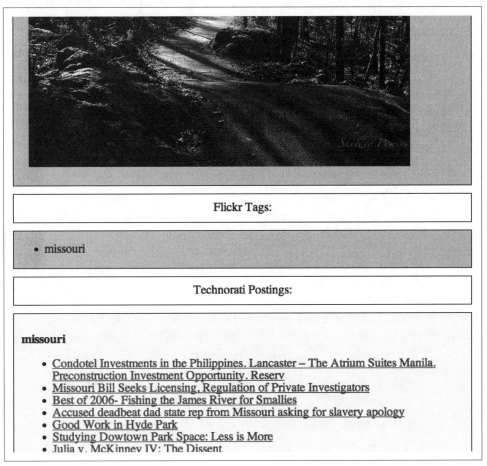

Flickr Tags:

• missouri

Technorati Postings:

missouri
- Condotel Investments in the Philippines. Lancaster – The Atrium Suites Manila. Preconstruction Investment Opportunity. Reserv
- Missouri Bill Seeks Licensing, Regulation of Private Investigators
- Best of 2006- Fishing the James River for Smallies
- Accused deadbeat dad state rep from Missouri asking for slavery apology
- Good Work in Hyde Park
- Studying Dowtown Park Space: Less is More
- Julia v. McKinney IV: The Dissent

Figure 9-6. First page of the Flickr/Technorati/Google mashup

The code makes two service requests, one to get the tags and one to get the location. The location processing function, Photo.placeLocation, is much simplified from previous examples because it doesn't have to wrangle a Google map. All that happens now is that the location is assigned to the photo object and a Google Maps link is added to the front page:

```
//for Google maps
placeLocation  : function(obj) {
  var lat = parseFloat(obj.photo.location.latitude);
  var lon = parseFloat(obj.photo.location.longitude);
  this.photos[this.currentPhoto].setLocation(lon,lat);
  var ul = aaElem('maplinks');
  var li = document.createElement('li');
```

```
    var a = document.createElement('a');
    var url = "http://maps.google.com/maps?f=q&hl=en&q=" + lat + "," + lon +
"&ie=UTF8&z=15&om=0&iwloc=addr";
    a.setAttribute('href',url);
    a.appendChild(document.createTextNode('Link to Google Maps for this
location'));
    li.appendChild(a);
    ul.appendChild(li);
}
```

The `Photo.createTagArray` function processes the Flickr tags into the tags collection for the individual photo. By caching the tags for the photo, we can limit the number of foreign web service requests we make:

```
// attach array of tags to picture
createTagArray : function(obj) {
  var pic = this.photos[this.currentPhoto];
  var tags = obj.photo.tags.tag;
  for (var i = 0; i < tags.length; i++) {
    if (tags[i].machine_tag != 1) {
      var tag = tags[i].raw;
      pic.tags[pic.tags.length] = tag;
    }
  }
  this.resetTags();
},
```

The `Photo.resetTags` method processes the tags, building the Flickr Tags page. Again, much of this code consists of DOM method calls to build page elements:

```
// reset tags tab to current photos tags
resetTags : function() {
  var pic = this.photos[this.currentPhoto];
  aaElem('techpostname').style.visibility="hidden";
  var tagArea = aaElem('flickrtags');
  var ul = aaElem('tagUl');

  // reset display
  if (ul)
    tagArea.removeChild(ul);
  if (pic.tags.length > 0) {
    ul = document.createElement('ul');
    ul.id = 'tagUl';

    // add each tag
    for (var i = 0; i < pic.tags.length; i++) {
      var li = document.createElement('li');
      var a = document.createElement('a');
      a.setAttribute('href', 'http://technorati.com/tag/' + pic.tags[i]);
      a.appendChild(document.createTextNode(pic.tags[i]));
      li.appendChild(a);
      aaManageEvent(li,'click',aaBindEventListener(this,this.getTechPosts));
      ul.appendChild(li);
    }
```

```
        tagArea.appendChild(ul);
    }
},
```

When a Flickr tag link is clicked in the application, the Technorati Posts tab is made visible. The message "…working" is also added to the Flickr page and is managed through Photo.getTechPosts. This message provides a clue that the application is processing the request. When the Technorati request returns, the message is removed from the Flickr Tags page at the same time that the Technorati Posts tab is made visible, and the results are printed.

The request in this instance is made using the XMLHttpRequest object rather than an endpoint, mainly because I wanted to mix up the two techniques. Another reason to use one over the other is if we want to keep the local web service more private:

```
// get technorati posts matching flickr tag
  getTechPosts : function(evnt) {
    var tagarea = aaElem('flickrtags');
    var p = document.createElement('p');
    p.setAttribute('id','working');
    p.appendChild(document.createTextNode('...working'));
    tagarea.appendChild(p);

    evnt = evnt ? evnt : window.event;
    aaCancelEvent(evnt);
    var target =  evnt.target ? evnt.target : evnt.srcElement;
    var tag = target.childNodes[0].nodeValue;

    // reset technorati post area
    var content = aaElem('techpostcontent');
    if (content)
       aaElem('techposts').removeChild(content);

    // get XHR, prep, and send request
    if (!xmlhttp) xmlhttp = aaGetXmlHttpRequest();
    var qry = "tag=" + tag;
    var url = 'technorati.php?' + qry;
    xmlhttp.open('GET', url, true);
    xmlhttp.onreadystatechange = this.processTechPosts;
    xmlhttp.send(null);

}
```

The last Photo method is Photo.processTechPosts, which processes the returned Technorati XML, creating links to posts for the third page. Again, most of the code is DOM element methods. If nothing else, you're getting some good exposure to DOM techniques with this example:

```
// process the tech posts
  processTechPosts : function( ) {
    if(xmlhttp.readyState == 4 && xmlhttp.status == 200) {
        var working = aaElem('working');
        working.parentNode.removeChild(working);
```

```
var items = xmlhttp.responseXML.getElementsByTagName('item');
var content = document.createElement('div');
content.id = 'techpostcontent';

// append links to posts
if (items.length > 0) {
   for (var i = 0; i < items.length; i++) {
      var name = "";
      if (items[i].getElementsByTagName('name')[0].firstChild)
         name = items[i].getElementsByTagName('name')[0].firstChild
         .nodeValue;
      var title = "No title";
      if (items[i].getElementsByTagName('title')[0].firstChild)
         title = items[i].getElementsByTagName('title')[0].firstChild
         .nodeValue;
      var link = "";
      if (items[i].getElementsByTagName('permalink')[0].firstChild)
         link = items[i].getElementsByTagName('permalink')[0].firstChild
         .nodeValue;

      var a = document.createElement('a');
      a.appendChild(document.createTextNode(title));
      a.setAttribute('href',link);
      var p = document.createElement('p');
      p.appendChild(a);
      p.appendChild(document.createTextNode(' by ' + name));
      content.appendChild(p);
   }
} else {
   content.appendChild(document.createTextNode('no technorati posts'));
}
aaElem('techposts').appendChild(content);
aaElem('techpostname').style.visibility="visible";
   }
}
```

Figure 9-7 shows the last page with several Technorati posts displayed.

Without the Google Maps, the application does perform much more efficiently, and at little loss of functionality since the one link does take us to the main Google Maps page.

One last change for this application to make it truly accessible is to add good keyboard support for accessing the different tab pages and well as the different links within the pages. Tab page navigation should be built into the Tabs library.

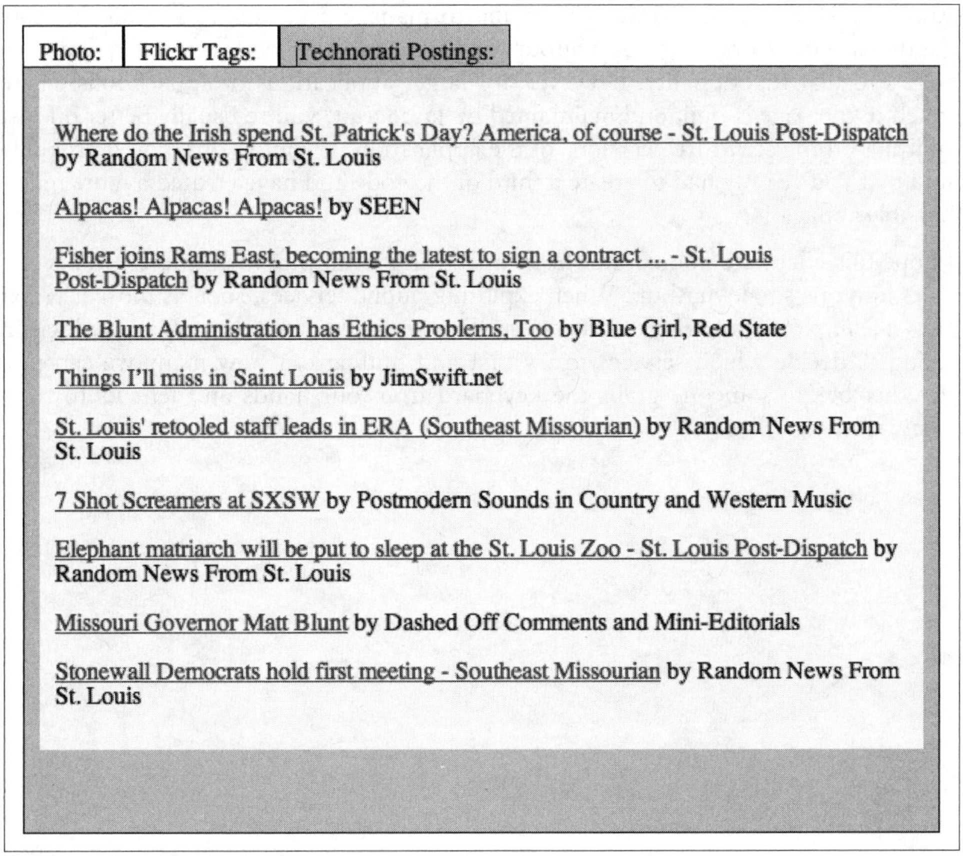

| Photo: | Flickr Tags: | Technorati Postings: |

Where do the Irish spend St. Patrick's Day? America, of course - St. Louis Post-Dispatch by Random News From St. Louis

Alpacas! Alpacas! Alpacas! by SEEN

Fisher joins Rams East, becoming the latest to sign a contract ... - St. Louis Post-Dispatch by Random News From St. Louis

The Blunt Administration has Ethics Problems, Too by Blue Girl, Red State

Things I'll miss in Saint Louis by JimSwift.net

St. Louis' retooled staff leads in ERA (Southeast Missourian) by Random News From St. Louis

7 Shot Screamers at SXSW by Postmodern Sounds in Country and Western Music

Elephant matriarch will be put to sleep at the St. Louis Zoo - St. Louis Post-Dispatch by Random News From St. Louis

Missouri Governor Matt Blunt by Dashed Off Comments and Mini-Editorials

Stonewall Democrats hold first meeting - Southeast Missourian by Random News From St. Louis

Figure 9-7. Last page of the Ajax client in the Flickr/Technorati/Google mashup

Summarizing Mashups

Creating mashups is like creating any Ajax application (or any other kind of application) in that there's more to the effort than just code (though the code can be considerable). One of the biggest risk factors associated with Ajax applications is an unwillingness to drop an original idea when it proves overly difficult to implement or not practical. There's a strong belief that developers can code their way around any problem, and maybe that's true, but it doesn't necessarily mean the application is going to be any good once you've gone through the pain.

Another risk factor has to do with trying to manage accessibility and all the Ajax goodness within one page or a group of pages. Most Ajax effects complement a page's regular functionality. However, for larger applications or applications where much of the page is built and maintained by JavaScript, you're usually better off just splitting off the script-free versions of the application. If you do this, you'll probably find that you've only had to create a third of the code and have created a more maintainable application.

I hope this chapter demonstrates how much fun it is to pull in all these various services into one single mashup. When exploring public services, such as those listed at sites like *http://programmableweb.com* and *http://mashup.com*, the only difficulty is in trying to decide which services to try first and finding out how many we can pull together before someone grabs the keyboard from our hands and tells us to back away, slowly.

CHAPTER 10

Scaling, Infrastructure, and Starting from Scratch

In some ways, Ajax is just another way to build a web application; people interact, users request data and invoke services, and web pages are created or modified. Ajax is dependent on the same things that any other application is dependent on, including a well-designed database, secure web services, efficient transactions, and having to deliver standard, accessible pages that work in most browsers and other user agents.

Ajax adds its own challenges, though, especially regarding the "work in most browsers" part. There's a partnership between our browsers and the web servers that we're effectively breaking when we use Ajax. In the traditional Web, browsers download a page with data already in it, and when the page is accessed again, since the data hasn't aged, the page is pulled from cache; there are no restrictions on where a service is invoked or where data is retrieved for the server-side application; data built into web pages is visible to screen readers or viewable when the user clicks View Source. It doesn't matter whether scripting is enabled. Then we toss Ajax in, and all of this goes to heck.

Still, as I hope I have demonstrated throughout the book, when used properly, Ajax can really add to the positive experience of web readers, clients, and application users. It just makes building web pages and applications that much more challenging. The payback, though, can be worth it.

In this chapter, we'll look one more time at the added infrastructure requirements of an Ajax application, as well as points to consider when developing a site or application from scratch. This includes the language to use for the server-side functionality, and whether to use a framework, or perhaps even multiple frameworks.

All the examples in the book up to this point were based on the idea that the Ajax technologies were being integrated into an existing application or framework. PHP has been the primary language used for the examples because it is the most common server language used with existing applications. It's also the one that requires the least setup and is provided with most hosting systems. However, the examples would have worked equally well with Java web services, Perl, or other web services languages. None of the examples were dependent on the language or environment used to create the web services. None of the examples are dependent on any new framework, either.

In this chapter, that restriction drops away, creating the chance to explore the concepts associated with creating a new site from scratch. This includes looking at new server languages in addition to new frameworks. In fact, the choice of framework could determine language.

That's not to say that you have to scrap every bit of an old site to use these new frameworks. You could isolate areas of a web site and convert over to a new framework while the rest of the site exists as-is. The only time this won't work is if you use a server-side framework that requires a specific operating system or environment that might not be compatible with your existing application, but this becomes rarer as time goes on.

Regardless of whether you start from scratch or enhance an existing application, there are decisions to be made. Should you use a framework or code from scratch? When you create a web service, should you expose it to public access? What's the best course: use an external library or create your own? How extensively should you integrate Ajax? If choosing a framework, which one and why?

And you thought all you had to worry about with Ajax is writing code.

Frameworks: Tight Versus Loose Coupling

In Chapter 1, we examined tight versus loose coupling. This really is an important consideration when building a site from scratch. Enough so that we will revisit the topic one more time.

All examples in the book are based on the premise that Ajax effects are being integrated into an existing application. They're also based on the concept of "loose coupling" in that they were all developed in such a way that there is no dependency from client to server or from server to client.

If an Ajax request to a service expects data in a certain format, it doesn't matter how this is accomplished, or by what language. Conversely, if a web service is completely decoupled from the client, it doesn't matter if the application making the request is a page in a web browser or another server application. The server application is designed to be used by a variety of clients, not necessarily those based in Ajax. The Ajax client accesses web services that can be created in any number of ways, and it doesn't matter how they were created. The only "handshake" between Ajax and the web service is the format of the request and the structure of the returned data.

Tightly coupled applications, though, require that the client and the server be tightly intertwined. Typically, much of the client interface is generated by web server calls.

A change in the server is immediately reflected in a change in the client, and a change in the client requires a change in the server.

This tight coupling between the server and client has advantages and disadvantages. The advantage is that application developers familiar with Java, Ruby, or another language don't necessarily have to learn JavaScript and the DOM in order to create Ajax applications. In addition, server-generated components could be fine-tuned to work with the server application, making for a potentially better-performing application. The code base may also be easier to maintain if it doesn't require a clean split between the server and the client in development.

Many frameworks that have a tightly coupled client and server also make it much simpler to get an application up and running. Rather than having to code the web service and then the JavaScript in the client, you write a few lines of code in the server application, which then generates both server- and client-side components. A task that could otherwise take days may only take hours.

The disadvantages, though, are that the generated code may not be as efficient as code that is created manually. It may be much more difficult to debug the application to fully understand what's happening between the client and server. As new browsers are released, the code may not keep up with changes or enhancements, and the application may become out-of-date.

Which to choose? There's no set of rules that provides a definitive answer as to which is the best course to take. If most of your applications are based in Java, chances are you've had some level of coupling already invested into your applications, and with the libraries and infrastructures available, tight coupling might be a good course. However, there are PHP-based infrastructures that require tight coupling, also—tight and loose coupling are general issues, not something specific to a particular language.

Having said that, though, there is one language where tight coupling between server and client in an Ajax application makes sense, and that's with Ruby and Ruby on Rails. This is an environment that has grown up in and around Ajax. It's one of those instances where the server-side functionality is heavily integrated with one of the more popular Ajax libraries (Prototype), and is also young enough so that moving from loose to tight coupling doesn't necessarily require massive changes.

Finally, it could be that a specific framework or library is what drives the design decision. If you're determined to use Google's Web Toolkit, you're going to be using Java, and you're going to be tightly coupled.

One thing to be aware of with this choice is that a change from one type of coupling to the other will require significant effort. It's worth it to spend time exploring the options before making a decision.

The Web Service: Resource and Security

When you're creating Ajax applications, unless you're using only others' web services, you'll be creating your own. When developing web services, you have choices such as whether to provide a public interface, and if so, what is your plan if your service suddenly becomes popular? If you do decide to keep your services private, what kind of security do you need to ensure this privacy?

In the hours before del.icio.us released its *tagometer*, web widgets that show tags associated with a page, a discussion broke out about its JSON endpoint. "Why not provide an API that provides XML or supports other services?" was the comment. Of course, once the badges were released, it became obvious that the JSON endpoint was for use in these badges, but by that time, enough interest was generated that the company that owns del.icio.us (Yahoo!) left the endpoint "exposed."

This is an excellent demonstration of the dangers inherent to an Ajax application—if the data is easy for your application to access, it could also be easy for other people to access. The question then becomes, "Do you want to expose your web service APIs or endpoints to external access?"

If yours becomes a popular service, you could be looking at a significant expense in bandwidth and server costs, but think of all the free publicity, not to mention the goodwill you'll accrue.

If you do provide a popular service, and bandwidth and resource usage becomes a problem, one way you can cut costs is to use third-party services, such as Amazon's Web Services, to host or run applications or to manage application messaging. The advantage to this is that companies like Amazon have years of experience dealing with balancing loads and demands and managing security, and they have the bandwidth and CPUs to meet even sudden surges of interest.

 The Amazon Web Services (AWS) is a for-pay service and can be found at *http://aws.amazon.com*.

Of course, if you do build in a dependency on a third-party service, you'll want to develop a layer of abstraction between your application and the service so you can swap out the external dependency if the need arises in the future. This, of course, adds even more complexity, but sure can contain costs.

You could also see about open sourcing your services, hopefully leading to a mirroring of your web server application, so that your own mirror isn't overly burdened. Even with a commercial application, spreading out your resources doesn't mean losing control of or exposing proprietary code.

If you don't want to expose your services for public access, you're going to want to be careful about the use of dynamic scripting, callback functions, JSON endpoints, and services that respond to GET requests. Neither of these work well behind secure walls, and none is really intended for a closed system. You can also take a hint from Google and restrict service requests based on IP address or host or file access, though these, unfortunately, can be spoofed and should only be relied on as a first level of defense.

If your web service needs to be secure, you can consider using HTTPS to manage the communication, and encryption and digital signatures to protect your data. You can also pass usernames and passwords as part of each XHR request, but whatever you do, make sure to eliminate those open endpoints.

Ajax Libraries: Homegrown or Borrowed

Most of the examples in the book don't use libraries other than the Adding Ajax library, addingajax.js, which we "growed up" as we went along. This leads to another major decision when beginning Ajax development—whether to create your own Ajax library, or use one or more of the many free libraries available on the Internet.

Some libraries such as Prototype provide basic functionality and are quite small. Others, though, can be rather large, and unless you have a real commitment to integrate them into your application, the bandwidth needed for the library isn't justified.

You can mix libraries as long as each uses some form of namespacing to prevent conflicts, and as long as the libraries are using event handlers that don't tromp all over each other or your own code, of course.

As for creating your own library, you can take a minimal, basic library such as addingajax.js and add your own components. One such addition is simplified processes to add and access DOM elements in order to cut down on the amount of code. The following example creates a two-item unordered list, with each item containing an anchor element:

```
// create unordered list container
var ul = document.createElement('ul');

// create two anchor elements
var a1 = document.createElement('a');
var a2 = document.createElement('a');
a1.setAttribute('href','http://someurl.com/');
var txt1 = document.createElement('some text');
a1.appendChild(txt1);
a2.setAttribute('href','http://someotherurl.com/');
var txt2 = document.createElement('some other text');
a2.appendChild(txt2);
```

```
// create list items and attach links
var li1 = document.createElement('li');
li1.appendChild(a1);
var li2 = document.createElement('li');
li2.appendChild(a2);

// attach to ul
ul.appendChild(li1);
ul.appendChild(lil2);
```

There's a lot of code associated with the DOM, and this example isn't even the most complex. Packaging some of this up into a library can not only cut down on how much code has to be written, but can also make applications easier to read and maintain. You can also eliminate bugs in an application by packaging commonly used groups of elements into libraries that, once tested, can be used as-is without having to code and recode:

```
var a[0] = aaCreateAnchor(link,text);
var a[1] = aaCreateAnchor(link,text);

// create unordered list, passing in array of items to package as list items
var ul = aaCreateList(listype, a);
```

If you do decide to use one or more external libraries, make sure you go through the entire library and understand how the code works before using it. That's one thing I can't emphasize enough: if you don't know what's happening in the library, you're not going to know how your own code or another library's code could impact, and you could end up with odd side effects or bugs that are difficult to trace.

The issue is not as critical when you're using a self-contained API, such as Google Maps. However, even with this API, we're constrained to serving pages as HTML and not XHTML.

If the library is provided only in a compressed, obfuscated format or is too big to review, and you need to integrate it with your code or other libraries, it's too cryptic and too large for you to use.

Designing Ajax from the Ground Up

In some ways, adding Ajax to an existing site is much easier than developing an application with Ajax as a component from the beginning. First of all, you already have your script-free application versions, and you won't be tempted to skip this essential component.

After doing the preliminary development planning discussed in Chapter 1, and after you have a good idea of where you want to use Ajax (and why), you now have design issues related purely to the development process.

Packaging Your Functionality into Units

It's a given that we'll package our JavaScript into reusable libraries, but we don't think about packaging our CSS or our HTML, not to mention also packaging our server-side code. A framework takes care of much of this, but we also need to look at going beyond the framework and discovering how much functionality we can package into complete units, such as CSS, HTML, server-side framework, and Ajax/scripting. This is dictated by common sense, of course, because we can easily make our sites impossible to maintain in our efforts to reduce it all to the lowest common denominators.

For instance, rather than having the CSS for an entire site in one file, we could split it out into separate CSS files for individual effects, and then load each of the CSS files only when the page needs a particular effect. Of course, the more we do this, the more HTTP requests are made, so another approach is to manually merge the CSS for all the effects into one file based on the page request. Or we could automate this in a manner similar to that used by MochiKit; you pick an effect, it highlights which libraries are required for the effect, and then it generates the JS library for you. MochiKit can even provide a deeply compressed library, or one that's wide open and easily viewable.

The more we break our web applications down into functional units, the more we can reuse these units, which can also simplify maintenance. It also makes it simpler to test changes.

Maintenance and Testing

I use Firebug extensively, but that's more of a tool for debugging as you're developing, rather than a testing tool. There are tools and techniques you can use to test your applications other than slapping a "beta" across a big, bold star and hoping you can get enough people willing to put your application through its paces.

 Regardless of the tool, getting users or potential users involved in testing should always be a part of your plan. No matter how good the test, it takes real users to really break an application.

The Open Web Application Security Project (OWASP; *http://www.owasp.org/index.php/Main_Page*), has an article on Ajax testing at *http://www.owasp.org/index.php/Testing_for_AJAX:_introduction*. What are some of the vulnerabilities to watch out for? SQL injection, cross-site scripting, memory leaks (IE is particularly vulnerable), and even the Ajax bridge, where one web service acts as a proxy to another completely unrelated web service. In other words, Yahoo! can provide a JSON endpoint that provides a way into a Google web service. All well and dandy, but do you trust the data traveling to and from such a bridge?

As for testing from a performance standpoint, Dan Wahlin published a list of testing and debugging tools, located at *http://weblogs.asp.net/dwahlin/archive/2007/02/16/ list-of-ajax-automated-testing-and-debugging-tools.aspx*. This is probably about the most extensive list I've seen on Ajax testing.

Among some of the automated testing tools that work with Ajax are JsUnit (*http:// www.jsunit.net*), HttpUnit (*http://httpunit.sourceforge.net*), and Selenium (*http:// www.openqa.org/selenium*). Selenium is a Firefox extension that acts as a recorder, allowing you to save a test case in a language such as Ruby, and which can also be extended to enable wait for conditions in an Ajax application test. A subtle advantage to this and other tools is they also demonstrate how important it is to make sure your application has keyboard access built into all the Ajax effects, as well as using links for any clickable item, as it records those.

Another is Fiddler, available at *http://www.fiddlertool.com/fiddler*, which logs all HTTP traffic between your computer and the Internet. You can actually stop the process and "fiddle" with the data as it's sent and as it's returned. This is a terrific intermediary that lets you test a variety of cases without necessarily having to adjust code. One limitation? Windows only.

The Ajax Patterns site, discussed earlier in this book, also lists information about testing and provides lists of tools at *http://ajaxpatterns.org/System_Test*. My recommendation is to look for those tools created specifically for your environment and try each, and then try out some of the tools that don't have a restricted environment. Your testing will probably incorporate two, three, or more tools.

Memory Leaks, Local Storage, and Robustness

In addition to the testing tools, which can help to drive out coding problems, you also have to be aware of items such as memory leaks, memory usage, individual CPU usage, database access, and server response times.

IE memory leaks can be detected using Drip/IE Sieve (*http://sourceforge.net/projects/ ieleak*), and most databases have usage monitoring tools as well as utilities that measure efficiency. The same applies to web applications, and though you're using Ajax, you're still making web requests.

One way to enhance the performance of an Ajax application is to make use of local storage. There are some techniques you can use that are platform-specific, such as DOM storage in Firefox and userData in IE. You should avoid these, though, and also avoid relying too heavily on the Flash Local Shared Object.

The lowly cookie doesn't seem like it can store much, but you'd be surprised at how much you can store in a cookie if you keep your caching and persistent data to a minimum.

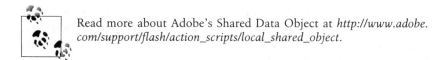
Read more about Adobe's Shared Data Object at *http://www.adobe. com/support/flash/action_scripts/local_shared_object*.

Reducing Every Effect to Its Simplest

The best applications are not the most clever, they're the most useful. I know the amount of work it takes to create a paint program that runs in a browser, but I love web applications that allow me to create, edit, or remove information directly in the page. An online chat application seems impressive, but I'd trade all of them for a really good Ajax-enabled photo slideshow or presentation.

From a design perspective, the all-important criteria to follow is not what will impress your developer peers, but what will impress your users. For example, a one-click update to add an item to a shopping cart and immediately check its availability is more impressive than having to click on that item and drag it over to a pseudo shopping cart.

I will repeat one more time, I don't like drag-and-drop, though I am forced to acknowledge that with the direction of future computers and other equipment, the use of the finger as an instrument is becoming the de facto standard. When Apple came out with its iPhone, it was entirely based on using your finger to perform every function, including dragging to resize.

Leaving aside the accessibility aspects of drag-and-drop, it's a cumbersome method if you're using a laptop with a touch pad, or even a handheld control such as Firefly's remote. Drag-and-drop requires the user to click on an item, move it across the page, then lift the finger (or release the mouse button), just to perform an action that often can be done with just a click of the mouse.

This does demonstrate that the best Ajax applications are the ones that follow users' intuitive actions, and that keep all actions as simple as possible to facilitate such actions. Dragging and dropping an item into a shopping cart might look cool, but it's simpler for a user just to click a Buy button.

Critical Areas of a Site

As much as I've repeated this throughout the book, I don't mean to be a nag and bring it up again, but critical functionality of an application, areas of a site, or data must be accessible via means other than Ajax-enabled navigation or techniques.

This isn't just a matter of good design; it could eventually be mandated by your government, or could leave you open for a lawsuit if you "blow off" users with special needs. In addition, as security continues to be a concern, users are turning off scripting. Assume scripting is turned off and that you have to earn your web page readers' trust before they'll turn it on.

Your pages also have to look good regardless of whether scripting is enabled. It makes no sense to make any visitor to your site or user of your application feel like she's been made to come in the back door and that she's here at your sufferance. Your application should tell her, "I'm glad you're here. If you have scripting, turn it on. If not, no worries."

Don't Over-Mash

Some users will access your pages via modem, and even with broadband access, resource usage should always be an issue. One situation in which resources can be abused is if you begin to add too many external services to a site, causing great delays as material is pulled in from many heterogeneous sites.

I have gone to some web pages and watched my status bar as 20 different web sites are accessed for data, images, and services. I've watched the status bar because I can't do anything with the page until all the stuff is loaded.

A Multitude of Devices

This has more to do with web design than Ajax, but pages are accessed by all sorts of devices now: phones, PDAs, televisions, and who knows what. Most of the time, these devices don't have JavaScript support, or the support is based on whichever built-in browser the device supports. The biggest problem with these types of devices occurs when you build in hardcoded sizing (which can be required to create any number of effects) or require certain actions like the aforementioned drag-and-drop.

You can drive yourself batty, though, worrying too much about all the various ways a page can be accessed. A good rule of thumb is to provide script-free pages and then provide mobile and print stylesheets, as well as pages that limit images, and you should be OK. Knock on wood, and don't forget to test.

Limit "Cool"

Cool effects are fun, and they make a web site seem so active and interesting at first. Typically, however, the cooler the effect, the more resources it requires and the more difficult it is to maintain, not to mention the more restrictive its environment has to be.

You can create an entire web site based on Ajax, and other Ajax developers might think the effect is awesome, but it's all lost as soon as you switch off scripting using the Firefox NoScript extension.

Early in 2007, the hosted weblogging company Wordpress.com enabled an Ajax functionality called *Snap* in all of its hosted sites. With Snap, as your mouse cursor hovered over a link, a miniature example of the linked site would be displayed in a little window above the link. I joined with many others in that we hated this effect— it was distracting, hid other material, made it more difficult to click the link, and pushed the page around. It was a cool effect that some people liked, but oddly enough, most web developers actually loathed it.

Cool should not get in the way of your web page readers. The glittery bits of imagery following around your mouse cursor, the floating bubbles, the pop-up ads that move down the page with you or cover the article you're reading, the drag-and-drop shopping cart—all these techniques, while seemingly cool, get in the way of what the site is about. Ajax and Ajaxian effects should enhance a site, add to the purpose, and enable ease of use, rather than detracting from what's important in the page.

Autocomplete is great, but not if you're running it against a data set with thousands of records. Pagination can work in some limited circumstances, such as with a database or other query. It's not a great way, though, to control your entire web page, especially if you're not incorporating any caching.

When used correctly, such as with in-place editing in addition to traditional editing techniques, Ajax can really add to the overall enjoyment of the application or site. Used for its own sake, it can really mess up a good web page.

But Cool's Good, Too

Having gone through the disadvantages of cool, cool can be good, too. I personally love the new graphics. I included the chapter on graphics as a treat for you and for me.

Be willing to explore the use of SVG/VML for a visual representation of data that complements your text-based delivery. Support active menus that work regardless of whether scripting is enabled. Providing in-place editing is one of my favorites, as is the accordion to make better use of space.

Providing fades to highlight a change can really add polish to a site, especially when added to existing means of notification. Pulling in data from external sites can help you create an application that really demonstrates the power of the concept behind tags, much more so than just talking about how useful they are for a "semantic" Web.

Providing a pop-up map to go with your company's address is better than providing the address alone. Providing live filtering of data can increase the overall efficiency and performance of your web application, as can live sorting and form validation.

I have become dependent on the autocomplete feature of my Google toolbar in Firefox. I use it to check almost all of my spelling now.

Even the bugaboo of Ajax pagination can work in limited circumstances, with really good caching built in. One of the most fun web applications I did for this book was the paginated database query mixed with SVG and Canvas from Chapter 8. It was a kick watching the little comment frequency graphics, but the regular text-based data was still present. What would have made it even better, though, would be to provide a static database table that scrolled within a container and then added the SVG so the data would be available for screen readers and the like.

One last issue to consider before starting from scratch: if you do decide to use a framework, which one should you use? In the last section of this chapter, we'll take a brief look at some of the ones available.

Frameworks du Jour

It doesn't matter what your favorite programming language or environment is, there's probably an Ajax development framework that matches your interest. I've seen ones for LISP, Cold Fusion, and Smalltalk, in addition to the usual suspects. Ruby and Ruby on Rails is one of the more publicized, but frameworks based in .NET and Java will most likely achieve the widest usage. Not to be outdone, there's more than one framework to work with PHP, and Python also has its Ajax goodies.

Most of the frameworks are not specific to Ajax, but provide support for a model-view-controller (MVC) paradigm, where the framework provides most of the controller component, integrating access to the data and services on the backend while contributing to or even generating the user interface (the "view"). Ajax enters the picture by providing another component of the application environment, but it isn't the focus of most of the frameworks. Sometimes Ajax is integrated into the overall environment, and other times it's an add-on or extension.

> An excellent resource for finding out which frameworks exist in your language and/or environment is the Ajax Patterns Frameworks page at *http://ajaxpatterns.org/wiki/index.php?title=AJAXFrameworks*.

ASP.NET and AJAX

Microsoft's Active Server Pages, or ASP, has been around for years, migrating from ASP to ASP.NET when Microsoft began the .NET initiative years ago. Microsoft has now provided a framework, AJAX, to add Ajax to your ASP.NET applications.

The major limitation with ASP.NET 2.0 and Ajax is, of course, that you can only use Windows as the server. All the other frameworks can work in different operating systems, including Linux, Unix, and Mac OS X. However, if you've worked with .NET in the past, then you're used to a Windows environment anyway, so this isn't a significant restriction. If you don't host your own server, there are some AJAX .NET hosting companies, and the number is growing.

ASP.NET AJAX is a free framework and can be downloaded from the main AJAX web site at *http://ajax.asp.net*. Once installed, you can leverage your Visual Basic or C# skills to create Ajax applications.

> Though the industry has moved to using "Ajax," Microsoft uses "AJAX" for its framework.

The ASP.NET AJAX framework was originally developed under the code name "Atlas," which was dropped when it was officially released. There are differences between the environments so if you've worked with Atlas in the past, you might want to read the migration guides that Microsoft provides.

Microsoft provides a decent set of documentation for this framework. Rather than a lot of handcoding, most of the documentation is based on how to build applications using Visual Studio. If you don't have the full version of Visual Studio 2005, there is a free "light" version of Visual Studio, called Visual Studio Express (at *http://msdn. microsoft.com/vstudio/express*) that does work with ASP.NET AJAX.

Once you've gone down this route, there is no turning back. Like most frameworks, you're locked into the environment. Again, though, this is no different than creating a regular ASP.NET application, or one in Java and EJB.

Microsoft also provides a nice set of videos to demonstrate how to develop in this environment, in addition to the extensive set of documentation. With the new release of Vista, development within the Windows environment should see a sudden growth in the next couple of years, and if you've worked with ASP or ASP.NET in the past, check it out.

The company, in cooperation with its community of developers, also provides the ASP.NET AJAX Control Toolkit, which is the client-side to the ASP.NET AJAX environment, providing visual elements such as the accordion, animations, filtered search and so on. The Toolkit's main site is at *http://www.codeplex.com/ Wiki/View.aspx?ProjectName=AtlasControlToolkit*.

You don't have to develop within the Visual Studio/.NET world to use all of Microsoft's Ajax offerings. The Microsoft AJAX Library is a pure JavaScript library, and can be used in other frameworks, or in individual applications. Since this book has focused so much on PHP as the backend language, I wanted to point out Steve Marx's PHP for Microsoft AJAX Library, a PHP backend that integrates with the Ajax frontend library. It can be downloaded at *http://codeplex.com/phpmsajax*. The MS AJAX Library can be downloaded independently from the rest of the .NET download.

Java and GWT

JavaScript and Java have always had a close association, though there really is no physical similarity between the two languages, or any actual connection, other than an early idea, quickly dropped and now long forgotten. The one thing they have shared is a mutual association with the Web, and that's now extended to a mutual association with Ajax.

Unlike enterprise applications built on middleware, such as EJBs and IBM's WebSphere, Java and Ajax don't have to walk through perilous canyons of complex frameworks and rigid protocols in order to be either useful or interesting. Thanks to frameworks and toolkits like Google's own Google Web Toolkit, it's astonishingly easy to begin producing Ajax applications using Java.

It starts with downloading and installing the toolkit. There are three varieties, one each for Windows, Mac, and Linux. Installation doesn't require the usual Java voodoo with 150 different environmental variables being set. In fact, when I first downloaded GWT to my Mac, I had my first GWT application up and running in less than a minute—and without really looking at the documentation.

OK, that's something you may not want to get into the habit of doing, but it does demonstrate that GWT has not followed the enterprise software path, but stays more closely aligned with the Java servlet/JSP/Web path, which means it's simpler to learn and easier to implement, but perhaps not something you want to use to maintain your company's deepest secrets. It is, after all, web-based.

Once installed, the `samples` directory under the main directory has several samples, each with a shell script that opens the sample within the GWT-hosted environment. Figure 10-1 shows the KitchenSink sample application on my Mac, running in Host mode.

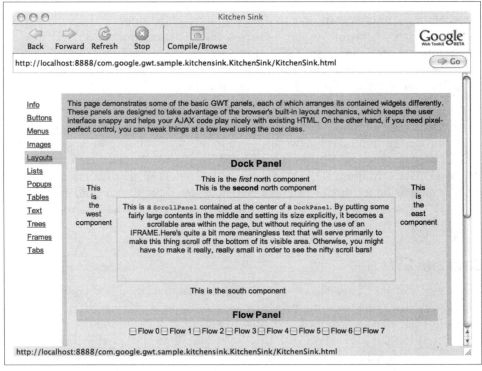

Figure 10-1. Google's GWT KitchenSink sample application running in Host mode

Once an application is compiled, it can be opened up in a browser and integrated into a Tomcat environment. The latter is the biggest restriction on using GWT: it is a Java framework, which does require a Java/Tomcat environment to host on the Web.

You can use your own JavaScript, though the GWT warns against this. This is typical, though, with a framework—you run risks when you move outside of the contained environment. If you use Eclipse, you can integrate this toolkit into your development environment, but there's also a command-line utility that can generate the application from source files. You can also integrate this application into your JUnit testing.

If your environment is already Java-based, this is a good option.

PHP Frameworks

Though we don't normally think of "frameworks" when working with PHP, there are Ajax PHP frameworks. In fact there are quite a few. One version is the open source Sajax: *http://ajaxpatterns.org/wiki/index.php?title=AJAXFrameworks*. Sajax has probably the smallest amount of documentation I've seen of all the frameworks—just a couple of paragraphs and a few examples.

Another, Zephyr (*http://zephyr-php.sourceforge.net*), provides an MVC framework that works with the Smarty template system. Smarty is in fairly widely used, so this framework should be of interest to anyone using a Smarty-based application.

One of the most popular PHP frameworks is Symfony, available at *http://www.symfony-project.com*. Not only does this framework provide libraries that facilitate development, it also provides the functionality to generate the directories and stubs to begin a project. Just glancing through the examples, you can see a strong Ruby on Rails influence to the framework, which also inspired similar frameworks in other libraries.

The only thing that concerns me about the framework and other frameworks is that the applications that are generated fail most of the code obscurity requirements, embedding scripting all through web pages. Still, it's a fun framework to use, and if you're a PHP developer, I would recommend giving it a trial run.

Python, GWT, and Django

The Google Web Toolkit is based on Java, but you can also get a Python version in pyjamas, available at *http://pyjamas.pyworks.org*. One of the advantages of this version, other than the fact that you might prefer Python, is that it's easier to locate a host that supports Python than one that supports Java.

Still, the big kid in Python frameworks is Django, available at *http://www.djangoproject.com*. Rather than build its own JavaScript library, the Django folks have incorporated Dojo, probably the second most popular JavaScript infrastructure after Prototype. It's a very open and extensible environment, but also a bit heavy at times, and unfortunately, too sparsely documented. Still, it's a powerful and a very open team.

Hey! It's Perl!

At one point in time, Perl powered the Web. Its usage has fallen off rather dramatically, especially in the last few years with the increased popularity of Java and PHP applications. However, who says Perl is no longer a hep cat?

There are two Perl modules for working with Ajax. One is CGI::Ajax, which is used for exporting Perl methods to JavaScript for Ajax, which is quite interesting. The other is HTML::Prototype, which generates HTML and JavaScript integrated with the Prototype library.

As for a fully rounded MVC Perl Framework, the hands-down winner in this category is Catalyst (*http://www.catalystframework.org*), providing as rich and as complete a development and production environment as any other framework in this list.

Ruby on Rails, Ajax, and Tight Coupling

From the oldest to the newest: from Perl to Ruby. Ruby is the new kid on the block from a language perspective, but it's catching up with other languages by the legions of fans that swear by its usefulness. Its popularity is mainly due to the succinct syntax and built-in object oriented support. As for frameworks in Ruby, there really is only one and that's Ruby on Rails (RoR or more commonly, Rails).

There's a close association between Rails and Ajax. For instance, the Prototype library consists almost entirely of Ruby-like artifacts, not surprising when you consider that Sam Stephenson, the creator of Prototype, is also on the Rails core development team. The use of the dollar functions in particular are very Ruby-like, as is the object structure created for all of the main classes. The use of Rails in Ajax development is facilitated by tightly integrating both Prototype and script.aculo.us into the actual installation; Rails tags are provided to include the libraries, as well as to provide access to several "helper" functions that generate the client-side code.

As intriguing as Rails is, one misconception about it is that it is the "only" environment for Ajax development. At any tech conference, when you mention "Ajax" and "framework," the tendency is to think of Rails, but it's really not the most commonly used server-side application for Ajax applications. That distinction has to go to none other than the ubiquitous PHP.

Go Forth and Ajax

Ajax can't make a bad application good, but it can make a good application better. When used as a means to progressively enhance a site, it adds additional functionality without sacrificing the original accessibility and usability.

Some of the edgier Ajax effects should give us some pause, but as the number of Ajax developers and interest in Ajax development grows, I expect to see more widespread usage of functionality such as in-place editing, flash notification, some of the space usage techniques, and live updates.

Best of all, working with Ajax doesn't require an initial investment in anything other than our time, nor does it require large frameworks. It doesn't require that we work in only one language or on one type of machine. All we need is a text editor and a browser and a place to put the page, and we're in action.

Index

We'd like to hear your suggestions for improving our indexes. Send email to *index@oreilly.com*.

Applet element, 17
apply method
    Function object, 125
    JavaScript, 228
appName property (Navigator), 45
appVersion property (Navigator), 45
array notation, 78
Array object, 78, 79
arrays
    associative, 78, 335, 337
    Flickr mashup, 306
    Google Maps mashup, 300
    JavaScript object notation, 54
    of nodes, 248
    slideshow infrastructure, 227
    tabbed pages, 163, 165
    Technorati mashup, 320
ASP (Active Server Pages), 360–361
ASP.NET AJAX, 360–361
associative arrays, 78, 335, 337
asterisk (*), 19
asynchronous requests, 68–70
attachEvent function, 100
autocompletion, 81, 180, 359
AWS (Amazon Web Services), 352
AWStats web tool, 21

B

Back button
    backtracking with, 223
    JavaScript support, 222
    remembering place, 244, 248
background color
    color fades, 123–132
    mouseover event and, 182, 186
    tabbed pages, 163, 166, 167
beta testing, 22
bind method (Prototype), 125, 126, 228
bindAsEventListener method
        (Prototype), 155, 159, 169
blending, 267
blink element, 16
Blockbuster, 97, 114, 117, 196
Bloglines, 202–208
BlueForm web site, 218
BOM (Browser Object Model), 5
bookmarks, 223, 244
Bosworth, Alan, 222
Browser Object Model (BOM), 5
browsers
    Ajax preview, 123
    Ajax support, 349

browser-specific quirks, 17–20, 43
    Canvas element, 290
    determining support for, 21
    Dojo Event System and, 102
    Dojo support, 86
    event handling support, 100
    Flickr/Google to tabbed pages, 313
    JavaScript sandbox model, 85
    library support and, 80
    live echo preview, 120
    namespace support, 195
    preparing XMLHttpRequest object, 37,
        38
    reengineering mashup, 329
    remembering place, 244, 248, 251
    scripting support, 4, 5
    sending requests, 43
    SVG support, 266, 277, 279, 281, 282,
        286–287, 289
    tracking statistics, 21
    (see also specific browsers)
bubble up phase, 99, 100, 101
Burkett, Wayne, 110

C

caching
    design considerations, 216
    Flickr mashup, 306, 336
    local storage and, 356
    performance considerations, 181, 194,
        223
    S5 framework and, 264
call method, 154–160, 310
callback functions
    defined, 42
    deleting table entries, 201
    Flickr API, 304, 308, 312
    Google Maps mashups, 300
    JSON endpoints, 63
    reengineered clients, 341
    Technorati support, 318
    web service considerations, 353
    XMLHttpRequest object and, 39, 42, 44
Camino browser, 266, 282, 314
cancelEvent method, 101
canedit variable, 185
Canvas element, 266, 290–293, 359
capturing phase, 99
cascading stylesheets (see CSS)
Catalyst framework, 364
Çelik, Tantek, 20
center element, 16

JSON (JavaScript Object Notation)
    abstracting web services, 335
    Ajax support, 4
    comments management, 207
    endpoints, 63–65, 352, 353, 355
    Flickr support, 304, 308, 332
    Gmail security gap, 67
    pages slideshow, 240
    processing responses, 54–58
    Prototype support, 73
    syntax standardization, 58
JSON evaluator, 74
JsUnit testing tool, 356
just-in-time effects (see JIT effects)

K

Keith, Jeremy, 2
key parameter (Technorati API), 317
keyup event, 118, 119
keyword/value pairs, 54
Knapp, Matt, 231
Konquerer browser, 280
KSVG plug-in, 280

L

labels, clickable, 109
li element, 17, 169, 202
Limit parameter (Technorati API), 318
limit property, 239
line shape (svg), 283
lineTo method, 291
live preview, 118–123
live validation, 211–215
LiveGrid encapsulated behavior, 84
load event handler, 99, 142
local storage, 356
localized functions, 309–313
locking, database, 216
logfile analyzers, 21
loose coupling, 26, 351
Lucovsky, Mark, 7

M

machine tags, 319
Mahemoff, Michael, 80
maintenance considerations, 355, 356
makeDraggable function, 276
manageEvent function, 99, 100
Map object, 312

map view (Google Maps), 298
mapping with Google, 297–299
margins
    browser-specific quirks, 17, 18
    manipulating, 133
    reengineering mashup, 328, 329
    resetting globally, 19
markers, 300, 305, 306
Markup Validation Service (W3C), 8–9
Marx, Steve, 361
mashups
    abstracting web services, 332–336
    adding Technorati, 317–326
    cautions overusing, 358
    creating Photo object, 309–313
    event handling support, 99–101
    Flickr, 304–308
    Flickr/Google to tabbed pages, 313–317
    Google Maps, 300–303
    reengineered clients, 336–346
    reengineering, 326–336
    risks with, 296, 347
MathML, 283, 284
memory leaks, 355, 356
menu element, 17
menus
    scripting and, 359
    web-friendly, 274
metadata, 312
Meyer, Eric, 20, 261
Michela, Adam, 197
Microsoft
    Active Server Pages, 360–361
    SVG support, 289
Migurski, Michael, 231
MIME type, 120, 282
MochiKit library
    browsers and, 80
    dynamic data effects, 220
    identifying needed libraries, 355
    overview, 94
    rounded corners, 268
    SVG support, 289
model-view-controller (MVC)
        paradigm, 360, 363, 364
moo.fx library, 94, 258
mooTools library
    dynamic data effects, 220
    overview, 94
    web site, 258
mouseout event, 288

Prototype library (*continued*)
  bindAsEventListener method, 155,
      159, 169
  Class.create method, 159, 169
  controlling animations, 125, 126
  dollar F function, 72, 75
  dollar function, 72, 75
  external libraries and, 79, 80
  getting style attributes, 140
  localized functions vs., 309–313
  overview, 72–77, 353
  prototype property, 77, 78
  Rico Accordion library and, 144, 145
  Ruby on Rails and, 351
  Ruby support, 364
  script.aculo.us library and, 80
  Tabs object and, 169
prototype property, 77, 79, 125
proxies
  defined, 63
  JavaScript security and, 85
  web services as, 355
PUT request (HTTP)
  deleting table entries, 201
  description, 40, 41
  Prototype support, 73
pyjamas framework, 363
Python framework, 363

Q

qForms API, 95, 217
question mark (?), 41
quirks mode, 5

R

RDF (Resource Description
      Framework), 296, 319
readyState property (XMLHttpRequest), 37,
      44
rect shape (svg), 283
rectangle shape (svg), 284
RegExp object, 78
rel="external" attribute, 110
removeEventListener method, 101
Representational State Transfer (see REST)
Request object, 73, 75
requests
  preparing and sending, 39–45
  synchronous, 68–70
  (see also DELETE request; GET request;
      POST request; PUT request)

require function (Dojo), 87
resetTags method, 344
Resource Description Framework
      (RDF), 296, 319
resources, web services and, 352–353
responses
  HTML fragments, 46–50, 58–62
  innerHTML property, 46–50
  JSON support, 54–58
  overview, 45–46
  requests and, 42
  XML support, 50–54
responseText property (XMLHttpRequest)
  description, 37
  processing responses, 45, 55
  sending requests, 44
responseXML property
      (XMLHttpRequest), 37, 50
REST (Representational State Transfer)
  Ajax responses and, 46
  Flickr support, 304
  HTTP support, 40
  PHP support, 318
  reengineering mashup, 331
RGB settings, 284
RIAs (Rich Internet Applications), 265
RichDraw library, 290
Rico library
  accordion effects, 144–147, 157
  Ajax pagination, 83
  dynamic data effects, 220
  functionality, 83, 85
  Prototype library and, 72
  rounded corners, 267, 268
  widget demo, 84, 85
Rico Weather Watch, 84
RoR (see Ruby on Rails)
rounded corners, 267–268
route marking, 300, 301
Ruby language, 351, 356, 364
Ruby on Rails (RoR)
  client-server architecture and, 351
  overview, 364
  Prototype library and, 72, 73
  Symfony framework and, 363

S

S5 framework, 261–264
Safari browser
  Ajax preview, 123
  browser-specific quirks, 18
  Canvas element, 290

About the Author

Shelley Powers is a software developer/architect, photographer, and writer who has authored numerous computer books on web development and technologies, including the O'Reilly titles *Developing ASP Components*, *Unix Power Tools*, Third Edition, *Essential Blogging*, *Practical RDF*, and *Learning JavaScript*. Through the years, Shelley has also contributed several articles on cross-browser development, standards, RDF, JavaScript, CSS, and XML for several publications, and has worked with some of the world's leading companies. Shelley's tech web site is *http://burningbird.net*.

Colophon

The animal on the cover of *Adding Ajax* is a forked mouse lemur, usually called a fork-marked lemur (*Phaner furcifer*). Like almost all lemurs, the fork-marked lemur is only found on the island of Madagascar. It is native to the rainforests in the northern and western parts of the country. The fork-marked lemur measures about 18 to 22 inches long, but its tail makes up half of that length. This lemur's name comes from the black markings that run from each eye over the top of its head in the shape of a two-pronged fork. This particular primate depends on gum from the temperate deciduous trees for its sustenance, but will sometimes eat the honeydew from insect larvae as well as insects for protein. The fork-marked lemur is the most vocal of the lemurs, with more than seven documented calls—including *ki*, *kiu*, *kea* (only made by males), *hon*—as well as alarm, distress, and fighting calls.

Like most animals around the world, the fork-marked lemur's habitat is being threatened by increased land development and farming. Its extinction status is currently near-threatened. However, efforts are being made to preserve this lemur; it can be found at a number of parks and reserves around the country.

The cover image is from *Lydekker's Library of Natural History*. The cover font is Adobe ITC Garamond. The text font is Linotype Birka; the heading font is Adobe Myriad Condensed; and the code font is LucasFont's TheSans Mono Condensed.

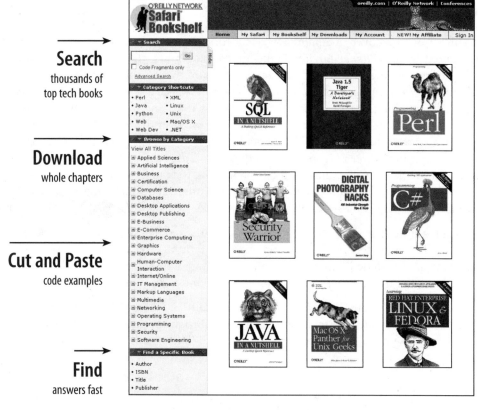